Exploring *Star Trek: Voyager*

Exploring
Star Trek: Voyager
Critical Essays

Edited by ROBERT L. LIVELY
Foreword by Lincoln Geraghty

McFarland & Company, Inc., Publishers
Jefferson, North Carolina

This book has undergone peer review.

LIBRARY OF CONGRESS CATALOGUING-IN-PUBLICATION DATA

Names: Lively, Robert L., editor. | Geraghty, Lincoln, 1977– writer of foreword.
Title: Exploring Star trek: Voyager : critical essays / edited by Robert L. Lively ; foreword by Lincoln Geraghty.
Description: Jefferson, North Carolina : McFarland & Company, Inc., Publishers, 2020 | Includes bibliographical references and index.
Identifiers: LCCN 2020008066 | ISBN 9781476678214 (paperback : acid free paper) ISBN 9781476638737 (ebook)
Subjects: LCSH: Star trek, Voyager (Television program) | Star Trek television programs—History and criticism.
Classification: LCC PN1992.77.S736 E97 2020 | DDC 791.45/72—dc23
LC record available at https://lccn.loc.gov/2020008066

BRITISH LIBRARY CATALOGUING DATA ARE AVAILABLE

ISBN 978-1-4766-7821-4 (softcover : acid free paper) ∞
ISBN 978-1-4766-3873-7 (ebook)

© 2020 Robert L. Lively. All rights reserved

No part of this book may be reproduced or transmitted in any form or by any means, electronic or mechanical, including photocopying or recording, or by any information storage and retrieval system, without permission in writing from the publisher.

Front cover image by Janez Volmajer (Shutterstock)

Printed in the United States of America

McFarland & Company, Inc., Publishers
 Box 611, Jefferson, North Carolina 28640
  www.mcfarlandpub.com

Acknowledgments

No collection can be completed as a solitary endeavor. A scholarly collection is at its heart a collaborative effort. As such, I want to thank the many people who helped make this volume possible. First, I want to thank Gary Mitchem and Layla Milholen at McFarland for making this process as smooth and supportive as possible. Their kind words of support and advice helped immensely. I would like to thank the authors in this collection who worked diligently on their essays, and who made my job as editor so much easier. I would also like to thank Dr. Lincoln Geraghty. When I first floated the idea of the collection, I wrote to Dr. Geraghty and asked him to spread the word about this collection because I have admired his previous work on *Star Trek* and popular culture. He was so kind that he volunteered to write the foreword for this collection. A special thanks to the peer reviewers of this collection who offered support and advice to make the volume better. Finally, I would like to thank my family. Thanks to my wife, Shelby, for putting up with my endless days compiling and editing and confiscating the TV to double-check something on an episode of *Voyager*. Thanks for helping me sort out long lists of citations, as well. Thanks to Erek for double-checking citations of episodes—I think I still owe you. And thanks to Jared for helping with technical issues during the final editing stage.

Table of Contents

Acknowledgments — v

Foreword
    LINCOLN GERAGHTY — 1

Introduction
    ROBERT L. LIVELY — 5

Part I. Ties to The Past: *Voyager* and Our Literary Heritage

"Far from gay cities and the ways of men": Exploring Wandering and Homecoming in *The Odyssey* and *Star Trek: Voyager*
    KWASU DAVID TEMBO — 15

"From hell's heart, I stab at thee": Villain Typologies of the Delta Quadrant
    ANDREW HOWE — 32

"Caught between worlds": Religion and *Star Trek: Voyager*
    CAMILO PERALTA — 49

Part II. Gendering the 24th Century: Problems, Solutions, Pathways

Where No Woman Has Gone Before: Kathryn Janeway Breaking the Glass Ceiling or Reinforcing Stereotypes?
    MICHELLE M. TABIT — 67

Millennial Girlhood and the End of Kes
    PETER W.Y. LEE — 82

"Tuvix" and Feminist Ethics in the Delta Quadrant
 JEFFREY BORUSZAK   98

"There's a woman in there if you'd take the time to look!"
Seven of Nine's Problematic Feminism
 SARAH CANFIELD   112

Part III. Negotiating Identities in the Delta Quadrant

Disabling Resistance: *Voyager* and Federation Ideology
 DANIEL PRESTON *and* CRAIG A. MEYER   133

B'Elanna Torres and the Hated Half: Negotiating Mixed-Race/Species Identity
 SHERRY GINN   149

Foreheads, Bad Attitudes and Mothers: Dismantling the Nuclear Family
 EILEEN TOTTER   164

Please State the Nature of Your Humanity: The Doctor and the Quest to Find Personality in Technology
 IAN THOMAS MALONE   179

Disturbing Parallel: The Shifting Politics of Racial Inclusion and Exclusion in *Star Trek: Voyager*
 CHRISTIAN JIMENEZ   194

Part IV. Broader Perspectives of the Future

The Politics of Nurturing: Gender, Care and Colonialism in *Voyager*'s Female Friendships
 ROSY B. MACK   213

Lost in Space Without an Idea of Home: The Triumph of Neoliberal Depoliticization in *Star Trek: Voyager*
 ALEX BURSTON-CHOROWICZ   231

Confessions of an Anti-Fan: *Voyager*, Fandom and Dislike
 MURRAY LEEDER   248

About the Contributors   265

Index   269

Foreword

LINCOLN GERAGHTY

Star Trek Voyager first aired in 1995, as part of Paramount's new UPN cable channel line-up. It was bold and brash and provided a somewhat different twist on *Star Trek*'s familiar motif of a starship-orientated show; the Voyager ship and its crew were lost 70,000 light years away from home and the security of Federation space. Still, like previous series, it continued in the vein of Gene Roddenberry's vision for the future. *Star Trek*'s goal is to promote the multicultural future of America, however impossible it may seem. Roddenberry's ideological foundation for the series was to show that there was such a thing as "Infinite Diversity in Infinite Combinations" (IDIC). That through a constant "didactic project to engage the experiences and politics of the 1960s," *Star Trek* could address real problems America was facing when it came to race and the politics of pluralism.[1] *Voyager* was no different in intent from the mission of its predecessors. Its crew, made up of a mixture of aliens and humans, was thrown together to form a miniature version of America's multicultural community. However, this time the show would be aware of the mistakes that past series had made when it came to addressing issues of race and identity on America's imaginary final frontier. It endeavored to re-examine the meaning of the "IDIC" ideology and to re-assess the assimilationist rhetoric that had plagued *Star Trek*'s earlier representations of different races and cultures during the Cold War era.

It is interesting to note that *Voyager* followed several major events that turned the clock back on American race relations. In 1991, Rodney King was brutally beaten by Los Angeles police, the evidence of which was broadcast to the whole nation. Yet that did not stop a white jury from letting the accused policemen go free a year later, sparking the worst race riots since Watts in 1965. Then in 1995 the widening gap between black and white America was made into a television event when the football star O.J. Simpson was tried and acquitted of murder. Causing civil unrest in parts of Los Angeles, the case showed that there was still an underlying racism eating away at interracial relations in American cities. Yet, *Voyager*'s vision of the future remained steadfastly multicultural: Janeway the first female Captain and lead, Chakotay the Native American First Officer, Vulcan Tuvok played by an African American, Asian American Harry Kim, and the half–human, half–Klingon B'Elanna Torres, played by a Latina actor. Later, as the series developed, the blurred lines between humanity and technology were brought sharply into focus through the introduction of a Borg character, Seven of Nine. *Voyager* attracted a loyal fan base distinct from the other series because of the diversity and mix of characters, which in turn offered great storytelling potential. However, as I have noted elsewhere, problems with race and representation did crop up: Chakotay was not only largely portrayed as the stereotypical American Indian, but his character often seemed isolated from the group. To that extent, he had been left alone to act and represent the Native American; singled out as the cultural "Other" even in a crew that was made up of many so-called "Others."[2]

These specific problems with representation aside, *Voyager* was able to offer more challenging storylines. Freed from the usual plots tied to Federation politics, as seen most often in the contemporary *Star Trek: Deep Space Nine* (1993–1999), and the already well-established canon, laid out in *Star Trek: The Next Generation* (1987–1994), the series could play with format and characters while at the same time return to Roddenberry's trick of challenging the audience's perception of the past and present through a look to the future. A number of episodes dealt with contemporary newsworthy topics such as capital punishment, genetic engineering, and organized healthcare. In the episode "Repentance" (7.13) the crew encounter a prison ship returning to its home world. The convicts are being transported to their death, returning home to be executed. This causes problems for those onboard Voyager who do not agree with such a harsh form of punishment. In "Lineage" (7.12) lieutenants Torres and Paris get the chance to see their baby in the mother's womb. Torres, who is half–Klingon, sees that the baby will be born with the distinctive head ridges and so decides to have the Doctor change its DNA to be born without them. Torres' own childhood experiences dictate how she wants her child to be born. "Critical Care" (7.5) sees the Doctor having to administer treatment to an alien race infected with a curable disease; however, the cure is only available to the rich upper class who can afford the drug. The Doctor takes it upon himself to treat all those infected, even those who have not been designated as "worthy." This concern for current affairs is not a new plot device for *Star Trek* but it characterized *Voyager*'s ethos more than past series. *DS9* finished its run in 1999 which meant *Voyager* was left as the stand-alone series on the relatively new UPN network. In the great *Star Trek* tradition, it took the lead in addressing important issues in America at that time; not least because 2000 was an election year where those issues proved to be important battlegrounds for the presidential candidates. Perhaps now, in this increasingly hostile environment of identity politics and the divisive rhetoric of hate, *Voyager*'s message of humanity and the collective search for understanding is more important than ever.

Voyager should be seen as part of what M. Keith Booker calls an "Age of Plenty" for science fiction television; where the 1990s saw a proliferation of new series.³ As well as concurrent series like *Quantum Leap* (1989–1993) and *Deep Space Nine* there followed *The X-Files* (1993–2002), *Babylon 5* (1994–1998), with its own spin-off *Crusade* (1999), *Sliders* (1995–2000), *Space: Above and Beyond* (1995–1996), *Stargate SG-1* (1997–2007) and spin-off *Stargate: Atlantis* (2004–2009), *Lexx* (1997–2002), Roddenberry's *Earth: Final Conflict* (1997–2002) followed by his *Andromeda* (2000–2005), a new version of *The Outer Limits* (1995–2002) that followed the renaissance of *The Twilight Zone*, and one might also include genre hybrids like the teen science fiction/horror series *Roswell* (1999–2002), *Buffy the Vampire Slayer* (1997–2003) and *Angel* (1999–2004). Of course, *Voyager* would be quickly followed by *Star Trek: Enterprise* in 2001. The impact of *Voyager* and series like these series meant that the concept of prime time "quality television" was firmly established by the mid–1990s, and their episodic formats also encouraged cable networks such as the Sci-Fi Channel (founded in 1992) to continue investment. The genre attracted a loyal and relatively affluent audience that could afford to buy into the ever-growing merchandising and DVD market. Series that started on the major networks would also end up on cable through syndication, adding to the pleasure of the rerun marathon which had become a staple cable marketing tool to attract science fiction fans. With the advent and popularity of streaming platforms Netflix and Amazon Prime, *Voyager* remains an ever-present example of quality science fiction television, attracting new audiences every year.

The essays in this collection represent a welcome reappraisal of a *Star Trek* series that was perhaps ahead of its time. *Enterprise* failed to ignite fan passion and was canceled after only four seasons in 2005, *Voyager* lasted the seemingly requisite seven seasons, but the inevitable return home to Earth felt rushed and could have been extended into another year of examining the physical and mental impact of being so far from familiar territory had on the crew. Now, with the success of Season 1 of *Star Trek: Discovery* (2017–) on CBS: All Access and Netflix as context, we might be able to see how innovative *Voyager* was in sending its crew and the *Star Trek* franchise into uncharted space. Like *Voyager*, *Discovery* offers a new twist on exploring the notion of "going where no one has gone before" through its inclusion of spore drive technology and the mycelial plane (a network that allows ships to travel vast distances to previously unexplored parts of normal space). Like *Voyager*, some of *Discovery*'s crew are at odds with the Federation and in rejoining have found it difficult to reconcile their personal beliefs with the ideology of peace and non-interference. And, like *Voyager*, *Discovery* plays with concepts of home and family where either can be found on the surface of a barren planet or the deck of a sterile ship. So entrenched in popular media culture, *Voyager* has also inspired comedic variations on the space opera theme. *The Orville* (2017–), created by Seth MacFarlane and *Voyager* Executive Producer Brannon Braga, charts the adventures of a ragtag crew of misfits. Episodes range from ones that focus on the private lives of crew members to others that tackle larger issues such as gender reassignment, religious idolatry and genocide. These sorts of ideas, these stories, can be found in *Voyager* and thanks to the contents of this much-anticipated volume, they are finally given the attention and recognition they deserve.

NOTES

1. Daniel L. Bernardi, *Star Trek and History: Race-ing Towards a White Future*. (Rutgers UP, 1998), pp. 29–30.
2. See Lincoln Geraghty, "'Neutralising the Indian': Native American Stereotypes in *Star Trek: Voyager*." *U.S. Studies Online*, Autumn (2003).
3. M. Keith Booker, *Science Fiction Television*. (Praeger, 2004), p. 111.

Lincoln Geraghty is a reader in popular media cultures in the School of Film, Media and Communication at the University of Portsmouth. He serves as editorial advisor for The Journal of Popular Culture, Transformative Works and Culture, Journal of Fandom Studies *and* Journal of Popular Television. *He is senior editor for* Cogent Arts and Humanities *and is the author or editor of several books, including* Living with Star Trek *(I.B. Tauris, 2007),* American Science Fiction Film and Television *(Berg, 2009) and* Cult Collectors *(Routledge, 2014).*

Introduction

ROBERT L. LIVELY

The 1990s were a time of great transition for the United States. The decade began with the break-up of the Soviet Union in 1991. This change felt optimistic. The Cold War was over, and the values of the West had won. Yet in the aftermath of the dissolution of the Soviet empire, questions began to arise about the alliances in the West. How would the old order react and adapt to the new change? What did the old treaties mean in the "New World Order" as President George H.W. Bush described it? As the world scrambled to redefine itself in the wake of the massive shift in international powers, political uncertainties affected the worldview of peoples across the globe.

The shakeup in world order was mirrored, if not amplified, at home in the U.S. The 1990s were the heyday of conspiracy talk radio, led by *Coast to Coast AM* with Art Bell. This genre of radio fed into the uncertainty of the changing world by proposing absurd governmental conspiracies, positing large corrupt governmental agencies experimenting on an unwilling and unknowing population. In a time when the government was adapting to the changing political reality, conspiracy talk radio fed into the fears of a population unsure of how these changes would affect them.

And changes were happening on the home front. In 1991, the Anita Hill testimony during the Supreme Court confirmation hearings for Clarence Thomas brought the term "sexual harassment" to the public eye for the first time in a major way. The all-male panel of senators grilling Anita Hill shed a light on the "Old Boys Club" of the Senate, and the aftermath of his confirmation spawned third-wave feminism. Coined from an article by Rebecca Walker, third-wave feminism challenged accepted stereotypical binaries, such as male-female, as ways to keep status quo power structures. Instead, third-wave feminism introduced the term intersectionality to the American public. Instead of viewing social categories in terms of binaries, intersectionality posits people as having interconnected and overlapping identities. The reaction to the Anita Hill/Clarence Thomas controversy led to several women being elected to the U.S. Senate and was popularly called "The Year of the Woman."

Demographically, America was changing as well, challenging the white majority power structures. For the first time in American history, the idea that white people would become the majority minority stirred a fear in the white population. The demographics were shifting across America, but especially on the coasts where diversity was always more common. The booming Latino population was changing the fundamental makeup of many U.S. urban populations, and it made older, white citizens fearful. This simmering racial tension came to a head in 1992.

The police beating of Rodney King led to the L.A. Riots which devastated parts of the second largest city in the U.S., and it brought police brutality into the public eye in ways it hadn't been seen before. The brutal beating of a man caught on videotape. The new technological medium of citizen video changed the way Americans thought about public interactions, and it helped catalogue abuses perpetrated by police. Race relations could no longer be swept under the rug because abuses could be recorded and aired on local news programs. The public sphere became increasingly bigger.

The greatest technological change occurred in 1990 when the World Wide Web launched. Never before in human history would a piece of technology affect the way humans interacted as much as this. The world became a smaller place. In the blink of an eye, an email could be sent anywhere in the world where the internet was set up. Online communities began to form. By 1994, the first major online community, Geocities, was up and running. Online technology held the promise of enlightening the world.

While the 1990s began with the optimistic view at the end of the Cold War, the transformations and upheavals quickly changed the '90s into a decade of uncertainty. Into this cultural crucible, *Star Trek: Voyager* launched on January 16, 1995. Rather than retreat from these cultural conundrums, *Voyager* speculated on what these changes might look like in the 24th century. *Voyager* cast the first female captain; it had the most diverse cast in *Star Trek* history. The series dealt with questions of humanity and identity. Moreover, the series creators set *Voyager* 70,000 light years away in the Delta Quadrant of space far from the safety of the Federation, which made the idea of lasting treaties and old alliances obsolete. *Voyager* tackled the uncertainties of the '90s and offered new ways of looking at an evolving cultural paradigm.

Yet *Voyager* has persisted remarkably well in popular culture. In a recent Netflix survey, six *Voyager* episodes placed in the top 10 *Star Trek* reruns people liked to watch. Moreover, the Italian astronaut Samantha Cristoforetti posted a picture of herself in Janeway's uniform on the International Space Station (see Michelle M. Tabit's essay in this volume). And even more recently congressional candidate Alexandria Ocasio-Cortez (D-NY) tweeted "As a kid, my parents let me stay up late to watch Captain Janeway lead her crew home through desperate straits, while lost in the galaxy. Couldn't have had a better example of a leader for these times. Thank you @The Kate Mulgrew!"[1] Kate Mulgrew responded with words of support for the House candidate.

This volume offers fifteen essays separated into four sections which investigate *Voyager*'s cultural context and the lessons the series offers readers today. The authors examine *Voyager* from cross-disciplinary perspectives to give a wide-reaching analysis of the series from its literary predecessors to broader cultural contexts, exploring the cultural mores reflected in the series. And much like the critics of the '90s, the authors themselves offer differing perspectives on *Voyager* as a cultural artifact. For all of its greatness and its flaws, *Voyager* captured the *zeitgeist* of the 1990s. In a time of change and uncertainty, *Voyager* was there to offer insights into the way things could be, even if its conjectures were sometimes a stretch. Viewers were lucky to find a show which explored the values of a changing world in a time of dramatic paradigm shift.

Part I. Ties to the Past: Voyager *and Our Literary Heritage*

The Homeric hymns are foundational texts in the Western tradition, and a longstanding source for narrative material. In "'Far from gay cities and the ways of men': Exploring Wandering and Homecoming in *The Odyssey* and *Star Trek: Voyager*," Kwasu David Tembo explores the similarities in the ideas of homecoming in both *The Odyssey* and *Voyager*. Using narrative theory to examine the texts, Tembo draws parallels between Captain Janeway and Odysseus, their motivating goals to bring their ships home while tossed about in hostile seas with the ever-present danger of forgetting about home.

Andrew Howe's "'From hell's heart, I stab at thee': Villain Typologies of the Delta Quadrant" explores the archetypal villains encountered in the Delta Quadrant. Rather than casting these villains as stock bad guys, Howe examines and categorizes villainy based on their moral codes; thus, he looks at various types of evil as misguided principles. He argues that each villain is consistent within their own moral stance. Whether this makes them sympathetic or not isn't the point of his analysis; he argues that the villains are consistent in what they hope to achieve. Their antagonism to *Voyager*'s crew makes them considered villains in ways they may not be to their own people.

In the Judeo-Christian tradition, references to biblical allusions are broadly referenced, both inside and outside of science fiction. Camilo Peralta explores these concepts in "'Caught between worlds': Religion and *Star Trek: Voyager*." Gene Roddenberry didn't value religion in storytelling, and he often chose to secularize materials written for the various series. Peralta shows how *Voyager* challenges this edict from Roddenberry in interesting ways. The conflicts between science and religion are still present in *Voyager*, yet the series is a bit more ambiguous in drawing harsh lines of distinction between them.

Part II. Gendering the 24th Century: Problems, Solutions, Pathways

Michelle M. Tabit's "Where No Woman Has Gone Before: Kathryn Janeway Breaking the Glass Ceiling or Reinforcing Stereotypes?" looks at the development of women in society and explains this development alongside the evolution of the *Star Trek* series. Tabit's historical view inevitably leads to Janeway as the first female lead captain in a regular series. She, in many ways, breaks the mold of the science fiction aesthetic for women to be othered. Janeway is a scientist and a leader who all follow. She struggles to find a balance as she has no forms of support from the Federation, and she must navigate her ship through unknown space with a disparate group of followers. As Tabit points out, "The development of feminist concerns in *Voyager* reflects the development in American culture throughout the 1990s."

Peter W.Y. Lee addresses the millennial generation growing up in the '90s in "Millennial Girlhood and the End of Kes." With the debates about feminism, the conservative backlash, and arguments that equality had been achieved for women, millennial girls heard mixed messages growing up. Lee charts these contradictory ideas through the character of Kes. Lee's treatment of Kes, often described as a weak or boring character by fans, shows that she is situated in an environment millennial girls also found themselves in as they grew into women. Lee's analysis of the story threads in which Kes appears gives a richer reading of her character.

In "'Tuvix' and Feminist Ethics in the Delta Quadrant," Jeffrey Boruszak examines one of the most controversial episodes in *Voyager*'s seven-year run. One of the enduring legacies of *Star Trek* has been to pose thought-provoking questions as episodes, and the episode "Tuvix" lives up to that tradition. Boruszak looks at Janeway's ultimate decision about the fate of Tuvix in terms of a feminist ethics of care, and why that supersedes other concerns in her decision even though it may run counter to usual Federation ideology.

Sarah Canfield's "'There's a woman in there if you'd take the time to look!' Seven of Nine's Problematic Feminism" confronts the problem of including Seven of Nine in the series. On one hand, she is a more-than-capable shipmate who runs the astrometrics lab. She is often referred to as the smartest person on the ship, and the Borg enhancements make her almost superhuman at times, yet the writing and costuming often display her as the "Sexy Cyborg."[2] To examine this conundrum, Canfield explores Seven's character in terms of Donna Haraway's "Cyborg Manifesto" to show the complicated space Seven inhabits, and how she challenges "gender hierarchies."

Part III. Negotiating Identities in the Delta Quadrant

In the 24th century, *Star Trek* offers a utopian view of the Federation. In this essay those Federation values are challenged by Daniel Preston and Craig A. Meyer's "Disabling Resistance: *Voyager* and Federation Ideology" because the ideology expressed is a dominant narrative which marginalizes populations inside the Federation. Drawing upon disability studies, Preston and Meyer argue that tensions onboard Voyager between the Maquis crewmen and Seven of Nine can draw parallels with the struggles faced by People with Disabilities to function in society. Can the utopian world create a place of inclusivity, or is *utopia* really a "no where" as the Greek name implies?

Sherry Ginn's essay, "B'Elanna Torres and the Hated Half: Negotiating Mixed-Race/Species Identity," explores B'Elanna Torres' story arc to find peace with her identity. *Star Trek* is no stranger to looking at issues of identity; episodes and story arcs across all of the series have raised the question of identity versus "otherness." B'Elanna's quest to accept her mixed Klingon/human identity is a strong arc throughout the series. Drawing on Erik Erikson's theory of development, Ginn suggests B'Elanna's character arc is about conflict resolution in her psyche which is slowly resolved over the course of the series, suggesting that the Voyager ship is her space of actualization.

Eileen Totter addresses changes to the family structure in "Foreheads, Bad Attitudes and Mothers: Dismantling the Nuclear Family." For all of its progressive vision, spearheaded by Gene Roddenberry, the average *Star Trek* family is heteronormative. Even in the 24th century, the nuclear family reigns supreme. Totter's essay examines the dysfunction of these families through the character of B'Elanna. Interrogating the changing dynamics of the family in American culture as expressed through B'Elanna was significant in that it allowed audiences to view intersections of non-traditional families with a sympathetic eye.

In her essay, "Please State the Nature of Your Humanity: The Doctor and the Quest to Find Personality in Technology," Ian Thomas Malone examines whether our advancing technology has human limits. Can technology become human? Is this even a correct way to phrase the idea of an evolving sentient Artificial Intelligence? Taking the analysis beyond the intellectual level of the Turing Test, Malone interrogates the ideas of emotion and free will in AI technology. On *Voyager*, The Doctor challenges the viewer's assumptions about the human/technology divide. Malone probes the limits of The Doctor's humanity and growth as a being with free will. With the current growth of AI such as Siri and Alexa, Malone's essay poses uncomfortable questions as we move into a new age where the lines become blurred.

Finally, Christian Jimenez examines race and politics in his essay, "Disturbing Parallel: The Shifting Politics of Racial Inclusion and Exclusion in *Star Trek: Voyager*." Chakotay as a character is interesting because he is one of the first Native Americans shown in a major science fiction role. However, his background is something of a conglomeration of Native tribes and the character lacks a clearly cohesive role during the series. Jimenez investigates the use of Chakotay to explore the ways in which *Voyager* is inclusive, but also in ways which show the series excludes certain ideas about colonialism and diversity, thus making Chakotay more palatable to an average viewing audience.

Part IV. Broader Perspectives of the Future

In Rosy B. Mack's "The Politics of Nurturing: Gender, Care and Colonialism in *Voyager*'s Female Friendships," she analyzes Captain Janeway's relationships with her crew, and more particularly Seven of Nine and B'Elanna Torres, using a feminist ethic of care as a lens to more fully understand how Janeway fulfills her leadership role. Rather than relying on the previous *Star Trek* series' use of colonial logics in their leadership structures, Janeway embodies a new way of looking at command/crew interactions on a Federation vessel.

Alex Burston-Chorowicz examines shifting political paradigms in "Lost in Space Without an Idea of Home: The Triumph of Neoliberal Depoliticization in *Star Trek: Voyager*." The 1990s saw a radical change in Western government. The paradigm of the New Deal in America was fading. President Clinton's "Third Way" politics merged conservative economic theories and social freedoms favored by the left. However, as Burston-Chorowicz points out, *Voyager* ends up in a political vacuum. Far from the Federation, it lacks much of the previous political narrative which drove *Star Trek: The Next Generation* and particularly *Deep Space Nine*. *Voyager* occupied a space where the new economics and lack of political messaging left the series in a political void.

The concluding essay, "Confessions of an Anti-Fan: *Voyager*, Fandom and Dislike," by Murray Leeder, addresses *Voyager* as the product of the internet age. Fandom always relied on a time gap before the internet. Bad episodes of a series could be brushed aside, and positive ones would be elevated because the results of watching were not immediately dissected by the public in an online environment. However, Leeder's thought-provoking essay critically examines why *Voyager* has faced a fan backlash online. The rise of internet immediacy just as *Voyager* began its series led to one of the first internet-age fan critiques. Seemingly every episode could be parsed and evaluated in the crucible of the public eye. This new era of fandom created super fans, but also as Leeder points out, anti-fans as well.

These essays represent a wide array of scholarship, written across several disciplines, and meant for multiple audiences. The purpose of the collection is to expand and analyze *Voyager*'s continuing interest among scholars who question it through different lenses across the academic spectrum, as well as fans who are interested in *Voyager* as a popular culture phenomenon. While this is not an exhaustive treatment of *Voyager*'s potential scholarship, we offer an interdisciplinary look at *Voyager*'s themes and tropes as a way of exploring what *Voyager* exemplified to a mid-'90s culture, and what we, as viewers in the 21st century, might learn from revisiting the series.

NOTES

1. See "Kinky Borgs and Sexy Robots: The Fetish, Fashion, and Discipline of Seven of Nine" (from *Channeling the Future* 2009). Mia Conslavo's "Borg Babes, Drones, and the Collective" (from *Women's Studies in Communication* 2010).

2. @Ocasio2018. "As a kid." Twitter, 11:05 a.m.—24 Jul 2018, https://twitter.com/Ocasio2018/status/1021818727371886593.

PART I

Ties to the Past: *Voyager* and Our Literary Heritage

"Far from gay cities and the ways of men"

Exploring Wandering and Homecoming in The Odyssey and Star Trek: Voyager

Kwasu David Tembo

> Many cities did he visit, and many were the nations with whose manners and customs he was acquainted; moreover, he suffered much by sea while trying to save his own life and bring his men safely home.
> —Homer, *The Odyssey* Book I

To Boldly Return: Introduction

When placed alongside the rest of the *Star Trek* television and cinematic franchise, *Star Trek: Voyager* (1995–2001) (hereafter *Voyager*) is comparatively novel. Unlike *The Original Series* (*TOS*) (1966–1969) or *The Next Generation* (*TNG*) (1987–1994), Voyager forgoes previous series premises which, not unlike Homer's *The Iliad* (800 BCE), explore the complex interplanetary sociopolitical, socioeconomic, and martial issues and tensions in the Alpha Quadrant. While these interspecific encounters and negotiations occur on an intergalactic scale in *Voyager,* the underlying impetus compelling the series' narrative is less concerned with a voluntary exploration of the universe than with a crew trying to survive a 75-year journey home to Earth through hostile uncharted space. The narrative of *nostos,* or the homeward journey, forms the ostensible narratological link between the story of Captain Kathryn Janeway (Kate Mulgrew) and her crew, and Odysseus, son of Laertes, king of Ithaca. The narrative of *The Odyssey* (800 BCE) is set a decade after the Trojan War. Due to Odysseus' hubris, and the mutinous hunger of his men, the theft, slaughter, and consumption of Helios' cattle pastured on the island of Thrinacia, Odysseus and his men are shipwrecked by Zeus and further waylaid by Poseidon who carries a lingering grudge against the king. *Voyager* interpolates the basic narrative of a crew stranded far from home as a result of the command decisions of its captain and their *nostos*, thereby reterritorializing the Greek precedent established by Homer within the context of contemporary science fiction.

Like *The Odyssey*, the narrative in *Voyager* is predicated on stranding, wandering, and the homeward journey. The series follows the Federation starship Voyager stranded in the Delta Quadrant, 75,000 light-years from Earth due to the near-omnipotent technological abilities of a near-omniscient alien being known as the Caretaker. Since that the Caretaker has the technology to pull vessels from across the galaxy, this being resembles the same ability possessed by Zeus to control the fate of millions of beings. The encounter between Janeway and the Caretaker occurs as a result of Voyager being deployed to find and apprehend a group of Federation rebels known as the Maquis, who are operating in an unstable nebula known as the Badlands. During an engagement near a space station called the Caretaker's array, both Voyager and the escaping Maquis ship are flung across space-time into the Delta Quadrant. Through much inter-crew tension, The Maquis crew reluctantly assimilate and join Voyager's crew in search for a way home.

Beyond the ostensible similarities in the underlying narratological and thematic basis of *The Odyssey* and *Voyager* there is a paucity of commentary, less even so for scholarship, concerning the broader similarities between the two texts. What little scholarship and commentary on said similarities tends to focus on a specific episode "Favorite Son" (3.20), or present sporadic and limited commentary on narrative and thematic similarities encountered in a comparison of the two texts. More specifically, such approaches have failed to discuss the broader relationship between wandering and homecoming in the respective mythologies of the two texts. With an aim to redressing this deficit, this essay will explore *nostos* in each text. *Nostos* here refers to an important theme in Ancient Greek literature that details the epic and perilous journey undertaken by a hero in his/her return home by sea. *Nostos* can therefore be defined as return, homecoming, a song or canto concerning the journey of homecoming, and/or a return to both life and light. Odysseus's *nostos* is one of many "*nostoi*," a group of songs describing the homecomings of other Greek heroes following the Trojan War. While Achilles has to make a choice between glory ("*kleos*") or a safe return home ("*nostos*"), both themes are one and the same for Odysseus who attains fame and immortalization by succeeding in his *nostos* (Harvard). Typically shipwrecked in an unknown land, the hero's nostos is often benighted with arduous trails, temptations, and dangers both subtle and obvious which all act as both natural and supernatural forces to delay or totally waylay his/her homecoming. There is, moreover, an important psychological and emotional aspect of the hero's *nostos*, namely the hero's reclamation of his/her status in the community he/she returns to, as well as assessing and maintaining her/his identity throughout the return journey itself (Alexopoulou 2–5; Bonifazi 48).

I have used Butler's translation for sake of ease as well as the fact that it, along with a second text *The Authoress of the Odyssey* (1897), forms a joint investigation into the authorship of the epic whereby Butler hypothesizes that the epic belongs not to Homer, but, rather, "was entirely written by a very young woman, who lived at the place now called Trapani, and introduced herself into her work under the name of Nausicaa" (Butler 2). In view of the fact that the comparative analysis to follow predominantly contrasts two captains, one male and one female, I feel that Butler's translation, directly and indirectly, speaks to a sensitivity toward gender politics with regard to the burdens, failures, and successes of command within the context of an epic journey/*nostos*. To do so as holistically as possible within the scope of this essay, I will compare numerous episodes in each narratives namely, Calypso, the Cyclopes, Aeolus, Circe, Hades, and the Sirens in relation to "Night" (5.1), "The Voyager Conspiracy" (6.9), "The Gift" (4.2), "Timeless" (5.6), "Dark Frontier" (5.15), and "Endgame" (7.25). I have chosen these particular episodes because the guiding narrative principles of each express a specific concern regarding the relationship between wandering and homecoming.

Wandering in Voyager *and* The Odyssey

In *Gods, Goddesses, and Mythology Volume 1* (2005), the entry concerning Odysseus and his inspirations, Anna Claybourne acknowledges the similarities between *The Odyssey* and *Voyager*, narratives in which a crew encounters numerous beings and strange worlds on their long journey home (Claybourne 1039). Similarly, in Chapter VIII of David Greven's *Gender and Sexuality in* Star Trek: *Allegories of Desire in the Television Series and Films* (2009), the author makes the astute observation that,

> if Homer's *The Iliad*, in its recounting of the Trojan War, tells us everything we need to know about war, courage, and human suffering, his *Odyssey* illuminates the fundamental human yearning for *nostos*, or homecoming, the ardent desire for which impels the wily trickster protagonist Odysseus to make his mazy way back from the Trojan War to his ever-faithful wife, Penelope. *Voyager* instructively accesses both the view of classical epic as the greatest of art forms and the intensity of nostalgia that permeates *The Odyssey*. Ostensibly, the primary difference between *Voyager* and *The*

> *Odyssey* is the different sexes of each narrative's captain. Though numerous female admirals and other high-ranking Starfleet officials had been seen in the franchise preceding Voyager, no series before it explicitly focussed on the adventures of a female captain and her crew. Recasting Homer's homeward-bound epic in feminist-sci fi terms, *Voyager* gives us an epic narrative about a female hero who seeks—with increasing obsessiveness—to bring her crew back home to Earth. In doing so, it grants a female protagonist access to the grand human truth of epic [Greven 166].

Greven also importantly draws attention to the fact that *Voyager* represents a confluence of gender and identity politics, science fiction and epic poetry. *Voyager's* status as one of the most daring representations and engagements of and with femininity in popular culture rests on the fact that its feminist accomplishments are predicated on "its determination to grant women access to epic narrative" (Greven 165).

In "'Every Old Trick Is New Again': Myth in in Quotations and the Star Trek Franchise" (2001), Djoymi Baker establishes the franchise's relationship with broader mythical texts and traditions by pointing out the fact that

> the *Star Trek* of the 1960s may quote non–*Star Trek* myths, but a popular cultural mythology based around the series itself had not yet begun. By contrast, the *Star Trek* of the 1980s and beyond is aware of its own place within the history of popular culture, an awareness activated whenever it quotes itself. Within such a context, to retell a story appropriated from an outside source is to simultaneously and necessarily retell the *Star Trek* story in a new guise [Baker 84].

In this way, Berman, Taylor, and Bragas' interpolation of Homeric aesthetic and thematic content "quotes external myth" in a "twofold [manner] because [*Voyager*] is aware not only of its source material, but also of its own status as (and deliberate construction of) a form of popular mythology" (Baker 84). As such, I affirm Baker's position in terms of the relationship between the *Star Trek* franchise and the antiquarian myths, particularly the Homeric texts, from which it draws when she states that "*Star Trek* not only contextualizes outside myths within *Star Trek's* fictional realm, but also attempts to contextualize its own mythology through that quotation" (Baker 84–5).

The preponderance of Baker's exploration of the similarities between *The Odyssey* and science fiction, specifically regarding the figures of the Sirens, is based on her discussion of "Favorite Son" (3.20). In so doing, Baker explicitly situates *Voyager* within the context of Greek myth and, vice versa, situates Greek myth within the context of *Star Trek*. The episode focuses on Ensign Harry Kim (Garrett Wang)-as-Odysseus, encountering and escaping a species of female aliens whose genetic manipulation of males of various species transforms them into suitable mates for procreation at the cost of their lives. The Taresians, inhabitants of a planet comprised of 90 percent females, are here portrayed as the Sirens Odysseus encounters in Book XII, whose technological manipulation of potential mates represents an updated instance of the Siren's song, drawing Kim to the occluded dangers of Taresia in the same way the Siren's song lures Odysseus and his men to the dangerous sea cliffs of their island.

Baker notes how the parallels between contemporary science fiction and ancient myth are drawn through quotation as Kim retells the story of Odysseus and the Sirens to his fellow crewmates in Voyager's mess hall. Though remodeled to conform to the concerns of a primarily science fiction program, ancient Greek myth forms the basic framework for this episode's narrative. However, Baker makes the important move of suggesting that the quotation of ancient Greek myth, particularly Homer's *Odyssey*, in fact forms a broader narrative and thematic backdrop for the entire series. Baker states that

> the Sirens story is, therefore, told twice within the context of the episode, but it has a third resonance in relation to *Voyager*'s series structure of the return home. While Homer's *Odyssey* tells of Odysseus' encounter with the Sirens in flashback, the episodic nature of Odysseus' adventures within a quest to return home against great odds is a structure which *Voyager* follows as a series. Whether or not the viewer is aware of this alignment is another matter, given the "Favorite Son: gives no more information about the *Odyssey* than Harry's brief retelling of the Sirens at the end of the episode. The use of the *Odyssey* nonetheless situates *Voyager* within its mythic framework, inviting the viewer to relate two tales to one another and directing us specifically to Odysseus over a myriad of other Siren myths" [Baker 86].

As it is later, particularly in Season 5, the Taresians-as-Sirens embody what Charles Segal refers to in *Singers, Heroes, and Gods in the Odyssey* (1994) as "the temptation of 'forgetting the return,'" as do numerous other beings, spaces, and times encountered by both Janeway and Odysseus' crews that encourage a forgetting of the desire to return to Earth/Ithaca respectively (Segal 215). As such, the fundamental problem faced by both captains concerns the circumvention of waylaying, the countermanding of any and all impediments to the *nostos*. In *The Odyssey*,

> Odysseus continually chooses the glory of nostos (return home) over the possible delights to be had elsewhere, so too the crew of Voyager consistently pass up opportunities to settle on hospitable alien planets. Although aliens often aid their journey, alien planets themselves always pose the potential of a replacement Earth that will divert the crew from their quest [Baker 86–7].

Baker claims that the threat of forgetting posed by the Taresians in "Favorite Son," predicated on their sexuality, falls square into the series' characterization of female agency as treacherous and manipulative in nature, whereby "the edict of equality of races" in *Voyager* is "little improved upon [in] *The Odyssey*'s own distinction between Greek and non–Greek women" (Baker 87). While Baker further asserts that

> although the allure of Homer's Sirens lies in their promise of knowledge and epic poetry, the language they use is distinctly sexual, as is their location on a "flowery meadow," a setting of sexual entanglements in early Greek poetry. The Taresians bypass such allusions, instead overtly offering the lure of no less than group sex [Baker 87].

While limited in scope, Baker's discussion of the tensions between the return home and delays represented in this episode as both a literal and figurative Siren song underpinned by issues and debates concerning the diversionary aspects of female sexuality does not account for the manifestations of waylaying female agency expressed by other characters in *The Odyssey*, particularly Calypso and Circe.

Baker claims that following explicit references can only take one so far in terms of the intertextual boundaries between *The Odyssey* and *Voyager*. I disagree. For example, Baker claims that

> while *Voyager* is much celebrated for having a female captain, it is a male ensign through which the Sirens story is told, not Captain Janeway [the implication here being that] although *Voyager's* ensemble cast allows different characters to feature prominently in different episodes, Janeway is closer to Odysseus in rank and function as the leader of her crew. The choice of Harry as the hero, and the addition of procreation as the source of the Taresian threat, suggests a return to the type of gender stereotyping often present in the original series (Baker 88).

In so doing, Baker overlooks the fact that not only do Janeway and her senior command all, to varying degrees of depth and frequency, express Odyssean characteristics regardless of species, age, or gender, the most Odyssean character in terms of the tension between a Siren song luring her away from her homeward journey is not Kim or Janeway, but Seven of Nine (Jeri Ryan), a similarity I will touch on later.

In terms of the inextricability between suffering calamities that serve to disable the *nostos* as well as boons, often supernatural/alien, that abet it, the thematic tension between leaving and returning, between wandering and homecoming manifest throughout *Voyager* and *The Odyssey*. Following on from Baker's comparative analysis of Harry Kim and Odysseus, "Timeless" (5.6) also focuses on the Odyssean qualities of Ensign Harry Kim. The episode is set fifteen years in the future where Chakotay (Robert Beltran) and Kim discover Voyager frozen on the surface of an ice world. After recovering the body of Seven of Nine and re-activating the ship's doctor, an Emergency Medical Hologram or E.M.H Doctor (Robert Picardo), Kim explains that fifteen years prior, the crew had attempted to use slipstream engine technology to expedite Voyager's journey home. The maneuver involved Chakotay and Kim guiding Voyager through the slipstream in the Delta Flyer. Calamity ensues when the slipstream becomes unstable due to a phase variance, causing Voyager to spill out of the slipstream and crash into the ice world. Voyager remains in the Delta Quadrant while Chakotay and Kim make it back to the Alpha Quadrant. Kim tells The Doctor that he and Chakotay have spent the last nine years searching for Voyager against Starfleet orders, going so far as to steal the Delta Flyer from a Starfleet shipyard as well as a Borg temporal transmitter. Kim explains that he can use the combination of Seven's interplexing beacon, located in her skull, and the transmitter to send a message back in time and warn Voyager, thus allowing them to make the requisite corrections and get his crew safely back home.

This particular episode focuses on what I call Kim's Odyssean dilemma, a reference to both character's facing ethical decisions when presented with means, be they technological or supernatural, to expedite their respective homecomings. The danger of malfunction Kim faces resembles the consequences of Odysseus accepting divine powers, which are tantamount to unpredictable alien technology within the science fiction context of *Voyager*. A notable example of the unpredictability and/or failed use of divine assistance comes in Book X. Odysseus recounts an episode in his *nostos* concerning his encounters with the Laestrygones, Circe, and Aeolus to king Alcinous of Scheria. Before arriving at Ogygia, the island of the goddess Calypso, Aeolus, son of Hippotas and master of the north, south, east, and west winds. winds and wind gods who lives on the floating island of Aeolia, entertains Odysseus for a month. He hears the hero's lamentatious tale of his time at Troy, the fate of the Argive fleet, and the *nostos* of the Achaeans. After retelling said events, Aeolus

> flayed [for him] a prime ox-hide to hold the ways of the roaring winds, which he shut up in the hide as in a sack—for Jove had made him captain over the winds, and he could stir or still each one of them according to his own pleasure. He put the sack in the ship and bound the mouth so tightly with a silver thread that not even a breath of a side-wind could blow from any quarter [Homer 161–162].

Unfortunately for Odysseus, after sailing for nine days and nights, and with the "stubble fires" of Ithaca visible on the horizon, Odysseus' men fall to talking among themselves regarding the contents of the sack, mistaking it for a trove of treasure taken from Troy (Homer 162). They open the sack and release a gale that sends them not only off course, but back in time so to speak, all the way back to the Aeolian island from which they had recently set sail. The risks presented in each instance, the dangers of a slipstream flight for Harry on the one hand, and being significantly blown off course for Odysseus on the other, must be weighed against their impatience to get home. The consequences of Kim and Odysseus making rash decisions that cost the lives of their respective crews predicated on the desire to get home by any means necessary are summed up by The Doctor who asks if Harry ever paused to look beyond his intense desire to return to Earth to consider what he and Chakotay are actually attempting. He warns that using radical alien technology to alter "the timeline may make things worse," offering the solace of the simple fact that though their crew perished because of a decision he made, he and Chakotay still survived. For Kim, the question is "get home in 15 years, or save your crew?" ("Timeless" 5.6).

Like "Timeless," "The Voyager Conspiracy" (6.9) deals with the moral, ethical, and physical dangers inherent when weighing alien technology and its risks against the ever-pressing desire for the *nostos*. In the episode, Voyager encounters an alien, a Saurian named Mr. Tash, who has constructed a space catapult capable of sending a ship several hundred light years in a matter of a few hours. Voyager assists with repairs to his array with the hope that they will be able to use the catapult after Mr. Tash's successful test flight with it. The episode concludes with Voyager being able to successfully use the catapult to travel closer to the Alpha Quadrant, reducing the completion of their *nostos* by three years. This particular episode explores the decisions captains make as well as the consequences of said decisions being inextricable from the time-saving opportunities presented by alien technology that would expedite their homeward journey.

Similarly, there are numerous episodes in Odysseus's journey in which his command decisions relating to his homeward journey are based on the ancient equivalent of alien technology, namely the supernatural powers of the gods, goddesses, giants, nymphs, kings, queens, heroes, and monsters he encounters. Examples include Circe, The Sirens, Hermes, Calypso, Athena, Zeus, and Aeolus. These examples find their quotation, interpolation, and reterritorialization in *Voyager's* plot structure for example, in "The Gift" (4.2) wherein Borg hull grafts, alien technology, allow Voyager to avoid capture and destruction, much in the same way Odysseus and his men evade capture and/or being eaten alive by the Cyclops Polyphemus in Book IX by using his own sheep as camouflage against him. In certain instances, the associative link between alien technology and supernatural powers, from ostensible displays like Athena's protective mists used to conceal Odysseus on his return to Ithaca seen in Book XIII and cloaking technology in "Dark Frontier" (5.15), or more subtle manifestations like Borg transmissions calling wayward drones back to the Collective in the same episode and Odysseus' ordeal with the Sirens in Book XII appear throughout *Voyager*. In the last instance, the ability to disrupt space-time for the purposes of lengthening or shortening the *nostos* of Odysseus and Janeway's respective crews means that the Aeolian wind in Book X is commensurate not only with Mr. Tash's catapult, but also with the Borg's temporal transmitter in "Timeless," as well as the Borg transwarp coil in "Dark Frontier" (5.15). Furthermore, the tractor beam of the Caretaker's array is synonymous with Zeus' lightning used to destroy Odysseus' ship as he fled from Calypso's island in Book XII. Similarly, the Pathfinder array Voyager uses to communicate with Starfleet in "Pathfinder" (6.10) serves a similar function and carries with it a similar *nostosic* value as Odysseus using the supernatural prescience of the shades in Hades to gain information about his *oikos* or home before the completion of the *nostos* in Book XI. Perhaps the clearest manifestation of this relationship between enabling and disabling the *nostos* through the intercession of alien technology or supernatural powers pertains to the process of Borg assimilation as expressed throughout the series and franchise more broadly, particularly in "Dark Frontier": a process whereby the bodies of individuals are forcibly transformed into drones by first injecting nanoprobes into them, then subsequently surgically augmenting their bodies with cybernetic components. Borg assimilation finds its ancient analogue in Circe's transmutation of Odysseus' crew into docile and obedient animals under the goddesses' thrall, seemingly trapped in the Delta Quadrant–like seclusion of her mysterious island, Aeaea in Book X.

In "The Gift" (4.2), Kes (Jennifer Lien), an Ocampan medical assistant aboard Voyager, is presented as a Calypsan/Circean danger/boon to the Voyager's *nostos*. In the episode, Kes and Tuvok (Tim Russ) meditate as an exercise in Kes further controlling her heightening telepathic abilities. She reveals that she has, in very many ways, become god-like, becoming not only able to manipulate matter on a subatomic level, but also "see" beyond it. This leads to Kes being a danger to both herself and Voyager as her uncontrolled powers destabilize both the ship and her body's structural integrity at the subatomic level. Kes and Janeway agree that in order to protect the rest of the crew, the former should leave the ship lest it be destroyed. Kes boards a shuttle and, after putting some distance between herself and Voyager, begins to destabilize. Before completely dematerializing, she contacts Voyager with a "gift." After vanishing, Voyager's warp core begins to function at over 120 percent capacity, sending the ship 9,500 light-years closer to Earth in an instant. The crew learn that they are not only safely beyond Borg space, but also ten years closer to the Alpha Quadrant.

Her possession of supernatural psychokinetic powers and abilities and her using them to expedite the Voyager's homeward journey align Kes and her powers with both the instability and possible transmutative danger of supernatural power, as with Circe in Book X. In Book X, Odysseus tells Alcinous that he was housed/imprisoned on Aeaea. For interloping outsiders like Odysseus and his men, the threat of this magical isle is inextricable from the feminine and magical power embodied and controlled by the sorceress Circe, its patroness, mistress, and queen. This threat and power is represented as being predominantly magical as opposed to geographical or topological in that after Circe offers Odysseus and his men hospitality and food—stools, chairs, drink, cheese, barley meal, yellow honey, and Pramnian wine—they are described as losing all memory of their homes. On the one hand, such a total erasure of memory could be seen as a utopian moment allowing for or facilitating the opportunity for radical existential restructuring, *tabula rasa*, allowing each man in Odysseus's company the chance to live a new life in which to create or re-create themselves and forget the ardors of the *nostos* and escape the danger and death they inevitably fill have to face in pursuing its completion. That said, the complete loss of memory is described as indiscriminate. Therefore, while Odysseus and his battle and sea-weary comrades may take solace in the magical erasure of the horrors of war and death they had witnessed at and since Troy, so too would they lose the memories of their wives, lovers, children, siblings, parents, and any and all moments of both joy and sadness experienced up to and including the moment of erasure. As such, Homer's construction of the island as a literary device or narrative space allows the author to explore seemingly contradictory themes or ideas. For example, feeling psychological and emotional relief in forgetting the very reason for one's journey home. In losing or forgetting this reason, one also loses or forgets a very important sense of purpose. It is a site on which and through which functions a double-craft, a space in which time and its recollection can be subtly, albeit totally, countermanded, evoking the unstable, unpredictable, and dangerous powers Kes possesses. As such, the sacred groves of Aeaea, in their resplendence, mystery, and horror, represent both the utopian and dystopian attributes of Kes's powers as means of both enabling and disabling Voyager's *nostos*: where both the attractive and equally dangerous aspects of Aeaea and Ocampan power are under the absolute control of a female authority.

This theme of the ethical complexes concerning the desire to complete the *nostos* contra the dangers of alien/divine techno-magical assistance persists to the very end of the series. For example, in Episodes 25 and 26, Season 7 "Endgame" (2001), the future Admiral Janeway uses stolen Klingon spacetime technology (a chrono deflector) in conjunction with a Borg transwarp hub (one of only six known examples) to intercede in her own history. Her plan here bears startling similarities with Homer's epic in terms of Admiral Janeway's expression of a now mature aptitude for Odyssean craft, wily escapes, subterfuge and deception. Not only does the transwarp network that allows for the manipulation of spacetime resemble a kind of wind or maelstrom through space-time, but time-travel is portrayed as a particularly unreliable type of techno-magic that can ensure or obliterate the *nostos*. In the series finale, an interesting transformation has occurred with regard to the psycho-emotional and command character of Janeway. On a purely narratological level, the journey has transformed Janeway into her own *deus ex machina*, a time-travel-capable entity with access to technology that allows her to be able to intercede in her own fate. Using the nebula of wormholes making up the Borg transwarp network, she is able to travel across space time and rewrite history. However, the instability and danger of this corridor home itself as well as the danger presented by those that guard it resembles the narrow strait in *The Odyssey*, both guarded by monsters, as it is with the Charybdis and Scylla in Book XII.

Journey Versus Homecoming in Voyager *and* The Odyssey

The association between *The Odyssey* and *Voyager* does not solely rest on a direct comparison between the captains. "The Gift" (4.2) explores the severance of the former Borg drone, Seven of Nine, from her destroyed Borg cube and the Borg Collective by extension. Now able to function as a physical, psychological, and emotional individual, her comparative isolation from her usual experience of a hive mind leaves her confused and angry. Regardless, her unsuppressed human immune system begins to reject her Borg implants. The Doctor decides to remove them after receiving the order from Janeway. During the procedure, Seven experiences violent convulsions caused by an unseen and seemingly inoperable implant attached to her brain. Kes uses her increasingly powerful telepathic abilities to disable the implant, stop the seizure, and dissolve the apparatus entirely. Having as much of her Borg implants removed as possible without killing her, Seven wakes and is displeased with her continuing humanization. She repeatedly demands she be returned to the Collective, protesting her individuality. After attempting to contact the Collective using a Borg transmitter that had been grafted onto Voyager, Seven is held in the brig where she and Janeway deliberate and argue about her separation from the Collective. After an unsuccessful attempt to escape the brig, Janeway presents Seven with information about her past, revealing that before she was Seven of Nine, she was a human girl named Annika Hansen. Enraged, Seven's wish to return to the Collective remains unchanged. In this episode, Seven's Borg and human sides competing for psycho-emotional dominance within her resemble the call of the Siren's Song Odysseus must contend with, and experience that each character endures alone of their respective crews. Similarly, precisely what the Borg Collective and the Siren Collective offer Seven of Nine and Odysseus respectively is most accurately summarized by Janeway when speaking to the newly liberated Seven in Voyager's sickbay, where she notes how Seven used to be "part of a vast consciousness, billions of minds working together. A harmony of purpose and thought. No indecision, no doubts. The security and strength of a unified will. And you've lost that" ("The Gift" 4.2). The sense of sequestration, confusion, rage, fear, and homelessness shared by Odysseus and Seven is encapsulated in the following exchange between Janeway and the latter:

> JANEWAY: It's obvious that you're in pain. That you're frightened. That you feel isolated. Alone.
> SEVEN: You are an individual. You are small. You cannot understand what it is to be Borg.
> JANEWAY: No, but I can imagine. You were part of a vast consciousness, billions of minds working together. A harmony of purpose and thought. No indecision, no doubts. The security and strength of a unified will. And you've lost that.
> SEVEN: This drone is small now. Alone. One voice, one mind. The silence is unacceptable. We need the others! ["The Gift" 4.2].

In this way Seven is Odysseus: both are stranded and alone, one in the ostensibly paradisiacal island spaces of gods, goddesses, kings and queens, and the other stranded within her own individuality, both looking to return to a Collective familiarity, be it Ithaca or Unimatrix Zero-One. The void of individuality Seven must invariably cross in order to arrive at the rediscovered space of her humanity resembles the psychological, physical, and emotional hardships endured by Odysseus throughout his return home. As with Seven, Odysseus reassuming his identity, however, exposes him not only to the dangers of the Cyclops, or the Borg as it is with Seven, but also to all the subsequent sufferings that Polyphemus' prayer to Poseidon, or the Borg queen's vendetta against Janeway and desire for Seven's re-collection, will bring down. In each character (re)claiming their respective identities, or keeping their identities in view, not forgetting one's identity and the identity of the home to which both travellers return to are both onto-existential and psycho-emotional processes steeped in identity politics. In this sense, both Seven and Odysseus' identities carry associations of pain (*odunai* in Greek) and hatred (*odussesthai*) with which both their respective Ithacan and Terrestrial existence and provenance are connected (Segal 33).

This notion of the Void is taken from "Night" (5.1). In this episode, Voyager is forced to travel through a sector of space the crew calls "the Void"— a region of space completely devoid of visible phenomena. Seven informs Chakotay that an astrometric scan reveals the nature of the Void. In it, there are no star systems for 2,500 light-years, with dense concentrations of Theta radiation blocking their sensors, depriving them of any insights as to what might be on the other side of the Void. As such, when Tuvok or Chakotay or Kim looks at the ship's bridge viewscreen, all they see is uniform blackness. In an exchange with Seven, Chakotay describes the Void as "every sailor's nightmare," that is like "being becalmed in the middle of the ocean. If it weren't for sensors [they] wouldn't even know [they] were at warp" ("Night" 5.1).

With nothing to do but contemplate time, distance, and patience, the crew of the Voyager become increasingly agitated. Janeway uses her time in the empty darkness of the Void to isolate herself and reflect on her crew's overarching predicament, succumbing to her feelings of guilt. Noticing crew morale suffering due to Janeway's prolonged absence and saturnine demeanor, Chakotay first seeks an audience with her during which he stresses that the crew "needs a Captain" and attempts to assuage her guilt over Voyager's situation.

Failing to hear reason, Janeway retreats back into silhouette, telling Chakotay to give the crew her regards if they ask for her. Chakotay leaves silently and seeks out Tuvok's counsel regarding his concern for both captain and crew. The problem he faces as first officer is the fact that while crew morale is significantly damaged by the Void, the captain's is lowest of all. Tuvok proceeds to tell Chakotay of Janeway's experiences on the USS *Billings* upon which she was sent to survey a volcanic moon as part of an away team. During that mission, the away team's shuttle was damaged by a magma eruption which severely injured three. Wracked with guilt, Janeway took a shuttle and returned to the moon to complete the mission alone, risking her own life to do so. On learning this, Chakotay fears that Janeway's guilt over the decision that stranded her crew in the Delta Quadrant will lead to another potentially catastrophic decision predicated on the pressure of guilty desire to get them out of the Void.

In the comparison of the captains, this episode does the important work of drawing attention to the fact that said comparison is based on both personal and command matters. Janeway's existential and command crisis mirrors Odysseus' in that Odysseus' return to Ithaca "is measured also in terms of his relationship with his companions. He is gradually divested of them— as of his ships, clothes, and all his Trojan accoutrements—through increasing emotional estrangement" (Segal 33–4). In Book I, *The Odyssey* opens with a description of Odysseus that bespeaks a clear sense of responsibility for his men:

> Many cities did he visit, and many were the nations with whose manners and customs he was acquainted; moreover he suffered much by sea while trying to save his own life and bring his men safely home; but do what he might he could not save his men, for they perished through their own sheer folly in eating the cattle of the Sungod Hyperion; so the god prevented them from ever reaching home [Homer 13].

In Book IX, Odysseus also shows a concern that his men are not left behind among the Lotus-eaters, a command concern further expressed, albeit with paucity, when Odysseus takes ultimately ineffective measures to pass Scylla without further loss of men in Book XII. While there seems to be a direct proportion between Odysseus' level of concern and the degree of the danger he and his crew face, his concern not only for his crew but also for the *nostos* is seemingly suspended (temporarily) on islands of Ogygia and Aeaea which function like Void spaces: odd places that do not function the same way other mortal space-times are bound to do. It is within this space that Odysseus' sense of command breaks down, leaving him little recourse but traumatic recollection of the failures of his command. In these voids, Odysseus "can no longer fulfill the functions of protective king and general, and he becomes increasingly less able to save his men from the ravages of this dangerous world" (Segal 34). In contrast to the "instability of these relationships [between Odysseus and his men], which are based only on temporary circumstances and a common desire for self-preservation," this line of relation is inverted in Janeway to such a degree that the crew becomes her family, and the ship itself both the means of and completion of *nostos* (Segal 34). As such, while "the bond begins to dissolve as [Odysseus's] companions' desire for self-preservation weakens," the dire circumstances, staggering distance, and narrow odds of Janeway's success do not corrode but rather strengthen her relationships with her crew, even highly onto-existentially complex ones like that between herself and Seven (Segal 34).

It would seem that the Void would suggest that circumstance, the burdens of command, failure, loss, being becalmed, and the ever-present likelihood of cataclysm, failure, death and destruction cause a similar caustic despondency in Odysseus and Janeway. For the former, by the time he arrives at Alcinous' palace, "even Odysseus' wish to save [his crew], along with his former position of authority, becomes increasingly meaningless" (Segal 34). While this is true of Janeway's self-reflection and self-criticism in the Void, the imperative nature of the *nostos*, the lives and well-being of her crew, and, according to Kim in the series finale, the value of the journey never falter to the point of meaninglessness.

In terms of the similarities between Janeway, Odysseus, and their respective Voids, Circe and Calypso's island have similar effects on Odysseus' psychological and emotional well-being. For each, they represent both spaces of reflection and of suffering. In certain respects, Ogygia and Aeaea have similarities with the holodeck, but in reverse. While the holodeck on the Voyager gives the crew respite from the monotony of the journey, a monotony whose psychological and emotional strain is intensified by phenomena like the Void, Circe's and Calypso's respective islands function as traps, impediments that waylay both the wandering and homecoming of Odysseus and his crew. Further similarities exist between the psycho-emotional profiles of both becalmed captains in that Janeway's despondency matches the despondency of Odysseus described in Book V after Odysseus arrives, by raft, to Scheria, Calypso's island. Similarly, when confronted by becalmed space which, like the title of Ensign Kim's clarinet concerto ("Echoes of the Void") aptly describes, acts as an echo chamber wherein memories of lapses in leadership and, more broadly, the significance, weight, and failures of the homeward journey and wandering manifest as psycho-emotional echoes in the Void. In the Void, the weight of the journey, the scale of its distances, the suffering/loss of their respective crews, and the inescapable prospect of further distances still untraveled on their homeward wanderings are the only things to resound in becalmed space. As such, Janeway's introspective self-criticism reflects that of Odysseus during his entrapment on the nymph/goddesses' respective islands. They are to Odysseus what the Void is to Janeway: an oppressive stillness, a deafening silence only broken by divine/alien intervention. Spaces wherein which both captains have nothing but inexhaustible time to think about their failures past and long road home ahead of them.

Janeway pining for days when the crew was under constant threat from the Borg is like Odysseus pining for the days of Troy, action, distraction, movement, and purpose as an alternative to the unavoidable dirge-like lamentations, recollections, self-criticism each captain has of their respective commands. On the one hand, Janeway's self-criticism is somewhat modulated by the presence of her senior officers, especially her first officer Chakotay who, though also experiencing the psychological and emotional strain and discomfort caused by the Void, is still able to offer an alternate opinion of the captain's decision making and general consequences of her command performance up to and including their entry into the Void. On the other hand, Odysseus has nobody to speak to on Ogygia save his captor-rescuer-seductress because his crew is all lost at this point in his homeward journey. It is for this reason that Odysseus's island void is, ironically, a space of psychological and emotional hardship. Despite the fact that Calypso's and Circe's islands have "hints of both an Elysium-like paradise of rest after life's trials and a Hades-like oblivion in a remote ocean," the Edenic external scene, topography, largess, and fecundity of these islands are the complete inverse of the black desolation Odysseus feels there upon (Segal 24).

In comparing the way each captain deals with her/his respective self-reflection, the isolation Odysseus experiences on said islands in said goddesses' keep versus Janeway in the Void illustrates that the latter is not only a better person, but also a better captain precisely because she takes the opportunity to, albeit depressively, reflect on her relationship with her command. The questions each captain must grapple with, questions that no *deus ex machina*, that is divine or technological intervention, can waylay include but are not limited to: What is a captain to do to get her/his crew safely home? How is a captain to balance their own psycho-emotional well-being against the insufferable odds amassed against the chances of success of their homecoming? The answers to these questions, which neither captain arrives at in any conclusive way, reveal how each views themselves as a commander and the status/profile of their own commands. With *Voyager*, we have other perspectives (Chakotay's and Tuvok's). With Odysseus, we have only his telling of his own command performance. Even in his trip to Hades in Book XI, his former crewmen and soldiers do not comment on his command, but rather take the opportunity to air their own personal grievances with him—for example, Ajax's sullen despondency regarding the fact that Odysseus outsmarted him to win the armor of the fallen Achilles.

By the conclusion of both narratives, the difference in value of the *nostos* in *The Odyssey* and *Voyager* can be summed up by Kim in "Endgame" (7.25):

> KIM: I think it's safe to say that no one on this crew has been more obsessed with getting home than I have. But, when I think about everything we've been through together, maybe it's not the destination that matters. Maybe it's the journey. And if that journey takes a little longer so we can do something we all believe in, I can't think of any place I'd rather be, or any people I'd rather be with ["Endgame" 7.25].

In this sense, by the end of the series' exploration of wandering and homecoming, its burdens, pleasures, mysteries, and heartaches, any typified notion of "home" is outgrown and becomes redundant. In *Voyager*, *nostos* is not as important as the journey. In this sense, Voyager, the ship, is *both* home and journey. In contrast, Odysseus cannot think about the value of the journey because he is convinced he will make it home. Over seven seasons numerous opportunities emerge for the crew of the Voyager to make it home. However, these encounters and opportunities, most missed or only partly achieved, catalyze an interesting evolution in the *nostos* narrative, the value of wandering, hardship, survival, tenacity, and teamwork. It is only because the crew of the Voyager come to accept that there is little to no chance of them successfully returning to Earth that the value of homecoming itself becomes lesser than that of the voyage itself.

WORKS CITED

Alexopoulou, Marigo. *The Theme of Returning Home in Ancient Greek Literature: The Nostos of the Epic Heroes*. Edwin Mellen Press, 2009.
Baker, Djoymi. "'Every Old Trick Is New Again': Myth in Quotations and the Star Trek Franchise." *Star Trek as Myth: Essays on Symbol and Archetype at the Final Frontier*, edited by Mathew Wilhelm Kapell, McFarland, 2010, pp. 80–93.
Bonifazi, Anna. "Inquiring Into Nostos and Its Cognates." *American Journal of Philology*, vol. 130 no. 4, 2009, pp. 481–510. Project MUSE, doi:10.1353/ajp.0.0078. Accessed 30 Jan. 2019.
"Dark Frontier." *Star Trek: Voyager*, written by Joe Menosky and Brannon Braga, directed by Terry Windell and Cliff Bole, Season 5, episodes 15 and 16, Paramount, 17 Feb. 1999.
"Endgame." *Star Trek: Voyager*, written by Rick Berman, Kenneth Biller, and Brannon Braga, directed by Allan Kroeker, Season 7, episodes 25 and 26, Paramount, 23 May 2001.
"Favorite Son." *Star Trek: Voyager*, written by Lisa Klink, perf. Garrett Wang, Season 3, episode 20, Paramount, 19 Mar. 1997.
"The Gift." *Star Trek: Voyager*, written by Joe Menosky, directed by Anson Williams, Season 4, episode 2, Paramount, 10 Sept. 1997.
Greven, David. *Gender and Sexuality in Star Trek*. McFarland, 2009.
Homer. *The Odyssey*. Translated by Samuel Butler, W.J. Black, 1944.
Marshall Cavendish Corporation. *Gods, Goddesss, and Mythology Vol. 1*. Marshall Cavendish, 2005.

"Night." *Star Trek: Voyager*, written by Brannon Braga, directed by David Livingston, Season 5, episode 1, Paramount, 14 Oct. 1998.

"Nostos." Harvard, http://sites.fas.harvard.edu/~lac14/glossary/nostos/index.ghtml. Accessed 30 Jan. 2019.

Segal, Charles. *Singers, Heroes, and Gods in the "Odyssey."* Cornell University Press, 2001.

"Timeless." *Star Trek: Voyager*, written by Joe Menosky, Brannon Braga, and Rick Berman, directed by LeVar Burton, Season 5, episode 6, Paramount, 18 Nov. 1998.

"The Voyager Conspiracy." *Star Trek: Voyager*, written by Joe Menosky, directed by Terry Windell, Season 6, episode 9, Paramount, 24 Nov. 1999.

"From hell's heart, I stab at thee"
Villain Typologies of the Delta Quadrant

Andrew Howe

Star Trek: Voyager has been celebrated as the first Trek with a narrative primarily told through the storylines of women, first and foremost with Captain Kathryn Janeway and later Seven-of-Nine, the latter Voyager's equivalent to Spock and Data, characters who, through the discovery of their humanity, allow us to see with fresh eyes. The series has also been noted for, like Homer's Odyssey (see Kwasu David Tembo's essay, this volume), focusing upon the complexities of home as both a physical destination and a meta-physical idea. One dimension that has received little attention involves the many new villains created for the show, a diversity of antagonists with widely disparate agendas and attitudes against whom Janeway and her crew must compete, in so doing defining and deepening their own values. In the first Star Trek series to be set exclusively outside the Alpha Quadrant, the writers behind Voyager were given a nearly blank slate upon which to create these villainous characters. The major portion of this essay will examine villains that exist within two different typologies, focusing on several for sustained analysis. The first general category involves villains who have a moral code. These characters know the difference between right and wrong, although somehow their code is a bit twisted or at odds with Voyager. Such villains are often driven by a need for order or some other higher ideal, although they do not care if their goals are achieved at the expense of others. In this regard, they are utilitarian, and would very much resonate with the saying "when making an omelet, you have to break a few eggs." To continue this metaphor, such characters do not break eggs wantonly, but only when they feel it to be necessary. As such, they are not necessarily marked as "evil" within Voyager. Examples of this villain type include Captain Braxton of Starfleet, Species 8472, and Annorax of the Krenim. The Borg also fit into this category, although this species has been explored in a variety of publications and as such analysis will not be offered in this essay. The second general category involves villains with no moral code whatsoever, those who are motivated purely by selfish desire—e.g., the Kazon and Seska, or the Vidiians and their organ harvesting—or by a rigidly narrow ideology, such as Kashyk of the Devore. Kazon characters are generally morally bankrupt with no ethos other than pure Darwinian survival. The Devore, on the other hand, have a clear and consistent code, but one that is immoral in its rejection of basic civil rights. For the two categories, sub-types will be identified, e.g., the mastermind, the Ahab figure, and the betrayer. It will become clear that the boundaries between those with a moral code and those without are murky indeed, linking *Voyager* as a close spiritual cousin to *Deep Space Nine*, the *Star Trek* show most often noted for its moral complexity. The final portion of the essay will examine the two-part episode "Equinox" (5.26 and 6.1) which serves as a microcosm of the various forms of villainy on display in the Delta Quadrant, ironically amongst a ship full of humans from Starfleet.

The villains in *Voyager* that exhibit a moral code tend towards orderliness and consistency, perhaps a narrative ploy on the part of the writers when it comes to short-term plans for rehabilitation at the end of an episode (Annorax) or in future episodes (Species 8472). From the Klingons (*The Undiscovered Country*, Worf, Martok) through the Cardassians (Garak) and even the Borg (Hugh, Seven), the rehabilitation of former enemy species has been a consistent thread throughout the *Star Trek* canon. In general, such villains tend to contribute something to an institution or to their culture, and their goals are more collective than individual. That's not to say that these aliens are sympathetic, or that they are necessarily rehabilitated. For instance, in "The Scientific Method" (4.7), the Srivani are never apologetic for the medical experiments to which they subject Voyager's crew. As Anthony Rotolo notes, this species' "high-tech form of anonymity" allows them distance from the damaging effects of their ministrations (Rotolo 35). He goes on to identify that the episode "asks us to consider what we are willing to sacrifice in the name of science, especially as new technologies make it easier to hide from the consequences of our actions" (Rotolo 35).

Spock's statement "The needs of the many outweigh the needs of the few" is empty and illogical, resulting in moral codes that, like the Srivani's, suffer from mission creep over time. Despite this mark against them, at the end of the day the Srivani are on one side of the villainy divide, as their experiments are for collective benefit, while the Vidiians, with their organ harvesting involving personal gain, are on the other. That's not to say that personal gain does not apply to some of the moral villains, however. A case in point is Annorax, whose desire to return his family to the timeline gets in the way of his mission. Furthermore, for species such as the Hirogen, maintaining culture has in essence become about individual needs, due to the rigid hierarchies predicated upon trophies from successful hunts. When it comes to general features, one final point deserves to be raised when it comes to the villain with a moral code. Although it often serves as a cheap narrative trick, numerous *Voyager* episodes humanize a single member of a species as a way of recapturing some semblance of morality and decency while allowing the maintenance of general species-level culpability as villains (e.g., Seven of Nine and Annorax).

The first villain analyzed in this section illustrates a critical point that will be driven home in the later analysis of "Equinox" (5.26 and 6.1): some of the worst villains that Voyager encounters in their travels—Braxton, Seska, and Ransom—are from the Alpha Quadrant. Captain Braxton crosses paths with Voyager twice, in "Future's End, Part I" (3.8); "Future's End, Part II" (3.9); and in "Relativity" (5.24). On both occasions, he attempts to destroy Voyager, in the former episode because he believes they are responsible for a temporal explosion that destroys 29th century Earth, in the latter because he realizes that removing Voyager from the timeline will allow him to regain his career and former standing. In "Future's End" (3.8 and 3.9), his villainy has its roots in hubris, and he is punished by being stranded for decades on Earth amongst, as he denotes them, the "postindustrial barbarians" of the late 20th century. In "Relativity" (5.24), his villainy is one of illness, as he experiences temporal psychosis. In both cases, Braxton is presented as a singularly humorless character devoid of emotion and focused obsessively upon his mission. In this, he is a bit of an Ahab character, although not to the same degree as Annorax. Like the ship's captain from Herman Melville's famous novel *Moby Dick*, Braxton is so focused on his mission that he does not realize when his obsession begins to destroy innocent lives, including his own. Indeed, when Voyager first crosses paths with Braxton, his justification for why he is attempting to destroy the ship sounds very much like the Borg assimilation mantra: "My mission is your destruction. You must not resist."

Karma Waltonen notes that Braxton's experiences with time do "not make him question the wisdom of attempting to use time travel to 'fix' the timeline" (Waltonen 164). Indeed, "Future's End" (3.8 and 3.9) is an example of a Pogo Paradox, a concept invoked in "Relativity" (5.24) involving a causal loop whereby the interference of an agent in attempting to stop an event is actually its cause. Waltonen continues by noting that Braxton's attempts to destroy Voyager arise out of a desire to save lives: "Braxton's intentions are good, but his incomplete understanding of causality almost renders the timeline permanently damaged" (Waltonen 169). Despite being unlikable as a character and having twice tried to destroy Voyager—in "Future's End" (3.8

and 3.9) by shooting them with a subatomic weapon, in "Relativity" (5.24) by planting a temporal disruptor on the ship—Braxton is rehabilitated at every turn. In "Future's End" (3.8 and 3.9), when the Voyager crew encounters him after both are stranded on 20th century earth, he is homeless, paranoid, and constantly being harassed by police.

In a well-used narrative trick, much worse villains are introduced as contrasts to Braxton's villainy, including (briefly) members of a racist, anti-government militia in Arizona who menace Chakotay and Torres, and Henry Starling, the CEO of Chronowerx Industries. Starling, a hippy who happened to be camping in the Sierras when Braxton's ship crashed in 1967, took parts from the time ship and became a sort of twisted, Bill Gates–type entrepreneur, creating the micro-computer revolution. Although he claims that his goal is "the betterment of mankind," Starling is purely selfish in his designs. While playing pinball, he coldly orders the murder of an employee who knows too much, then sadistically tortures The Doctor, into whose holographic code he has introduced pain receptors. Next to Starling and his species of villainy, Braxton begins to become something of a sympathetic character.

Rehabilitation is also evident in "Relativity" (5.24). Again, Braxton is humorless—at one point dismissing Seven as "a pedantic drone"—and bent upon the destruction of Voyager. Once again, however, he is portrayed as paranoid, this time not due to exile on earth but temporal psychosis: "That woman has been responsible for three major temporal incursions.... And who do you think had to repair the damage? Me. She's reckless; she has no regard for the integrity of the timeline. I asked for her help once. She refused, and I ended up stranded in the late 20th century" ("Relativity"). Braxton's statement is ironic, as he is guilty of the same thing of which he accuses Janeway: recklessness. In "Future's End" (3.8 and 3.9), he concludes on scant evidence that Voyager is responsible for the 29th century destruction of earth. And in planting the temporal weapon in "Relativity" (5.24), he has no regard for the integrity of the timeline. When one realizes, however, that Braxton is suffering from psychosis, his actions become more understandable. Other evidence of his rehabilitation comes in the fact that he uses a temporal disruptor that will only fracture space-time within 150 meters (so as not to hurt anyone else), and that once caught he freely admits when he plants the bomb, allowing Janeway to capture him in the past. Braxton is an unpleasant character, to be sure, and a villain of note in the *Voyager* canon. However, the origins of his villainy come out of a sense of mission and preservation rather than selfish design. He does have a moral code, although one that, in the end, is easily overthrown by his obsession and tendency to jump to conclusions without complete information.

Annorax is another Ahab-type villain who appears in a temporal storyline, although his specific obsession manifests itself in not knowing when to put an end to his project rather than from psychosis or paranoia. In "The Year of Hell, Part I" (4.8) and "The Year of Hell, Part II" (4.9), Annorax uses a temporal weapon to tinker with the timeline, attempting to restore the Krenim Imperium to its former glory. Of course, he is never able to bring the empire back to 100 percent of its former capacity, the linchpin for his continued quest the fact that the world upon which his family lived is never part of the recaptured space. There is a coldness about Annorax, such as when after zapping a city with his temporal beam, his officer Obrist tells him: "All organisms and manmade objects have been eradicated." Annorax calmly replies: "Probe the continuum. Has our target event been achieved?" ("The Year of Hell, Part I"). When removing smaller targets from the timeline proves ineffective, he broadens the scope of his temporal experiments: "Eradicating a single Zahl colony wasn't enough for a total restoration. We have to work on a larger scale. Take us to the Zahl home world. Prepare a new set of calculations. We must erase the entire species from time, every life-form, every molecule" ("The Year of Hell, Part I").

One might think that Annorax is a monster, and that he is able to justify that he isn't really murdering these species, just ensuring that they never existed in the first place. Despite the chilling aspects of his statements, however, there is humanity and nobility to Annorax, particularly as comes through in his relationship with Chakotay, whom along with Paris he captures after trying unsuccessfully to remove Voyager from the timeline. His mission is rooted in both patriotism to his species and love of his family, and we find out that he has been tinkering with the timeline for over 200 years. He develops a relationship with Chakotay, serving as a mentor when he recognizes that Voyager's commander has a gift when it comes to temporal mechanics. At one point, he treats Chakotay and Paris to a feast consisting of the gastro-remnants of civilizations that, in this timeline, never existed. What might seem like a celebration with trophies, however, is actually about remembrance and loss. As Annorax tells Chakotay: "You can't imagine the burden of memory that I carry—thousands of worlds, billions of lives, gone, brought back, gone again. I try to rationalize the loss. They're not really being destroyed because they never existed. Sometimes I can ... almost convince myself" ("The Year of Hell, Part II"). In the end, Annorax does *not* do the right thing. Voyager prevails not because of his conscience, but because Obrist realizes that his captain will never be satisfied and disables the Krenim ship so that Janeway might survive. Still, it would be a mistake to denote Annorax anything other than a moral villain, and it is important to note that, at the end of the episode, the writers included a scene with Annorax reunited with his wife.

Sometimes, rehabilitation is possible on a species-wide level. When they first debuted at the end of Season 3, Species 8472 introduced a complex, multi-season story arc that further troubled the notion of villainy in the series. Initially, in "Scorpion, Part I" (3.26), Species 8472 was presented as having an ideology at odds with Voyager, as in her telepathic communication one of them tells Kes: "The weak shall perish." Although Janeway's first instinct is to enlist 8472 as a potential ally against the Borg, she quickly decides that this new species is the bigger threat based upon the alien's attack on both Voyager and Harry Kim, as well as Kes' premonitions. The fact that the Voyager crew so quickly embraces the clinical Borg name for this species indicates a full acceptance of villainy, with no attempt to humanize or understand. As it turns out, Kes' glimpse of the alien and its communication are unrefined, and the threats representing the false bravado of one who feels cornered. True, some of the aggression displayed by the single alien is later reflected on the species level when, after Voyager enters fluidic space, Kes is told that humans have contaminated their realm and the threat is made that "Your galaxy will be purged" ("Scorpion, Part I"). Again, this statement should not be taken at face value, and it is important to note that 8472 is the only species in its realm, which means that they are more likely to be xenophobic, making Voyager's actions that much more invasive. Both 8472 and Voyager are operating out of fear, demonstrating that villainy can be a construct rooted in false perceptions, distracting from what might have been more cordial relations had these two species met under different circumstances.

In two later episodes, Species 8472 enjoys a full rehabilitation, moving from terrifying villain to a place of mutual respect and détente. In "Prey" (4.16), Janeway agrees to help a member of Species 8472 stranded outside fluidic space and hunted by Hirogen. Unable in the end to protect the hunted, Janeway and her crew are nevertheless exposed to Species 8472 as a victim. The fruits of this turn are born in the episode "In the Flesh" (5.4), when Chakotay visits a simulation of Starfleet headquarters, where 8472s train for what will theoretically be a mission of reconnaissance, if not invasion, of Earth. This concept episode is interesting in that it allows the Voyager crew to vicariously return home, re-introduces a character—Boothby—who first appeared in the *TNG* episode "The First Duty" (5.19), and allows Chakotay a brief romance with an 8472 who takes on the guise of Commander Valerie Archer. The 8472 operatives have taken drugs that will allow them to hold a shape that appears human, and are enjoined to "Think Human. Talk Human. Be Human" ("In the Flesh"), reminiscent of the KGB training towns in Russia where operatives trained so that they could optimally blend into American society. Indeed, the spirit of the Cold War pervades this episode. The 8472 take the human threat very seriously, not only in creating these training simulations, but also in the manner in which a captive taken by Chakotay and Tuvok responds when questioned by Janeway, shrieking "Disease! Humans!" before releasing a cellular toxin into his bloodstream.

Clearly, the 8472 are as terrified of Voyager as the crew is afraid of these aliens. In managing the threat, the senior staff discusses WMDs (in this case, a torpedo containing nano-probes) and diplomacy; fortunately, the latter wins the day. In a sit down between Janeway and the Boothby 8472, it becomes clear that each leader's perception of the other is in error. Species 8472 isn't a villainous species, their actions colored by a perception of the Federation as a conquest-driven empire like the Dominion in *DS-9*, and whose first act was to make an alliance with the Borg and invade their realm. Janeway takes the torpedoes offline, invoking Starfleet Directive 101: "Before engaging alien species in battle, any and all attempts to make first contact and achieve non-military resolution must be made" ("In the Flesh"). The two sides arrive at an uneasy détente, although *Voyager* is far too good a show to wrap things up so neatly. True, those who have met the Voyager crew might be convinced, but the Boothby 8472 indicates that he will have to try and win over his superiors, who are not nearly as open-minded as he. Once a villain is created, it's a long road indeed for full rehabilitation, even if they are discovered to hold the same values and follow the same moral code.

Although there have been several different flavors of villainy analyzed thus far, they all share in common some aspect of consistency of vision geared toward the preservation of culture or embrace of a greater good. Such villains are villainous mostly because they are matched up against Voyager and her crew. They have a moral core that informs their actions, and thus are somewhat predictable in their behavior. Such a distinction does not apply to all of the villains in the series. There are those who lack a moral code and are motivated by pure selfish design. Such villains appear in different forms, all of them antithetical to Starfleet values. For the first few seasons, Seska is arguably the primary villain, once again an Alpha Quadrant antagonist rising to a level of prominence. Chakotay and the other Maquis crew knew her as a clever and formidable operative fighting against Cardassian rule in contested space. In reality, Seska was a Cardassian agent genetically altered to look Bajoran, planted in the Maquis in order to gain intelligence that would undermine their mission. She is archly manipulative, willing to employ seduction, intimidation, or even murder to get her way, using others for the alliances they offer but willing to throw them over at a moment's notice.

Seska does have some redeeming qualities, clearly having feelings for Chakotay. Her ongoing relationship with him serves as a prism not only for her selfishness, but also for his rehabilitation as a former Maquis. As Will Nguyen notes, the prior relationship between the two "adds depth to Chakotay in the sense that it shows him to be vulnerable and also intensely loyal, even to a fault" (Nguyen). Linked as former Maquis, Seska's lack of loyalty demonstrates Chakotay's growth as a character. In the early episodes, Chakotay is vulnerable to her manipulation, as is Mike, another Maquis whom, in

"Lifesigns" (2.19), she both bullies and cajoles in order to extract information. In "State of Flux" (1.11), in order to make Chakotay jealous she mentions that she has become attracted to Harry Kim before cooing: "Can we make up now?" Voyager's first officer, however, eventually figures her out. In "Maneuvers" (2.11), when Chakotay dialogues with Maje Culluh of the Kazon-Nistrim, he attempts to warn Seska's latest ally about her weapons: "Flattery, devotion, sex."

Seska is one of *Voyager*'s arch villains not due to the frequency of her appearance, but in that she almost always, except for in the final frame, gets the better of the Voyager crew. In "Maneuvers" (2.11), she sets a flawless trap for Voyager and anticipates Janeway's every move, demonstrating her superiority to B'Elanna at transporting when she successfully beams Chakotay onto her ship. In "Shattered" (7.11), she is the villain that Chakotay and Janeway leave until last, enlisting crew from different time periods in order to defeat her. And in "Worst Case Scenario" (3.25), the *trace* of Seska is deadly, as one of Tuvok's training program's involving a Maquis rebellion runs amok, threatening Voyager. Seska had found the program during her time on the ship and re-programmed it to take over, nearly proving a match for Voyager's combined crew even *after* her death.

All villains have reasons for what they do, but not all have a moral code. Despite what clearly amounts to affection for Chakotay and a mother's love for her child, Seska's decisions are very much rooted in self-interest. Yes, she does have long-term goals, but those are rooted in a myopia that does not stand up to scrutiny. In "State of Flux" (1.11), after being exposed as a Cardassian Seska explains to Chakotay why she shared technology with the Kazon: "We are alone here, at the mercy of any number of hostile aliens because of the incomprehensible decision of a Federation captain who destroyed our only chance to get home.... We must begin to forge alliances. To survive, we must have powerful friends." There is no real pattern or long-term stratagem at work, however. The Kazon are simply one of the first species that Voyager encounters, and clearly one that has nothing to offer the ship. Seska's assertion is thus empty, her act one of self-interest in hedging her bets by making an alliance should her secret identity as a Cardassian spy be uncovered.

The Kazon are an entirely different type of villain. Much like Seska, they are very much about selfish gain, but more of a direct, brutish flavor than the Cardassian's manipulations. Maje Culluh and most of the other Kazon characters of note appear to be ruled by impulse. Consistently, the species is portrayed as crude, barbaric, simplistic, violent, and paranoid. When shown on Voyager's view screen, a Kazon leader's face is nearly always too close to the camera, almost as if they are invading the screen. They are reactive in their decision-making, tribal in their organization, patriarchal and misogynist in their hierarchy, and territorial in their outlook. When seeing Voyager's shuttle in "Initiations" (2.2), the captain of one ship solemnly intones: "We should teach them the price of displaying their markings in our space," without having a clue as to how powerful an enemy they are provoking. The Kazon are cunning, no doubt, but not very strategic, their actions often as violent as they are expedient. They are no real threat to Voyager, at least without Seska's master planning, other than in their numbers and implacable nature.

As Paul Ruditis notes, the Kazon have suffered from factors outside of their control, factors that might explain their belligerence and propensity for violence. For starters, they suffer from a cultural legacy of a colonial species known as the Trabe (Ruditis 92). In "Alliances" (2.14), Janeway hears the backstory from Mabus, a member of the Trabe that Voyager rescues from captivity.

> I was 8 years old when it started. I wasn't even particularly aware of the Kazon. They lived in restricted areas that children weren't allowed to go near. I didn't know they lived in poverty, and filth. I didn't know they were persecuted by the Trabe police. I was told they were violent and dangerous, and had to be kept isolated, so they wouldn't get loose and kill us, which is exactly what they did, but we brought it on ourselves ["Alliances"].

The imagery of segregation begins to move into the terrain of Nazi ghetto policy as Mabus continues: "The Trabe treated them like animals, fenced them in, encouraged them to fight amongst themselves so they wouldn't turn on us" ("Alliances").

In the episode "Initiations" (2.2), a young Kazon whom Chakotay befriends notes that the revolution happened 26 years ago, and that the infighting between sects started immediately after. The Kazon legacy is thus one of the early phases of de-colonization. This point is made abundantly clear in "Alliances" (2.14), an episode where Voyager attempts to facilitate a peace summit between the various Kazon sects and the Trabe. In a scene similar to *Godfather III*, Mabus tries to convince the Voyager delegation to leave the room right before it is strafed by a ship. Clearly, the Kazon not only have their own kind to fear, but a resurgence of power by the Trabe. One can understand why they might be paranoid, selfish, and even violent when it comes to outsiders. As Wei Ming Dariotis notes, the Federation does have an awful lot to answer for, with the ideological and geo-political conflicts that arise out of its "scientific" exploration leading to "border-changing and identity-challenging convergences" that, inevitably result in empire building (Dariotis 71). Even though Voyager merely wants to proceed quickly through Kazon space, and Seska is the agent of Maje Culluh getting his hands on a transporter, Voyager's technology *does* change the balance of power in the sector. Perhaps the Kazon are justified in their attempts to destroy Voyager.

Ruditis also notes another manner in which the Kazon's path may have been somewhat pre-ordained, at least in the short-term: the lack of resources in their sector has served to magnify the infighting (Ruditis 92). This is certainly true, as in the very first episode ("Caretaker" 1.1); it is clear that the Kazon live hand-to-mouth, evidenced by the fact that they are willing to barter for water. As Maje Jabin tells Janeway: "How can we help someone so powerful they can create water out of thin air?" Much later, in "Relativity" (5.24), Seven underscores the primitive nature of the Kazon in discounting them as the source for the temporal disruptor placed on Voyager: "The Kazon are an inferior species. They don't possess the technology to create such a complex weapon." Her first statement is judgmental, her second precise. Clearly, Seven has no use for the Kazon, for as a species they could not help the Borg in their goal of perfection. The seeds of sympathy for the Kazon are sown in these earlier episodes, with the culmination of a partial rehabilitation coming with the character of Kar in "Initiations" (2.2).

Kar is a young Kazon who cannot bring himself to kill Chakotay, and who must bear the shame of his inaction. Throughout the rest of the episode, Kar is caught between the philosophy of Voyager's first officer, who befriends him, and of his upbringing, symbolized by the violent Maje Razik of the Ogla, who in the first of several episodic connections to the Hirogen displays around his ship trophies from enemies he has vanquished. In the end, Kar announces that he will shoot his enemy, but turns his phaser upon Razik instead of Chakotay. Clearly Razik was not a popular leader, as instead of being sanctioned Kar is accepted into the group and given his adult name. Kar is a young character who signals a hope for the future in potentially abandoning the self-destructive practices and attitudes of his species. Kar has been taken back into the embrace of his people, a group he might one day grow to exert influence over. When it comes to the Kazon and their villainy, there is sympathy and hope for the future. That's not to say, however, that they have a moral code. Clearly, Kar does, but on the species-wide level the consistent application of naked aggression in pursuit of expedient gain suggests the lack of a moral code. With the passage of time, better access to resources, the continued consolidation of the sects, and voices like Kar's gaining prominence, the Kazon may get there eventually. They do, however, have quite a long way to go.

Not all villains of this typology are grounded in self-interested greed. As is evident in "Counterpoint" (5.10), there are examples of societal-level ideology that is more immoral than amoral in nature. In their widespread, systematic persecution of others (in this case, all telepathic species), the Devore are reminiscent of the Nazis, not an uncommon villainous trope in the *Star Trek* canon (see Jimenez's discussion in this volume), seen most notably in the form of the Cardassians (Carney 313). The Devore are a clean, orderly, record-keeping society, much as were the Nazis. Prax is the mindless Gestapo goon who quotes protocol, follows orders, and prefers physical intimidation. Kashyk is more sophisticated, employing false intellectual crutches to prop up arguments as to why species such as the Brenari deserve to be scooped up and placed in relocation centers, from which the implication is that there is no coming back. There are distinct overtones of racial purity when it comes to Kashyk and what is a national project of cleansing based upon telepathic ethnicity. The Devore ideology is distinctly flawed, however. No two telepathic species are alike. Brenari are not Vulcan are not Betazoid, and furthermore variation will exist within a species as to how easily a telepath can read a mind, as well as the degree to which an individual will exercise that power. In this episode, Voyager has become something of a Schindler's Ark, using the transporters to suspend the ship's telepaths and some refugee Brenari during the routine inspections to which Voyager is subjected while in Devore space.

The plot twist in "Counterpoint" (5.10) comes when Kashyk shows up, unannounced, claiming to be on the run from the Devore Imperium and requesting sanctuary, offering his help in securing the safety of the telepaths he knows to be on board. Despite her misgivings, Janeway goes along with him, as the Brenari admit that there are sympathizers among the Devore. On the surface, it seems as if Kashyk is another example of an individual pocket of conscience amidst larger societies of villainous antagonism, and that he is another who chooses not to subsume his moral compass to the immoral agenda of his species, much like Danara Pel of the Vidiians, who realizes that organ harvesting is wrong. Kashyk shares with Janeway his moment of epiphany:

> Three months ago, my teams were inspecting a plasma-refining vessel. We found a family of telepaths hiding in one of the extraction tanks. There was a child, very young. She'd been inside it for days, barely able to breathe. When I lifted her out and set her down on the deck, she thanked me. I sent her to a relocation center with the others, knowing full well what would happen to her ["Counterpoint" 5.10].

Naturally, Kashyk's change of heart is a deception to capture the Brenari, although true to form Janeway hedges her bets and everyone makes it out safely.

Chillingly, Kashyk admits to Janeway that his anecdote was in fact true, but that instead of overwhelming him with empathy it reinforced his obligation to protect his people from a very real threat. Much like the Hirogen, the Devore have made a determination as to who deserves which rights. The difference is that the Hirogen are utterly predictable in their *actions*, following a specific and inviolate code. There are certain things they will do, and certain things they won't, in the pursuit of their prey. They don't really have an overarching ideology, but they do have a moral code guiding their behavior. The same cannot be said for the Devore, however. For them, ideology trumps everything else, leading to a complete lack of a moral code. They are willing to do anything to anyone at anytime in pursuing their goals. When it comes to their telepathic xenophobia, there are no checks or balances on behavior.

The two-part episode "Equinox" (5.26 and 6.1), which spans the end of the fifth season and beginning of the sixth, is fascinating for a variety of reasons. First of all, it provides insight into how another Federation ship with different personnel and a different leadership model reacted to being stranded in the Delta Quadrant. Certainly, it is important to note that the Equinox was not a deep space-capable ship, perhaps explaining why its captain and crew began to cut corners, culminating in capturing and killing a nucleogenic species as a source of super-fuel in order to get back to Earth more quickly. It's also possible, however, that the lack of a blended crew had something to do with the descent into moral decay. After the events of "Caretaker" (1.1), the Voyager crew was not only tested by external forces, but also by internal ones involving ongoing tension between the two crews and the revelation that Seska was a Cardassian spy, factors that perhaps resulted in an immediate need to define identity and values. Perhaps, however, it simply has to do with top-end leadership and the personalities of Janeway and Rudolph Ransom, the Equinox Captain. Aside from providing the opportunity to see how another Federation crew fares after making different decisions, "Equinox" is yet another example of how some of the worst villains Voyager encounters are from the Alpha Quadrant. And finally, the episode is critical to this study as multiple threads of nuanced and complex villainy are manifest. At the outset of the episode, after Voyager saves the Equinox from an alien attack, Seven indicates that she would like to meet Ransom and his crew in order to "expand [her] knowledge of humanity." She will, just not in the fashion that she expects.

The two crews bond quickly: Ransom and Janeway over the responsibilities that they share; First Officer Maxwell Burke and B'Elanna over the time they spent together at Starfleet; and Noah Lessing and Seven of Nine, who saved his life after the alien attack. Quickly, however, it becomes clear that the two crews have gone in very different directions in the face of adversity. Ransom, whom his crew calls "Rudy," suggests that Janeway throw out the rule book when she invokes a Starfleet regulation and implies that he has broken the prime directive on multiple occasions. Clearly, Janeway feels the opposite, that order, hierarchy, and regulations are what have kept them not only Starfleet, but also human. In a secret meeting, it becomes evident that the Equinox crew are planning to pilfer Voyager of some key technology that will allow them to return to their project of getting home. Equally as clear, however, is that there are divisions amongst the senior staff. Ransom and Burke want to push the plan forward whereas Marla Gilmore is worried that Voyager will be left vulnerable. Lessing wants to stay on with Voyager, believing that together the two ships are more powerful. Ransom wins the day, shaming his staff over their ambivalence: "A shower and a hot meal. I guess that's all it takes for some of us to forget what's at stake here. We're going home" ("Equinox" 5.26).

As an Ahab figure, Ransom only focuses on his own obsession—getting home—not acknowledging that there is also something at stake for Voyager's crew, as indeed when Equinox does leave the nucleogenic aliens transfer their attacks to Voyager. The reasons why all four of the Equinox senior staff participate in the capture and murder of alien life forms are varied. Ransom wants to get his crew home, feeling as if he owes them as their Captain. As such, he is a double of Janeway, although one whose choices led him down a darker path. Burke has no pretense of lofty justification: he just wants to get home, although both he and Ransom are willing to use as bullets in their arsenal the argument that "we owe it to those who died for us to get this far." Gilmore and Lessing, however, are not fully on board, going along out of a mixture of duty to their captain and crew and desire to go home.

The division amongst the Equinox staff is mirrored on Voyager, where Janeway relieves Chakotay of duty after he stops her from nearly killing Lessing during an interrogation. A series of conversations during this episode tease out the competing philosophies of Ransom and Janeway, as reflected in different quantities in different individuals. The first is between the two captains. After she accuses him of meticulous brutality, he notes that the Equinox accidentally killed the first alien prior to discovering its properties—perhaps an instance of unreliable narrator—and that only 63 more such sacrifices are needed in order for the ship to return home. Their next exchange gets at the heart of Starfleet and its core mission of exploration:

> JANEWAY: [Our responsibility] is seek out new life, not destroy it.
> RANSOM: It's easy to cling to principles when you're standing on a vessel with its bulkheads intact, manned by a crew that's not starving.
> JANEWAY: If we turn our backs on our principles, we stop being human ["Equinox, Part I" 5.26].

One might think from this exchange that Ransom is valuing his crew over his principles, and Janeway the opposite. That is faulty logic, however, as clearly Janeway is investing in the health of her crew such things as culture and identity. She has the bigger picture in mind, whereas Ransom has allowed himself a singular determinant for being an effective leader. To Janeway, adherence to a moral code is a large part of a crew's overall health. In the second conversation, Gilmore tells Chakotay that she is glad that Voyager will be putting a stop to the experiments, noting how she dealt with what she knew was an immoral project: "I concentrated on the work. I tried not to think about how it was going to be used" ("Equinox, Part I" 5.26).

Of course, after this confession, Gilmore facilitates the Equinox escape by incapacitating Seven, indicating that while confession may be good for the soul, it does not necessarily equate to a full embrace of new patterns of behavior.

As the Equinox flees despite the aliens attacking Voyager—Ransom clearly not only puts his crew before the aliens, but also before fellow Starfleet personnel—he tells Seven that Janeway's mistake was in putting her morals before the welfare of her crew, again missing the point that morality is a key part of a crew's welfare. The final critical conversation is between Janeway and Chakotay when the latter gets the captain to admit that for once she has let the identity of an antagonist impact her decision-making:

> JANEWAY: He's a Starfleet Captain, and he's decided to abandon everything this uniform stands for. He's out there right now, torturing and murdering innocent life-forms just to get home a little quicker. I'm not going to stand for it. I'm going to hunt him down no matter how long it takes, no matter what the cost ["Equinox, Part II" 6.1].

In the end, even though Janeway has Chakotay confined to quarters, his words get through to her. Before being relieved of command, he tells her: "It's not about rules and regulations, it's about right and wrong" ("Equinox, Part II" 6.1), reminding her that morality trumps allegiance to Starfleet.

Ransom, too, has second thoughts. Although his crew once again go about harnessing aliens for fuel, he as well as Gilmore and Lessing start to doubt their mission. It is as if their encounter with Voyager, and specifically a crew that despite hardships worked diligently to uphold their Starfleet values and principles, reawakened in them an upwelling of conscience. In the end, Burke is the only one who is unrepentant, seizing control when Ransom attempts to surrender to Janeway.

Ransom is able to turn the tables, however, transporting several of the Equinox crew to Voyager, in his own words "those worth getting," absolving some crew members—such as Gilmore and Lessing—while implicating others, most notably Burke and himself. These two, and the majority of the Equinox crew, die in the subsequent all-out alien attack, victims of their decision to put the safety of their cohort ahead of the moral principles that guided them.

The *Star Trek* canon is crowded with varied and complex villains, not the least of which is Khan Noonien Singh, whose paraphrase of a quote from *Moby Dick*—"From Hell's heart, I stab at thee"—provides the title for this essay. Like Khan and Ahab before them, many of the most fascinating figures in *Star Trek: Voyager* are its villains, characters who chart a range both broad and subtle when it comes to specific brands of villainy. Having a strong antagonist is key to producing a rich narrative tapestry, something that American artists as diverse as Herman Melville and Gene Roddenberry have long realized. For a long arc *Star Trek* narrative, one might think that *Voyager* was at a disadvantage in a directional storytelling that rarely involved the same physical space more than once (unlike, for instance, the richness of location afforded in *Deep Space Nine*, with villains like Gul Dukat returning again and again to the station). Although there are a few villains who do make multiple appearances—Seska, Maje Culluh, the Borg Queen—in general *Voyager* draws its strength from having to continually invent new and novel villains, the antithesis to *Deep Space Nine* and the ongoing gag of "yet another Weyoun clone" arriving on the station to fence verbally with Captain Sisko.

Among all of the *Star Trek* television series, *Voyager* often seems to get short shrift; perhaps the lack of a centralized villain in the vein of Gul Dukat or Q (who, despite appearing in three *Voyager* episodes, never really rises to the same level as he does in *The Next Generation*) does the show harm in the collective fandom. Evidence of this latter assertion appears in the online mock trial "The Court Martial of Captain Kathryn Janeway"—in which she was found not guilty by fans of being the series' primary villain (Davenport)—as well as YouTube videos dedicated to identifying show runners Rick Berman, Michael Piller, and Jeri Taylor as the principal villains (Macleod). Holding *Voyager* to the same standard as its predecessors, however, is unfair. It's hard to rehabilitate a villain in *Voyager* when the ship is a moving target that rarely stays put long enough to see the long-term impact of its influence, but the series does chart this territory by returning to certain *species* time and again, allowing for a realistic portrayal of character and even species-level evolution. And finally, in having so many of the most interesting villains—Braxton, Seska, and Ransom—derive from the Alpha Quadrant, *Voyager* advances a thesis that, despite Roddenberry's pro-humanistic vision, wells up in the *Star Trek* canon from time to time: humans are often their own worst enemy, true from such topical concerns as the impact of whaling upon Earth's vitality in *Star Trek IV: The Voyage Home* through the villains of *Voyager*, many in the mold of Ahab, who through their interaction with the ship allow Janeway and her crew to understand, and reinforce, their humanity.

Works Cited

"Alliances." *Star Trek: Voyager*, written by Jeri Taylor, directed by Les Landau, Season 2, episode 14, Paramount, 22 Jan. 1996.

"Caretaker." *Star Trek: Voyager*, created by Jeri Taylor, Gene Roddenberry, Rick Berman, and Michael Piller, performance by Roxann Dawson, Season 1, episodes 1 and 2, Paramount, 16 Jan. 1995.

Carney, Amy. "Nazis, Cardassians, and Other Villains in the Final Frontier." *Star Trek and History*, edited by Nancy R. Reagin, Wiley, 2013, pp. 307–22.
"Counterpoint." *Star Trek: Voyager*, written by Michael Taylor, directed by Les Landau, Season 5, episode 10, Paramount, 16 Dec. 1998.
Dariotis, Wei Ming. "Crossing the Racial Frontier: *Star Trek* and Mixed Heritage Identities." *The Influence of 'Star Trek' on Television, Film and Culture*, edited by Lincoln Geraghty, McFarland, 2008, pp. 63–81.
Davenport, Caillan. "The Court Martial of Captain Kathryn Janeway." *Trek Today*, www.trektoday.com/articles/court_martial_janeway_intro.shtml. Accessed 15 April 2018.
"Equinox, Part I." *Star Trek: Voyager*, teleplay by Brannon Braga and Joe Menosky, Season 5, episode 26, Paramount, 26 May 1999.
"Equinox, Part II." *Star Trek: Voyager*, teleplay by Brannon Braga and Joe Menosky, Season 6, episode 1, Paramount, 22 September 1999.
"The First Duty": *Star Trek: The Next Generation*, written by Ronald D. Moore and Naren Shankar, Season 5, episode 19, Paramount, 30 Mar. 1992.
"Future's End, Part I." *Star Trek: Voyager: The Complete Series*, written by Brannon Braga and Joe Menosky, directed by David Livingston, Season 3, episode 8, Paramount, 6 Nov. 1996.
"Future's End, Part II." *Star Trek: Voyager: The Complete Series*, written by Brannon Braga and Joe Menosky, directed by Cliff Bole, Season 3, episode 9, Paramount, 13 Nov. 1996.
Gunkel, David J. "Resistance Is Futile: Cyborgs, Humanism, and the Borg." *The 'Star Trek' Universe: Franchising the Final Frontier*, edited by Douglas Brode and Shea T. Brode, Rowman and Littlefield, 2015, pp. 87–98.
"In the Flesh." *Star Trek: Voyager*, written by Nick Sagan, directed by David Livingston, Season 5, episode 4, Paramount, 4 Nov. 1998.
"Initiations." *Star Trek: Voyager*, written by Kenneth Biller, directed by Winrich Kolbe, Season 2, episode 2, Paramount, 4 Sept. 1995.
Jones, Charles Evans, Jr. "The Borg: Fan Pariah or Cultural Pillar?" *Fan Phenomena: Star Trek*, edited by Bruce E. Drushel, Intellect, 2013, pp. 92–101.
"Lifesigns." *Star Trek: Voyager*, written by Kenneth Biller, directed by Cliff Bole, Season 2, episode 19, Paramount, 26 Feb. 1996.
Macleod, Liam. "Why Do Star Trek Fans Hate Voyager." *Den of Geek*, www.denofgeek.com tv/star-trek-voyager/23099/why-do-star-trek-fans-hate-voyager. Accessed 17 May 2018.
"Maneuvers." *Star Trek: Voyager*, written by Kenneth Biller, directed by David Livingston, Season 2, episode 11, Paramount, 20 Nov. 1995.
Nguyen, Will. "Twenty Years Later, Looking Back at Voyager." *Trek News*, www.treknews.net/2015/05/02/star-trek-voyager-first-Season-20-years-later/. Accessed 17 May 2018.
"Prey." *Star Trek: Voyager*, Brannon Braga, directed by Allan Eastman, Season 4, episode 16, Paramount, 18 Feb. 1998.
"Relativity." *Star Trek: Voyager*, story by Nick Sagan, directed by Allan Eastman, Season 5, episode 24, Paramount, 12 May 1999.
Rotolo, Anthony. "*Star Trek* and the Information Age: How the Franchise Imagined/Inspired Future Technologies." *The 'Star Trek' Universe: Franchising the Final Frontier*, edited by Douglas Brode and Shea T. Brode, Rowman and Littlefield, 2015, pp. 29–40.
Ruditis, Paul. *Star Trek: The Visual Dictionary*, Dorling Kindersley, 2013.
"Scientific Method." *Star Trek: Voyager*, teleplay by Lisa Klink, directed by David Livingston, Season 4, episode 7, Paramount, 29 Oct. 1997.
"Scorpion, Part I." *Star Trek: Voyager: The Complete Series*, written by Brannon Braga and Joe Menosky, directed by David Livingston, Season 3, episode 26, Paramount, 21 May 1997.
"Shattered." *Star Trek: Voyager*, teleplay by Michael Taylor, directed by Terry Windell, Season 7, episode 11, Paramount, 17 Jan. 2001.
"State of Flux." *Star Trek: Voyager*, story by Nick Sagan, directed by Allan Eastman, Season 1, episode 11, Paramount, 10 Apr. 1995.
Waltonen, Karma. "To Boldly Go When No One Has Gone Before (or After): *Star Trek*'s Timelines." *Star Trek and History*, edited by Nancy R. Reagin, Wiley, 2013, pp. 158–175.

"Worst Case Scenario." *Star Trek: Voyager*, created by Rick Berman and Michael Piller, directed by Alexander Singer, Season 3, episode 25, Paramount, 14 May 1997.

"Year of Hell, Part I." *Star Trek: Voyager*, written by Brannon Braga and Joe Menosky, directed by Allan Kroeker, Season 4, episode 8, Paramount, 5 Nov. 1997.

"Year of Hell, Part II." *Star Trek: Voyager*, written by Brannon Braga and Joe Menosky, directed by Mike Vejar, Season 4, episode 9, Paramount, 12 Nov. 1997.

"Caught between worlds"
Religion and Star Trek: Voyager

Camilo Peralta

In a 1991 interview with *The Humanist*, Gene Roddenberry was asked to reflect on his religious views and upbringing as a Southern Baptist. "I didn't really take religion that seriously," the creator of *Star Trek* responded. "I guess from that time it was clear to me that religion was largely nonsense—largely magical, superstitious things. In my own teen life, I just couldn't see any point in adopting something based on magic, which was obviously phony and superstitious" (Alexander 6). The earliest scripts of his "wagon train to the stars" TV show certainly reflect a view of religion as something "phony and superstitious." *The Original Series* famously lampooned spiritual belief in a number of episodes, including the very first one to air, which featured Kirk in a bare-fisted brawl with an aspiring deity, whose glowing eyes and telekinetic powers turned out to be no match for the cold, calculating blast of a phaser. *The Next Generation*, likewise, kicked off with a premiere that found the crew battling a seemingly omnipotent, yet inherently ridiculous, figure, though John de Lancie's Q was at least charming enough to make for a decent recurring villain. When he died a few months after that interview, in October of 1991, Roddenberry had every reason to believe that *Star Trek* would always adhere to his "expressed desire that the future of humanity be essentially atheistic" (McGrath 473).

But all of the shows that have been produced since his death have found one reason or another for rejecting this overly narrow and irreligious vision of the future. With its sympathetic portrayal of Bajoran spiritual practices and series-spanning mystery over Sisko's role as Emissary to the Prophets, *Deep Space Nine* immediately set out to challenge the notion that religion had no place in *Star Trek*, offering a glimpse of a future for humanity which was able to find room for faith and science alike. Though one contemporary reviewer found the show "obsessed with religion" (Edwards 88), its portrayal of the Federation as an imperfectly pluralistic society now seems much richer and more realistic than that offered by either of its forerunners. Even the much-maligned *Enterprise* managed to portray the spiritual beliefs and practices of its characters in a favorable light. Dr. Phlox, especially, seems to exhibit the kind of intellectual curiosity and respect for other cultures that is the hallmark of genuine humanistic thinking. The series which aired between both of these, *Voyager*, seems to have been largely overlooked in recent discussions of *Star Trek* and religion. In many ways, *Voyager* is even more of an outlier than its immediate predecessor, despite being set on an actual ship and relying less on the kind of serialized, long-form storytelling that DS9 employed in its latter seasons. It is, after all, the first series in the franchise to feature a female captain, a black Vulcan, and a Native American as regular crew members.

Perhaps more notably, it is set 70,000 light-years from the Federation, far away from familiar species like the Klingons, Cardassians, and Romulans. "Unlike all of the other *Star Trek* narratives," Aviva Dove-Viebahn notes, "*Voyager* does not embark on a journey to explore space; rather, its adventure is one of returning home" (598). Led by the scientifically inclined Captain Janeway, the crew often devises technological solutions to the crises they face. But the show frequently explores the personal aspects of faith, juxtaposing characters whose spiritual beliefs are essential to their identities (like Chakotay and Neelix) with situations that force them to constantly reevaluate—and, more often than not, reaffirm—those beliefs. The show's unique treatment of science and religion provides us with an excellent model for how we talk and think about these subjects today. In its sympathetic treatment of the latter, *Voyager* manages to remind us of something we seem to be losing sight of in this STEM-obsessed era: that science and religion do not have to be mutually exclusive, and that there are some questions to which science may never be able to formulate an answer.

The Voyage Home

The show's premise has much to tell us about its attitude towards religion. No matter how many opportunities the crew members are given to get home, regardless of how many god-like beings with teleportation powers or advanced alien warp drives they come across, it isn't until the final episode that they are once again able to look upon Earth. In the series premiere, they face the kind of moral dilemma that will soon become familiar to loyal viewers: either use the Caretaker's array to transport themselves across the galaxy in an instant, or destroy it in order to protect a defenseless species. In fact, the crew has another option that nobody seems willing to acknowledge, let alone consider: abandon the idea of ever making it home, and find a nice, M-class planet somewhere in the Delta Quadrant to settle on. This is really the only sensible solution. The prospects of completing the 75-year journey home are worse than slim-to-none. How many of the original crew would even be alive to guide the ship as it limped back into orbit around Earth? It would take the kind of dumb luck or providential miracle no self-respecting scientist would allow himself to trust for *Voyager* to survive the journey home. Why not stay?

Indeed, the idea is flirted with on more than one occasion. In the Season 2 premiere, "The 37's" (2.1), the crew discovers a group of humans who were kidnapped from Earth during the 1930s and taken to a Class L planet. Centuries later, their ancestors had grown to over 100,000, and had managed to build a more than comfortable life for themselves, which they offer to share with any member of *Voyager* who wishes to stay. Several debate the idea, including the ambitious Ensign Kim, who bemoans the idea of spending the rest of his life "on a starship, day after day, with no end in sight." Surely, he is thinking about the practical aspects of the journey home: the countless battles that await them, the endless wandering through unknown space. If even one of the youngest members of the crew doubts their ability to make it home, it seems likely that many of the others are seriously considering the offer, as well. Ultimately, however, no one chooses to stay behind, and they continue on their way. At the end of Season 3, as the ship prepares to enter Borg territory for the first time, Janeway herself raises the issue of settling down ("Scorpion" 3.26). Of course, the idea of turning back is never seriously considered. She chooses, instead, to lead her crew into the heart of Borg space, and they follow, trusting they will somehow be able survive repeated encounters with the Federation's most deadly enemy. Surely, the desire to go on never faltered so much, or the desire to stay seemed so tempting.

It is worth noting here that most of the world's major religions feature a journey as part of their central narratives. The faithful are always on the move, whether they are Christians trying to find their way to Heaven, or Jews searching for a homeland after thousands of years in exile. For the earth's billions of Buddhists and Hindus, the wandering of our souls only ends when we reach Nirvana and achieve perfect union with our Maker. The English word, "religion," is at least partly derived from the Latin *religare*, "to bind back," which suggests something else about the journey. It entails a kind of promise or a sense of obligation on the part of the faithful, not to give up despite whatever hardships they may face, or however long they must stay on the road. The millions of Muslims who travel to the Hajj each year in an attempt to "affirm a common identity" clearly take this promise quite seriously (Clingingsmith et al. 1134). And they receive a promise in return: that it will all be worth it in the end, that, someday, they will finally be able to rest. Moses does not lead the Jews out of Egypt merely to escape slavery, but to deliver them "unto a good land and a large, unto a land flowing with milk and honey," as God assures him, they will eventually discover (Authorized King James Version, Exo. 3:8).

The overriding imperative to return to Federation space lends *Voyager* a narrative arc that should be familiar to anyone who has ever read the foundational texts of world literature, including *The Odyssey* and *The Iliad*. Together, these comprise "a journey out from the Greek homeland and, after suitable conquest and discovery, an emphatic return home" (Jeffrey 18). Likewise, the heroes of *The Epic of Gilgamesh* and the 16th century *Journey to the West* set out on a circular journey that ends up back where it started. Along the way, they must overcome a variety of dangerous foes, as well as the intractable temptation to abandon the quest. Of course, whereas the journeys in all of these works are explicitly religious in nature, *Voyager*'s is decidedly secular. It is not God or Zeus who has stranded them in the Delta Quadrant, but the Caretaker, whom no one can possibly mistake for a god. Even the Ocampa decline to identify him as such, though his importance to their society is surely intended to evoke such a comparison. The crew's hostile reception of Q indicates that, despite his pretensions to the contrary, he has no more of the divine in him than the Caretaker. *He* may think of, and indeed even refer to, himself as a god, but from his first, comical, introduction in *TNG*, it becomes difficult to take such a claim seriously.

As with all of the *Star Trek* series, *Voyager* frequently relies on supernatural elements to serve as a plot device, but it attempts to wave them away at the last moment with a natural or technological explanation. In "Spirit Folk" (6.17), a failure in the ship's "perceptual filters" causes the holograms to become sentient. "We've pushed the limits of holo-technology, and they pushed back," Torres somehow manages to say with a straight face. In Season 3's "Coda" (3.15), an alien entity assumes the shape of Janeway's father and leads her through a series of near-death experiences. It turns out that it was all a scheme to lure her spirit away from her body, as the alien feeds upon the spirit or "consciousness" of life forms. (Of course, in claiming as such, the show raises the question of where that spirit is supposed to come from, if not from a supernatural source.) The fate of the Emergency Medical Hologram, known simply as The Doctor, tells us much about the show's uneasy appropriation of religious elements. Throughout the series, he is depicted as undertaking his own sort of quest for self-identity and fulfillment. It is taken for granted that a hologram—or an android—might win the right and deserve to be treated as a human, but the trickier implications of that decision, which lie beyond the purview of science, are ignored or glossed over. To put it simply, no amount of programming can turn a neural network into a soul.

All of this is, of course, symptomatic of larger trends in Western society regarding religion and science. Even for many Christians, overt, unambiguous expressions of faith may seem "utterly irrational, a by-product of the I simplicity of previous evolutionary stages" (Levering 32). We did not arrive at that point overnight, any more than the show is the first work of art to feature a hero who embarks upon a long and perilous journey while steadfastly denying the role of providence in guiding him to his destination. Robert J. Forman points to Vergil's *Aeneid* as an important step in adapting the holy quest of Homer for secular audiences:

> Though the *Aeneid* employs elements of Homer's *Odyssey* and *Iliad*, it entirely avoids the supernatural elements of these poems. There are no lotus flowers that make a warrior forget his home, no Sirens with seven rows of teeth to devour mariners, no witches like Circe who turn men into swine. Aeneas sails past the island of the Cyclopes, but they do not influence the narrative of the poem.... In essence, all that happens in the *Aeneid* can be seen in purely natural terms [3].

Since the Enlightenment, there has certainly been a greater tendency to try to explain things "in purely natural terms," even when all of the evidence points to the contrary. Everyone tuning into *Voyager* for the first time on January 16, 1995, knew that the ship would eventually find its way back to earth. But confirmation of that inevitable ending during the course of its seven-year run would have led to a great deal of dissatisfaction, not to mention an immediate decline in viewers. Modern-day humans do not want to see the strings, or the person holding them, even when we know that both are there.

But there is something else worth noting about the journey that *Voyager* is on. Not only does the audience know that the crew will survive the trip— it knows exactly where the ship is going, which is back to where it started. As such, the show represents a dramatic break from the long history of heroic quests descended from the *Aeneid*. In Vergil's epic, Aeneas and the storm-tossed Trojans must wander around the whole Mediterranean in search of their new home. "Through varied fortunes, through countless hazards," Aeneas says, "we journey towards Latium, where fate promises a home of peace" (I.190). The pious warrior would never see him homeland again. Subsequent works, from the *Divina Commedia* of Dante to Spenser's *Faerie Queene*, would also features journeys that either have no clear end in sight, or end up in an entirely different place from where they started. In its premise, *Voyager* seems to hearken back to the epics of Homer, the ancient Babylonians, and the Bible, which are all circular in nature. Like Odysseus and the ancient Israelites, Janeway knows exactly where her journey will end. She has no idea how long it will be, or how she will get there. So it is with all humans, who invariably end up returning to dust, regardless of how well or long they lived.

Janeway: Captain, Scientist, Mother

The modern scientific method is often said to begin with Sir Francis Bacon, but a case could be made instead for Leonardo da Vinci. Like Bacon, who was born a century later, Leonardo pursued a wide range of interests, though he kept his observations on these to himself, recording them in a series of letters, notes, and drawings that number over 10,000 items. M. Jourdain describes the effect of reading through his collected journals as one that begins with "a feeling of disappointment in the meagerness of the scientific result," which is then "counterbalanced by the realization that he is the first of the moderns in his belief in experimental methods, his distrust for mere authority in science as in the arts he practised" (284). And yet, for all of his prophetic observations on optics and flight, for all of his keen insight into mechanical and anatomical processes, Leonardo will always be better known to us as a painter of such masterpieces as *The Mona Lisa* and *The Last Supper*. Most of his surviving works are deeply religious, and an early biographer records that Leonardo requested Holy Communion on his deathbed (Vasari 270). Perhaps, like Descartes, Newton, and so many others, "the first of the moderns" never fully abandoned his faith in God.

Given his enduring popularity as "the Renaissance ideal of the universal man," in whom "powerful intelligence and scientific curiosity were harmoniously combined with a love of nature," it is not surprising that Leonardo and his works have made a number of appearances in popular culture (Puceković 36). Recently, he has appeared in the *Assassin's Creed* video game franchise, the best-selling *Da Vinci Code* series of novels by Dan Brown, and, as portrayed by John Rhys-Davies, in two episodes of *Star Trek: Voyager*, as the holographic confidante of Captain Janeway. His first appearance is in the third season finale, "Scorpion" (3.26), though he has a much more prominent role in Season 4's "Concerning Flight" (4.11). The producers and writers probably had in mind the Leonardo da Vinci who has come down to us through his journals: skeptical, empirical, and highly suspicious of tradition and authority. But he works even better as a friend and mentor for Janeway if we remember that he was, first and foremost, inclined to creative and spiritual pursuits. She is the kind of leader who always tries to find logical solutions to her problems; he is there to remind her that, sometimes, there aren't any to be found. Indeed, their relationship functions well as a kind of metaphor for the show's overall treatment of science and religion.

Most of the scholarly interest in Janeway has focused on "the complexities of female leadership" and how her choices and behavior as captain contrast with those of her male peers (Bowring 389). More than just a "female leader," she actually wears three different hats: those of captain, scientist, and mother. From the start, the show goes out of its way to emphasize that it will be her interest in science—not her gender—which distinguishes her from her predecessors in command. We learn in the first episode that she served as science officer aboard the *Al-Batani* under Tom Paris's father, now an admiral, who was known for taking only "the best and the brightest" ("Caretaker" 1.1). She soon reveals herself to be adept at investigating complicated phenomena like spatial distortions and astral eddies ("Parallax" 1.3, "Real Life" 3.22). In "Coda" (3.15), the alien entity who assumes the form of her father reminds Janeway that she was brought up "to be a doubter and a sceptic, to look at the world with a scientist's eye." Though not the words of her actual father, they confirm what the viewer has already come to know about Janeway during the first three years of the show. Unlike the impulsive Kirk, cerebral Picard, or emotional Sisko, she demonstrates all of the characteristics of a good scientist. She is rational, methodical, and empirical, not above risking the safety of the crew to explore a strange-looking nebula or spatial oddity.

Like all modern-day scientists, she usually begins from a position of doubt, and relies on logic to explain things that seems supernatural or metaphysical in nature. Season 3's "Sacred Ground" (3.7) provides a nice example of how Janeway typically approaches these matters. After Kes is injured while attempting to enter a holy shrine, the Nechani monks insist that she is being punished by the gods for not undergoing the appropriate rites, and that nothing can be done about it. As a rationalist and an empiricist, who trusts that a scientific and logical explanation can be found in every situation, Janeway is initially skeptical. She insists on undergoing the ritual of purification herself, so that she can determine the *something* that explains why the monks are able to enter the shrine themselves without fear of reprisal. "If you're asking if I expect to speak to the Ancestral Spirits, no, of course not," she explains to Chakotay. "But something happens to the monks when they go through that ritual. Something that allows them to withstand the effects of the biogenic field." As it turns out, there *is* a perfectly logical explanation—there is a *something*—which the doctor happily provides at the end of the episode. Most of the time, when *Voyager* encounters something strange or mysterious, the crew is able to discover a *something* that satisfies their need for a rational explanation.

At the same time, the experiences Janeway undergoes in "Sacred Ground" raise some important questions about how unwavering her faith in science truly is. "I imagine if we scratch deep enough," she declares confidently at the start of the episode, "we'd find a scientific basis for most religious doctrines." But it is difficult to see one in the actual experiences she undergoes during the ritual, which she is more or less forced to acknowledge at the end. At one point, she encounters a group of spirits who openly ridicule her trust in science: "Even when her science fails right before her eyes, she still has full confidence in it," one observes dryly. "Now *there's* a leap of faith." They encourage her to "Let go of all that," to go back into the shrine with Kes and "trust the spirits to return her soul." Janeway must believe, in other words, and it is important that she does so sincerely, because if she goes in "with any doubt, with any hesitation," she and Kes will both die. Having no other choice, Janeway decides to take their advice. In the end, she is forced to reject the need for a rational *something*, and embrace instead the kind of blind faith she has long denied. Her hesitant response to The Doctor's offer of a scientific rationale for what has happened indicates that, despite being offered a *something*, it may not suffice in this instance.

Janeway is more than just a scientist, however. With the small size of the crew and the limitations of its particular mission, the show offers her a unique opportunity to serve as head of the ship's "family," which she eagerly assumes. Early in the first season, while the possibility yet remains that the crew will be able to find its way home, Janeway remarks upon a theme that will soon become integral to *Voyager*: "Here in the Delta Quadrant, we are virtually the entire family of man. We are more than a crew and I must find a way to be more than a captain to these people, but it's not clear to me exactly how to begin" ("The Cloud" 1.6). The answer soon reveals itself: by adopting the role of a mother in her relations with the crew, Janeway will be able to maintain appropriate boundaries between herself and the others, even as their journey seems likely to persist for decades. In "The Thaw" (2.23), we learn that she has already succeeded in establishing this kind of relationship between herself and Ensign Kim. In resurrecting Paris's career, nurturing Torres, and, especially, in the mentoring roles she adopts with Kes and Seven, Janeway demonstrates her willingness and ability to serve as the crew's "mother," despite what contemporary critics might decry as the "hyperfeminine" associations of such a role (Bowring 392). Q's request for her to carry and give birth to his child only makes the importance of her special relationship with the crew more explicit ("The Q and the Grey" 3.11).

All captains must be willing to sacrifice themselves to protect their ships and save the lives of their crew. The frequency with which Janeway offers to so is striking, however, and suggests that her need to protect others may arise out of more than just professional duty. "Emanations" (1.9), "Resolutions" (2.25), and "The Thaw" (2.23) provide early examples of the captain putting her life on the line to save others. She is willing to do this for practically anyone, whether human or alien, friend, foe, or complete stranger. In "Unimatrix Zero, Part I" (6.26), for instance, she leads a small party into the heart of a Borg cube in an attempt to liberate scattered members of the Collective, most of whom she will never meet or know. But her greatest act of sacrifice surely comes in the show's final episode, "Endgame, Part I" (7.25). It is set 32 years in the future, a decade after the ship finally makes it home after wandering for so long through the Delta Quadrant. Dissatisfied with her inability to get everyone home faster, Vice-Admiral Janeway undertakes an ambitious and daring plan to travel back in time and undo what she regards as her past mistakes. It is not for her own sake or reputation that she wants to get the ship home faster, but for that of her family: "You said you and The Doctor wanted to keep things in the family," she tells Captain Kim when he arrives to stop her. "But our family's not complete any more, is it?" It was a minor miracle that she managed to get some of them back at all. But Janeway wants to perform a greater one. And, having experienced so many things over the years that she could not explain via logical or rational means alone, she might have learned that such miracles can happen, if you are willing to believe in yourself, and in them.

Perhaps it is not her identity as a captain, scientist, or mother which best defines Janeway, but her ability to keep an open mind. Although she approaches every situation from a rational and skeptical perspective, she will abandon it when faced with a problem that cannot be solved through scientific means alone. In Season 1's "The Cloud" (1.6), for example, after running through the usual technological solutions, she is obliged to seek more creative means for escaping the nebula in which the ship has become trapped. She even enquires into Chakotay's Native American beliefs about animal guides, and accepts his offer to teach her how to contact her own. Long before The Doctor decides to explore his humanity, she encourages him to let her know if there is anything she can do to make him feel like a more welcome member of the crew ("Eye of the Needle" 1.7). She is always respectful of other culture's religious beliefs, especially, and is careful to avoid dismissing them as fanciful or mistaken, even if she naturally assumes that to be the case. In "Emanations" (1.9), she comforts an alien who is distraught over finding herself aboard a starship filled with aliens, instead of in her people's version of the afterlife. "I know this must be frightening for you," Janeway assures her. "You've been through a very traumatic experience. It would frighten me. But please try to understand. *Just because I don't have the answers to your questions doesn't mean there aren't any*" (emphasis mine). Her attitude is quite a contrast to the outright scorn and hostility with which so many prominent scientists today greet religion.

Though he is only featured in two episodes of the series, her choice of confidant seems to make perfect sense, after all. When Janeway comes to Da Vinci on the eve of her first major battle with the Borg, he warns her against trusting too much in science, in the single-minded pursuit of easy facts and yes-or-no answers that blinds so many today ("Scorpion, Part I" 3.26). "When one's imagination cannot provide an answer, one must seek a greater imagination," he says. "There are times when even I find myself kneeling in prayer." He invites her to join him in making an "appeal to God" at the chapel of Santa Croce. She declines the offer then, but one can't help but wonder how she might respond to it if he were to offer it to her again later, after she has come to realize that there isn't always a *something* to be found in every situation.

Far from the Bones of Our Ancestors: The Two Chakotays

By putting Bajoran spiritual practices—and politics—front and center for much of its seven-year run, *Deep Space Nine* more than earns its reputation for being the "religious" Trek. One recent reviewer credits it for having "our first (and I'd argue only good) portrayal of religion in the franchise," which is uses to teach "tolerance and understanding" to its viewers (Elderkin). Perhaps no character does more to contribute to the positive impression of religion on *DS9* than Major Kira Nerys, who manages to combine the impeccable credentials of a former terrorist with a respect for organized religion (as opposed to mere "spirituality") that remains unique in the *Star Trek* universe. The show always portrays Kira's beliefs as sincere, and, unlike certain characters on *Voyager*, she never admits to the possibility that they might not be *true* in every sense of the word. Even so, for all its sympathy and toleration, *DS9* is careful not to validate those beliefs, but leave open the possibility that a *something* might be found for her, too, if she were willing to look for it. The wormhole aliens she regards as celestial prophets might belong, in the end, to the same kind of powerful race we've seen in Q and the Caretaker; likewise, the *pah-wraiths* who seize control of Keiko and Gul Dukat are dismissed as mere "legend" ("The Assignment" 5.5).

There is no one on *Voyager* quite like Kira, but of the expansive cast, Commander Chakotay probably comes closest to fulfilling her role. He, too, is the ship's executive officer, often tasked with providing advice or a dissenting opinion to his mercurial captain. In a close examination of the character as depicted on the show and in the voluminous amount of fan fiction that has been written in the years since it went off the air, V. Somogyi describes Chakotay as "respectful, supportive, admiring, [and] unthreatened by Janeway's power" (400). As with Kira, his faith is an important aspect of his identity, though it often portrayed in inconsistent terms, as something he fervently believes, or doesn't, as suits the needs of the episode. "I remember when my mother taught me the science underlying the vision quest," he tells Janeway in "Sacred Ground" (3.7). "In a way I felt disappointed. Some of the mystery was gone." His dialogue here suggests that, as with most of the crew's encounters with religion and supernatural phenomena, there is even a *something* to explain the fundamental practices of his faith. "The Cloud" (1.6) features at least two scenes in which Chakotay seems to acknowledge as much himself. In the first, he equates the use of animal spirit guides by his people to the "active imagination technique" of Carl Jung. Then, as if to kill two birds with one stone, he assures Janeway (and the audience) that, although his ancestors had to rely on "psychoactive herbs" to attain the meditative state necessary for undertaking vision quests, Federation scientists have, fortunately, discovered "more modern ways to facilitate the search."

All of this is rather silly, and it is to Robert Beltran's credit that his character is able to escape such scenes with his credibility intact. Consistency has never been cited as one of *Voyager*'s strengths, so it is not, perhaps, surprising that Chakotay would just as often be called upon to sell the opposite approach: that, far from being something which needs to be prefaced with an apology or excuse, religion can sometimes provide us with the only possible solution to a certain problem or question. In "Cathexis" (1.13), for instance, B'Elanna attempts to use Chakotay's medicine wheel to revive him after he is knocked unconscious by some sort of energy discharge. Despite The Doctor's skeptical dismissal of "psycho-spiritual beliefs," even he is unable to explain the subsequent chain of events, which ends with Chakotay's disembodied spirit using the wheel to guide the crew to safety. "Basics" (2.26), meanwhile, sees the commander employ one of his much-derided vision quests to communicate with the ghost of his long-dead father. "I ask on this day of sorrow and uncertainty," he prays, "that the wisdom of my father find me and help me understand my dilemma." Almost immediately, the old man appears and speaks to him. In this scene, at least, the show demonstrates its willingness to accept religious practices and belief at face value. It does not merely present Chakotay having an imaginary conversation with his father, but depicts it as something that really happens.

Chakotay is featured prominently in Season 3's "Distant Origin" (3.23), an episode which might be said to best reflect the show's nuanced take on the relationship between faith and science. The premise is based on the story of Galileo Galilei, the Renaissance astronomer whose support of the heliocentric model of the universe leads him to incur the ire of the Catholic Church. The episode is unusual, in that it is told mostly from the perspective of an alien race, the Voth, which has never before been featured or mentioned on the show. The Galileo role is taken by a Voth scientist, Gegen, who has discovered a link between his people and humans that seems to suggest that we share a common ancestor on earth. It may be "the most important discovery in Voth history," as he declares, but it also, unfortunately, contradicts the central Doctrine of his people, that the Voth are a "First Race" who originated in the Delta Quadrant, and can therefore claim it as their ancestral homeland. As with Galileo, he is charged with heresy, brought to trial, and eventually forced to recant his position. If Galileo's trial represents a milestone in the "timeless conflict between 'faith and reason'" for humans (Gorman

284), it is implied that Gegen's will play a similar role for the Voth. He is, after all, *right* in a rational and empirical sense. All of the evidence supports what he has to say. In refusing to even consider it, the Voth Minister who presides over his trial comes across as dangerously tyrannical and intolerant.

But the message of the episode, and of the show as a whole, may be more complicated that. It is not only the stubbornness of the Voth Minister which proves worthy of blame, but that of Gegen, as well. At no point does anyone demand that he either reject his research entirely or embrace the truth of Doctrine. All that is asked of him is that he be willing to admit the possibility that he might be wrong. "Will you at least do that?" the Minister wonders. Later, she rephrases the question to make it even less damaging to his pride: "Could you be mistaken?" Again and again, he refuses to admit to even the slightest chance of being wrong: "No! Why should I? You've already made up your mind!" he declares. "Well, it won't work. I'll never retract my claims." Perhaps his refusal to do so would make better sense if it were coming from a scientist who was defending a position that had undergone rigorous testing and analysis by his peers, and could therefore safely declare it as more likely true than not. But no matter how often Gegen speaks of having "evidence" or "proof," it cannot be denied that his theory is radical and unproven. He and his circle of friends and colleagues are the only members of his species who have really had a chance to test his hypothesis. Even Darwin admitted to having doubts about the theory of evolution. How can Gegen be so sure that he is right? Should we be so quick to accept the *something* we've discovered as the best or only solution to the problem?

Ultimately, *Voyager* rejects both unquestionable doctrine and scientism, a "speculative worldview" that regards science as "the only source of human knowledge," and which has become increasingly popular in recent years (Burnett). The show seeks to promote instead a reconciliation between religion and science, and of the respective truths towards which they are able to lead us. As in "Distant Origin," Chakotay often serves as a kind of spokesperson for this position. "I know from the history of my planet," he tells the Voth minister, "that change is difficult. New ideas are often greeted with skepticism, even fear." Doctrine, he adds, may be changed without being denied completely. The Voth can modernize, while remaining completely faithful to their ancient beliefs. In a similar manner, the Catholic Church has managed to endure for over 2000 years. Recently, Pope Francis has spoken out on the need for Christians to accept scientific theories that enjoy widespread acceptance, even if they seem to undermine or even contradict the truth of Scripture. "God is not … a magician, but the Creator who brought everything to life. Evolution in nature is not inconsistent with the notion of creation, because evolution requires the creation of beings that evolve" (as qtd. In Tharoor). His wisdom and humility contrasts sharply with the arrogance of some of his own predecessors, as well as with his counterpart among the Voth.

There is a lesson here for all of us in the modern day, when it is no longer the power of religious institutions that must be feared, but orthodoxies of the political and social kind. It is a lesson that prominent atheists such as Richard Dawkins, Neil deGrasse Tyson, and all of their followers must bear in mind if we are to avoid making the same kind of error Gegen does, in believing that it is possible for any one person or theory to have all of the answers. As *Voyager* at its best never hesitates to acknowledge the possibility of there being a kind of truth that lies beyond the ken of science, so should we always seek to balance the legacy of the Enlightenment with the inheritance of the ages that came before it. Humans are, by nature, a rational species, and we shall need all of our scientific and logical prowess to build the kind of optimistic future envisioned by the creators and writers of *Star Trek*. But we have always been, and shall continue to be, a spiritual, if not religious, people; and it seems safe to assume that it will be easier to achieve that dream if we keep that aspect of our collective identity in mind.

Perhaps *Voyager* had to get itself stranded in the Delta Quadrant in order to explore these issues fully. Far from earth, and from the familiar races of the Federation, the ship is free to encounter any number of alien species, each with its own, unique spiritual beliefs and practices. And the show's creators were able to distance themselves a bit further from Roddenberry's short-sighted insistence that religious themes in *Star Trek* be either marginalized or ignored. Instead, they could tackle these subjects freely, without fear of disturbing long-established canon, resulting in a nuanced take on the relation between religion and science that just might be the most genuinely humane the franchise has ever offered. Like the crew of *Voyager*, we are all on a journey, and though some of us may have a different sense of where the destination lies, no one knows for sure what will happen once we get there. As Janeway prays, "We are far from the sacred places of our grandfathers and from the bones of our people. But perhaps there is one powerful being who will embrace this good crew and give them the answer they seek" ("The Cloud" 1.6). Who can say that the same "powerful being" she hopes will guide the crew safely through the Delta Quadrant back to earth, is not also watching over us?

Works Cited

Alexander, David. "Gene Roddenberry." *Humanist*, vol. 51, no. 2, Mar/Apr 1991, pp. 5–38. *Academic Search Premier*, EBSCO*host*. Accessed 13 July 2017.

"The Assignment." *Deep Space Nine*, teleplay by Bradley Thompson and David Weddle, directed by Allan Kroeker, Season 5, episode 5, Paramount, 25 Oct. 1996.

"Basics, Part I." *Star Trek: Voyager*, written by Michael Piller, directed by Winrich Kolbe, Season 2, episodes 26, Paramount, 20 May 1996.

"Basics, Part II." *Star Trek: Voyager*, written by Michael Piller, directed by Winrich Kolbe, Season 3, episodes 1, Paramount, 4 Sept. 1996.

The Bible. Authorized King James Version, Oxford UP, 1998.

Bowring, Michèle A. "Resistance Is Not Futile: Liberating Captain Janeway from the Masculine-Feminine Dualism of Leadership." *Gender, Work and Organization*, vol. 11, no. 4, July 2004, pp. 381–405. EBSCO*host*, doi: 10.1111/j.1468-0432.2004.00239.x. Accessed 22 July 2017.

"Caretaker." *Star Trek: Voyager*, created by Jeri Taylor, Gene Roddenberry, Rick Berman, and Michael Piller, performance by Roxann Dawson, Season 1, episodes 1 and 2, Paramount, 16 Jan. 1995.

"Cathexis." *Star Trek: Voyager*, teleplay by Brannon Braga, directed by Kim Friedman, Season 1, episodes 13, Paramount, 1 May 1995.

Clingingsmith, David, et al. "Estimating the Impact of the Hajj: Religion and Tolerance in Islam's Global Gathering." *Quarterly Journal of Economics*, vol. 124, no. 3, Aug. 2009, pp. 1133–1170. *Business Source Premier*, EBSCO*host*. Accessed 1 Nov. 2017.

"The Cloud." *Star Trek: Voyager*, story by Brannon Braga, directed by David Livingston, Season 1, episode 6, Paramount, 13 Feb. 1995.

"Coda." *Star Trek: Voyager*, written by Jeri Taylor, directed by Nancy Malone, Season 3, episode 15, Paramount, 29 Jan. 1997.

"Concerning Flight." *Star Trek: Voyager*, teleplay by Joe Menosky, directed by Jesús Salvador Treviño, Season 4, episode 11, Paramount, 26 Nov. 1997.

"Distant Origin." *Star Trek: Voyager*, written by Brannon Braga and Joe Menosky, directed by David Livingston, Season 3, episodes 23, Paramount, 30 Apr. 1997.

Dove-Viebahn, Aviva. "Embodying Hybridity (En)Gendering Community: Captain Janeway and the Enactment of a Feminist Heterotopia on *Star Trek: Voyager*." *Women's Studies*, vol. 36, no. 8, Dec. 2007, pp. 597–618. EBSCO*host*, doi: 10.1080/00497870701683894. Accessed 13 July 2017.

Edwards, Gavin. "*Star Trek: Deep Space Nine* (Film)." *Rolling Stone*, no. 929, 21 Aug. 2003, p. 88. *Academic Search Premier*, EBSCO*host*. Accessed 10 Dec. 2017.

Elderkin, Beth. "*Deep Space Nine* Is *Star Trek*'s Best World, Because It's the Real World." *io9*, Gizmodo, 7 Sept. 2016, io9.gizmodo.com/deep-space-nine-is-star-treks-best-world-because-its-t-1786060432. Accessed 16 Dec. 2017.

"Emanations." *Star Trek: Voyager*, written by Brannon Braga, directed by David Livingston, Season 1, episode 9, Paramount, 13 Mar. 1995.

"Endgame, Part I and II." *Star Trek: Voyager*, teleplay by Kenneth Biller and Robert Doherty, directed by Allan Kroeker, Season 7, episodes 25 and 26, Paramount, 23 May 2001.

"Eye of the Needle." *Star Trek: Voyager*, teleplay by Bill Dial and Jeri Taylor, directed by Winrich Kolbe, Season 1, episode 7, Paramount, 20 Feb. 1995.

Foreman, Robert J. "On the *Aeneid*: Biography and Allegory." *Critical Insights: The Aeneid*, 16 Sept. 2011, pp. 3–16. *Literary Reference Center*, EBSCO*host*. Accessed 11 Dec. 2017.

Gorman, Michael John. "A Matter of Faith? Christoph Scheiner, Jesuit Censorship, and the Trial of Galileo." *Perspectives on Science*, vol. 4, no. 3, 1996, pp. 283–320. *Academic Search Complete*, EBSCO*host*. Accessed 18 Dec. 2017.

Green, Mandy. "The Virgin in the Garden: Milton's Ovidian Eve." *Modern Language Review*, vol. 100, no. 4, Oct. 2005, pp. 903–922. *Academic Search Premier*, EBSCO*host*. Accessed 14 Dec. 2017.

Jeffrey, David Lyle. *Houses of the Interpreter: Reading Scripture, Reading Culture*. Baylor UP, 2009.

Jourdain, M. "Leonardo Da Vinci. (Born 1452. Died 1519.)." *The Monist*, vol. 30, no. 2, 1920, pp. 281–291. *JSTOR*, www.jstor.org/stable/27900803. Accessed 10 Dec. 2017.

Levering, Matthew. "The Logic of God." *Christian Century*, vol. 133, no. 9, 27 Apr. 2016, pp. 31–33. *MasterFILE Premier*, EBSCO*host*. Accessed 10 Dec. 2017.

McGrath, James F. "Explicit and Implicit Religion in *Doctor Who* and *Star Trek*." *Implicit Religion*, vol. 18, no. 4, Dec. 2015, pp. 471–484. EBSCO*host*, doi: 10.1558/imre.v18i4.29087. Accessed 13 July 2017.

Milton, John. *Paradise Lost. Complete English Poems, of Education, Areopagitica*. Edited by Gordon Campbell, Everyman, 2000.

Nowalk, Brandon. "*Star Trek: Voyager* Accidentally Presided Over the Franchise's Decline." *The A.V. Club*, tv.avclub.com/star-trek-voyager-accidentally-presided-over-the-franc-1798238334. Accessed 8 Dec. 2017.
"Parallax." *Star Trek: Voyager*, created by Rick Berman, Michael Piller, and Jeri Taylor. Dir. Kim Freidman, Season 1, episode 3, Paramount, 23 Jan. 1995.
Puceković, Branko. "Leonardo Da Vinci and His Contributions to Cartography." ["Leonardo Da Vinci I Njegov Doprinos Kartografiji"]. *Cartography and Geoinformation*, vol. 12, no. 20, Dec. 2013, pp. 34–52. *Academic Search Complete*, EBSCO*host*.
"The Q and the Grey." *Star Trek: Voyager: The Complete Series*, written by Kenneth Biller, directed by Cliff Bole, Season 3, episode 11, Paramount, 27 Nov. 1996.
"Real Life." *Star Trek: Voyager*, teleplay by Jeri Taylor, directed by Anson Williams, Season 3, episode 22, Paramount, 23 Apr. 1997.
"Resolutions." *Star Trek: Voyager*, written by Jeri Taylor, directed by Alexander Singer, Season 2, episode 25, Paramount, 13 May 1996.
"Sacred Ground." *Star Trek: Voyager*, teleplay by Lisa Klink, directed by Robert Duncan McNeill, Season 3, episode 7, Paramount, 30 Oct. 1996.
"Scorpion, Part I." *Star Trek: Voyager: The Complete Series*, written by Brannon Braga and Joe Menosky, directed by David Livingston, Season 3, episode 26, Paramount, 21 May 1997.
"Scorpion, Part II." *Star Trek: Voyager*, written by Brannon Braga and Joe Menosky, directed by Winrich Kolbe, Season 4, episode 1, Paramount, 3 Sept. 1997.
Somogyi, V. "Complexity of Desire: Janeway / Chakotay Fan Fiction." *Journal of American and Comparative Cultures*, vol. 25, no. ¾, Fall 2002, pp. 399–404. *Academic Search Premier*, EBSCO*host*. Accessed 10 Dec. 2018.
"Spirit Folk." *Star Trek: Voyager*, written by Bryan Fuller, directed by David Livingston, Season 6, episode 17, Paramount, 23 Feb. 2000.
"The Thaw." *Star Trek: Voyager*, teleplay by Joe Menosky, directed by Marvin V. Rush, Season 2, episode 23, Paramount, 29 Apr. 1996.
"Unimatrix Zero, Part I." *Star Trek: Voyager*, teleplay by Brannon Braga and Joe Menosky, directed by Allan Kroeker, Season 6, episode 26, Paramount, 24 May 2000.
"Unimatrix Zero, Part II." *Star Trek: Voyager*, teleplay by Brannon Braga and Joe Menosky, directed by Mike Vejar, Season 7, episode 1, Paramount, 24 May 2000.
Vasari, Giorgio. *Lives of the Artists*, translated by George Bull. Revised ed., Penguin Classics, 1965.
Vergil. *The Aeneid*. Translated by Sarah Ruden, Yale UP, 2009.

Part II

Gendering the 24th Century: Problems, Solutions, Pathways

Where No Woman Has Gone Before

Kathryn Janeway Breaking the Glass Ceiling or Reinforcing Stereotypes?

MICHELLE M. TABIT

In an interview Gene Roddenberry, the creator of *Star Trek*, noted, "I have no belief that STAR TREK depicts the actual future, it depicts us, now, things we need to understand about that." David Gerrold, a writer for the series, elaborated on that comment, explaining that "[t]he stories are about the twentieth century man's attitudes in a future universe. The stories are about us" (Asherman, *The Star Trek Interview Book* 155). To that end the writers of the five *Star Trek* series offer critical commentary on numerous social issues including but not limited to racism, sexism, feminism, and militarism. The images of women presented in *Star Trek* are in many ways as complicated as the changing roles of women. Nevertheless, the various *Star Trek* series reflected the more traditional expectations of society and showcased the gradual expansion of women's roles over the last forty years culminating in the character of Captain Kathryn Janeway. Although Janeway is not the first female starship captain, she is the first to become a role model for female viewers, representing Gene Roddenberry's dream of a future where gender did not define women, but rather they could aspire to be anything.

The original *Star Trek* series began in the mid–1960s as the contemporary feminist movement took root. Social change on this scale should have provided the writers with the opportunity to explore how women used the changing social and technological landscape to forward their goals. Initially, the writers took the opportunity to place a woman in a position of authority. Leonard Nimoy explained in the documentary *Star Trek Memories* that in the pilot episode "The Cage" produced in 1964, the writers created a female first officer referred to as Number One portrayed by Majel Barrett. She portrayed the character as an extremely competent, authoritative officer, committed to her ship, crew, and captain. However, when NBC executives viewed the pilot they wanted Number One removed (Curtis). M. G. Dupree explains in her chapter "Alien Babes and Alternate Universes," published in Nancy Reagin's *Star Trek and History*, that executives found Majel Barrett's character unacceptable. They called her "pushy" and "annoying" and criticized her for "trying to fit in with the men" (Reagin 280–295). Dupree further notes that both men and women disliked female characters outside traditional roles, which meant that writers would remove women from leadership positions in the *Star Trek* universe, thereby reinforcing traditional gender norms of men in power and women in subservient roles (Reagin 280–295). Karin Blair explains in her article "*Star Trek* and Sex" that the writers "objectified women" and created the "disposable female." She notes that when women appeared in an episode they were often "fantastic, exotic, and erotic" (292–3). In "Space and the Single Girl: *Star Trek*, Aesthetics, and 1960s Femininity" Patricia Vettel-Becker points out that "the women of Starfleet wore short close-fitting tunics that emphasized their feminine curves and highlighted their legs, their thighs sheathed in transparent black hose, their calves and feet in snug black high-heeled boots" (Vettel-Becker 146). She goes on to explain that contrary to what many believe in the 21st century, no woman saw the attire as demeaning. In fact, women in the 1960s believed the miniskirt symbolized sexual liberation. As a result, the female members of the cast argued that in the 23rd century women would be respected for their intellect and abilities, not their clothing (Vettel-Becker 146–47). In the early episodes of *Star Trek* women were caught in the constructs of the male imagination. Nevertheless, *The Original Series* failed to provide female viewers with strong women in leadership positions.

Dupree explains "that it would take twenty-nine years and two more iterations of *Star Trek* before a woman—Kathryn Janeway took command of a starship" (280–295). The series returned to the original format of trekking across the universe with a unique twist; instead of embarking on a traditional mission of exploration, the crew was abducted by a powerful alien and stranded in the Delta Quadrant, 70,000 light years from Earth. Janeway and her diverse crew sought a route home. Some suggest that *Star Trek: Voyager* [hereafter referred to as *Voyager*] is a ground-breaking series; others have referred to it as *Gilligan's Island* in space, as each week the crew makes progress towards home, but it is slow, tedious, and often foiled by circumstances beyond their control. What makes *Voyager* unique is that for the first time in a *Star Trek* series a woman is cast in a lead role surrounded by other women in key leadership positions. The timing of Janeway's placement as captain is reflective of several changes taking place in the 20th century. Not long before *Voyager* debuted President Bill Clinton made women's issues an important part of his presidential agenda. Throughout his tenure in office he placed women in high office in his administration, sought equal opportunity for women in the labor force, and encouraged greater participation of women in business. On August 26, 1995, Clinton announced the formation of an Interagency Council on Women. This intragovernmental body was charged with coordinating the implementation of the Platform for Action, the goals of which were to further women's progress and engage in outreach and public education to support women. First Lady Hillary Rodham Clinton served as honorary chair of the President's Interagency Council on Women; Secretary of Health and Human Services Donna Shalala chaired the council (1995–1997); Secretary of State Madeleine Albright would take over the leadership role in 1997 ("U.S. Society and Values" 5). Therefore, a case can be made that in the mid–1990s when *Voyager* began, the writers were responding to calls for a more diverse and feminist-oriented perspective in the *Star Trek* world.

The backstory of *Voyager* is important to keep in mind. The ship leaves Earth with orders to capture a Maquis ship led by Captain Chakotay when suddenly both ships are caught in an energy field that transports them 70,000 light years to the Delta Quadrant in a matter of seconds. The "Caretaker," a strange, yet powerful, alien life force, is searching for a mate with compatible DNA so that he may reproduce. Unfortunately, the DNA of neither crew is compatible. The Caretaker realizes he is dying and requests that Janeway not allow the Kazon to use his array, forcing the Starfleet captain to destroy it, thus leaving the two ships stranded. As Captain Janeway prepares for the long journey home (a minimum of 75 years at maximum warp), she proposes that the two crews—Starfleet and Maquis—merge, and on the journey the crew will encounter strange new worlds, new civilizations, and aliens. Co-executive producer Michael Piller explained that the writers wanted to "go back to the original show in the '60s and the spirit of that was: one ship with a bunch of people, out there alone, exploring the unknown, never sure what they were going to find around any corner. That's what we wanted, so that *Voyager* wouldn't be a pale imitation of *The Next Generation*" (Kim). When the creative threesome of Jeri Taylor, Michael Piller, and co-executive producer Rick Berman insisted that *Voyager* be led by a woman the network executives initially resisted the idea. And when word reached the fans that a woman would lead the new ship, Kim notes that one America Online subscriber wrote, "Do they want it to sink?" Despite many doubts executives greenlighted the project as long as Berman agreed not to "close the door to men ... and to look at men as well" (Kim). The process of selecting Kate Mulgrew for the project resulted in numerous auditions.

To round out the cast Janeway invites two aliens from the Caretaker's planet—Neelix, a Talaxian, and Kes, an Ocampan—to join the crew. At the end of the third season when Kes decides to leave *Voyager*, the writers created "Seven of Nine," a former Borg drone and a character foil to Janeway. Thus, *Voyager*'s crew is the most diverse in the *Star Trek* canon. In fact, *Voyager* casts Garrett Wang, a Chinese American, as communications officer; Robert Beltran, a Mexican American, as a Native American first officer; Tim Russ, an African American, as a Vulcan security officer; and Roxann Biggs-Dawson as a half-Latina and half–Klingon chief engineer. This creates a multicultural mixture of humans and aliens, both traditional Starfleet and outsiders. Captain Janeway is confronted with the same challenges reflected in American society during the late 1990s. As historian Samuel Huntington notes, one of the most important questions of the Cold War is pondered by Rabbit Angstrom, a central character in John Updike's novels: "Without the cold war, what's the point of being an American? If being American means being committed to the principles of liberty, democracy, individualism, and private property, and if there is no evil empire out there threatening those principles, what indeed does it mean to be American, and what will come of American national interests?" (Huntington 29). *Voyager* writers assembled a group of outsiders who were forced to work together under Janeway's leadership, ultimately providing the audience a venue to explore the nature of human destiny, to confront the conflicts of living in a diverse society, and thereby demonstrating the ability of society to work together with those who are different.

Placing *Voyager* in the Delta Quadrant is essential to the development of Janeway's character. By employing an abduction narrative, the ship is taken out of the Alpha Quadrant and as in the old captivity narratives that first appeared in the 17th century, traditional and proper roles were pushed aside, and women could step out of their "normal" roles. For instance, in the case of Mary Rowlandson, a woman kidnapped and taken prisoner by the Wampanoag Indians in February 1676 during King Philip's War. Rowlandson was kept prisoner for three months, returning to her family in May 1676 after her husband paid a £20 ransom. During her time in captivity she became accustomed to a meager diet, but her skill in sewing and knitting earned her better treatment that other less fortunate captives. Rowlandson wrote and published an account of her captivity which would be published in 1720 called *The Sovereignty and Goodness of God, Together with the Faithfulness of His Promises Displayed: Being a Narrative of Captivity and Restoration of Mrs. Mary Rowlandson*. In it Rowlandson testified to the Lord's strength in carrying her through her ordeal "so much that I could have thought of it had I not experienced it" (Mulford 45). Her statement emphasizes that her experience is unique; by enduring captivity, Rowlandson achieved understanding of the Lord's power that she could not have otherwise achieved. This knowledge sets her apart from the rest of the community; through her challenges, she achieved redemption of herself and her community. Mulford explains

> that the American perception of the wilderness changed because of captivity narratives. Before the publication of captivity narratives people believed the wilderness was a frightening wasteland. Yet, female captivity narratives depicted survival in the wilderness; thereby, the colonists' view of the wilderness changed. Colonists came to see the wilderness as a place of opportunity for success and enlightenment. Rowlandson's isolation from her community tested her faith, while simultaneously it provided her with a unique chance to rely on herself and her faith for success [Mulford 45].

Placing *Voyager* in this context created a separate space away from Starfleet where Janeway could lead the way; however, her crew is a mismatched collection of characters. Neelix and Kes are aliens from the Delta Quadrant with no connections to Starfleet; Chief Engineer Torres is a Starfleet Academy drop-out with a chip on her shoulder; Tom Paris is a convict; Harry Kim is fresh out of the Academy without hands on experience; Chakotay is the captain of the rebel Maquis ship; Seven of Nine is a Borg; and the Doctor is a holograph. Perhaps the lack of strong male figures and the crew's distance from the male-dominated Starfleet created a space where women could be free to be the heroes or bond with other women. The development of feminist concerns in *Voyager* reflects the development in American culture throughout the 1990s. During this time women saw huge gains in the law, education, jobs, and politics. Thanks to President Clinton's Interagency Council on Women an atmosphere of increased sensitivity to the demands for equal protections, opportunities, and rewards for women in public life took root.

Throughout the journey back to Earth Janeway is meticulous about upholding Starfleet principles, particularly the Prime Directive. Janeway never wavered from the rules; in fact, they seemed immutable. The captain always had to be right, and the prime directive could not be breached for any reason. For example, in the episode "Alliances" (2.14) to ensure Voyager's survival, Janeway attempted to negotiate with a group of enemies to create a Federation in the Delta Quadrant. Ultimately, Janeway attempted to fulfill Roddenberry's vision of a utopia where worlds were not in conflict. Yet, for many viewers she does not embody the "right" characteristics for a captain. As Sara Eileen Hames notes in her *TOR.COM* article "Janeway Doesn't Deserve This Shit," criticism of Janeway tended toward the skeptical and dismissive, with much of the commentary being vitriolic or sexist. Hames explains that her favorite piece of criticism of Janeway was:

> What they needed was a take charge, dynamic female Captain, what they gave us was a moralizing, overly-liberal pushover all too willing to throw her crew's life away for no reason at all if it made her seem superior and at least as interesting in prancing around in frilly dresses on the holodeck as she is in leading her crew [Hames].

Comments like this abound on Internet chat boards. Nevertheless, the writers of *Voyager* provided viewers with a complicated, capable, brave leader, who made difficult decisions. She has no shame or pride, no false sense of ego, and one single, unwavering, certainly monomaniacal goal: to get her crew home. Over the course of seven years on the way back from the Delta Quadrant, she uses everything she has and more to succeed.

We learn in the pilot episode, "Caretaker" (1.1), that Janeway is a complete professional. She begins her mission to locate the members of the Maquis, and when it becomes clear that *Voyager* is in trouble, she steps up her game. She forges an alliance with the rebels and sets about getting her crew home. Janeway realizes that the promise to her crew to get them home is the only thing she will ever be judged on. As a result, she sacrifices her personal comfort, her friendships, and her privilege time and time again to make it happen (Vlack). As Michèle Bowring notes, "it seems the producers and actor are trying to portray a female leader who is not mired in the heterosexual matrix of the 20th century" (*Gender, Work, and Organization* 392). The writers present Janeway as a complete professional and throughout much of the series Janeway refrained from pursuing romance. Unlike Kirk or Picard, Janeway embraced the long-established tradition that military officers should not fraternize with lower-ranking shipmates because it threatens the chain of command. This sacrifice is meant to highlight her leadership and character. Hames explains that "Janeway is a strong female character to rock all strong female characters: a leader who is female-gendered, in touch with her sense of gender, and yet invested with a non-gendered position of highest responsivity which she executes with capability and compassion" (Hames). It is important to note that before being swept away to the Delta Quadrant Janeway said farewell to her fiancé, not realizing that they would be separated for years. During the first two seasons the writers toyed with a relationship between Janeway and Chakotay, which became a reality in the episode "Resolutions" (2.25) when the characters are quarantined alone on a planet for four months. Viewers are left to their own interpretations of the episode; however, when they returned to *Voyager* Chakotay accepted the role of helpmeet, a man who enables a woman leader, yet is not involved in a romantic relationship (Light, "Geek Post"). This is not to say that Janeway relinquished her sexuality, but viable partners were virtually nonexistent. Ultimately, she formed a relationship with an Irish hologram during the final season.

Throughout *Voyager's* seven year run only two characters questioned her ability to lead. The first challenge came from "Q," the impudent, superior, and sometimes malevolent being from the mysterious Q Continuum that many refer to as a "space-jerk." In the episode "Death Wish," Q appears and accuses Quinn, another member of the Continuum, of sending humans to the Delta Quadrant where they do not belong yet. When Q realizes that Quinn is not responsible for this action, he demands to know who let Quinn out of his prison. When Janeway explains the *Voyager* crew let him out, Q turns to Janeway and says, "that's what you get for having a woman in the captain's seat." Q goes on to state that he thought "Riker would get this command" (2.18). The second challenge came from the Kazon, an alien species characterized by their violence and division along gender lines. The Kazon are a patriarchal society with a low opinion of women. Women in the Kazon society were spoken down to and treated as second class citizens. Moreover, male Kazon did not tolerate being given orders by a woman ("Maneuvers" 2.11 and "Alliances" 2.14). Nevertheless, Janeway's gender is never an issue for her crew and the writers never focus on her gender as a challenge to her ability to serve as a capable leader. Gladys Knight explains in her book *Female Action Heroes: A Guide to Women in Comics, Video Games, Film and Television* that many critics believed that women do not identify with Janeway—because she is too self-reliant and sure of herself, because she does not easily give in to fear. Still others claim that Janeway is not military enough, because she touches people and cries in front of subordinates and asks for second opinions (Knight 196). Critics compare Janeway with Kirk, Picard, and Sisko who they believe are strong men. This comparison is unfair; Kathryn Janeway is a woman in command, not a woman trying to do a man's job. She is the first female captain in *Star Trek* history and is a work in progress (Asselin). It is important to note that most criticism of her focuses on her emotions, decision-making, leadership ability and work/life balance followed by the tag line, "because she is a woman." Nevertheless, throughout the series she takes the viewers on a journey of discovery, helping them understand what it means to be a woman in authority, without being expected to behave like a man. Women in leadership positions, prior to Janeway, often subdued their feminine side to fit in with their male counterparts. Janeway is a complex female captain who leads with confidence; she is by no means a flawless leader, but she provides a woman's perspective on leadership.

Claire Light explains in her article "Maiden, Mother, Crone: Why Voyager Was Awesome" that Janeway's character started on shaky ground, because executives believed a male lead would be more acceptable. In fact, Genevieve Bujold, a French-Canadian actress, only lasted one day ("Kate Mulgrew Talks Sex and Seven of Nine"). Nevertheless, Paramount chose *Voyager* as the centerpiece of the new United Paramount Network (UPN) and placed a woman at the helm. According to Michèle A. Bowring's article "Resistance Is *Not* Futile," Kate Mulgrew embodied important characteristics that swayed Paramount executives. Mulgrew's dynamic performances came from her training as a stage actor, which provided a rich source of nuanced talent and performances (389). Additionally, Bowring notes that it would be difficult to write Janeway as obviously stereotypically masculine or feminine. She doesn't have the physique to be the kick-ass heroine Ripley of the *Alien* movies, nor does she have the young, nubile looks required for a campy space-vixen heroine. She is a slim, short woman in her forties with classic looks and a strong screen presence. This balanced moderate appearance suggested a balanced moderate character whose identity would come more from her personality rather than her looks [389–90].

In essence, the writers did not have an archetype for Janeway to embody. Writers explore a possible relationship with Chakotay, but the flirtation did not progress. By Season 3 the writers realized that Janeway could be a strong authority figure without having to totally give up her feminine side in her professional persona. Writers eventually got rid of her "bun of steel" and she "gradually let her hair down" by converting to a ponytail, which showed she was more comfortable inserting more feminine elements. During this same period, writers realized that Janeway juggled the conflicting responsibilities of being Starfleet's only envoy in the quadrant with the ultimate task of getting her crew home alive without external support. Writers made her ruthless and creative, finding compromises for the sake of survival. Moreover, they tried to make her a "motherly" figure that fostered nurturing motherly relationships with each of her crew to varying degrees of success. B'Elanna and Janeway seemed destined to be in conflict throughout the series. In "Parallax" (1.3) Chakotay proposes making Torres Chief Engineer. Janeway is resistant to this idea, believing Torres to be a "loose cannon," while B'Elanna believes that Janeway is too "Starfleet"—uptight and by the book. Nevertheless, as the series progresses the two grow very close. In "Barge of the Dead" (6.3) B'Elanna realizes that Janeway is dedicated to Starfleet in the same way her mother believed in Klingon traditions. Janeway also mothered Harry Kim, "the good son" who always obeyed orders and never broke the rules. Yet, like a child testing his boundaries in the episode "The Disease" (5.17) Harry Kim and Janeway have an argument about his relationship with an alien woman. Harry rails at Janewa, "I have served on this ship for five years and said, 'yes, ma'am' to every one of your orders. But not this time." Perhaps Janeway, the disappointed parent in this case, is harsher on Harry than others under her command when she issues a formal reprimand for his professional file. As with Harry Kim we see flashes of anger and rage, particularly when it comes to protecting her crew from the hazards of the Delta Quadrant. During a 1995 interview Mulgrew explained that "women have an emotional accessibility that our culture not only accepts but embraces" (Kim). Unlike her male counterparts who stoically reprimanded errant crewmembers, when *Voyager* personnel let Janeway down she often called them to her ready room where she expressed her emotions and feelings about their behavior and in no uncertain terms expressed her dissatisfaction with their performance. According to the essay "Captain Kathryn Janeway," "a man would be more interested in enforcing rules; Janeway is more interested in enforcing relationships always putting the needs of her people first even to her own peril because she recognizes that as their leader she has a responsibility to keep them safe" ("Captain Kathryn Janeway: Feminist Role Model for the 24th Century?"). In turn, her crew is willing to walk through fire for her.

The women of *Voyager* mentored by Janeway demonstrate what socially responsible women can achieve. As Gladys Knight explains in *Female Action Heroes: A Guide to Women in Comics, Video Games, Film, and Television,* "it was rare on television to see a female leader in her forties in a position of unquestioned power mentoring two younger action heroes about duty and social responsibility in addition to family and emotional happiness" (198). She goes on to explain that in American society age, associated with experience, prestige, wisdom, and other positive terms, is socially acceptable for men in positions of leadership. In contrast, women who embody those characteristics are portrayed as older women and passive grandmothers on television. Janeway defied the stereotype and proved that she could successfully mentor B'Elanna Torres and Seven of Nine. This trio represent a group of science oriented intelligent individuals. Through these characters' collegiality, camaraderie, and conflict, as well as numerous plots that focused on feminist ethics, the series presented a version of science that embraced feminist ideas about how women can alter the practice of science. They debated each other's actions without resorting to name-calling, catfights, and hysteria. For instance, in "Parallax" (1.3), B'Elanna and Janeway bounce ideas back and forth to help the ship break free of an anomaly. At times the viewer feels as though they are of one mind as they finish each other's sentences. Seven and B'Elanna clashed on occasion over professional issues as in "Day of Honor" (4.3), but they found professional ways to settle their differences and by the end of the series had become friends. According to Mulgrew, "Many times, you'll see Janeway change a thought or an opinion in mid-sentence because she understands that B'Elanna has an angle on a situation that she missed or Chakotay says something that makes sense and she changes her thinking. There is a wonderful flexibility in this tower of strength" (Mulgrew). The women of *Voyager* represented empowered women who could lead a rescue mission, rather than always being the damsel in distress in need of a rescue (Asselin). Viewers were not subject to them gossiping, whining about their sex lives, or comparing fashion notes to remind us that they are women. They have sex appeal without becoming sex objects and show that women can be more than caregivers and counselors. In *Star Trek: The Next Generation,* counselor Deanna Troi and Dr. Beverly Crusher were essentially taking on traditional female roles. In *Star Trek: Deep Space Nine,* Kira was a first officer, a subordinate to a male captain. Only in *Voyager* do we finally see a female captain, a female chief engineer, and a unique female who prefers to play by her own rules. In short, they displayed the values of importance in the mid-1990s intelligence, strength, and femininity.

Janeway inspired many girls and women to enter or advance in the sciences, including Italian astronaut Samantha Cristoforetti, who tweeted a photo of herself wearing a Janeway uniform aboard the International Space station (Hodge, *Gender Focus*). Cristoforetti quoted Janeway when she tweeted "There's coffee in that nebula'" ("The Cloud," 1.5) perhaps paying homage to Janeway who was always searching for ways to produce coffee as she trekked home (Cofield). Julie Tizard explains that Captain Janeway offered her inspiration during a particularly difficult time in her life:

> I was the Squadron Commander of an Air Force flying training unit and I had to select, hire, and train 110 instructor pilots.... I had to deal with a difficult Wing Commander, an insubordinate Operations Officer, and remote desolate location. Watching Captain Janeway fight enemies in the Delta Quadrant, deal with insubordinate crewmembers, and lead her ship on difficult and dangerous missions.... Kate Mulgrew did an amazing job as an actor breathing life into a complex, multifaceted, woman in command [Tizard].

Janeway's character helped women question conventional wisdom, gender roles, sexism, racism, and homophobia—inspiring her to look for a better, broader definition of feminism that is more akin to humanism (Hodge, *Gender Focus*). Watching women in positions of leadership is not just a story line for viewers—decisive, self-confident, and courageous women like Captain Janeway provided a generation of young women a role model which they could aspire toward.

The Mary Sue, a popular culture website which celebrates the diversity of women's representation in all its cultural forms, put every episode of every *Star Trek* incarnation up to the Bechdel Test, sometimes referred to as *Mo Movie Measure*, that examines the following three criteria:

1. It must include at least two women in it, who
2. talk to each other
3. about something besides a man [Bechdel Test].

The results revealed that the series that depict women in positions of power passed the test.

Voyager scored an 86.9 percent and every single episode of the fifth season received a passing score; *Deep Space Nine* earned a 57.8 percent; *The Next Generation* scored 44.9 percent; followed closely by *Enterprise* with 39 percent. The Original Series ranked in last place with only 7.5 percent (Hodge, "How Does Your Favorite *Star Trek* Series Fare on the Bechdel Test?"). One reason that *Voyager* ranked so high is that Janeway often conversed with B'Elanna about transporters, the warp drive, the impulse engines, or other ship related issues. It is also interesting to note that many of the *Voyager* episodes that did not pass the test were Janeway-centric but focused on her interactions with men. This demonstration of improved roles for women enhances *Star Trek's* claim of a utopian vision for the future where women and minorities are integrated more completely in the grand narrative. Yet, the series' feminist dynamism encounters challenges during the last two seasons when *Voyager* achieves contact with Starfleet command.

At the 2016 Montreal Comic-Con the issue of future diversity and inclusivity in *Star Trek* became a topic of conversation. Brent Spiner, William Shatner, and Katie Mulgrew, representing various *Star Trek* franchises, highlighted the forward-looking narrative of various series; however, Shatner then commented that he had never seen *Voyager*. A supportive audience member cheered that "A woman's place is on the bridge." According to Jarrah Hodge, Mulgrew sarcastically said, "Or in the kitchen as the case may be." Shatner immediately responded by saying, "A woman's place is in the fridge," a comment that he repeated several times. A woman came to the microphone to ask Brent Spiner a question about what it was like playing a non-human character, when Shatner again reiterated his comment. The questioner responded by stating "It's Mr. Spiner's turn now." The audience responded with sustained applause. Spiner responded by stating that the writers do most of the work. The woman responded by stating "All you had to do was show up"; Shatner responded, "This woman is dangerous: put her in the fridge." Later in the session when a fan asked Mulgrew about how it felt to wrap filming on *Voyager*, her response was heartfelt: "I wept, I wept, because you're in the trenches for seven years (Mr. Shatner doesn't know about this). You've invested so much. I loved being the Captain." Shatner responded, "You say you wept? Wow. That's so female. I can't imagine the captain of a starship weeping." Shatner's commentary does not sit well with many fans and is disrespectful of women (Hodge, "William Shatner Says, 'A Woman's Place Is in the Fridge'"). Moreover, it demonstrates the deep divide that remains in our society concerning the role of dynamic women in leadership positions.

The *Star Trek* franchise has not always treated authoritative women kindly. As previously noted, NBC executives removed Majel Barrett as first officer, a downfall for *Trek* feminists. The final *Original Series* episode, "Turnabout Intruder" (3.24), showcased Dr. Janice Lester driven insane by the chauvinistic Starfleet that denied women the right to command starships. Nevertheless, *Star Trek* has come a long way since 1966, and it is still breaking new ground. Captain Rachel Garrett of the *Star Trek: The Next Generation* episode "Yesterday's Enterprise" (3.15) suggested that women made progress. Garrett is the only female captain of the *Enterprise* as far as we know. She commanded the *Enterprise-C*, which emerged through a temporal rift into the 24th century mid-battle, changing history and putting the Federation at war. When she learned that the defeat of her ship could save thousands of others and prevent years of war, she did not hesitate, agreeing to go back and make the supreme sacrifice for the sake of the future and the possibility of a future of peace instead of war. She set an example for her crew, which they followed even after she died in the effort. For approximately thirty minutes before an untimely death she demonstrated the true meaning of Starfleet principles and saved the timeline along with thousands of lives, even though it meant the loss of her own.

In a 1995 interview Kate Mulgrew states, "it took balls for these guys to hire me in this capacity ... the first woman to lead a *Trek* series onto TV.... It's a bold choice, and an appropriate one for 400 years in the future" (Kim). Ultimately, what *Star Trek: Voyager* makes clear is that women can be capable, effective leaders and retain their femininity. Janeway was a scientist and a leader who made difficult decisions, set high standards for the behavior of her crew. She got to know them personally; she was a captain that you could go to with a personal problem as well as a professional one. Janeway knew when to be hardcore and when to go easy, when to trust someone and when not to, and she had impeccable principles. During the seven-year run, Captain Janeway fought the Borg, rallied against prejudice, fought new enemies, welcomed new friends, outwitted her foes, and in "Year of Hell," sacrificed her life. In essence, Janeway was a pioneer, who had a deep understanding of what things were like for Captain James Kirk and his crew during the early days of deep space exploration. In the article "18 Awesome Women in Star Trek," Mulgrew commented,

> It's not surprising that they had to bend the rules a little. They were a little slower to invoke the Prime Directive, and a little quicker to pull their phasers. Of course, the whole bunch of them would be booted out of Starfleet today. But I have to admit, I would have loved to ride shotgun at least once with a group of officers like that [Ulster].

But as Janeway told her crew: "In a part of space where there are few rules, it is more important than ever that we hold fast to our own. In a region where shifting allegiances are commonplace, we have to have something stable to rely on. And we do.... The principles and ideals of the Federation. As far as I'm concerned those are the best allies we could have" ("Alliances" 2.14). She knew it was not easy to stand by one's principles in the Delta Quadrant, but she was steadfast, telling Captain Ransom in "Equinox, Part I" (5.26), "It's never easy, but if we turn our backs on our principles, we stop being human." Standing by her principles, Captain Kathryn Janeway got her people home.

During her individual Comic-Con session, Mulgrew noted that "hopefully with the introduction of Mrs. Clinton as the next President of the United States, we can start to put aside this very odd notion that women are not equal. Equal screen time is now at hand. Equal sex time. Equal gender time. Equal color, race and creed time." She is correct that this was Gene Roddenberry's dream those many years ago; hopefully, despite Mrs. Clinton's presidential loss women will not lose traction in their quest for equality; however, if they do there is a 24th century woman reminding us what women throughout history have been telling us all along—that women are just as capable as men in top roles ("Captain Kathryn Janeway: Feminist Role Model for the 24th Century?"). During her concluding remarks, Mulgrew reflected on her role as Captain Janeway; "I think it is fairly clear that to play Kathryn Janeway in the time that I played her, was not only history-changing, but was a major blow to the glass ceiling of the boys' club in Hollywood." In Mulgrew's opinion, "Captain Kathryn Janeway was about more than being 'politically correct' or just letting *Star Trek* tick off the woman captain box" (Hodge, "William Shatner Says, 'A Woman's Place Is in the Fridge'"). Representation matters! As Sally Ride said, "You can't be what you can't see" (Hodge, *Gender Focus*). Perhaps now that we are in the 21st century, the time has come for the entertainment media to focus on the roles of women in the real world and stop focusing on archaic images of the past. Television needs more characters like Captain Kathryn Janeway to inspire women and young girls to aim high.

WORKS CITED

"Alliances." *Star Trek: Voyager*, written by Jeri Taylor, directed by Les Landau, Season 2, episode 14, Paramount, 22 Jan. 1996.

Asherman, Allan. *The Star Trek Compendium*. Pocket Books, 1986.

_____. *The Star Trek Interview Book*. Pocket Books, 1988.

Asselin, C.K. "My Tribute to the Women of Star Trek: Voyager." *TrekToday*, 22 Feb. 2001, www.trektoday.com/articles/tribute_to_women_of_voyager.shtml. Accessed 9 April 2017.

"Barge of the Dead."*Star Trek: Voyager*, created by Jeri Taylor, Gene Roddenberry, Rick Berman, and Michael Piller, Season 6, episode 3, Paramount, 6 Oct. 1999.

Bechdel Test Movie List, The Mary Sue, bechdeltest.com. Accessed 9 Aug. 2018.

Bernardi, Daniel. *Star Trek and History: Race-Ing Toward a White Future*. Rutgers University Press, 1999.

Blair, Karin. "Sex and 'Star Trek' (*Le Sexe Dans* 'Star Trek')." *Science Fiction Studies*, vol. 10, no. 3, 1 Nov. 1983, pp. 292–297.

Bowring, Michèle. "Resistance Is *Not* Futile: Liberating Captain Janeway from the Masculine-Feminine Dualism of Leadership." *Gender, Work and Organization*, vol. 11, no. 4, 4 July 2004, pp. 381–405.

Calla, Cofield. "Space.com." Space.com, Space.com, 25 Apr. 2015, www.space.com/29161-astronaut-star-trek-uniform-space.html. Accessed 9 August 2018.

"Captain Kathryn Janeway: Feminist Role Model for the 24th Century?" allreaders.com/book-review-summary/captain-kathryn-janeway-feminist-role-model-203. Accessed 9 Aug. 2018.

"Caretaker." *Star Trek: Voyager: The Complete Series*, written by Michael Piller and Jeri Taylor, directed by Winrich Kolbe, Season 1, episode 1, Paramount, 16 Jan. 1995.

"The Changing Roles of Women in the United States." *U.S. Society and Values*, June 1997, usa.usembassy.de/etexts/soc/ijse0597.pdf. Accessed 15 Aug. 2018.

"The Cloud." *Star Trek: Voyager*, story by Brannon Braga, directed by David Livingston, Season 1, episode 6, Paramount, 13 Feb. 1995.

Cranny-Francis, Anne. "Sexuality and Sex-Role Stereotyping in Star Trek (*Sexualité Et Rôles Sexuels Stéréotypés Dans 'Star Trek')*." *Science Fiction Studies*, vol. 12, no. 3, 1985, pp. 274–284.

"Day of Honor." *Star Trek: Voyager*, written by Jeri Taylor, directed by Jesús Salvador Treviño Season 4, episode 3, Paramount, 17 Sept. 1997.

"Death Wish." *Star Trek: Voyager*, teleplay by Michael Piller, directed by James L. Conway, Season 2, episode 18, Paramount, 19 Feb. 1996.

"The Disease." *Star Trek: Voyager*, story by Kenneth Biller, directed by David Livingston, Season 5, episode 17, Paramount, 24 Feb. 1999.

Douglas, Susan J. *Where the Girls Are: Growing Up Female with the Mass Media*. Times Books, 1995.

"Equinox, Part I." *Star Trek Voyager*, created by Jeri Taylor, Gene Roddenberry, Rick Berman, and Michael Piller, performance by Roxann Dawson, Season 5, episode 26, Paramount, 26 May 1999.

Geraghty, Lincoln. *American Science Fiction Film and Television*. Berg, 2009.

_____. *The Influence of Star Trek on Television, Film, and Culture*. McFarland, 2007.

Gerrold, David. *World of Star Trek*. BenBella Books Inc., 2016.

Hames, Sara Eileen. "Janeway Doesn't Deserve This Shit," TOR.com, 27 Aug. 2012, www.tor.com/2012/08/27/janeway-doesnt-deserve-this-shit/. Accessed 15 Aug. 2018.

Heller, Lee. "The Persistence of Difference: Post-Feminism, Popular Discourse, and Heterosexuality on 'Star Trek: The Next Generation.'" *Science Fiction Studies*, vol. 24, no. 2, 1997, pp. 226–244.

Henderson, Mary. "Professional Women in Star Trek, 1964–1969." *Film and History*, vol. XXIV, no. 1, 1994, pp. 48–59.

Hodge, Jarrah. *Gender Focus*, 14 June 2015, www.gender-focus.com/2015/06/14/captain-janeway/. Accessed 9 Aug. 2018.

_____. "How Does Your Favorite Star Trek Series Fare on the Bechdel Test," The Mary Sue, 1 Sept. 2014, www.themarysue.com/star-trek-bechdel-test? Accessed 9 Aug. 2018.

_____. "William Shatner Says, 'A Woman's Place Is in the Fridge,'" *Remains the Worst*, The Mary Sue, 18 July 2016, www.themarysue.com/set-phasers-to-sexist/. Accessed 9 Aug. 2018.

ADD Huntington_____

Jameson, Frederic. "Progress Versus Utopia: Or Can We Imagine the Future." Science Fiction Studies, 1982, p. 151.

"Kate Mulgrew Talks Sex and Seven of Nine on 'Star Trek: Voyager.'" TrekMovie.com, edited by TrekMovie.com Staff, 2 July 2017, trekmovie.com/2017/07/02/kate-mulgrew-talks-sex-and-seven-of-nine-on-star-trek-voyager/. Accessed 20 Aug. 2018.

Kim, Albert. "Star Trek Voyager's First Female Captain," *Entertainment Weekly*, 20 Jan. 1995, ew.com/article/1995/01/20/star-trek-voyagers-first-female-captain/. Accessed 9 Aug. 2018.

Knight, Gladys L. *Female Action Heroes: A Guide to Women in Comics, Video Games, Film, and Television*. ABC-CLIO, 2010.

Light, Claire. "Geek Post: Why Voyager Rocked," 21 Aug. 2009, clairelight.typepad.com/seelight/2009/08/geek-post-why-voyager-rocked.html. Accessed 9 Aug. 2018.

_____. "Maiden, Mother, Crone: Why Voyager Was Awesome," Nerds of Color, 12 Sept. 2013, thenerdsofcolor.org/2013/09/12/maiden-mother-crone-why-voyager-was-awesome/. Accessed 9 Aug. 2018.

"Maneuvers." *Star Trek: Voyager*, written by Kenneth Biller, directed by David Livingston, Season 2, episode 11, Paramount, 20 Nov. 1995.

Mulford, Carla. "Early American Writings." *Mary White Rowlandson*, edited by Carla Mulford, Oxford, 2002, pp. 306–07.

Mulgrew, Kate. *Trekkie Feminist*, Apr. 2014, trekkiefeminist.tumblr.com/post/81858160543/leadership-style-command-has-to-embrace-but-it. Accessed 15 Aug. 2018.

Nimoy, Leonard. Interview by Kevin Curtis. *Star Trek Memories*, 1983.

Norwalk, Brandon. *AV/TV CLUB*, 28 May 2013, tv.avclub.com/star-trek-voyager-accidentally-presided-over-the-franc-1798238334. Accessed 15 Aug. 2018.

"Parallax." *Star Trek: Voyager: The Complete Series*, written by Brannon Braga, directed by Kim Friedman, Season 1, episode 2, Paramount, 23 Jan. 1995.

Reagin, Nancy. *Star Trek and History*. Wiley Pop Culture History Series, 2013.

"Resolutions." *Star Trek: Voyager*, written by Jeri Taylor, directed by Alexander Singer, Season 2, episode 25, Paramount, 13 May 1996.

Rowlandson, Mary. *Project Gutenberg's Captivity and Restoration*, edited by David Widger, Gutenberg Project, 9 Nov. 2009, www.gutenberg.org/files/851/851-h/851-h.htm. Accessed 15 Aug. 2018.

Snyder, William J. *Star Trek: A Phenomenon and Social Statement on the 1960s*, 1995, www.ibiblio.org/jwsnyder/wisdom/trek.html. Accessed 9 Aug. 2018.

Tizard, Julie. "Oh, Captain, My Captain: Images of Women in Command." *Woman at Warp*, 1 Nov. 2017, www.womenatwarp.com/oh-captain-my-captain-images-of-women-in-command/. Accessed 20 Aug. 2018.

"The Turnabout Intruder." *Star Trek*, story by Gene Roddenberry, directed by Herb Wallerstein, Season 3, episode 24, Paramount, 3 June 1969.

Ulster, Laurie. "18 Awesome Women in Star Trek: Who Are the Female Heroes of Star Trek? Freedom Fighters to Science Nerds, They Make Their Mark," screenrant, 1 Feb. 2017, screenrant.com/awesome-women-star-trek-voyager-next-generation/. Accessed 15 Aug. 2018.

Vettel-Becker, Patricia. "Space and the Single Girl: Star Trek, Aesthetics, and 1960s Femininity." *Frontiers*, vol. 35, no. 2, 2014, pp. 143–72.

Vlack, Tarah Wheeler Van. "Star Trek's Captain Kathryn Janeway, CEO Role Model," 25 Nov. 2014, www.wework.com/creator/run-your-business/hr-human-resources/star-treks-captain-kathryn-janeway-startup-ceo-role-model/. Accessed 15 Aug. 2018.

"Yesterday's Enterprise." *Star Trek: The Next Generation*, directed by David Carson, perf. By Patrick Stewart, Season 3, episode 15, Paramount, 19 Feb. 1990.

Millennial Girlhood and the End of Kes

PETER W.Y. LEE

On stardate 50348.1, a little girl grew up and hated it. In "Warlord" (3.10), *Voyager*'s resident gentle chronological toddler, Kes, turned into a tyrant. The episode wasn't a phase of the terrible twos; rather, a malevolent alien invaded her mind. Possessed, Kes dumps her guardian/lover Neelix, kills a hapless shipmate, and conquers a planet. While the episode ends with Starfleet triumphant, as usual, Kes somberly tells the ship's expert mentalist, Tuvok, that mind-melding with Federation values of self-exploration and improvement doesn't necessarily make for a happy ending. Kes initially joined *Voyager*'s crew to seek out new life and civilizations—to boldly go beyond the limits of her isolationist home world. But in doing so, she realizes that human ideals of self-discovery and maturation aren't exactly as Captain Kathryn Janeway had advertised. Rather, the captain's role model of a mother figure who can do it all has limits outside the enlightened standards of twenty-fourth century Alpha [Quadrant] womanhood.

Or even millennial American girlhood during the 1990s.

The end of the twentieth century supposedly heralded the end of feminism. Various female "firsts," including Sandra Day O'Connor's ascent to the Supreme Court in 1981, Geraldine Ferraro's 1984 nomination as U.S. Vice President, and Hillary Clinton's overachievement as First Lady, led the public to declare 1992 as the "Year of the Woman" (Collins 343). By 1994, *Star Trek* was poised to trail-blaze the trend into the future. While actress Geneviève Bujold didn't have the temperament to handle the required technobabble befitting a Starfleet officer, Kate Mulgrew relished the notion of manning the captain's chair to take humanity's intrepid explorer into the next millennium. Mulgrew described Kathryn Janeway as "an extraordinary woman" and predicted that "400 years from now, women will have transcended all of these stereotypes that so limit us today or certainly have in the past" (Roller 63). Mulgrew noted Janeway combined character traits of traditional womanhood—"her femininity, her great heart, her empathy, her need for personal contact"—with the rigors of command. "When she needs to take over, she takes over like nobody's business" (Roller 63–64). Actress Jennifer Lien, prepping for her role as Kes, agreed: "The captain is a thoughtful, courageous woman and that is appealing regardless of sex" (Dilmore "Jennifer," 58). By crossing the boundaries of gender roles, strong-willed women seemingly embodied the best of both worlds.

But not every woman had it good as *Voyager*'s captain. Cultural critics, such as Susan Faludi and Gabriele Griffin, argue that women experienced a backlash during the 1980s and into the 1990s. Social conservatives dismissed second wave feminism as outmoded, with "postfeminism" signifying gender equality a reality. With feminism seemingly accomplished, few young women in the 1990s identified with the movement, and feminists largely focused on marginalized groups, such as "problem" youth: single teen mothers, child prostitution, and other tabloid-ready headlines (Morgan 135). While these topics were important—some found their way into *Voyager*—they focused on a minority of the population, largely ignoring mainstream girlhood. Despite some commanding presences on television such as the leading heroines in *Xena: Warrior Princess* and *Buffy: The Vampire Slayer*, a proliferation of images showing women as anorexic, thin, and hypersexualized dominated mainstream media. Women conceivably could do it all, but schoolgirls experienced conflicting images of supposed independence while forcing their bodies to conform to limited, rigid body types. Such identity crises voyaged into the twenty-fourth century's Delta Quadrant.

A Mess of Kes: What Are Little Girls Made Of?

Star Trek: Voyager did not just celebrate the first female lead in the franchise's history. The series introduced the franchise's first little girl, Kes. Unlike other Trek kids, like the toddler Molly O'Brien, the non-conformist Alexander Rozhenko, the mischievous Nog and Jake Sisko, or teen *wunderkind* Wesley Crusher, Kes was a blank slate: an innocent, charming child, curious about the galaxy around her. The series character bible describes Kes as "delicate, beautiful, young—and has a life span of only nine years" (Rennit 5). Her life span renders Kes a legal-aged minor who approached life with wide-eyed wonder. But unlike Data, whose built-in aging program gave the android a sagging chin and wrinkles like any normal human, Kes's short shelf life indicates a real potential to never grow old.[1]

Kes's short life span, however, confined the character's development as a perpetual child. An alien who dies of old age before a human child enters double digits connoted vulnerability and the need for guardian figures. Kes has adult figures in abundance. The crew's entrance to the Delta Quadrant is due to an elderly guardian whom the Ocampa literally call a "Caretaker." This banjo-strumming old-timer provides the Ocampa with the comforts of home, claiming that their maximum age of nine denies them self-sufficiency, let alone individual maturity. The elderly Caretaker's guilty conscience—his race is responsible for devastating the Ocampan home world—leads him to pamper the Ocampa lest they fall prey to galactic heavies, notably the Kazon. Little more than schoolyard bullies, the Kazon prey on the hapless child-race, forcing the Caretaker to devote his golden years to protecting his "children," and leading Janeway to give up her crew's initial chance to get home when the Caretaker dies. The producers built up the Kazon as *Voyager*'s early antagonists, but, unlike the honorable Klingons, the Kazon lack a moral code—even a set of house rules to acquire stuff that drive the Ferengi. Instead, the Kazon sects are simply thugs brawling for Starfleet technology—a zero-sum game that the audience knows they will never win. The Borg even considers the Kazon unworthy of assimilation, a sign of universal neglect that enables these bullies to pick on the Ocampa with abandon ("Mortal Coil" 4.12).

Although one-dimensional, the Kazon effectively frighten the Ocampa from leaving their underground haven. However, Kes doesn't scare. Executive producer Jeri Taylor emphasized Kes wasn't just a sweet girl; she was a "strong-minded, independent character" (Spelling "Now," 45). Taylor called Kes a rebel who believes the Ocampa have "grown lazy mentally" thanks to the Caretaker. Kes dares to know more than her underground life affords her and leaves the sanctuary for the harsh glare of the surface world. But like other would-be philosophers who turn from their dark caves to stare at the sun, she's in for a rude awakening. The Kazon abduct and enslave her. Her introductory shot, a scarred and sullen face in the shadows, signifies not only Ocampan helplessness without an adult presence, but an innocent needing perpetual protection.[2] Kes herself says as much at the end of the series pilot, telling Janeway she hopes *Voyager*'s course home will be the same as hers.

Kes's decision to leave her home planet opens her world, but also threatens to strip her innate child-like wonder. As the series progressed, Kes walks a fine line between maintaining her innocence and growing alongside the crew making their way through the Delta Quadrant. This duality didn't make for the best storytelling. Executive producer Rick Berman later called Kes "an elfin female" who "became somewhat superfluous"; her mission to poke around the cosmos was no different than the Starfleet (and Maquis) officers aboard the ship: "It was just really hard for the writers to work on it, so eventually we wrote the character out of the show" (Gross and Altman 567). Indeed, many episodes short-changed Kes, minimizing her presence to a passive observer ("The 37's," 2.1) or giving her a throwaway line about how she's interested in interstellar phenomena ("The Q and the Grey" 3.11). Kes does not appear in "Resistance" (2.12) or "Non Sequitur" (2.5). The inquisitive little girl is also an ideal victim: in "Basics, Part II" (3.1), some primitive cave-aliens abduct Kes and Neelix (Neelix is kidnapped off-camera, Kes is ambushed and dragged into the bushes in moonlight); in "Deadlock" (2.21), Kes falls through a space-time rift and the crew works to rescue her; in "Sacred Ground" (3.7), Kes wanders into a religious shrine, thereby committing sacrilege, and is condemned to death in a comatose state, leaving Janeway to take an endurance test to save her.

Despite a limited role, Kes fully embraces Starfleet's mandate as a guide for growing up. Jennifer Lien enthused over this wide-eyed innocence as her central trait: "Everything is new to Kes. She's seeing it all for the first time. It's all wondrous and different for her, and I love playing that" (Spelling "Jennifer," 34). With her life span counting down, Kes believes in being "a free thinker" and employing an "appetite for knowledge and the sense of curiosity" before her time runs out (Spelling "Jennifer," 35). Lien further singled out relationships with The Doctor, Neelix, and Janeway as teacher-pupil dynamics, with the two-year-old soaking up information from the hologram, cook, and captain (Spelling "Jennifer," 36). She settles with a "caretaker" role as the ship's gardener and field medic. Her taking charge of creating an airponics bay enables her to indulge in her love of flowers and plant life to feed the crew, fulfilling a traditional feminine role as food provider.

Kes's stint as a nurse is more substantial. The Doctor's subroutines are thrilled when Kes starts training, giving him downtime for opera and holonovels. As for the crew, Kes exceeds The Doctor's first medic, Tom Paris (whose sole qualification is taking two semesters of biochemistry), and even the hologram itself, who Kes notes has no bedside manner. As a nurse, Kes is a nurturer, encouraging the nameless hologram to find an identity. While the rest of the crew treats The Doctor as if he was just a tool, Kes urges him to get in touch with his feelings and fiercely defends his sentience. When The Doctor's program starts deteriorating in "The Swarm" (3.4), Kes plays nursemaid, balking at Torres's suggestion to simply reboot the program and start anew. She persuades The Doctor—and even The Doctor's feisty self-built troubleshooting program—to take steps to preserve his individuality. In doing so, Kes fulfills Starfleet's mission to investigate new life, even if such exploration takes place in the crew's own sickbay.

While Kes's jobs on the ship are stereotypically feminine, the ultimate role of mother eludes her. With a nine-year life span, Kes's toying with motherhood would subject her to the human standards of legal maturity and sttutory rape. Rick Berman initially thought of Kes as "this kind of funny-looking gremlin's girlfriend. It just didn't work" (Gross and Altman 567). The relationship fizzled as the producers worried about sending the wrong message; the idea of an alien child having sex with a hairy alien old enough to be her father daunted writers. Executive story editor Ken Biller noted producers Berman and Taylor "had some concern that she was so young. Are we sending the right message that they are screwing?" (Kutzera 80). Such fears killed Kes's first romance lest the fears of twentieth century headlines about teenage moms sully Gene Roddenberry's utopian future. Historian Joanna Gregson notes that although rates of teenage motherhood decreased from the 1990s to 2005, the press projected an "epidemic" of teenage promiscuity in sensationalized news and in popular culture (1). For Kes, having a child requires her losing her virginity, and by connotation, her girlhood innocence.

Kes considers having children throughout the series. She becomes a mother in an alternate reality in "Before and After" (3.21), but the viewer knows the timeline would never come to pass, if only because the episode's premise includes the deaths of Janeway and Torres during a year of hell that never really materializes. In the episode "Elogium" (2.4), Kes has the opportunity to have a child when she enters puberty. Kes wants to give birth, but the father figure of choice, Neelix, isn't willing to settle down. The episode "Jetrel" (1.15) reveals Neelix lost his first family during a war and he has never fully recovered. On the rebound, he sees Kes as a lover, albeit they don't share quarters aboard the ship. Despite Neelix' reluctance, Kes prepares for motherhood, turning to her surrogate parents—Janeway, Tuvok, and The Doctor—to prepare her mind and body. Mulgrew commented that the episode effectively paralleled a mother aiding "Janeway's surrogate daughter" (Spelling "Kate," 21) who was entering puberty: "It showed my involvement with her on a very female level, a very maternal level, which I liked" (Spelling "Kate," 24). Screenwriter Ken Biller noted the episode came closest to *Star Trek* presenting "a metaphor in there about teen pregnancy. Does Kes, just because she is capable of having a child, have to make the decision to have a child? It's certainly one of the biggest social problems of our day" (Kutzera 79).

"Elogium" (2.4) answered Biller in the negative. With teenage parents regarded as one of the "biggest social problems," the episode showed viewers the downs and outs facing young moms. Kes faces a reluctant father, the uncertainties of child rearing, and the realization that her life would change. The show's tantalizing promise of a little girl "doing it"—Kes states she isn't even two years old yet, and she and Neelix would be joined for six days of intercourse—tap into the racy perceptions of child sexuality and the loss of innocence surrounding girlhood. Indeed, viewers have a glimpse of Kes in heat, with her sweaty face and palms, her wanton appetite as she devours bugs and plants, and arousal via a foot massage as she talks about giving birth through her back. However, unlike previous forays into social issues like racism and miscegenation, Biller sidestepped the issue; Neelix ultimately does the noble thing of accepting fatherhood, but Kes opts out. She preserves her virginity and her role as the ship's sweetheart, resolving the "big social problem" by avoiding it. Kes emerges from puberty still a little girl, with the sanctity of marriage and the nuclear family as ideals she can explore in the future. Kes leaves open the possibility of having a child, but viewers might suspect Kes never will. After all, if she has a child, she would no longer be the ship's little girl.

Innocence Mislaid: Needling Neelix

Kes's flirtation with motherhood and her abuse at the hands of the Kazon demonstrate that the little girl's innocence is at constant risk from internal and external pressures. Her child-like persona, heightened by her status as a legal minor, connoted an erotic quality paralleling other television shows and film. As media scholars note, the image of a highly sexualized and infantilized female dependent on a male provider blossomed in the 1990s through incest fantasies and various "May–December" relationships. If women could seemingly "do it all," then the male fantasy of a young, submissive, needy girl buttressed the structure of a benevolent patriarchy, where daddies took care of adoring daughters (Karlyn 59). Such themes found high acclaim in movies like *Lolita* (1997), *Wicked* (1998), and *American Beauty* (1999), which won the Academy Award for best picture. The sexualized girl had grownup counterparts in media, notably with Pamela Anderson's *Baywatch* filling the boob tube, or Demi Moore's *Striptease* (1996) titillating the silver screen (Madrid 284–285). Popular culture indicted women could straddle multiple personas, like the sexy soccer mom who scores in the bedroom and the workplace, but many girls struggled to reconcile the images of supermodel and pornstar with independence, empowerment, and fulfillment.

Star Trek's producers also tried to keep Roddenberry's optimistic vision of the future current. The relationship between Neelix and Kes paralleled the father-daughter romance cycle in popular culture, but, as Rick Berman noted, it didn't click for writers and the relationship faded. The franchise's legion of Trekkies also had their say; Kes's innocent demeanor proved alluring and fans wanted her to pair up with someone other than the ship's cook. The fans' demand for the little girl to outgrow her puppy love for the ship's morale officer took Jennifer Lien by surprise. The actress resisted the idea of being a "sex person," negated the suggestion that she was "one of the sexiest woman [sic] on any *Star Trek* program," and dismissed suggestions Kes hook up with other men, like The Doctor—whose program was younger than Kes, but, appearance wise, also looked old enough to be her father (Snauffer "Space,"

18).[3] This promiscuousness flew in the face of Kes's assertion that her people mate for life and, befitting their status as innocent "children," had no concept of distrust, envy, or betrayal regarding their spouses ("Parturition" 2.7). Nevertheless, that fans wanted Kes to break out of her shell echoed contemporary concerns that teenage girls were doing just that. Sociological studies, including *Reviving Ophelia* and *Schoolgirls*, observed that many girls felt pressure to push the boundaries of simply being familial "princesses." Girls struggled with drug use, experimented with sex, fought eating disorders, and expressed a general victimization with growing up. Such themes made for hot Nielsen ratings bait, box-office boffo, and best-selling lists across the country.

Star Trek's vision of the twenty-fourth century is supposedly above that sort of thing—at least, on the part of the progressive Federation. However, as Kes broadens her experiences, her body remains a focus for the viewers' and fellow crewmembers' eyes. An openly curious child with a developing body, Kes's first guardian figure is Neelix, who takes it upon himself to preserve her innocence—if only for his own carnal desires. The character bible describes the pair: "Neelix adores her, is protective of her, is insanely jealous of her. Kes doesn't give him any reason for those feeling; she loves Neelix and is loyal to him. But she is inquisitive and eager to absorb knowledge about this starship and its fascinating crew. She is an innocent who sees humanity through a fresh perspective, and the crew of *Voyager* never cease [sic] to fascinate her" (Ruditis 5). Kes's eagerness in knowing the crew's male members irks Neelix who depends on the Federation to provide Kes a home. "Kes helps him cook and serve, but she'd much rather be roaming the ship, getting to know the people," the character bible explains (Ruditis 6). In return, Neelix's jealousy means "he's always sure she's standing in a closet with a sailor" (Ruditis 6) Kes is an innocent child, but Neelix fears she veers close to becoming a nymphet.

As a galactic trader and drifter, Neelix has been around the quadrant a couple of times and knows there are sailors in every port. In part, he idealizes Kes, a vision of purity and virtue in a violent universe filled with phages. Neelix has first-hand experience, having lost his first family in a holocaust thanks to a mad scientist during an interstellar war ("Jetrel" 1.15). In mourning, bitter, and on the run from alien bullies, Neelix sees Kes as a rarity, like running water in a sun-baked, desert planet. Neelix hopes to keep Kes uncontaminated while keeping her for himself. Given her short life span, he wants to prolong her innocence—the duo doesn't even kiss on screen until "The Cloud" (1.6), the sixth episode.

However, Neelix's purity campaign runs into a snag; production wise, it became a stumbling block for writers wary of offending viewers with scenes of figurative father-daughter sex. In terms of characterization, Neelix comes across as overly possessive and downright jealous. Actor Ethan Phillips noted envy played a large role in Neelix's makeup as a father figure who wants to keep a close eye on the two-year-old Ocampan: "He has thought about that an awful lot, the fact that in eight years this woman whom he loves *won't* be around anymore." (Spelling "Ethan," 20). Neelix's desire to keep Kes uncontaminated and exclusively *his* erupts when he suspects these Federation types mask their debased behavior under the polished technowizardry of food replicators and fancy holodecks.

Neelix is grateful for Janeway's giving him and Kes a home, a purpose, and a higher standard of living. However, as a loner, Neelix remains suspicious of governmental bodies; his distrust stems from personal experience with the Kazon, the organ-stealing Vidiians, and his home world's own failed conflicts. The bitter Talaxian remains wary of these Starfleet officers who stick their noses into any anomaly and planet, the Prime Directive notwithstanding. He recognizes the Federation can provide for Kes, but he insists on personally looking out for her best interests, especially when it concerned the innocent girl's moral sensibilities.

Neelix's moral precautions reflected a rise of popular discontent during the 1990s against what the public perceived as government conspiracies and the intrusion into the personal lives and businesses of "real Americans." Popular culture, notably *The X-Files*, fueled these ideas that ordinary citizens couldn't trust the government, the media, or even each other. Disgruntled citizens took up arms, forming make-shift militias and embraced gun culture as a way of protecting themselves lest the government unleashes the military against civilians. Writers like Karen MacNutt penned a column in the magazine *Women and Guns*, where she decried a liberal establishment hell-bent on disarming the population to institute tyranny (Homsher 12). In this environment, social conservative women shouldered firearms in the name of protecting their children, and, by extension, the family values surrounding innocent tykes growing up in a hostile environment of greed, sex, and corruption led by Madison Avenue and Hollywood (Homsher 147). Neelix steps in as Kes's watchdog, safeguarding her from universal corruption, including the Federation. However, as Kate Mulgrew has pointed out, Janeway likewise sees herself as Kes's protective mother figure watching out for her daughter. Janeway figuratively rebutted social conservative American women who stood ready to gun down negative influences from Tinsel Town. Indeed, representing 1990s sensibilities, Janeway made for a better guardian figure than Neelix, whose sexual interest in the "child" worried Berman's production staff. Kes's embracing Federation values refuted the negative image of Hollywood television while affirming the perceived need to shelter girlhood from malevolent forces, either in the Delta Quadrant or in American media and clandestine government forces. Once the Ocampan comes aboard, she doesn't need Neelix's protection anymore and their romance dissipates.

The Federation enriches Kes's life far beyond what Neelix can offer her, but, despite Janeway's protective guidance, Kes's naiveté endangers her as she lives aboard a ship filled with eligible bachelors. Kes selects Neelix as the father of her child, and while parenthood does not pan out, Neelix remains wary that his "sweetings" is playing around with the guys, turning his character into a suspicious and jealous dad. In "Twisted" (2.6) when Kes recites the locations of her fellow crewmen's quarters, Neelix wonders how she knows where these men sleep—her duties as the sole nurse notwithstanding—unless her innocence is "twisted," as the episode's title implies.

Neelix's wrath specifically targets Tom Paris, the ship's bad boy and former jailbird, who he suspects wants to seduce the two-year-old girl. At least one fan approved of Paris, commenting, "The far more attractive Paris has set his sights on Kes, a welcome development if it injects some tension and discord into what is a far too harmonious world" (Doherty 66). Paris himself sees the Delta Quadrant as a new start from his former life in a penal colony, but Neelix mistakes his gallantry as cradle snatching. In "Parallax" (1.2), Paris chivalrously pulls out a chair for Kes and Neelix shoots daggers in the helmsman's direction. When Paris gives Kes a locket for her second birthday in "Twisted" (2.6), Neelix glowers. In "Elogium" (2.4), Kes and Paris drop off some cabbages at the mess hall and the Talaxian wonders what else might be growing between them. The cook blows his lid in "Parturition" (2.7) when he attacks Paris with a plate of putrid pasta. In an alternate future, Kes and Paris wed and share a lifetime of bliss ("Time and Again" 1.4), but Neelix worries that, as long as they stay aboard *Voyager*, corruption and temptation remain. After all, they'll always have Paris.

Furious Growing Pains

In terms of storytelling, Kes's body was generally off-limits after puberty since she chose not to have a child. But her mental development became her main character arc as she overcomes the "mentally" lazy Ocampa under the Caretaker. Female students needed an encouraging shot in the arm; as sociologist Peggy Orenstein points out, in the 1990s, schoolgirls were marginalized in the classroom and in the public; the societal focus on their sexualized bodies downplayed their mental development. Girls fell behind boys in STEM classes; in 1994, one teacher divulged that boys saw math as their domain "that shows they're brainy and they like being able to show off that way," while girls were more passive and demurred risk-taking (Orenstein 15). Such views lingered into the *Star Trek* franchise, where the 1960s Theiss Titillation Theory—named after the costume designer of the Original Series who determined a woman's appeal by how her clothes seemed to fall off her body—

still played a role in female characterization. In contrast, Kes's girlpower rested in her brains, not her bared skin. In "Cold Fire" (2.10), Ocampa who have rejected their race's isolated outlook to nurture their latent mental powers warn Kes that, as she voyages further from their home world, she, too, will develop her mind and end up threatening her human enculturation. That warning comes to pass.

Kes's mental powers belied her physical appearance. As early as the third episode, Kes shows signs of seeing beyond the space-time continuum ("Time and Again" 1.4). She eagerly wants to expand her mind as part of her self-exploration and turns to Tuvok. Neelix has no problem with the emotionless Mr. Vulcan keeping her up at night in his quarters alone, unlike that cad, Tom Paris, but the security chief doesn't coach her beyond playing with blocks ("Flashback" 3.2) or candles ("The Gift" 4.2). Indeed, Tuvok's *kohlinar* training aside—a failed attempt in which he underwent severe discipline to purge all emotions, only to fall in love and start a family—Kes is simply out of his league, even overwhelming Tuvok's consciousness when he tries the famed mind meld ("Warlord" 3.10; "The Gift" 4.2). Kes's mental training accelerates at a fast pace, catalyzed by the telepathic life forms she encounters, such as Species 8472, who broaden her mind. In following the Federation's values of self-exploration and improvement, the inquisitive little girl's brain power threatens to destroy the ship itself.

In "Warlord" (3.10), Kes, whom writer Lisa Klink called "the least warrior-like character you can think of," tests the limits of her physical and mental maturity (Kaplan "Voyager," 98). When a dying tyrant implants himself in her mind, Kes's consciousness struggles to regain control. The warlord, Tieran, rejects the little girl persona, killing several extras, including a fellow crewmate, assassinates the head of his home world, assumes the throne, and then puts the move on the crown prince, much to Tieran's wife's annoyance. While Kes's love for botany and gardening surfaces at times, he refuses to yield to the little girl. The warlord even implies that's not necessarily a bad thing, telling Chakotay he's not a monster. Kes returns to normal, of course, thanks to Starfleet's medical technobabble, but the episode concludes with the Ocampan less sure of herself.

Ironically, only when Tieran usurps Kes's consciousness does the girl grow up in mind and body. As Tieran, she finally dumps Neelix, and Kes never resumes the relationship when she is Tieran-free; she assaulted members of *Voyager*'s crew; and temporarily ruled a planet. Kes finds strength and empowerment through physical and sexual aggression, and she can't regress to her old lifestyle. Her mentor, Tuvok, says as much, stating how she will adapt to this experience is up to her. Kes soon decides that a more aggressive womanhood and sexuality have benefits. She grows out her hair and styles it in wavy curls (Lien's actual hairdo sans the Ocampa wig to cover her elfin ears) and wears form-fitting jumpsuits instead of conservative overalls and aprons. Lien commented she never had a role like Tieran before and enjoyed playing a "strong and determined" character. One reviewer agreed, calling it "unfortunate" that Lien "only gets to do something active when possessed by an alien" (Kaplan "Voyager" 98). As Tieran, Kes becomes top-tiered in mind ... and body ... according to 1990s Terran standards.

Kes's maturation spells the end of her innocence and brings closure to her character arc. As the third season progresses, Kes gains experience and exposure to the great galaxy outside her airponics bay, but this violates her core characterization. After she breaks up with Neelix, she hooks up with a guest star, Zahir, who tempts her to leave *Voyager* for good to expand her mental power ("Darkling" 3.18). She declines, but she also can't go back to where she once was, even if she wanted to; Kes is soon undercut by cute kids like Naomi Wildman, the ship's new resident space cadet who has ambitions to become the Captain's Assistant. Fittingly, Neelix, who had taken to Kes's innocence, becomes an uncle to Naomi, filling in for the young girl's career mom to tuck her in at night. Either as a child or as a budding Starfleet officer, Kes has no place on the ship she can uniquely call her own. With the airponics bay incinerated ("Cold Fire" 2.10) and The Doctor fully mobile outside of sickbay ("Future's End" 3.8), Kes doesn't have a real job, save to continue exploring on her own. With her mental abilities surpassing Tuvok's, the logical course of action is for Kes to leave the ship.

From a production standpoint, the show needed a "shake-up" for ratings purposes, and Seven of Nine came on board to excite the fan boys. The physical opposite of Kes's "little-girl" persona, Seven of Nine's contempt/fascination for humanity's imperfection reverses Starfleet's mission. Seven is already well-versed with thousands of species, but, as Annika Hansen, she is a figurative child in Borg components; in "Scorpion, Part II" (4.1), Janeway notes young Annika went over to the dark side of the Delta Quadrant, assimilated alongside her parents who refused to follow Federation guidelines, even to the point of not filing a flight plan. Janeway regards Seven as a bratty little girl who needs to comply with humanity under the norms of Starfleet regulations. Since Seven's state of mind is not up to a human's maturity, Janeway asserts herself as a mother, making decisions in Seven's best interests, just as she had nurtured Kes.[4] Resistance was futile.

Seven's early opposition to Janeway contrasts sharply to Kes's wide-eyed obedience. As an eager pupil, Kes is open to exploring strange new worlds, but her innocence is a dead end in terms of keeping her sexually pure and wholesome once she acquires the ability to conquer entire worlds at a whim. Shaped in the mold of Starfleet personnel exploring the Delta Quadrant — from The Doctor's nurse to Tuvok's pupil — Kes has little to do. The writing staff, already stretched to cover ten main characters had Kes stayed, decided her "story arc had been fully realized and that she would have to leave the ship" (Ruditis 191). In part, her short lifespan undercut any potential for long-term growth; "Before and After" (3.21) already showed viewers Kes's life as an old woman in seven short years. Her possibilities simply ran out of time.

Kes's departure reflects the last stage of her story arc. The series had flirted with Kes's potential for destruction; after all, the little girl is a rebel who had left home to see what was out there. In "The Gift" (4.2), Kes decides to embrace her mental development by pushing it to the max. The titular "gift," that of human curiosity to expand her horizons, enables her to go into the subatomic level, truly where no one has gone before (In contrast, Seven violently rejects the "gift" of human individuality Janeway imposes upon her). Kes pays the crew back by adopting their standards and beating them at their own game: she performs surgery on Seven when The Doctor cannot, she trumps Tuvok when he tries to coach her in mental wizardry, she outperforms Torres in stopping Seven when the drone sends a homing beacon to the collective, she out-argues Janeway into letting her leave, and she outpaces Paris by sending the ship closer to home. In growing up, the little girl shows she has outgrown her home; even when she leaves her corporeal form behind, she demonstrates the embodiment of Starfleet principles.

Kes's final voyage, however, isn't quite complete. After almost three years away, she comes back, fast and furious. In "Fury" (6.23), an older Kes, disheveled, aged, and bitter, intercepts the Federation starship she once called home. After ramming *Voyager*, boarding it, and leaving a trail of destruction behind her, the Ocampan intrudes into Engineering, kills Torres, and travels back to the past—specifically, 56 days into the series.

Kes's retreat into the past isn't just a trip down memory lane. The furious Ocampan wants to save her childhood and the innocence she had willfully discarded. She later explains to Janeway that, after she left the ship, her pathfinder expedition of self-discovery bogged down. Like a human teenager leaving childhood, she is unable to handle the mental, physical, and psychological changes that accompany maturity. Lacking a guardian figure to guide her and sick of exploration and discovery, she wants to revert back to the girl left behind. She blames Janeway's crew for corrupting the innocent they brought aboard with grandiose ideas about new life and new civilizations. Since Kes doesn't think the naïve, dependent Ocampan will accept her learned self, she wants to preserve her younger, purer version from the next five years that spelled the end of her childhood. By going back to Ocampa, she, like others before her, knows there's no place like home. The thought of leaving her own backyard, where the Ocampa had a friendly caretaker to provide their every whim, now fills Kes with fury.

Viewers reacted with mixed feelings. One reviewer dismissed "Fury" (6.23), calling it "one of the flattest episodes of the year" with an "incoherent story and weak acting" (Fisher 31). One fan was shocked at the Ocampan's fate, stating that the crew, if forewarned about what the future would bring, "would have made better physical and emotional preparations or her future" (Ryan 70). The same fan questioned the premise altogether, stating that the younger Ocampan was "always such a positive, gentle and loving character that it made no sense that she would behave so very hateful and vindictive" to those she once loved and which "went against her own beliefs" (Ryan 70). She found it incomprehensible that this little girl could reject the optimistic, inclusive vision that Roddenberry had established. Women like Janeway can literally do it all, from taking command of a ship to enticing the omnipotent Q to take her as his mate ("The Q and the Grey" 3.11), and later to act as godmother for his son ("Q2" 7.19). For a Starfleet vessel filled with mentors to have let down Kes prompted the fan's disbelief, if not fury. For her part, Jennifer Lien wasn't filled with anger or even deep thoughts regarding the character's future. "The episode has nothing to do with Kes' growing up," she told one interviewer, asserting that the now eight-year-old Ocampan simply comes "out of nowhere" and her portrayal of Kes remained the same, even if Kes now neared old age. "If I played Kes differently because I have changed over the years, it wasn't consciously" (Dilmore "Kes," 12). In her eyes, Kes remains the same sweet-tempered girl, even though she now seeks to undermine everything she has accomplished.

Conclusion: Boldly Going…?

The accusations of "weak acting," character inconsistencies, and violations to the established canon strike at the millennial theme of abandoned girlhood. Contrary to Lien's take, the episode acknowledges that growing up is hard to do, even in a twenty-fourth century utopia. When the bitter Ocampan barters the *Voyager*'s organs to the Vidiians for safe passage to her home world, the past Janeway kills Kes's older, future self to save the ship. To prevent young Kes from going "bad," the captain, Tuvok, and Kes create a recording where the young Ocampan reminds her older self about taking responsibility and living with the consequences. Kes re-learns that making life choices is at the heart of growing up. She wasn't up to the task; she spent her entire life dependent on Neelix, then Starfleet, to guide her, encouraging her to explore even while preserving her innocence. When she left the crew, she was confident and comfortable, but adulthood overwhelmed her, and she lashed out at her surrogate parents. An older Kes re-learns the concepts of responsibility and duty; she breaks out in a smile and the fury dissipates. In the end, however, she declines Janeway's offer to stay onboard and continue to venture forth to Earth. Instead, she voyages home, alone.

The image of girlhood in the 1990s was also fractured and directionless. The so-called end of feminism led women to accentuate various facets of femininity. From a curious little girl to a know-it-all Borg clueless about her sexual allure, to a conflicted Klingon engineer who relied on brains instead of brawn, to an overachieving career woman captain, *Voyager* meanders the murky space of gender development—truly adrift in American culture. Producer Brannon Braga insisted the diversity among the crew wasn't a nod to political correctness, a concept he "was a little sick of," even as he introduced a black Vulcan and a Mexican Indian lead (Snauffer "Star," 14). Noting that *Star Trek* historically served as "a measuring rod for a lot of people's values" and with *Voyager* as no exception, he juggled proposals for homosexual characters, neo–Nazis, and other "outsiders" struggling to express their group identity (Snauffer "Star," 14). Girlhood, in the form of Kes and other characters' reactions to the ship's little girl, signified gender norms in transition.

Kes' girl power remains unresolved after she departs for good. Perhaps she returns home and becomes a shepherd to guide the Ocampa to the next phase of the species' transfiguration. Or, perhaps they reject her and Kes' fury reignites. Maybe she spends the last of her nine years regretting a wasted life. For the Starfleet crew, however, such concepts are irrelevant. Content to letting her former daughter figure return to an isolationist world, Janeway assumes that home is where the heart is. That Kes yearns to return to traditional Ocampan life—infancy without curiosity or fury—might not have even surprised Janeway. After all, her own mission isn't to go where no man has gone before, but to go back to the Federation safe and sound, like a child returning home.

Notes

1. Viewers have a glimpse of Kes as an old woman in "Before and After" (3.21), supposedly in her last year of life. However, this Kes hailed from a parallel universe and the "real" Kes looks nothing like a senior in her final appearance in "Fury" (6.23). In this episode, Kes's inability to cope with her mental powers causes her to age, although the episode shows Kes able to revert to a younger, wrinkle-free self on a whim. In "Cold Fire" (2.10), Ocampa who have elevated their mental powers defy aging; the Ocampa live well past their life expectancy and look decades away from the human standards of seniority.

2. In "Cold Fire" (2.10), the crew encounters another Caretaker who allows her Ocampa to develop their mental abilities unencumbered. These Ocampa literally grow up—the oldest is fourteen—but they still depend on the Caretaker for sustenance. In contrast to the elderly banjo-man, this Caretaker has the humanoid form of a little girl named "Suspiria," but is immature, impatient, self-centered, and has a short-temper—the opposite of the sweet-natured Kes.

3. In an early draft of "Darkling" (3.18), The Doctor creates a holodeck family. When Kes walks in, she sees he has created a Sickbay full of Keses, including one slit open on a biobed. The Doctor supposedly remarks, "Just getting to know you better." Screenwriter Michael Piller called the scene "perverse," and screenwriter Joe Menosky concurred; viewers would think "that somewhere in The Doctor was this horrible, dirty old man who as just waiting to get his hands on Kes. There was almost no way to erase that." Menosky also notes

96 Part II. Gendering the 24th Century

actor Robert Picardo wanted to keep the scene in the script, enjoying the "S and M Doctor" scenario (Kaplan "Star Trek," 94).

   4. Seven's regeneration chamber is set-up in the same cargo bay that once housed Kes's airponics bay. The alcove has slots for more Borg, which later leads Seven to acquiring "borglet" children in the sixth season.

WORKS CITED

"Basics, Part II." *Star Trek: Voyager*, written by Michael Piller, directed by Winrich Kolbe, Season 3, episode 1, Paramount, 4 Sept. 1996.
"Before and After." *Star Trek: Voyager*, written by Kenneth Biller, directed by Allan Kroeker, Season 3, episode 21, Paramount, 9 April 1997.
"Caretaker." *Star Trek: Voyager*, written by Michael Piller and Jeri Taylor, directed by Winrich Kolbe, Season 1, episode 1, Paramount, 16 Jan. 1995.
"The Cloud." *Star Trek: Voyager*, written by Tom Szollosi and Michael Piller, directed by David Livingston, Season 1, episode 6, Paramount, 13 Feb. 1995.
"Cold Fire." *Star Trek: Voyager*, written by Brannon Braga, directed by Cliff Bole, Season 2, episode 10, Paramount, 13 Nov. 1995.
"Darkling." *Star Trek: Voyager*, written by Joe Menosky, directed by Alex Singer, Season 3, episode 18, Paramount, 19 Feb. 1997.
"Deadlock." *Star Trek: Voyager*, written by Brannon Braga, directed by David Livingston, Season 2, episode 21, Paramount, 18 Mar. 1996.
Dilmore, Ken. "Jennifer Lien: The Power Behind Kes." *Star Trek Communicator*, no. 131, 2000, p. 58.
_____."Kes Returns—in a 'Fury.'" *Star Trek Communicator*, no. 128, 2000, p. 12.
Doherty, Thomas. "30 Years in Space: Gene Roddenberry's Enduring Vision of the Future Keeps Trekkin.'" *Cinefantastique*, vol. 37, no.4-5, 1996, pp. 64-66.
"Elogium." *Star Trek: Voyager*, written by Kenneth Biller and Jeri Taylor, directed by Winrich Kolbe, Season 2, episode 4, Paramount, 18 Sept. 1995.
Fisher, Deborah. "Voyager: Going Solo," *Star Trek Communicator*, no. 130, 2000, pp. 24-33, 68-69.
"Flashback." *Star Trek: Voyager*, written by Brannon Braga, directed by David Livingston, Season 3, episode 2, Paramount, 11 Sept. 1996.
"Fury." *Star Trek: Voyager*, written by Bryan Fuller and Michael Taylor, directed by John Bruno, Season 6, episode 23, Paramount, 3 May 2000.
"Future's End." *Star Trek: Voyager*, written by Brannon Braga and Joe Menosky, directed by David Livingston, Season 3, episode 8, Paramount, 6 Nov. 1996.
"The Gift." *Star Trek: Voyager*, written by Joe Menosky, directed by Anson Williams, Season 4, episode 2, Paramount, 10 Sept. 1997.
Gregson, Joanna. *The Culture of Teenage Mothers*, The State University of New York Press, 2009.
Gross, Edward and Mark A. Altman, *The Fifty-Year Mission: The Complete, Uncensored, Unauthorized Oral History of* Star Trek—The Next 25 Years: From The Next Generation to J.J. Abrams, St. Martin's Press, 2016.
Homsher, Deborah. *Women and Guns: Politics and the Culture of Firearms in America*, M.E. Sharpe, 2001.
"Jetrel." *Star Trek: Voyager*, written by jack Klein, Karen Klein, and Kenneth Biller, directed by Kim Friedman, Season 1, episode 15, Paramount, 15 May 1995.
Kaplan, Anna L. "*Star Trek: Voyager*: Jeri Taylor at the Helm, Seeking More Energy and Excitement in Third Season." *Cinefanastique*, vol. 29, no.6/7, 1997, pp. 83-101, 107, 109, 113.
_____. "Voyager Episode Guide." *Cinefantastique*, vol. 29, no. 6/7, 1997, pp. 85-113.
Kutzera, Dale. "Voyager Episode Guide." *Cinefantastique*, vol. 28, no. 4/5, 1996, pp. 76-107.
Madrid, Mike. *The Supergirls: Fashion, Feminism, and the History of Comic Book Heroines*, Exterminating Angel Press, 2016.

Morgan, Debi. "Invisible Women: Young Women and Feminism." *Feminist Activism in the 1990s*, edited by Gabriele Griffin, Routledge, 1995, pp. 127–136.
"Mortal Coil." *Star Trek: Voyager*, written by Bryan Fuller, directed by Allan Kroeker, Season 4, episode 12, Paramount, 17 Dec. 1997.
"Non Sequitur." *Star Trek: Voyager*, written by Brannon Braga, directed by David Livingston, Season 2, episode 5, Paramount, 25 Sept. 1995.
Orenstein, Peggy. *Schoolgirls: Young Women, Self Esteem, and the Confidence Gap*, Alfred A. Knopf, 1994.
"Parallax." *Star Trek: Voyager*, written by Brannon Braga, directed by Kim Friedman, Season 1, episode 2, Paramount, 23 Jan. 1995.
"Parturition." *Star Trek: Voyager*, written by Tom Szollosi, directed by Jonathan Frakes, Season 2, episode 7, Paramount, 9 Oct. 1995.
"The Q and the Grey." *Star Trek: Voyager*, written by Kenneth Biller, directed by Cliff Bole, Season 3, episode 11, Paramount, 27 Nov. 1996.
"Q2." *Star Trek: Voyager*, written by Robert J. Doherty, directed by LeVar Burton, Season 7, episode 19, Paramount, 11 April 2001.
"Resistance." *Star Trek: Voyager*, written by Lisa Klink, directed by Winrich Kolbe, Season 2, episode 12, Paramount, 27 Nov. 1995.
Roller, Pamela. "Kate Mulgrew: This Veteran Actors Begins Her 'Voyage' of Discovery as the First Woman to Captain a *Star Trek* Series." *Star Trek Communicator*, no. 100, 1994, pp. 62–65.
Ruditis, Paul. *Star Trek: Voyager Companion*, Pocket Books, 2003.
Ryan, Marianne E. Letter. *Star Trek Communicator*, no. 130, 2000, p. 70.
"Sacred Ground." *Star Trek: Voyager*, teleplay by Lisa Klink, directed by Robert Duncan McNeill, Season 3, episode 7, Paramount, 30 Oct. 1996.
"Scorpion, Part II." *Star Trek: Voyager*, written by Brannon Braga and Joe Menosky, directed by Winrich Kolbe, Season 4, episode 1, Paramount, 3 Sept. 1997.
Snauffer, Douglas. "Space Beauty: Jennifer Lien Talks About Life on and Off the Set of Her Hit TV Series." *TV Scene*, no. 1, 1995, pp. 16–18.
_____. "*Star Trek: Voyager*—Bringing a Universe Together." *TV Scene*, no. 1, 1995, pp. 12–15.
Spelling, Ian. "Ethan Phillips: Neelix." *Star Trek: Voyager*, no. 3, 1995, pp. 17–23.
_____. "Jennifer Lien: Kes." *Star Trek: Voyager*, no. 3, 1995, pp. 33–37.
_____. "Kate Mulgrew: Captain Kathryn Janeway." *Star Trek Voyager*, no. 5, 1996, pp. 19–25.
_____. "Now, Voyager." *Starlog*, no. 211, 1995, pp. 40–45, 66.
"The Swarm." *Star Trek: Voyager*, written by Michael Sussman, directed by Alexander Singer, Season 3, episode 4, Paramount, 25 Sept. 1996.
"The 37's." *Star Trek: Voyager*, written by Jeri Taylor and Brannon Braga, directed by James L. Conway, Season 2, episode 1, Paramount, 28 Aug. 1995.
"Time and Again." *Star Trek: Voyager*, written by David Kemper and Michael Piller, directed by Les Landau, Season 1, episode 3, Paramount, 30 Jan. 1995.
"Twisted." *Star Trek: Voyager*, written by Kenneth Biller, directed by Kim Friedman, Season 2, episode 6, Paramount, 2 Oct. 1995.
"Warlord." *Star Trek: Voyager*, written by Lisa Klink, directed by David Livingston, Season 3, episode 10, Paramount, 20 Nov. 1996.

"Tuvix" and Feminist Ethics in the Delta Quadrant

Jeffrey Boruszak

Originally broadcast on May 6, 1996, the *Star Trek: Voyager* episode "Tuvix" (2.24) remains one of the most polarizing televised entries in the franchise's long history. Despite a favorable reception from producers and critics, with then-showrunner Michael Piller citing it as evidence that its writer, Ken Biller, had become "the poet laureate of *Star Trek*" (Kutzera 77), David McIntee describes "Tuvix" as "by far the most debated episode in fandom, especially on the internet" (120). The episode concerns a transporter accident that combines Lieutenant Commander Tuvok and "Chief Morale Officer" Neelix into a single merged humanoid—the eponymous Tuvix, portrayed by guest actor Tom Wright. Tuvix quickly becomes an accepted member of the ship's crew, serving aboard Voyager for two weeks before The Doctor discovers a method that will restore Tuvok and Neelix while killing Tuvix in the process. In the episode's climax, Captain Janeway chooses to restore her former crewmen, a decision that a non-consenting Tuvix calls "an execution."

Fan debate centers on Captain Janeway's dramatic decision at the episode's end. By killing Tuvix, some viewers believe that she reneges on her duties as a Starfleet Officer by exterminating what is undoubtedly a form of "new life," to adopt a phrase from the voiceover that opens the title sequence in both *The Original Series* and *The Next Generation*. But the reason for her decision—and its implications for the utopian values of the Federation and the *Star Trek* franchise more broadly—are not as cut-and-dry as they may initially appear. In this essay, I explore the unusual dramatic structure of "Tuvix" in order to describe the scope and impact of one of the most difficult choices ever faced by a *Star Trek* captain. By comparing her predicament to similar situations faced by other captains over the course of the franchise's history, I argue that Janeway faces an ethical, rather than a moral, dilemma in this episode. In shifting discussion from the rhetoric of morality and its focus on evaluating an action as objectively "right" or "wrong" to the space of ethics, where competing obligations force one to make seemingly impossible decisions between equally valid choices, I engage with the feminist dimensions of *Voyager* beyond the issues of gender representation typically associated with the first *Trek* series to seat a woman in the captain's chair. More specifically, I present Janeway's choice to restore Tuvok and Neelix as an example of what contemporary scholars refer to as an "ethics of care," a philosophical system that by emphasizing mutual recognition and compassion as guiding principles in human social lives, interrogates the function of the United Federation of Planets beyond the Vulcan commitments to logic and reasoning that usually define its values.

Symbiogenesis, Sentient Life and Dramatic Structure

Transporter accidents occur frequently in *Star Trek*, with the holodeck being perhaps the only ship system more likely to produce unintended (but dramatically compelling) results on a regular basis. Dividing and/or merging humanoids during transport is not unusual for this futuristic technology: in *The Original Series* episode "The Enemy Within" (1.04), a transporter malfunction splits Captain Kirk into "good" and "evil" versions of himself, forcing Spock to use the transporter to recombine them at the episode's end; in *The Next Generation* episode "Second Chances" (6.24), the Enterprise-D crew discovers that Commander Will Riker's double (who eventually adopts the name Thomas Riker) was inadvertently abandoned on a planet for eight years after an energy distortion duplicated his transporter signal during an evacuation. Given that the *TOS* crew restored their captain without hesitation while the *TNG* crew offered Thomas the opportunity to pursue his own life as a sovereign individual, it is worth describing the transporter accident that created Tuvix in detail in order to highlight the degree to which he constitutes a lifeform endowed with inalienable rights under Federation law.

The merging of Tuvok and Neelix results from the introduction of an unknown flora sample to the transporter, which induces a reproductive process known as *symbiogenesis*. Also referred as endosymbiosis, it is a process that occurs on Earth, albeit at a much smaller scale than its high concept sci-fi presentation would otherwise suggest. During Terran symbiogenesis, two prokaryotes, or single-celled organisms without a nucleus, merge into an individual eukaryote, a multi-celled organism containing a nucleus. As an account for the emergence of multicellular organisms, scientists theorize that symbiogenesis may have played a crucial role in the early stage of life's evolution on our planet. Onboard the USS Voyager, this process indicates that the transporter did not malfunction as the crew initially suspects. Rather, the transporter signal functions as a catalyst that ignites an orchid's underlying endosymbiotic function. The subsequent symbiogenetic reaction produces Tuvix, a lifeform where "all biological material merged at a molecular level." The practical result of this accident is that Tuvix must remain on the ship until The Doctor can find a method for isolating and extracting Tuvok's and Neelix's DNA in order to restore them.

Tuvix is an entirely new creature that, pardon the cliché, is more than the sum of his parts. His physical features include the Vulcans' trademark pointed ears and the Talaxian forehead markings. He shows remarkable memory recall, as Tuvix can remember experiences—and even conversations—from both of his forbears with intricate detail. In fact, there is no indication that any memory or knowledge failed to transfer during his creation. Most notably, Tuvix does not have split personalities like other symbiotic species, such as the Trill and the Borg.[1] Instead, he possesses a unified consciousness expressed with a single voice, which he uses to articulate unique desires that are neither reducible to nor mediated by those of Tuvok and Neelix. As The Doctor notes, "he possesses Tuvok's irritating sense of intellectual superiority *and* Neelix's annoying ebullience." As a result, Tuvix ends up being a vastly superior cook and a more effective tactical officer. He is, above all else, an autonomous lifeform who consistently presents his connection to Tuvok and Neelix through the language of sexual reproduction and familial inheritance. In other words, they are his parents.

"Tuvix" shares thematic similarities with the celebrated *TNG* episode "The Measure of a Man" (2.09), which similarly hinges on questions about the importance of sentient life and a Starfleet captain's role in defending the inherent value of that life. Yet the stark contrast in *how* these two episodes dramatically structure their central debates demonstrates the difficulty of evaluating Janeway's situation in strictly moral terms. In "The Measure of a Man," a requisition order from Starfleet Command, under which Data would be disassembled for study, with no guarantee that he could be restored, leads Captain Jean-Luc Picard to defend Data's status as a sentient lifeform in a court of law. While the viewer likely agrees with Picard's position at the outset, the story's narrative structure develops the question of Data's sentience over the course of the entire episode in order to call on the viewer as an additional judge who will listen to arguments, weigh evidence, and make a ruling. And while this synoptic overview appears to suggest that Data is the episode's central character, it is fact Picard who navigates the story's dramatic stakes.

In the episode's opening scene, Picard encounters Captain Phillipa Louvois, a friend with whom he feels lingering unease after the earnestness with which she prosecuted his court-martial at an earlier point in his career. Their reunion introduces a thematic conflict between duty to the law—a necessity for Starfleet Officers operating in a hierarchized command structure—and truth as an objective criterion for evaluating the moral value of an action. That is, even with the prohibition on intrapersonal conflict that *Star Trek* writers refer to as "The Roddenberry Rule,"[2] close friendships like that of Picard and Louvois face disruption when inviolable social duties and moral convictions come into opposition with one another. Given that Picard also attempts to persuade Data to accept the transfer as an officer, then accepts the resignation of his subordinate's commission, then actively defends his friend's inherent rights before a judge, the episode's dramatic arc clearly centers on Picard as he attempts to "engage" the personal fallout from his court-martial alongside his obligations as both a Starfleet Captain and a citizen of the United Federation of Planets.

At the episode's climax, Picard delivers his closing argument in defense of Data with astounding gusto. As he declares:

> The decision you reach here today will determine how we will regard this creation of our genius. It will reveal the kind of people we are; what he is destined to be. It will reach far beyond this courtroom and this one android. It could significantly redefine the boundaries of personal liberty and freedom: expanding them for some, savagely curtailing them for others. Are you prepared to condemn him, and all who will come after him, to servitude and slavery? Your honor, Starfleet was founded to seek out new life: well, there it sits! Waiting ["The Measure of a Man" 2.9].

According to Picard, the reasoning the court adopts in its decision will determine the outcome of similar controversies in the future. There is an objective truth, he claims, a "purer product" that unconditionally embraces life as inherently valuable at the individual scale. Starfleet (and by extension, the Federation) were founded on this principle, and if one were to imagine that all future cases would return the same verdict, then there is only one decision that could ever be true, moral, or just: preserving life.

While he does not explicitly acknowledge the influence, a well-read and classically educated Renaissance man such as Jean-Luc Picard likely intends his argument to draw force from a theoretical cornerstone in the tradition of moral philosophy: *the categorical imperative.* As its originator, Immanuel Kant, first articulated its central premise: "act only according to that maxim through which you can at the same time will that it become a universal law" (71). In other words, determining the morality of an action requires one to call upon the human capacity for reasoning in order to examine the myriad consequences of said action. Lying is an excellent example of an immoral action according to the premises of the categorical imperative; while a single lie may provide pleasure, relief, or safety for the person who tells it, if every person in the world were permitted to lie at will there would be no way to establish trust and build a functioning society. Picard presents his case in similar terms: if the Federation is to position itself to declare beings either sentient or not and afford basic rights accordingly, then there is a moral obligation to support and preserve that life regardless of mitigating circumstances.

While "The Measure of a Man" (2.9) revels in its examination of the Federation's utopian commitment to radical inclusion over the course of the episode, "Tuvix" takes a markedly different approach to questions of life and sentience, particularly in its dramatic structure. For starters, Tuvix explicitly confirms his sentience and his status as an autonomous individual when speaking to Kes during his initial medical diagnostics. But just as viewers might mistakenly place Data at the narrative center of his court case, so too might they consider Tuvix to be the focus of the episode's philosophical and emotional poignancy. In such an approach, Tuvix occupies the center of the story's action, and his fearful pleading with Voyager's crew for help before security escorts him off the bridge serves as the height of the plot's action and stakes. With an external decision imposed on him by a commanding officer, Tuvix marches to a quiet and tragic execution for which Captain Janeway is solely responsible. The audience would therefore be inclined to identify with Tuvix as the perspective through which they encounter the story's events, and the Captain's unjust decision becomes irredeemably immoral. However, Tuvix is not the focus of the episode that bears his name. Instead, the dramatic weight of this narrative falls to both Kes and Janeway, who share the spotlight due to an atypical shift in perspective between the third and fourth acts.

For readers who may not be familiar with dramatic conventions, it is helpful to rehearse some of the technical terms informing the structure of nearly every televised entry in the *Star Trek* franchise. Episodes usually begin with a *cold open* that briefly introduces the hour's plot and themes through an *inciting action*, or a problem to be faced, following which the show's title credits play. After a commercial break, five *acts* air in sequential order, with four additional commercial breaks punctuating the transitions between each act. *Act breaks*, or the final moments that conclude an act by presenting a situation of heightened conflict, usually focus on the episode's central character(s), who encounter new knowledge or obstacles that disrupt their current plans and which they must confront head-on in the subsequent act. These moments are intended to serve as miniature cliffhangers that encourage the viewer to stay tuned through the advertisements. The final act break tends to present the story's featured character with their greatest obstacle thus far, and they confront this difficult situation during the episode's *climax*, the point near the story's conclusion where protagonists encounter the issues and challenges they must finally resolve.

Tracking act breaks demonstrates the important ways in which this story's conflicts and character drama fall to Tuvix's interlocutors, rather than Tuvix himself. After Tuvix initially appears in the cold open (the episode's inciting action), the first act is mainly expository. Characters explain the circumstances to the viewer, including Tuvix's status as a merged but autonomous being. This exposition concludes when Tuvix gives himself his new name. But this brief moment of resolution falters after Tuvix then instinctively refers to Kes as "sweeting," the pet name Neelix used when speaking to her. This linguistic slip of the tongue establishes conflict between the two characters, with Kes subjected to feelings of confusion and loss.

In the second act, Tuvix theorizes that symbiogenesis was the process that led to his creation. As the crew begins to search for a "cure," Tuvix and Kes head to the mess hall and the former reclaims his galley. Tuvix proves himself to be a talented and organized chef, and he shares an emotionally intimate exchange with Kes. But in the act's final moments, Tuvix tells her: "if the situation were reversed, if he [Neelix] found himself without you in his life, he'd be absolutely lost." A distraught Kes responds by announcing her departure. Note the asymmetry of their relationship, which informs the scene's emotional complexities. Tuvix may be new to the ship, but with the memories of both Tuvok and Neelix at his disposal, he knows Kes with the intimacy of both a lover and a mentor. While he may struggle with the strange situation, he finds himself in, those around him are not complete aliens (pun intended). He knows whom to trust, as well as where and how to find support. Kes, on the hand, must interact with someone who is effectively a stranger, but who also knows her to arguably the fullest extent possible (given that Tuvok trains Kes in developing her psychic abilities, this familiarity likely includes a mental connection extending far beyond what we can even imagine as humans).

Kes grows increasingly isolated and disturbed during the third act, which sees The Doctor explain that his initial experiments in reversing symbiogenesis failed. While The Doctor says he will continue his research, he also explains that the crew must accept the possibility that Tuvok and Neelix will be lost forever. In responding to this new status quo, Kes grieves alone in her quarters until Tuvix interrupts her with a declaration of his love. A shocked Kes requests an explanation and time to think about her decision. Tuvix acquiesces, leaving her with a kiss on the cheek and the weight of a life-changing proposition.

The fourth act includes a major dramatic shift of massive import to the episode's resolution. Viewers will likely notice this uncanny disruption in storytelling, even if they cannot identify why it seems so strange. The act opens with Kes standing at the door to the Captain's Quarters immediately following her conversation with Tuvix. She seeks advice, and Janeway comforts her by telling her she is not alone, as the rest of the ship's crew faces similar feelings of despondent uncertainty about their loved ones back home. Janeway encourages her to take her time developing a relationship with Tuvix, and Kes agrees with this suggestion. Suddenly, a voiceover culled from the Captain's Log informs the audience that two weeks have passed, with Tuvix having ably served as both tactical officer and chef during this time and formed friendships amongst the ship's crew as a result. Time jumps of such magnitude typically do not occur *within* an act; because they rupture an act's internal unity, such leaps forward in time tend to happen off-screen during commercial breaks. After this jump in time, Kes tells Tuvix over a candlelit conversation in Chez Sandríne that she would like to begin their relationship as friends, but she remains open to developing it further. Just then, The Doctor convenes a meeting in Sick Bay to announce he has discovered a medical procedure that will restore Tuvok and Neelix. The crew grows excited—Kes especially—until Tuvix quashes the celebration by telling them: "I don't want to die." Given the story's prior focus on Kes, we might reasonably expect her reaction to this statement to set the tone for the final act. But instead we are treated to a close-up shot of Captain Janeway as the camera zooms in on her worried expression.

Up until this moment, Janeway is surprisingly tangential to the episode's story. She is present for narrative exposition and directs the crew with her orders, but even in her late-night conversation with Kes, the plot largely mutes her ability to influence the situation's outcome. But the fifth act turns to her character with alacrity by bringing her role as Voyager's captain to the forefront of the action. The episode is no longer simply a story about Kes's grief. Instead the importance of a Starfleet captain's responsibility to—and for—their crew becomes central.

Morality and Ethics in Star Trek

There is a fine line dividing the fields of morality and ethics in the Western philosophical tradition, even though we use the two as largely interchangeable terms in everyday conversations. People tend to agree that ethical behavior (like returning a lost wallet to its owner without removing the cash inside) is undeniably moral, and unethical behavior (like an elected official who accepts bribes in exchange for favorable treatment) is clearly immoral. Despite this overlap, there are important distinctions between morality and ethics that become important when examining how *Star Trek* reflects utopian values during situations when democratic institutions, such as the United

Federation of Planets, come into conflict with the strict adherence to duty demanded by Starfleet's military hierarchy.

In broad and largely non-technical terms, *morality* concerns proper behavior that conforms to socially prescribed expectations. For example, we tend to consider killing another human being to be an immoral act in the United States because of its clear prohibition in our government's laws and influential Judeo-Christian texts. Killing enemy soldiers during military service, however, can be considered a morally permissible act that we describe with patriotic (and Klingon) language such as "honorable" and "noble." The difference between how the public perceives these two similar acts demonstrates the confusion that can attend the declaration of moral ideals as incontrovertible truths. What exactly makes an act moral or immoral—one's intent or the eventual outcome?

The short answer is that it is both and neither. Immanuel Kant's categorical imperative is an example of what is called a *deontological* approach to morals, which emphasizes the morality of the process instead of the results; one could lie to save a person's life, but the act is still immoral because one lied to achieve that outcome. *Teleological* or ends-based approaches to morality, on the other hand, consider the destination more important than the journey. *Star Trek* usually favors teleological approaches, particularly through its embrace of *utilitarianism*, a philosophical position aimed at maximizing the greatest amount happiness for the greatest number of people. As Spock famously presents this argument in *Star Trek II: The Wrath of Kahn*: "The needs of the many outweigh the needs of the few." In the logical culture of the Vulcans, morality is part of a mathematic calculus that gives particular weight to self-sacrifice in service of quantifiable results. If these positions seem complicated or contradictory, then rest assured that you are not alone in this feeling. Philosophers have been debating the merits and dangers of these positions for centuries without coming to clear conclusions about what constitutes objectively moral behavior.

The Prime Directive, Starfleet's paramount order that prohibits its members from making contact with pre-warp civilizations, highlights the difficulty that attends the assignation of clear-cut moral judgments to individual actions. Because it is a clearly articulated position that all officers swear an oath to uphold, violating the Prime Directive is considered categorically immoral within the confines of Starfleet. Yet crews repeatedly violate this order across the franchise's series and films, often to the audience's delight and adamant support. Typically, these violations invoke the Federation's commitment to the preservation of life—that is, a character defies their orders because they believe that allowing a death or multiple deaths to occur would be such a fragrantly immoral act that they eschew their obligations to Starfleet Command. While many fans (myself included) joke about the frequency with which characters invoke the Prime Directive only to subsequently disregard its proscriptions, stories that violate these orders often produce thought-provoking reflections on moral complexities and resonate with viewers.

Unlike morality, which attempts to determine whether an action should be considered right or wrong, *ethics* is the space where we confront moral duties and obligations when they come into conflict with one another. To phrase it another way: if morality determines the degree to which behavior conforms with a set standard, ethics examines the ways in which people weigh competing standards and subsequently choose one over the other. While my examples of the categorical imperative and utilitarianism present these concepts in moral terms, we could also describe each as an ethical position that argues *how* one ought to choose between options if they wish to behave morally. When a person "acts ethically," then, they are not adhering to a socially prescribed standard of right and wrong. Instead, they are paying close and careful attention to the conflicts between their competing obligations as they choose one over the other.

In a series of lectures given just months before "Tuvix" originally aired, French philosopher Jacques Derrida uses "hospitality" as an analogy for the field of ethics and the issues that arise when one desires to act ethically. Derrida states:

> absolute hospitality requires that I open up my home and that I give not only to the foreigner (provided with a family name, with the social status of being a foreigner, etc.), but to the absolute unknown and anonymous other, and that I *give place* to them, that I let them come, that I let them arrive, and take place in the place I offer them, without asking of them either reciprocity ... or even their names [25].

Derrida is a notoriously difficult writer, particularly because he intentionally uses words that in their original French either sound similar or share etymological roots that make them closer in meaning than one would otherwise think. For example, contemporary English speakers tend to use the word "foreigner" to describe a person who is not a legal citizen of a nation; Derrida, on the other hand, calls on the word's Latin root—*fores*, meaning "doors"—to describe any person who walks through the doors of your home as a kind of "foreigner." In this passage, Derrida describes "absolute hospitality," a theoretical extreme of hospitality in which every person is always obligated to invite any and all strangers inside their home without knowing their guests' names or origins, and without expecting to receive anything in return. While this description certainly varies with our real-life experiences of providing hospitality to guests, Derrida calls it "absolute" because it is the purer form after which we model our hospitable acts. The reason we do not practice "absolute hospitality" at all times, and instead ask names of our guests and exclude some who may want to enter is because how else, as Derrida asks, "can we distinguish between a guest and a parasite?" (59). That is, as much as we have an idealist obligation to offer our homes without condition, we also have other obligations to ourselves, to our families, to the upkeeping of our living conditions that require us to give careful consideration to who we ought to let in and keep out of our homes. Ethics resembles hospitality, then, because ethics is the place where our absolute duties and practical obligations come into direct conflict with one another, forcing us to make impossible choices between what otherwise appear to be equally valid options.

I describe these decisions as "impossible" and "equally valid" because if there were a case where a choice was easy, fast, or simple, then it would be more akin to an automatic or reflexive response instead of an ethical dilemma. Rather, the weight and importance of our competing duties forces us to prioritize one obligation over another as we come to a decision. What we are meant to contemplate, either within the scholarly tradition of ethical philosophy or in our daily lives as we attempt to act ethically, is not whether our actions are "right" or "wrong" in an objective sense. Instead, we are to pay close attention to *how* and *why* we prioritize some obligations over others before we act.

In "Tuvix," Captain Janeway's climactic decision is a clear example of an ethical dilemma. On the one hand, she is a citizen of the United Federation of Planets who, having sworn herself and her crew to uphold Federation ideals while stranded in the Delta Quadrant ("The Caretaker," 1.1), has an unyielding duty to seek out and uphold life at all cost. But on the other hand, she is a Starfleet captain who, travelling in dangerous and unknown circumstances, also has an infinite duty to her crew to keep them alive and bring them back home. When Voyager comes under attack by the Kazon, or the Borg, or the Hirogen, or Species 8472, Captain Janeway orders her crew to return fire because, except for cases involving genocide, her duty to those under her command becomes paramount to her general obligation to preserve alien life. Janeway's decision to "execute" Tuvix, however, breaks with this more common conflict because he is not a foe that poses an existential threat to the ship. There are no urgent circumstances that make one duty more important than the other, and Janeway is forced to choose between equally compelling options: should Tuvix live, or should Tuvok and Neelix live?

The Doctor's refusal to perform the separation procedure highlights the variety of available options for assessing conflicting obligations when engaged in ethical quagmires. Despite receiving an order from his Captain, The Doctor abstains on the grounds that he swore an oath to "do no harm." He draws this phrase from the original Hippocratic Oath, which includes the statement: "I will do no harm or injustice to them [my patients]" (qtd. in North). While contemporary medical practitioners do not swear an oath upon the Hippocratic

Oath as it was articulated in Ancient Greece, its principles continue to inform the central tenets of medical bioethics. As such, The Doctor's "ethical subroutines," as they are later called in the *Voyager* episode "Equinox, Part II" (6.01), determined that his duties as the ship's Chief Medical Officer outweigh his obligation to follow a command issued by his superior officer. As The Doctor's decision demonstrates, there are no standard criteria for navigating an ethical minefield. Ethical determinations are highly individual and contextual, and we could therefore describe both Janeway's and The Doctor's choices as ethical, even though they take opposite actions.

If we return to the categorical imperative and utilitarianism as representative (but by no means comprehensive) examples of mechanisms for deciding between competing options, we can begin to understand Janeway's difficulties in addressing her situation. According to the categorical imperative, she *must* choose to allow Tuvix to live because if we imagine that her action would become a "universal law," then every conflict between the lives of new beings and Starfleet officers would side with the latter. Such a hypocritical rule would be so inconsistent with the Federation's stated ideals that the integrity of its entire value system would be put at risk. Yet the categorical imperative has clear limitations in its inflexibility—Derrida notes that Kant was once asked if one could lie to assassins looking for a friend who is staying with you in your home, to which Kant immediately responded, "Yes, one should never lie, even to assassins" (Derrida 67). A utilitarian framework, meanwhile, initially suggests the mathematical importance of saving the lives of two crewmen over one. But if Tuvix is superior as a chef and a tactical officer, and one being would consume significantly fewer resources over the course of what was at that point still a seventy-year journey, then perhaps Tuvix's life would promote the greatest amount of "happiness" for the ship's crew. I present these arguments not as a series of rhetorical straw men, but as an attempt to highlight the sheer difficulty posed by ethical dilemmas and the complex decisions they demand. There are so many different methods for weighing competing duties that what becomes most important in ethical questions is not the choice itself but *why* one makes that choice. So, then, why does Captain Janeway ultimately decide to execute Tuvix in order to save the lives of Tuvok and Neelix, and what does her reasoning indicate about her position as Voyager's Captain?

Feminism and Star Trek

Given the episode's acrobatic narrative transition from Kes to Janeway as its featured dramatic subject, it may not be surprising that Kes provides us with an answer to this question. During their late-night meeting, Captain

Janeway begins the scene in a state of nostalgic reflection over Tuvok's "efficient" writing style before sitting adjacent to Kes. They hold their torsos facing each other, largely maintaining eye contact as Kes implores her captain for advice. While Janeway's initial responses seem confident and supportive, her vocal tone and body language change when Kes asks how *she* deals with her feelings of separation. "I struggle with it every day. Sometimes I'm full of hope and optimism," Janeway begins. But as she considers her own situation, Janeway slumps down her head and avoids direct eye contact. She clears her throat, presumably to keep her voice from cracking before continuing: "I dream about being with Mark. And it's so real. Then, when I wake up and realize it's just a dream, I'm terribly discouraged. In those moments it's impossible to deny just how far away he really is." Janeway then pauses, turning her head away from Kes. She begins rubbing her throat. Janeway refuses to tell Kes that she should give up hope, and at the scene's end Kes smiles at Janeway from the doorway before departing. Janeway's subtle body language in this scene is anything but tertiary to the story's trajectory. Even though Janeway refuses to tell Kes what to do about her despondency over losing Neelix, the two exit the scene in emotional and physical positions that are the exact opposite of the states in which they entered. While Kes finds counsel and practical advice, Janeway empathizes with Kes and their similar predicaments. In considering the depth of her own feelings of loss and separation, Janeway realizes what Kes feels because that is also how she herself feels.

As Janeway ponders whether to force Tuvix to submit to separation, Tuvix speaks to Kes in the Mess Hall. He implores her to intercede with the Captain on his behalf, reasoning that she could possibly sway Janeway and save his life. When Kes enters the Ready Room, however, she quickly begins sobbing as she tells the Captain: "I don't know how to say goodbye to Neelix and Tuvok. I know this sounds horrible, and I feel so guilty for saying it, and Tuvix doesn't deserve to die, but I want Neelix back." Janeway comforts Kes with a hug, and the camera lingers on Janeway, who makes an expression that Kes cannot see. The Captain found a resolution to her dilemma; in the next scene, Janeway orders Tuvix to Sick Bay for separation.

Captain Janeway's decision is an example of a feminist ethics founded in recognition, identification, empathy, and compassion between two women. That is, she recognizes the similar situations in which both she and Kes find themselves; she identifies and empathizes with Kes's feelings of pain, loss, and guilt; and she acts to remedy the situation by compassionately accepting total responsibility for the decision to subject Tuvix to what effectively is an execution. In the episode's final shot, Janeway exits Sick Bay alone after restoring Tuvok and Neelix. As she walks away from the celebratory atmosphere, she lowers her head and furrows her brow. Janeway feels the weight of her actions, having taken an innocent life so that Kes does not have to feel pain or guilt. With a look of resolve, she regains her composure and resumes her stride—as Captain, she will suffer for her crew without letting them know the depth of her sorrow.

The feminist ethics Janeway displays through her decisions in "Tuvix" reflect a field of study that contemporary thinkers refer to as an *ethics of care*. As articulated by writers such as Carol Gilligan and Nel Noddings, who approach the topic from diverse perspectives including psychology, philosophy, and social policy, an ethics of care proceeds from two observations. First, care is a fundamental component of human life. We usually recognize care most readily when it occurs in the family—caring for children, the elderly, and the disabled. But care informs larger group formations as well. "In most nation-states, some form of primary healthcare is available" (Robinson 1), and myriad social services, from income and nutrition assistance, to public education, to emergency police and fire services, can be described through the state's role in providing, organizing, and disseminating care on behalf of its citizens. Second, the importance of care outside of the family unit is rarely recognized because historically it was devalued as a field of feminine labor and therefore the exclusive concern of women. To elaborate on this statement, which may be prone to misinterpretation: neither care itself nor an ethics of care excludes the participation of men. On the contrary, writers who advocate an ethics of care frequently argue that the feminization of care negatively impacts both men and women. Rather, care was widely accepted as women's private domain during the same period of time that male Enlightenment figures revolutionized thinking across a number of fields (and moral philosophies such as the categorical imperative and utilitarianism were first articulated), meaning that the role of care in philosophy, science, law, and politics remains underdeveloped and awaits further investigation.

It is for this reason that Captain Janeway's decision to save Kes by restoring Tuvok and Neelix stands out as one of *Star Trek*'s mostly overtly feminist moments. There is no objectification of the female body in this episode, nor are there discussions grounded in heteronormative sexual desire. The narrative and emotional poignancy of the episode relies upon the interactions between women who recognize each other as autonomous and capable individuals engaged in mutual support and care. To reject Captain Janeway's decision outright as an immoral perversion of *Star Trek*'s values is to repudiate the diverse and complex philosophical questions about how we ought to act as humans that make the franchise a science fiction titan. Captains may make different choices than one another by emphasizing specific values and duties to varying degrees—but it is in the multitude of efforts they undertake in upholding the values of life, knowledge, equality, and a better future that Star Trek can be said to boldly go where no one has gone before.

Notes

1. The Trill were first introduced in "The Host" (*TNG* 4.23) as a larval-like species who symbiotically join with a humanoid host. A Trill takes on the personality of their host until their host body dies, following which they are transplanted into a new host body. This new Trill will have all of their previous memories, as well as a personality reflecting that of their new host. *Deep Space Nine* explores the specifics of Trill biology in more detail through the characters of Lt. Commander Jadzia Dax and Lt. Ezri Dax—including the fact that Trill have two brain wave patterns, and therefore two consciousnesses, functioning simultaneously (*DS9* 1.8). The infamous Borg, meanwhile, fuse humanoid species with cybernetic implants that turn them into hosts for a hive-mind consciousness. When individual drones are disconnected from the rest of the Borg, their previous personalities re-emerge and retain horrific memories of their actions as drones. See "Survival Instinct" (6.2) for more information on drone personalities during and after their connection to the Borg.

2. *Star Trek* creator Gene Roddenberry famously prohibited writers from including petty squabbles and personal conflicts between Starfleet officers in their scripts, reasoning that humanity would evolve beyond such needless dramatic behavior. This so-called "Roddenberry Rule" was not popular among writers, who nonetheless adhered to its demands until it was intentionally abandoned during the production of *Star Trek: Discovery*. For more on the Roddenberry Rule and its impact on the writing of *The Next Generation*, see the 2014 documentary film *Chaos on the Bridge*, directed by William Shatner.

Works Cited

"The Caretaker." *Star Trek: Voyager*, teleplay by Michael Piller and Jeri Taylor, directed by Winrich Kolbe, Season 1, episode 1, Paramount, 16 Jan. 1995.
Chaos on the Bridge. Directed by William Shatner, Ballinran Entertainment, 2014.
"Dax." *Star Trek: Deep Space Nine*, story by Peter Allan Fields, directed by David Carson, Season 1, episode 8, CBS, 14 February 1993.
Derrida, Jacques. *Of Hospitality*. Translated by Rachel Bowlby, Stanford UP, 2000.
"The Enemy Within." *Star Trek: The Original Series*, written by Richard Matheson, Season 1, episode 4, NBC, 6 October 1966.
"Equinox, Part II." *Star Trek: Voyager*, teleplay by Brannon Braga and Joe Menosky, Season 6, episode 1, Paramount, 22 September 1999.
"The Host." *Star Trek: The Next Generation*, written by Michel Horvat, Season 4, episode 23, Paramount, 13 May 1991.
Kant, Immanuel. *Groundwork of the Metaphysics of Morals: A German-English Edition*. Edited and Translated by Mary Gregor and Jens Timmermann, Cambridge UP, 2011.
Kutzera, Dale. "*Star Trek: Voyager*." *Cinefantastique*, November 1996, pp. 75–105.
McIntee, David. *Delta Quadrant: The Unofficial Guide to Voyager*. Virgin Publishing, 2000.
"The Measure of a Man." *Star Trek: The Next Generation*, written by Melinda M. Snodgrass, Season 2, episode 9, Paramount, 13 February 1989.
North, Michael, translator. "The Hippocratic Oath." *National Library of Medicine*, 2002. www.nlm.nih.gov/hmd/greek/greek_oath.html. 24 May 2018.
Robinson, Fiona. *The Ethics of Care: A Feminist Approach to Human Security*, Temple UP, 2011.
"Second Chances." *Star Trek: The Next Generation*, story by Michael Medlock, teleplay by René Echevarria, Season 6, episode 24, Paramount, 24 May 1993.
Star Trek II: The Wrath of Khan. Directed by Nicholas Meyer, Paramount Pictures, 1982.
"Survival Instinct." *Star Trek: Voyager*, written by Ronald D. Moore, Season 6, episode 2, Paramount, 29 September 1999.
"Tuvix." *Star Trek: Voyager*, teleplay by Ken Biller, directed by Cliff Bole, Season 2, episode 24, Paramount, 6 May 1996.

"There's a woman in there if you'd take the time to look!"
Seven of Nine's Problematic Feminism

SARAH CANFIELD

On paper, *Star Trek: Voyager* comes closest to gender equality of all the franchise's numerous incarnations. The show features *Trek*'s first female captain in a leading role, Kathryn Janeway, as well as a female chief engineer, B'Elanna Torres. With the inclusion of Kes (Seasons 1–3) and Seven of Nine (Seasons 4–7), women make up three of the series' nine main cast members. Twenty years later, the Center for the Study of Women in Television and Film finds only 11 percent of ensemble television shows have gender parity and two-thirds still feature majority male casts, with approximately 40 percent of major characters—including single-episode roles—being female (Lauzen 2). *Voyager* may be a show "inundated by femininity" (Casavant 153) in comparison to other *Trek* franchises, but it remains fairly typical of broadcast network television of its time. Where the show stands out is its direct confrontation of gender issues within the context of *Trek*'s utopian humanism. While conflict among the stranded crew drives some plot lines, gender rarely plays an explicit role in those struggles. Indeed, the aliens of the Delta Quadrant are far more likely to exhibit misogyny—explicit or implicit—than are members of Voyager's crew. In the series premiere, Janeway establishes the show's sensitivity to gender issues when she informs Ensign Kim that she prefers "Captain" as a form of address over either the Starfleet protocol "sir" or the gender-specific "ma'am" ("Caretaker" 1.1). Despite these apparent attempts to address the lingering gap between *Star Trek*'s egalitarianism and its portrayals of female characters, however, the show continues to struggle with gender bias in its portrayals of women.

Nowhere is this more evident than in the character Seven of Nine, the rescued Borg drone. As many critics note, Seven is a complex character with diverse motivations who "has never been easy to 'pin down' with a simple reading" (Consalvo 177). Seven stands up for herself and her Borg-derived subjectivity; her relationship with Janeway demonstrates the crucial significance of female mentorship; and her willingness to challenge the Voyager crew forces them to question as well as reassert the fundamental humanistic values of the Federation and, by extension, *Star Trek* as a whole. She exerts her authority as "the pre-eminent scientist aboard" (Roberts 216) with the greatest knowledge of the Delta Quadrant without hesitation, often bucking traditional chains of command to do so. She is the female Other who stands outside the system and through her difference demands we construct, and reconstruct, ourselves. As with the other female characters, Seven "exposes bias and proposes a feminist alternative" (Roberts 204) within patriarchal humanism. Nevertheless, Seven of Nine's character arc suggests that the surface feminism of her character is less than skin deep, no more significant than the token cybernetic implant on her face.

Donna Haraway, a postmodern feminist critic of science and culture, takes up the well-established science fiction trope of the cyborg (the term derives from "cybernetic organism") to critique the persistent patriarchal biases of traditional humanism. In this context, humanism has been a predominant philosophical view of Western European cultures since the Renaissance; it centers value in human experience and emphasizes the individual's capacity for free thought and moral judgment, as when the seventeenth-century French philosopher Descartes declared, "I think, therefore I am" (*Cogito, ergo sum*). As Haraway and other critics note, however, the particular experiences most often centralized, and assumed to be universal, by traditional humanism belong to European men, like Descartes himself. Straddling the border between human and machine, Haraway's "cyborg myth is about transgressed boundaries, potent fusions, and dangerous possibilities" (154) which question the coherence and rationality of the humanist subject, especially when the experience of that subject is gendered, and prioritize a posthuman subject that welcomes uncertainty as a source for transformation and liberation. Since its inception with The Original Series in 1966, *Star Trek* has advocated a progressive political agenda built on a humanist foundation as the pathway to achieve the Federation's technological utopia. That progressive politics has included a growing commitment to gender equality, but while female characters have "progressed ... they must still adhere to traditionally feminine ideals of beauty and ... subordinate status" (Consalvo 180). Tudor and Meehan ascribe this to neoliberal "negotiations between masculinized power centers and progressive feminist ideas" (131) where "the presence of female characters on the ship's bridge in *Star Trek* signals an egalitarian workplace, which the narrative contradicts by consigning these characters primarily to traditional female roles centered on family or romance" (132). *Voyager*'s use of Seven of Nine demonstrates the fundamental conflict between feminist politics and the franchise's optimistic humanism, especially in the context of mass-produced cultural entertainment. While *Trek*'s humanism is reaffirmed consistently when Janeway and the Voyager crew extol human virtues to Seven, the series' portrayal of Seven of Nine just as consistently reverts to essentialist and patriarchal gender politics, where Seven's female biology corresponds to a necessarily self-sacrificing, nurturing, and romantic femininity as the essential core of her identity.

While the Harawayan cyborg can advance a progressive utopian agenda, it exists specifically to contest the humanistic values that form the core of *Star Trek*. At her introduction in "Scorpion, Part II" (4.1), Seven of Nine embodies the Harawayan cyborg's destabilizing posthumanism that constantly questions the core assumptions of humanist identity. For humanism, the self exists as an individual, whole and complete, who interacts with the world around him and the other individual selves, likewise whole and complete, who populate that world. As the Borg liaison, Seven is skeptical of Voyager's ability to maintain its agreements specifically because she doubts that any singular individual, or a collection of such individuals, can achieve such wholeness and completion: "You lack harmony, cohesion, greatness," the very qualities that might normally sum up the Federation's idealized, humanist view of itself. In "The Gift" (4.2), she calls out Janeway for trampling her autonomy: "You are hypocritical, manipulative ... no different" than the Borg. Seven "expos[es] the limits of liberal individualism" (Consalvo 197) through equating the morals of the Borg and the Federation. She is both the asexual logician in the tradition of Spock and Data and the ultrasexual "babe in a bodysuit" in the tradition of green-skinned Orion slave girls and Deanna Troi. As the series pursues its oft-stated goal to reclaim Seven's humanity, the character's cyborg characteristics must be stripped away and replaced by human elements—and this "struggle ... between 'the human' and the 'posthuman' and how that struggle is configured, is always gendered" (Consalvo 178). Seven's humanity cannot be conceived without also re-asserting patriarchal gender stereotypes. Haraway's manifesto claimed that for feminists to escape Western humanism's deeply embedded and oppressive discourses of gender, they must leave humanism behind for the posthuman. The "white male body of liberal humanism" is "the site of ultimate authority" within *Trek* (Cranny-Francis 149). Seven of Nine's journey, from feminist challenger of humanist ideology to feminine supporter of humanity, suggests that *Star Trek*'s humanism may always undermine its ability to realize feminist ideals.

The cyborg "is resolutely committed to partiality, irony, intimacy, and perversity. It is oppositional, utopian, and completely without innocence" (Haraway 151). Seven demonstrates her own partiality by repeatedly arguing not only for the technological superiority of the Borg over the human, but also of the Borg's greater intimacy. Each member of the collective exists in constant communication with all the others, not so much a singular hive mind as a sustained mental intimacy in which the barriers between public and private, self and other, cease to matter. When first severed from the collective, she reacts to the absence of "the voices" of her fellow Borg ("The Gift" 4.2), and her greatest and most persistent fear throughout the series is being alone. Even as she transfers her loyalty from the Borg to her new "collective" ("Drone" 5.2), Seven maintains her sense of irony that she, a rehabilitated drone, should now devote her Borg skills to sustaining and protecting the human crew—to the point of cracking jokes about assimilation. Indeed, her failure to pursue normal social interactions prompts The Doctor to label her "intentionally perverse" ("One" 4.25). Her first encounters with Voyager's crew are defined by her opposition to everything they, and humanity, represent. Tuvok calls her "argumentative" and Janeway "headstrong" ("The Killing Game, Part I" 4.18).

Most importantly, Seven clings to her Borg identity even in the face of the Federation crew's active hostility. "We are Borg" is her mantra. She fully understands the crimes the Borg have committed—as a Borg drone, she participated in the assimilation of millions. While Janeway and The Doctor repeatedly assert Seven's essential human identity, Seven herself accuses them of "forcing" that identity on her ("The Gift"). She denies any childish innocence, wronged by the Borg. When Torres confronts her with her guilt, she expresses neither remorse for her actions nor blame for the treatment she receives. "Guilt is irrelevant" not only because she is indeed guilty, but also because her feelings will make no difference to herself or others ("Day of Honor" 4.3). Her dual refusals of human identity and Borg guilt combine with the explicit project to instruct Seven in human behavior to highlight the disconnect between Janeway's humanist idealization of an essential subjectivity (Descartes' *cogito*, the thinking self, whole and complete) that can be restored and the postmodern, posthuman condition of the cyborg that acknowledges identity as always already "contradictory, partial, and strategic" (Haraway 155). Where Janeway and the Voyager crew try to construct a narrative for Seven in which her girlish innocence must be redeemed through the restoration of human wholeness, Seven herself recognizes that any human identity she achieves will be as much a social and historical construct as the Borg, compiled from the "biological and technological distinctiveness" of every assimilated species. Her self-reconstruction "denaturalizes liberal humanism and reveals it to be a specific set of beliefs, attitudes, and values with its own demands" (Cranny-Francis 159). Where humanism tends to universalize experience in its construction of individual identity, Seven's posthuman position highlights the contingency of identity, where class, gender, race, sexual orientation and other distinctions within experience overlap and interact in complex ways. This intersectionality of multiple identities within any particular subject undercuts humanist assumptions that the self can be whole and complete, because all experience is multiple and contingent.

That the construction of Seven's humanity will also require construction of her gender identity becomes evident immediately. Physically, her transformation from cybernetic drone to silver-clad siren takes only a single episode, and soon enough male crew members respond. Harry Kim, whose character has been firmly established as hopelessly attracted to all the wrong women, is the first to identify Seven as more than a child in need of rescue: "There's a woman in there—if you'd take the time to look!" ("Revulsion" 4.5) Where Tom Paris sees a robotic Borg killing machine, Kim sees Seven as "vulnerable" ("Revulsion" 4.5). Correctly deducing Kim's romantic projections, Seven's response is quintessential cyborg, equally willing to "copulate" or resume work. The exchange leads quickly to a campaign to teach Seven how to correctly perform her gender. Kim urges her to cultivate her ability to make small talk ("Concerning Flight" 4.11); The Doctor develops a series of lessons to address Seven's complete lack of "social graces"; Janeway mandates she learn "compassion" ("Prey" 4.16). Despite her "claims to an ungendered existence" (Consalvo 186), Seven's sultry appearance and the demands of her human compatriots require that she do the work of her gender as part of establishing her humanity.

Seven's humanization falls into three categories, each linked to particularly feminine constructions of identity. In the first category, she must repudiate her collective, consensus-based Borg subjectivity and recast herself as a desiring subject within the acceptable hierarchies of authority and sociality on Voyager. This process corresponds to Seven's lost girlhood, where she should have learned proper social behaviors and control of her emotions under the tutelage of her parents. In the second category, Seven's reincorporation into humanity hinges on her ability to nurture and protect, rather than assimilate, vulnerable individuals. Specifically, she must learn to be a good mother, as in the episodes with the Borg children—whether she wishes to be or not. In the third category, which frames the first two and thereby dominates Seven's character development over the course of the show, Seven's subjectivity and desires must be appropriately channeled into heteronormative relationships. This set of lessons focuses on Seven's ability to flirt, date, and present herself as the object of romantic interest, beginning with her awkward encounters with Harry Kim ("Revulsion" 4.5) and concluding with her marriage to Chakotay ("Endgame" 7.25–7.26). These categories are not distinct and separate phases of development, but overlapping and reinforcing constructions. Where Seven begins as an ultimate case of intersectional identity—the cyborg crossing and blurring the boundaries of organism/machine, alien/human, sexual/asexual, self/other—she ends securely categorized and defined as a woman whose purpose derives, not from her own radically liberating position at the borders of all categories, but from the subordination of her desires to those of others and control of her behavior by the expectations of her gender. Where Haraway calls for cyborg writing to "reverse and displace the hierarchical dualisms of naturalized identities" (175), the writing on *Voyager* reasserts those dualistic hierarchies by fully naturalizing Seven's femininity.

Creating Subjectivity

Seven's first reconfigurations of herself and her relationships on Voyager center around her relationship as an individual to her community. Once a small piece of the vast Borg entity, Seven must now "find [her] place within liberal humanism and claim her role as subject" (Casavant 159). While first presented in *Star Trek: The Next Generation* as a faceless threat to the humanistic individual whose horror stemmed from the complete erasure of identity in the collective, the Borg quickly underwent a process of individuation through figures such as Locutus, Hugh, and the Borg Queen (Consalvo 183; Cranny-Francis 147; Joyrich 66). By the time Seven reaches Voyager, the Borg are no longer a simplistic black hole devouring individuals and assimilating their knowledge into a vast incomprehensible Other. Rather, they are a complex symbiotic subjectivity that contains multitudes. Seven repeatedly emphasizes that when Voyager severed her link to the collective, they did not free her original human self from enslavement, nor did they retrieve Annika Hansen from the hive mind as though they had separated her unique mental droplets from the ocean of the collective. Rather, they violently ripped her from the comfort of a constant, infinitely complex and sympathetic communion that is unavailable to the isolated individuals of humanity.

In contrast to Seven's explanation of her story, Janeway asserts a version of events that corresponds to Haraway's description of the masculinist narrative of Western humanist individuation, which "begins with original innocence and privileges the return to wholeness [and] imagines the drama of life to be individuation, separation, the birth of the self, the tragedy of autonomy" (177). To construct her identity, the crew encourages Seven to reconnect to her human childhood as Annika—an "infantilization" (Cranny-Francis 158) to which she strenuously objects. In "The Raven" (4.6), for instance, she experiences partial memories of the Borg in the form of nightmares. Although her behavior appears to be a reversion to Borg type (she attacks Harry Kim and steals a shuttle), Janeway recognizes that she is actually drawn to the wreckage of her parents' ship as the site of her childhood trauma. Nevertheless,

Seven refuses Janeway's offer to investigate the available records on her parents and background, accepting only the suggestion that she explore her ability to imagine outside the collective. When Janeway orders Seven to assist Species 8472 as a lesson in "compassion," Seven defies the Captain's orders and acts on her own assessment of the situation. The subsequent discipline provokes Seven's painful assessment of her attempt to assert her new self: "You claim to respect my individuality, but in fact you are frightened by it" ("Prey" 4.16). This articulates the fundamental conflict between humanism's validation of the individual and the limitations it places on gendered, female subjects.

Seven's volatile emotions and vulnerability to her recovered memories feature in "Retrospect" (4.17), where her nascent autonomy produces tragedy not for herself, but for another. After she punches an annoying alien and experiences a panic attack, The Doctor diagnoses her frayed impulse control as a delayed response to repressed trauma: a "brutal assault" by an arms trader. Seven describes feeling "violated" and "powerless, unable to stop them." This thinly disguised rape narrative triggers a fundamental conflict between Seven's cyborg response and the personal emotional upheaval expected by The Doctor and Voyager crew. Seven initially discounts her "human feelings" of anger and resentment because she sees them as pointless, much as she sees no need to regret her actions while part of the collective. The Doctor, however, insists that she reframe the assault as a violation of her individuality and an offense against both of her identities—as Borg and human. With The Doctor's naïve coaching, Seven calls for Janeway to bring her attacker to justice, insisting that as an individual, her rights must be respected. Indeed, with the human right to bodily integrity aligned with the Borg desire to collect and retain technological superiority, this marks one of the first moments where the disparate constructions of Seven's identity reinforce rather than disrupt each other. Voyager's investigation ultimately proves Seven's memories to be mistaken, however—rather than a recent assault aimed at stealing her Borg technology, she has transposed later events onto her terrified childhood recollections of assimilation. Far from reconciling her competing subjectivities, she learns that the root cause of her trauma is the moment that created her cyborg self. Her false accusations lead to Covin's death, and she learns both compassion and remorse, two emotions that are useless within the symbiotic consciousness of the Borg but essential to human individuals who must interact and form communities.

Consistently, Janeway and the Federation crew of Voyager invalidate Seven's cyborg interpretations of events and reconstruct new interpretations based on humanistic principles. Two episodes from the end of the fourth season require Seven to not only submit to the redefinitions, but to actively redefine herself in humanistically individual terms. In "The Omega Directive"

(4.21), Seven's Borg priorities once again conflict with the humanistic directives of the Federation. In this case, Janeway's directive to eliminate the dangerous omega particles directly conflicts with Seven's Borg appreciation for perfection. In her attempt to persuade Janeway to study them, Seven clearly expresses herself as an autonomous subject with her own desires for the first time. Although she witnesses the particles' spontaneous self-organization into a perfectly balanced, unified whole, this epiphanic moment comes after Seven has abandoned her own desire in service to the "greater good" as defined by the Federation hierarchy. Seven must learn not only to assert her autonomy, but also that "[b]ecause she is feminized ... and dominant discourses structure women as essentially connected to others, her individuality [and personal desire] is limited" (Casavant 178). In an ironic reversal, only when she accepts that the potential destruction of billions of individuals outweighs her personal convictions can Seven be granted her vision of perfection—a vision of "a final appropriation of all the powers of the parts into a higher unity" (Haraway 150) at odds with the disruptive transgressions of cyborg politics. The same moment that she witnesses what had been, as a Borg, her greatest desire, she must destroy it in accordance with her newly constructed human obligations. Roberts describes Janeway's position in this conflict as "a more feminist, site-specific response" because she "acts in terms of connection" (218); I would argue instead that Janeway's position is acceptable specifically because it confines Seven's desire within a framework of appropriate feminine behavior.

In the penultimate episode of Season 4, Seven asserts her autonomy again when she volunteers to safeguard the Voyager crew when they are incapacitated during the traverse of an unavoidable nebula ("One"). This gesture of sacrifice—Seven must exist alone for over a month with only limited access to The Doctor and holodeck, an extreme isolation which epitomizes her greatest fear—is explicitly framed by Janeway as an act of redemption, the proof that Seven has surrendered her Borg identification and accepted her existence as a reconstructed humanist subject. Battling fear and panic, Seven draws on her ethical obligation to protect the other people on the ship to sustain her, but her ultimate strength depends upon her embrace of herself as an autonomous being. In a direct reversal of her initial recitation of "We are Borg," she declares a new mantra: "I am an individual. I will survive as an individual." When all turns out well, her acceptance as one individual in the community is represented in the final scene of the episode, when she seeks out the crew for companionship.

Seven's autonomy recurs as a point of contention during the remainder of the show. In "Infinite Regress" (5.7), the constant voices which once comforted Seven when she was one part of the cyborg group consciousness threaten to overtake her personality. Recaptured during a raid on a Borg ship but not re-assimilated, ("Dark Frontier" 5.15–5.16) Seven learns that the Borg also value her individuality as the tool that will allow them to defeat humanity, but she thwarts their intention by preserving individual lives as often as possible. Her rescue comes not only from the Voyager crew, but when she stands up for herself against the Borg Queen, as a self-determining human subject, bolstered by her memories of her parents and her desire to prove herself to be not a "mindless automaton" but "Annika Hansen, human."

Janeway allows Seven to choose whether to stay with Voyager or join Kouros's Think Tank, much like a mother sending an adolescent into the world, or a mentor acknowledging the maturation of her protégée: "Until now I've kept a close eye on your progress, helped you with decisions, but I think you have learned enough as an individual to decide for yourself" ("Think Tank" 5.20). When former drones from Seven's own Unimatrix 01 seek her assistance to free themselves from their mini-collective, she must decide whether to return them to the Borg, so they can survive or to make them completely separate individuals, knowing they will die in a few weeks. She chooses individuality for her "distant cousins," and turns to the Voyager "family" for comfort ("Survival Instinct" 6.2).

Each of these challenges to Seven's human identification is answered by the assertion, both by Seven herself and by the humanist community into which she has reintegrated, of her self-determination. Captain Janeway, as mentor and mother-figure, praises her growth as an individual and encourages her to take on greater responsibility for the safety of the ship and its crew. Read through the lens of humanism, with its emphasis on the individual whose identity derives from an essential core nature, Seven's progress demonstrates personal growth and empowerment consistent with the egalitarianism that characterizes *Star Trek*'s philosophy. Seven remains outside the command hierarchy but becomes one of the most powerful figures aboard ship, alongside Janeway and Torres. Nevertheless, her journey to full humanity remains incomplete unless she can also reconstruct herself according to the demands of her gender. As an individual, she must limit the exercise of her autonomy in the service of her community "because she has been taught a feminine identity that focuses on one's connections to others" (Casavant 181). In addition, she must develop, accept, and even pursue both maternal and romantic relationships.

Making a Mother

Mothering and maternal relationships feature more prominently on Voyager than any other *Star Trek* series, not surprising considering the show's generally intensified concerns with gender and women's authority. All of the major female characters (Janeway, Torres, Kes, and Seven) must deal with literal and metaphorical crises of motherhood at various points in the show. In Seven's case, she finds herself caught between two models of motherhood (Janeway and the Borg Queen) even as she is forced to accept, however unwillingly, her own maternal responsibilities. In these narratives of familial obligations and maternal instincts, Seven confronts the centrality of motherhood to the feminine humanist subject: The narratives of humanism "are ruled by a reproductive politics ... [where] women are imagined either better or worse off, but all agree they have less selfhood, weaker individuation ... less at stake in masculine autonomy" (Haraway 177). Regardless of egalitarian principles, *Trek*'s humanism cannot conceive an autonomous female subject free of the choices surrounding reproduction: to become a mother or not, to nurture and guide children toward autonomy by sacrificing some of her own. Seven cannot evade such choices.

In "Dark Frontier" (5.15–5.16), the same episode in which Seven directly reclaims her identity as "Annika Hansen, human," Seven's choice is not simply between the Borg and humanity. She must also choose between the Borg Queen, the cyborg mother-figure "not of Woman born" (Haraway 177) who demands she submit to the posthuman project and Janeway, the mentor-mother who demands she preserve individual subjects, including herself and her companions. In an otherwise quite serious episode, the paired scenes where first the Borg Queen, then Janeway, each send Seven to bed provide a tongue-in-cheek nod that acknowledges Seven's child-like position—but also re-emphasize that *Star Trek* in general and *Voyager* in particular require gender identification even for posthuman villains like the Borg. When that gender identification is female, it must usually be linked as well to the maternal. The Borg Queen's twisted version of mothering, where she preserves Seven's individuality only to exploit it, justifies the continued vilification of the Borg and their posthumanity. Janeway, as a nurturing mother figure, reinforces the rightness of Seven's decision to embrace humanity—including both humanism and its gender implications.

This persistent linking of human individuality to gender, and of femininity to motherhood, forces Seven to address her own potential to be a mother as well. The egalitarian gender politics of *Voyager* align with mainstream liberal feminism's approach to motherhood as a choice, and the show takes as a given that parenting duties should be shared, as in the late-season plotlines around B'Elanna Torres and Tom Paris's daughter ("Lineage" 7.12). When a parent is single, the entire ship community will help, as in the case of Samantha Wildman and her daughter Naomi, whose father was left behind when Voyager was drawn to the Delta Quadrant. Seven, however, finds herself repeatedly forced into a mothering role rather than choosing it, and the crew—including her own mother-figure, Janeway—consistently step back and leave Seven to figure out what to do on her own. The sequence of episodes devoted to Seven's "maternal instincts" ("Child's Play" 6.19) demonstrate how essentialist gender constructions, especially those that suggest women, no matter their spoken preferences, are naturally nurturing and maternal, undergird the show's concept of humanity. If she cannot be a mother, Seven cannot be human—she would be missing a necessary element of her gendered humanity.

Seven's first experience with motherhood comes when her Borg technology fuses with The Doctor's mobile emitter and a convenient crew member's DNA to create an embryonic drone ("Drone" 5.2). This is not the usual Borg reproduction—as Seven notes, they "assimilate, they do not reproduce"—but an unplanned (though external) pregnancy. Seven argues to terminate, but Janeway overrides her objections and informs Seven she "will be the teacher." Despite Seven's misgivings, the plan is to repeat Seven's reconstruction as human with this new drone, to make it the kind of person the crew wants him to become. "How Starfleet!" exclaims a skeptical B'Elanna. The Doctor soon informs Seven that she is the new drone's mother, whether she wants to be or not. He follows her everywhere, and she names him One, identifying him as a self-contained, whole person. She teaches him both skills and Federation values, including that the Borg are a threat to individuals such as those on the ship, and himself. She develops an emotional bond and reassures him that although he was "an accident" and "unexpected," he has unique value and a right to his own thoughts and feelings. Despite her initial reluctance, her success as a first-time mother becomes evident when One sacrifices himself to protect his mother and the ship from assimilation by the Borg. Seven ends the episode both proud of her son's choice and deeply grieving his loss, more profoundly in touch with her humanity because of her experience of motherhood—a motherhood imposed on her as a necessary cost of that humanity, and directly in contradiction of the show's putative endorsement of a woman's right to control her own reproduction.

Seven's most dramatic and long-term engagement with motherhood comes when Voyager discovers a disabled Borg cube containing only "neonatal drones" ("Collective" 6.16). Unlike her first unintended experience, this time she chooses to step forward immediately to protect these children from their own recklessness as well as emotional pain when they realize they have been abandoned by the Borg. She midwives a premature infant and agrees to mother these "very troubled children" despite her concern that caring for them will be difficult. She soothes their fears and gives them names—activities that troubled her with One, but that she now recognizes as important. Her maternal intentions do not last long, however, and soon Tuvok chastises her for "le[aving] the children unsupervised" and Chakotay accuses her of being overly rigid in her discipline. Her declaration that she "no longer wish[es] to be guardian to the Borg children" because she is failing them does not elicit support from her community, however. Instead, Chakotay advises that chaos and children go together, and she should adapt ("Ashes to Ashes" 6.18). When Icheb, the touchiest adolescent in the group, learns that he is a genetically engineered bioweapon created by his parents to destroy the Borg, Janeway encourages Seven to rely on her "maternal instincts; they worked before" ("Child's Play" 6.19). Each time Seven seeks to step away from her maternal role, Janeway or another member of the Voyager crew stands in her way. Failure to mother these Borg children into successful individuals will mark a failure of her humanity—again, Seven's own rights to self-determination must give way to the insistence that she perform her gender.

This linkage of Seven's ability to mother with her successful reconstruction of her humanity culminates in the final season episode "Imperfection" (7.2), when her emotional ties to her foster children overlap with the symptoms of her malfunctioning Borg technology. As three of the orphaned Borg children leave Voyager to be reunited with their native species, Seven blames her tears not on sadness at their departure, but on a problem with her ocular implant. While this might seem to invalidate her grief, the failure of her Borg technology in fact reinforces her emotional maturation within the paradigms of gendered humanist individualism. She must come to terms with her individual mortality when she no longer has the multiplicitous consciousness of the collective to remember her. She theorizes that Janeway's refusal to accept her death stems from disappointment that she has not become truly human, despite her assertion of doctor-patient privilege, a first demand for her fundamental right to privacy and medical self-determination, including the right to refuse treatment. Janeway disagrees, declaring "You've become ... an extraordinary individual ... a friend." The evidence that Janeway, rather than Seven, has the right of it comes after Seven's foster son Icheb donates his own technology to save her. Her tears of relief that Icheb survived the risky procedure prove her deep attachment to her son as well as the genuine emotion she felt in the opening scene, when she let her other foster children go home. Again, despite her frequently expressed reluctance to be a mother, the insistence of Janeway and the Federation crew that she must do so to prove her own humanity controls the narrative.

More than the basic social ties between otherwise autonomous individuals that dominated the fourth season, the ability to form the deeper emotional ties of mother to child is the inevitable consequence as well as the proof of her reintegration into gendered humanist subjectivity. Seven's re-education in her purportedly instinctive role as nurturing mother inscribes her within the reproductive aspect of her humanity. The necessity of mothering to her character works against any radically posthumanist cyborg deconstruction of gender paradigms, which at least could allow the refusal of motherhood and might offer profoundly different forms of parenting independent of gender. Despite all of the ways in which Seven initially resists the assumptions made by the Voyager crew about her value as an individual as well as her ability, as a single woman, to care for these children, she ultimately embraces both roles, while the alternatives are villainized through their association with the Borg and the Borg Queen. Beyond reconstructing herself as a self-determined autonomous individual, Seven's journey to humanity hinges on her reintegration into gendered social relationships. As a mother, Seven demonstrates her empathy and her ability to nurture the budding individuality of her unplanned, foster, and adoptive children.

The Subject of Romance

From her first appearance in a silver skintight bodysuit to her last scenes in the series finale, Seven's humanity is measured repeatedly and most consistently against her ability to form appropriate heteronormative romantic attachments. While Harry Kim's awkward flirtation marks her place outside those relationships during her first days aboard Voyager, the crew—in this instance, represented most frequently by The Doctor—continually return to her ability, or lack of ability, to smile, flirt, and date as the main pathway by which her lessons in human interaction should progress. Until Seven not only accepts, but actively cultivates her own romantic attachments to an available man, her humanity remains in question.

The first steps in Seven's romantic education require her to "phrase things a little more diplomatically" ("Concerning Flight" 4.11) and develop her "ability to put others at ease, make them feel comfortable" ("Prey" 4.16). When the Hirogen trap the Voyager crew in holodeck simulations, she appears as a sexy cabaret singer, complete with flowing blond hair, a sparkling silver gown, and soft-focus cinematography ("The Killing Game, Part I" 4.18)—reinforcing her position as an object of romantic interest within the simulation, for the Voyager crew, and for the show's audience. Several other episodes feature her as an object of male desire—from Harry Kim fantasizing her as a sexually aggressive coquette ("Waking Moments" 4.13) and The Doctor fantasizing her as a nude model ("Tinker, Tenor, Doctor, Spy" 6.4), to an adolescent Q ogling her nude body ("Q2" 7.19)—but she initially lacks any romantic desire of her own. Still, she attempts to develop conversational skills and engage in small talk ("One" 4.25), and even practices smiling ("Drone" 5.2) and gets drunk as a way to work on her "social skills" ("Timeless" 5.6). Failure to push her own discomfort aside and accommodate the expectations of others results in criticism or disappointment.

Seven gradually shifts her understanding of dating from dismissing it as "a courtship ritual ... [that] seems an unnecessary and complicated precursor to the act of procreation" ("Unforgettable" 4.22) to fascinated, collecting "gigaquads" of data on Tom and B'Elanna's "mating behavior" ("Someone to Watch Over Me" 5.22). This last prompts Janeway and The Doctor to encourage her to try out "romance" for herself, as she is "a woman." The Doctor calls this "a simple biological fact with repercussions that are hard to deny" and prescribes dating as "an important stage in her social development," confirming the essentialist identification of her biological sex with certain gender norms and expected behaviors. Although she physically damages her first date, she masters the social graces to become an object not only of outright lust but genuine interest specifically because she learns, again, to moderate her behavior and conversation. This Pygmalion-style episode concludes with her toast "to all that makes us unique." Her increased appreciation for romance corresponds directly to her public expression of her increased appreciation of the individuality at the core of humanism.

The Doctor's ongoing lessons—which begin with "First Contact" and proceed through such topics as "Beguiling Banter," "Dress for Success," and "Shall We Dance?"—highlight that Seven's social skills, including dating and romance, must be taught ("Someone to Watch Over Me"). This might suggest that her gendered human identity is as much a construction as her nearly forgotten cyborg consciousness, but the reappearance of Seven's ability to dream—not seen since her first nightmares of her childhood assimilation—reveals that her romantic nature is essential to her human individuality. In these dreams, Seven sees herself walking through a misty forest with a strangely "familiar" man who calls her by her name, Annika, rather than her Borg designation. The Doctor eagerly proposes interpretations: "Is he a father figure? Or does he represent a repressed desire for male companionship?" ("Unimatrix Zero, Part I" 6.26). These options, while amusing for their very stereotypical nature, also indicate how her relationship to a man appears fundamental to the definition of Seven's humanity. Even more revealing than The Doctor's assumptions, however, is the actual origin of these "dreams." The man, Axum, is not a figment of Seven's unconscious, a representation of her disembodied wish for a relationship—he is, in fact, her lover in a virtual reality that preserved individual identity within the Borg collective. Within Unimatrix Zero, Axum encourages Seven to see her "essence," her true self. This self is remarkably similar to the siren from the holodeck in "The Killing Game" with soft lighting and her hair down, this time without any Borg implants. Lest we miss the significance of this relationship, The Doctor spells it out: "How ironic! All this time, we've been trying to develop this aspect of your humanity, and it's been there all along." Contrary to Seven's contention that she has no essential identity to recover, we now know that Seven has always already been a romantic at heart ("Unimatrix Zero, Part II" 7.1). When

Unimatrix Zero is destroyed and Seven loses Axum (his physical body is on the other side of the galaxy), Seven's humanity remains fundamentally incomplete.

Although cyborg logic suggests that Seven, who spent eighteen years as part of the Borg's collective consciousness, need have no necessary commitment to heterosexuality, as the series approached its conclusion the story of Seven's journey to humanity also required conclusion. Where she originally dismissed any notions of her initial innocence defiled by the Borg, and therefore any guilt for her actions, she must now release the guilt she acquired along with her human consciousness: "You've reclaimed your humanity," Janeway tells her. "It's time you stopped blaming yourself for the crimes of the Borg" ("Repentance" 7.13). More importantly, however, her humanity remains in doubt unless she proves herself both willing to seek out a romantic attachment and able to maintain it with an appropriate and available man. At this point, the only single men on Voyager's primary crew are Harry Kim and Chakotay. As Harry, by definition, cannot form lasting relationships, Seven's only available romantic partner within the heteronormative framework is Chakotay—a much older man in a superior position within Voyager's hierarchy. Over the course of a few episodes, Seven confirms her humanity by fantasizing about and then pursuing the relationship that conforms to gender expectations.

For most of her time on Voyager, Seven spends little time dreaming and rarely expresses personal desire. Indeed, the few occasions when she does so are called out as milestones on her journey to selfhood: the nightmares that draw her to her parents' ship and reconnect her to her human childhood, her longing for the perfection of the omega particle that calls her to express her own desire for the first time, her dreams of Axum that reveal her latent sexuality. Once Axum is forever lost to her, however, Seven turns to the holodeck to explore her desires: for humanity without any remnants of Borg technology, for children and a home of her own, for "intimate relations" and romantic love ("Human Error" 7.18). It seems no mistake that the sequence of her fantasies follows the same sequence as the milestone events along her road from posthuman cyborg to typical human woman. Called out on her distraction, having spent more attention on her imaginary crew quarters and flirting with a virtual Chakotay than on doing her job, she explains her motivation: "Unimatrix Zero…. Ever since it was destroyed, my life has seemed incomplete." Far from the curious but analytical cyborg willing to "copulate" with Harry Kim for the sake of experimentation, she now faces the challenge of finding "the right balance" between work and her personal life. Rather than short-circuiting patriarchal gender expectations and forging a new paradigm, she stands in the same position of many modern women, including almost all the major female *Star Trek* characters since *TNG*.

The series finale, "Endgame" (7.25–7.26), resolves Seven's story by resolving her romantic dilemma. The episode follows two timelines—a current time in which Seven and Chakotay are continuing to date, and one over a decade into the future, where they have married. Both branches of Seven's romance speak to the lingering conflicts between *Trek*'s feminism and the persistent gender hierarchy embedded in its humanism. At their picnic, Seven is tentative but Chakotay declares her romantic arrangements "perfection." As their longer-term romance progresses, they become a devoted couple so profoundly enamored of each other that Seven's death nearly destroys Chakotay. With Seven gone, Janeway declares, "our family is not complete anymore." The crew memorialize her as their lost daughter, sister, and wife—her perfect humanity found in the most traditional of feminine roles. In the short-term timeline, Seven's professional plans are vague and she is focused on her relationship. Warned of the danger to him should he lose her, Seven's last significant decision on the series comes with her declaration that she will "alter the parameters of the relationship," her attempt to break off their intimacy in order to protect him. He refuses to allow it, however, and they end with hands clasped. One final time, Seven's attempt at self-determination is overruled.

From her initial appearance aboard Voyager, Seven of Nine strikingly embodies an alternative feminist model that challenges traditional humanism and gender hierarchies. Indeed, she is a rare example of a true Harawayan cyborg in mainstream popular culture. She retains many of these qualities throughout her time on the show, a confident and intelligent woman who advocates for what she knows to be right. She even "manages to retain some Borg characteristics and not suffer the consequences" (Consalvo 187), including both her physical implants and most of her objectivity, throughout the series. Nevertheless, the radical disruptions to traditional gender paradigms that she represents must in time be contained through the narrative reconstruction of her humanity. Reading Seven of Nine's character arc through the lens of cyborg theory does more than demonstrate the limitations placed on women on screen. It highlights the ways in which gender is not just a construct, but a construct deeply embedded within our understanding of what it means to be human. Postmodernism and posthumanism may not be new concepts in philosophy and critical theory, nor were they when the show aired at the turn of the millennium. *Star Trek: Voyager*'s deployment and defusion of the cyborg confirms that while resistance may be futile, it is gender normativity, not cyborg potentiality, that triumphs in popular culture.

WORKS CITED

"Ashes to Ashes." *Star Trek: Voyager*, written by Ronald Wilkerson, directed by Terry Windell, Season 6, episode 18, Paramount, 1 Mar. 2000.

128 Part II. Gendering the 24th Century

Casavant, Michele M. *To Boldly Go Where No Other Has Gone Before: The Construction of Race and Gender in Star Trek*. 2003. U of Kansas, Ph.D. dissertation.
"Child's Play." *Star Trek: Voyager*, written by Paul Brown, directed by Mike Vejar, Season 6, episode 19, Paramount, 8 Mar. 2000.
"Collective." *Star Trek: Voyager*, teleplay by Michael Taylor, directed by Allison Liddi, Season 6, episode 16, Paramount, 16 Feb. 2000.
"Concerning Flight." *Star Trek: Voyager*, teleplay by Joe Menosky, directed by Jesús Salvador Treviño, Season 4, episode 11, Paramount, 26 Nov. 1997.
Consalvo, Mia. "Borg Babes, Drones, and the Collective: Reading Gender and the Body in Star Trek." *Women's Studies in Communication*, vol. 27, no. 2, 2004, pp. 177–203. *Omni-File Full Text*, doi:http://dx.doi.org/10.1080/07491409.2004.10162472. Accessed 18 Feb. 2018.
Cranny-Francis, Anne. "The Erotics of the (Cy)Borg: Authority and Gender in the Sociocultural Imaginary." *Future Females, the Next Generation: New Voices and Velocities in Feminist Science Fiction Criticism*, edited by Marleen S. Barr, Rowman and Littlefield, 2000, pp. 145–163.
"Dark Frontier." *Star Trek: Voyager*, written by Brannon Braga and Joe Menosky, Season 5, episode 16, Paramount, 17 Feb. 1999.
"Day of Honor." *Star Trek: Voyager*, written by Jeri Taylor, directed by Jesús Salvador Treviño Season 4, episode 3, Paramount, 17 Sept. 1997.
"Drone." *Star Trek: Voyager*, written by Bryan Fuller, Brannon Braga, and Joe Menosky, directed by Les Landau, Season 5, episode 2, Paramount, 21 Oct. 1998.
"Endgame." *Star Trek: Voyager*, written by Kenneth Biller and Robert Doherty, Season 7, episodes 25 and 26, Paramount, 23 May 2001.
"The Gift." *Star Trek: Voyager*, written by Joe Menosky, directed by Anson Williams, Season 4, episode 2, Paramount, 10 Sept. 1997.
Haraway, Donna. "A Cyborg Manifesto: Science, Technology, and Socialist-Feminism in the Late Twentieth Century." *Simians, Cyborgs and Women: The Reinvention of Nature*, Routledge, 1991, pp. 149–181.
"Human Error." *Star Trek: Voyager*, written by Brannon Braga and André Bormanis, directed by Allan Kroeker, Season 7, episode 18, Paramount, 7 Mar. 2001.
"Imperfection." *Star Trek: Voyager*, written by Carleton Eastlake and Robert Doherty, Season 7, episode 2, 11 Oct. 2000.
"Infinite Regress." *Star Trek: Voyager*, Directed by David Livingston, perf. Jeri Ryan, Season 5, episode 7, Paramount, 25 Nov. 1998.
Joyrich, Lynne. "Feminist Enterprise? Star Trek: The Next Generation and the Occupation of Femininity." *Cinema Journal*, vol. 35, no. 2, 1996, pp. 61–84. *JSTOR*, doi:10.2307/1225 756.
"The Killing Game, Part I." *Star Trek: Voyager*, written by Brannon Braga and Joe Menosky, Season 4, episode 18, Paramount, 4 Mar. 1998.
Lauzen, Martha M. "Boxed in 2016–17: Women on Screen and Behind the Scenes in Television." *Center for the Study of Women in Television and Film*, Sept. 2017. https://womenintvfilm.sdsu.edu/wp-content/uploads/2017/09/2016-17_Boxed_In_Report.pdf. Accessed 14 April 2018.
"Lineage." *Star Trek: Voyager*, written by James Kahn, directed by Peter Lauritson, Season 7, episode 12, Paramount, 24 Jan. 2001.
"The Omega Directive." *Star Trek: Voyager*, teleplay by Lisa Klink, directed by Victor Lobl, Season 4, episode 21, Paramount, 15 Apr. 1998.
"One." *Star Trek: Voyager*, written by Jeri Taylor, directed by Kenneth Biller, Season 4, episode 25, Paramount, 13 May 1998.
"Prey." *Star Trek: Voyager*, Brannon Braga, directed by Allan Eastman, Season 4, episode 16, Paramount, 18 Feb. 1998.
"Q2." *Star Trek: Voyager*, teleplay by Robert Doherty, directed by LeVar Burton, Season 7, episode 19, Paramount, 11 Apr. 2001.
"The Raven." *Star Trek: Voyager*, teleplay by Bryan Fuller and Harry Doc Kloor, directed by LeVar Burton, Season 4, episode 6, Paramount, 8 Oct. 1997.

"Repentance." *Star Trek: Voyager*, teleplay by Robert Doherty, directed by Mike Vejar, Season 7, episode 13, Paramount, 31 Jan. 2001.
"Retrospect." *Star Trek: Voyager*, directed by Jesús Salvador Treviño, perf. By Jeri Ryan, Season 4, episode 17, Paramount, 25 Feb. 1998.
"Revulsion." *Star Trek: Voyager*, written by Lisa Klink, directed by Kenneth Biller, Season 4, episode 5, Paramount,1 Oct. 1997.
Roberts, Robin A. "Science, Race, and Gender in Star Trek: Voyager." *Fantasy Girls: Gender in the New Universe of Science Fiction and Fantasy Television*, edited by Elyce R. Helford, Rowman and Littlefield, 2000, pp. 203–21.
"Scorpion, Part 2." *Star Trek: Voyager*, written by Brannon Braga and Joe Menosky, directed by Winrich Kolbe, Season 4, episode 1, Paramount, 3 Sept. 1997.
"Someone to Watch Over Me." *Star Trek: Voyager*, directed by Robert Duncan Mcneill, perf. by Robert Picardo and Jeri Ryan, Season 5, episode 22, Paramount, 28 Apr. 1999.
"Survival Instinct." *Star Trek: Voyager*, written by Ronald D. Moore, directed by Terry Windell Season 6, episode 2, Paramount, 29 Sept. 1999.
"Think Tank." *Star Trek: Voyager*, teleplay by Michael Taylor, directed by Terrence O'Hara, Season 5, episode 20, Paramount, 31 Mar. 1999.
"Timeless." *Star Trek: Voyager*, directed by LeVar Burton, perf. by Garrett Wang, Season 5, episode 6, Paramount, 18 Nov. 1998.
"Tinker, Tenor, Doctor, Spy." *Star Trek: Voyager*, directed by John Bruno, perf. by Robert Picardo, Season 6, episode 4, Paramount, 13 Oct. 1999.
Tudor, Deborah, and Eileen R. Meehan. "Demoting Women on Screen and in the Board Room." *Cinema Journal*, vol. 53, no. 1, 2013, pp. 130–164. JSTOR, doi: http://dx.doi.org/10.1353/cj.2013.0063. Accessed 30 Mar. 2019.
"Unforgettable." *Star Trek: Voyager*, written by Greg Elliot and Michael Perricone, directed by Andrew Robinson, Season 4, episode 22, Paramount, 22 Apr. 1998.
"Unimatrix Zero, Part I." *Star Trek: Voyager*, directed by Allan Kroeker, Season 6, episode 26, Paramount, 24 May 2000.
"Unimatrix Zero, Part II." *Star Trek: Voyager*, directed by Mike Vejar, Season 7, episode 1, Paramount, 4 Oct. 2000.
"Waking Moments." *Star Trek: Voyager*, written by André Bormanis, directed by Alexander Singer, Season 4, episode 13, Paramount, 14 Jan. 1998.

Part III

Negotiating Identities in the Delta Quadrant

Disabling Resistance

Voyager *and Federation Ideology*

DANIEL PRESTON *and* CRAIG A. MEYER

Introduction

The *Star Trek* universe changed the cultural discourse, allowing people to more easily discuss differences regarding race, gender, sexuality, and (dis)ability. However, a closer look at several *Star Trek: Voyager* episodes reveals a troubling pattern that discourages individuality. Through the lens of disability studies,[1] we examine ways that ablest language and dominant ideology can usurp even the most well-meaning groups.

The premise of *Voyager* suggests the greatest diversity of all *Trek* shows. Two starship crews with fundamentally divergent ideologies (Federation and Maquis) are flung into an unknown quadrant and forced together to make a 70-year journey home. While the pilot episode highlighted these differences, they were quickly folded into a Federation philosophy. In the series, there were several instances of Federation philosophy commandeering individual or group ideologies. The absorption of the Maquis into the Voyager crew is one example, but another more apparent example is Janeway's interactions with Seven of Nine.

Adding Seven gave producers and writers a constant sounding board for Federation ideology. Often, Federation ideology became paramount to the aspirations of Janeway's Borg protégé. Episodes like "Scorpion, Part I" (3.26) and "The Gift" (4.2) show debates about what it is to be human versus Borg, the virtues of individuality, and showcase Janeway's unflinching belief that the Starfleet way is the correct way. This parental relationship with Seven takes precedence over individual ideology that Janeway claims to respect. In effect, she disables Seven by limiting personal agency because Janeway "knows better."

In our essay, we discuss the incorporation of the Maquis into the Voyager crew and Seven of Nine's indoctrination into Federation/Janeway ideology. In doing so, we note the similarities between those journeys and struggles experienced by People with Disabilities (PWDs) to demonstrate how a dominant narrative can overwhelm and undercut individuality and, thus, (re)enforce compliance to the normalized status quo. We analyze certain scenes and highlight the ways that disability theory can be productively applied to a multi-cultural context. Lastly, we point to some lessons that *Voyager* and disability-related activism have taught us about our mutual challenges as we look toward an inclusive future. Through *Voyager*, we reveal representations of people who struggle to work together, achieve equal status, and express views that counter or challenge the dominant narrative. These challenges share common traits with the Disability Rights Movement and the strategies that are deployed for inclusion and a productive working environment between the crews, which is reminiscent of work done in disability studies.

Sociologist Erving Goffman describes the act of stigmatizing others and uses an early definition of *stigma* as one way to identify a person or a group of people. Stigma, according to Goffman, refers to physical markings or social behaviors that have become undesirable by members of a mainstream group. One "blemish" he specifically mentions as stigmatizing is "radical political behavior" (4). In *Voyager*, we contend that the Maquis and later Seven of Nine are blemishes, because of their divergent ideological perspectives and challenges to the Federation ideology. This ideology includes the Prime Directive as well as operating within Starfleet protocols and procedures. For Captain Janeway, the Maquis crew members and Seven of Nine exhibit these blemishes or challenges when they openly violate that ideology to accomplish goals.

Goffman further argues that the "normative expectations" we have on a particular category of person may not be realized (2). We reason, therefore, that a newly introduced person may not become part of the normalized group culture, which in our case is Starfleet. Yet at the very least, we recognize the Maquis and Seven challenge this culture. More still, we demonstrate through Seven that a "person with a stigma is not quite human," which can be seen in her discussions with Janeway about becoming human, since she does not recognize herself as human, but as a Borg (Goffman 5). Consequently, *Voyager* fashioned the Maquis and Seven as impaired by the Federation environment. *Star Trek* fan and fellow scholar Llana Lehmann provides insight into the 2002 International Classification of Functioning, Disability and Health (ICF). The ICF focuses on interactions through four categories: health condition, impairment, activity limitation, and participation restriction (Lehmann 2-3). For our purposes, we focus on this last category. Lehmann reports, "a *participation restriction* refers to the person's capacity to experience inclusion" (3). We utilize this insight to focus on the creation of disabling environments on *Voyager* that enhance or further an ideology and also the enforcement of certain social dynamics but not on any specific impairments.

As we analyzed *Voyager*, we were often reminded of the words of disability historian Douglas Baynton, who writes,

> Disability has functioned historically to justify inequality or disabled people themselves, but it has also done so for women and minority groups. That is, not only has it been considered justifiable to treat disabled people unequally, but the concept of disability has been used to justify discrimination against other groups by attributing disability to them [33].

Baynton introduces the *idea of disability*, whether marked by physical impairment or not, and how it can be just as damaging as physical differences. To that end, scholars in disability studies make clear distinctions between "impairments" and "disabilities," noting that impairments are physical, cognitive, or emotional differences that our bodies exhibit, while *disabilities* are created when those differences interact with the surrounding environment and create limitations of access and participation within the society. These represent the basic tenets of the social construction of disability and also suggest that the meaning of disability shifts throughout history and context.

As with all populations, physical impairments exist within the *Trek* universe, and this was no less true on *Voyager*. For example, audience members saw Tuvok dealing with blindness, ("Year of Hell" 4.9–4.10) or Neelix without lungs ("Phage" 1.5). Aside from these, and a few more discrete examples, it may be difficult to understand non–Federation crew members in terms of a disability framework. In such case, we share the thinking of I. M. Young: "for every oppressed group, there is a group that is privileged in relation to that group" (qtd. in Cameron 110). In *Voyager*, questions of otherness, minority status, and capability are often considered in episodes making *status* a narrative crutch of sorts. Additionally, the sometimes-blatant paternalism by Captain Janeway is reminiscent of outdated disability narratives, where (s)mothering takes the place of individual choice and agency, which effectively disabled or impaired the othered group or person. This created an oppressive and stigmatizing situation for minority groups, and we point to the other relationships within *Voyager* that mirror them, such as Janeway and Seven.

We remain comfortable with the choice to refer to these relationships and situations as disabling for two reasons. First, even though no specific disability is named, the Maquis and eventually other members of the crew who do not subscribe to Federation ideology are ostracized, treated differently, and presented with unique social challenges. This becomes akin to the ways that women and people of color were treated during the early (and ongoing) struggles for civil liberties. Second, we recognize that the addition of Seven functions as a constant test and measuring stick for Federation ideology, which Janeway embodies. Janeway reflects the larger culture of the Federation, all it holds dear, and all it hopes to be. Therefore, any slight against the captain is interpreted as a disavowal of Federation or "proper" values. Further, the relationship between Seven and Janeway operates in similar fashion to how PWDs are expected to understand, trust in, and function within mainstream society.

Starting with the earliest seasons of *Voyager*, Captain Janeway establishes Federation parameters aboard ship by continually reinforcing the notion of "the right way to do things." In turn, this created a binary among the crew and placed the beliefs and practices of the Federation against the beliefs and practices of the Maquis. While a strong belief in Federation ideology is crucial for a Starfleet captain, holding onto those beliefs can serve to create a social environment of disability for those who think and behave differently. Therefore, one need not look very far to see the assignment of impairment to the Maquis.

The Maquis as "Other"

The premiere episode of *Voyager* sets up two distinct groups of people who operate under two different ideologies. The prologue to the episode reads:

> Unhappy with a new treaty, Federation Colonists along the Cardassian border have banded together. Calling themselves "The Maquis," they continue to fight the Cardassians. Some consider them heroes, but to the governments of the Federation and Cardassia, they are outlaws ["Caretaker" 1.1].

In forty words, the writers establish and label the Maquis as "outlaws." This radical political behavior presents Chakotay (the Maquis ship captain) and the Maquis crew as impaired and as deviant, which establishes their stigma status. Throughout the first episode, the separation between the two groups is further established when the Maquis's B'Elanna Torres and the Federation's Ensign Harry Kim are captured. As they speak to each other, Torres uses the term "Starfleet" to label Kim, and he responds by calling her "Maquis." By the end of the first episode, Captain Janeway rescues both crews, names Chakotay her first officer, and tells the *new* crew that "Chakotay and I have decided that we will operate as one crew—a *Starfleet* crew." Within that one line, Janeway and the writers establish one of the main markers by which all characters will be judged and all decisions will be made. The crew's adherence to Federation standards, practices, and principles will be the guideline by which ability is measured. While this leap may not be properly set up in this opening episode, many viewers understood what *being* a Starfleet/Federation crew meant. At the time, it seemed that the writers wanted viewers to imagine a show where the two groups work together "to practice toleration and live together in peace with one another, and to unite our strength to maintain interstellar peace and security," à la the Federation Charter ("Federation Charter"). However, division among the crew quickly develops as the main source of the show's conflict.

"Parallax" (1.3), the second episode of the series, positions the Maquis crew as disabled due to their lack of Starfleet ideological indoctrination and training. The following scene between Captain Janeway and newly christened First Officer Commander Chakotay is about filling the vacant Chief Engineer position. Lt. Carey has been Acting Chief and Janeway posits that he is the most qualified, because he is the "senior officer":

> CHAKOTAY: I'm doing everything I can to integrate them into your crew, but frankly, you're not making it easy for me, Captain.
> JANEWAY: I can't make it easy, Commander. Surely you can understand that. They don't have the discipline. They don't have the training.
> CHAKOTAY: But some of them, like B'Elanna Torres, have the ability ["Parallax" 1.3].

Here, Janeway is defending the Federation and those beholden to its ideology as superior, proper, and correct. Since Janeway is the captain, she generally has the last word on all matters; therefore, decisions reflect her interpretation of Federation ideology. In this case, she sees the added crew members of the Maquis as unworthy, because the original Voyager crew were already part of the Federation. Thus, the formerly Maquis crew are disabled and stigmatized because they were not part of the more normalized society, culture, and ideology of the Federation. These crew "don't have the discipline" and "don't have the training" of Starfleet or its standards. However, the Maquis crew functioned as a crew without Federation oversight or values before being flung across the galaxy. Yet, Janeway fails to recognize that reality and positions all former Maquis crew, except Chakotay with his Starfleet training, as inferior. The scene continues with him pushing back:

> CHAKOTAY: You're asking them to accept me.
> JANEWAY: You're qualified. You're a graduate of the Academy, and you have Starfleet command experience. [...] Show me another qualified Maquis candidate and I'll consider him.
> CHAKOTAY: B'Elanna Torres ["Parallax" 1.3].

Within this conversation, careful attention reveals Janeway assigning impairments to Torres specifically and the Maquis in general. For Janeway, these

138 Part III. Negotiating Identities

educational gaps constitute what she considers insurmountable obstacles or flaws—these crewmen have impairments.

It should also be noted that Janeway's argument about Torres's qualifications for the job as Chief Engineer may have some roots within our own history as well. Consider the fact that "ability" has historically been linked in many ways to productivity or the impression of what productivity is and should be. For example, in his work on the ways that disability has been represented in the media, Charles A. Riley provides historical context and explains that the reception of Social Security benefits has always been tied to the ability to earn wages (3–5). However, our interpretation of the scene, based in the social model of disability, suggests that by limiting the Maquis' ability for promotion, Janeway creates a disabling environment based on her assumptions, supported by the Federation's general consensus, that the Maquis are outlaws. Chakotay, in turn, makes the argument for Torres's ability despite her Maquis impairment. Later during a crisis, Janeway calls a meeting of senior staff, which includes Torres and Acting Chief Carey. When asked for options, Carey offers a suggestion that is quickly shot down by Torres who says it won't work. Torres continues and explains another possible plan. Suddenly Janeway recognizes her ability, despite her Maquis impairment, and latches onto the idea, which saves them from the crisis. Janeway is suddenly convinced that Torres should be the Chief Engineer and promotes her accordingly. This exemplifies how the struggle for status is recognized only when it suits the needs of the dominant group, which we will return to later with Seven of Nine.

At the end of the first season, Janeway decides that the flaws she noted in "Parallax" can be compensated for through education and training (1.3). The episode "Learning Curve" begins with Janeway, Chakotay, and Tuvok discussing the possibility of a "Starfleet refresher course" for certain Maquis members, because as Janeway puts it, "It's not fair to expect Starfleet behavior from people who never went to the Academy" (1.16). They decide Tuvok should lead the course, and four crewmen are selected to take part. During their first session in a cargo bay, he explains its purpose:

> HENLEY: I think we need some clarification. Just why have we been singled out for this honor?[2]
>
> TUVOK: The answer to that question would seem to be self-evident, crewman. Interrupting a senior officer is not acceptable behavior. The purpose of this training is to familiarize you with Starfleet protocols so that mistakes like that will be minimized ["Learning Curve" 1.16].

The exchange continues as another, Crewman Chell, interrupts Tuvok again, and Tuvok responds by requiring Chell to do laps around the cargo bay. This example shows the ways in which Janeway uses discipline, through Tuvok here, to solidify the properness and unity of Starfleet regulations. The four crewmen selected for training initially defy orders and walk out on this first session. While talking with these crewmen later in the mess hall, the now common "there's a Starfleet way, and a Maquis way" refrain is uttered by Crewman Dalby as he tries to justify their actions of walking out to Chakotay. Dalby's insubordination leads Chakotay to punch him, sending him to the floor and, thus, demonstrating the "Maquis way." Chakotay orders the group to return to Tuvok's training, and notes that similar violence will be repeated daily if they refuse. Later in training, Tuvok has the group running laps around one of the ship's decks that has additional gravity to make the para-military exercise harder. At the same time, he continues espousing Federation ideology, again making it appear that the *Starfleet way* is the only way.

While the episode "Learning Curve" does present some problematic scenes relating to fitting into Federation ideology, we recognize that the concluding scenes suggest that both sides can benefit from a little bending of this ideology (1.16). The following scene comes after Tuvok and the select crew have been through physical training, battle simulations, and have come to a feasible working relationship. An explosion, which is presented as a real catastrophic event, occurs and endangers their lives; Tuvok orders them to save themselves by escaping into a Jeffries Tube and justifies his orders with, what equates to, the needs of the many outweigh the needs of the few or the one. Then, Tuvok goes back to save a fallen crew member that was left behind—breaking his own Federation, and logic driven, rule. Once all hands are safe, Dalby and Tuvok have a brief, but insightful discussion in which Tuvok acknowledges that "there are times when it is desirable to bend the rules" and wins Dalby's approval.

The intended resolution of the episode is for audiences to view these once problematic crew members as now folded into Federation ideology, but we highlight this was because of the *breaking* of that ideology. We also see a turning away from the dominant ideology in favor of another ad-hoc ideology, which worked out for both parties. This event can be viewed as an acceptance of different ideologies based on mutual experiences. By the end of "Learning Curve," we recognize that another important transition has taken place, too. While the senior officers agreed that education for the Maquis was paramount to the success of Voyager's mission, we cannot ignore the fact that an education of the Federation officers (primarily Tuvok) takes place as well. Like Janeway's eventual acceptance of Torres in "Parallax" (1.3), this episode demonstrates an observation made by David Mitchell and Sharon Snyder regarding the knowledge that disabilities create,[3] and that by interacting with PWDs, we can all learn and grow.

With the Maquis crew neatly folded into the Federation, writers moved beyond the simplistic Federation versus Maquis plotlines that were hallmarks of the first two seasons. At the end of Season 3, we are provided a new rivalry to explore Federation ideology, what it means to be human, and, more importantly for us, the application of stigma to a *not quite human* individual, Seven of Nine.

Collective Ideology: Federation vs. the Borg and the Disabling of Seven

When Seven of Nine is introduced ("Scorpion, Part I" 3.26), she is the enemy—a drone of the collective known as the Borg. Circumstances force Janeway to bring Seven aboard as an intermediary between Voyager and the Borg to mitigate the threat Species 8472 poses to both of them. But Seven is separated from Borg influence and is forced to confront her own aloneness. That aloneness is foreign to Seven, because she was assimilated by the Borg as a child and has always had millions of voices in her mind. This removal from the collective is the first time Seven sees herself as disabled—something has been taken from her that made her who she was. While Seven is human, the crew, Seven herself, and viewers see her as Borg, which is precisely how she is stigmatized because she, as Goffman cautioned us, is "not quite human." To further disable, but also normalize, her toward humanity, her appearance is changed. Several of her Borg implants are removed, and she becomes a stereotypically beautiful woman with mere Borg accessories adorning parts of her body. In a later episode titled "Dark Frontier," the Borg Queen notices Seven's changes and points to her indoctrination, by stating, "You've changed. Your exo-plating, your ocular implant. They've taken you apart and they've re-created you in their own image." (5.15–5.16). These changes provide for Seven's assimilation, again, into a new collective and steers the show into justifying a Federation ideology. Early in Season 4, episodes revolve around Janeway and Seven, their relationship, and the ongoing struggle to understand, enforce, and comply with Janeway's directives.

As such, Seven is set up as protégé to Janeway and as a prototype for human and Starfleet behavior. Many times, though, Seven embodies an obstacle for the crew to overcome because she is conflicted regarding which ideology she should follow. Additionally, Seven is often shown inconsistent applications of Federation policy and notes the complexity of following a seemingly non-existent standard of behavior (we point back to Tuvok bending the rules to save the crew member, as one example). Again, Captain Janeway has the final say regarding actions taken in any situation, so *her* ideology becomes paramount, and when Seven refers to the inconsistency, Janeway assumes a rather parental and sometimes dictatorial attitude that disables Seven even further by denying Seven her own agency. The first evidence of such an exchange is seen during "The Gift" (4.2). Seven attempts to contact the Borg (and escape Voyager) by accessing the communications array. In response, citing a security threat to the ship, Janeway places Seven in the brig. Janeway exercises her judgment over someone who doesn't follow her guidelines, this time going so far as to imprison Seven. Janeway's behavior may align with security concerns aboard ship, but Seven's recognition of the irony of "human freedom" is suggestive of the ways that many PWDs were, and are, historically placed in asylums and facilities for the *safety* and *betterment* of the public.[4] Despite Seven's objections, Janeway continues telling Seven more about the journey to humanity:

> SEVEN: You would deny us the choice as you deny us now. You have imprisoned us in the name of humanity, yet you will not grant us your most cherished human right. To choose our own fate. You are hypocritical, manipulative. We do not want to be what you are. Return us to the Collective!
> JANEWAY: You lost the capacity to make a rational choice the moment you were assimilated. They took that from you, and until I'm convinced you've gotten it back, I'm making the choice for you. You're staying here.
> SEVEN: Then you are no different than the Borg ["The Gift" 4.2].

Janeway cites Seven's inability to make "rational" choices and confirms that the only path to rationality is a complete acceptance of *Janeway's* philosophy and *human* ideology. Even after Seven points out the logical fallacy of Janeway's argument, and its similarity to Collective thinking, Janeway remains fixated on her belief that accepting the dominant culture she has established on Voyager is the only way to be successful.

Also in "The Gift," Kes, who is experiencing a metaphysical change that is damaging to the ship, has decided to leave Voyager in order to further explore who she is (or is meant to become) and to protect the ship (4.2). In a conversation that takes place in her quarters, Kes shares her plan, and Janeway struggles with it. While Janeway fails to concede, she does acknowledge that Kes has the right to make this choice for herself. This is troubling, because in this instance, Janeway is granting freedoms to one person, but denying them to another. This is further evidence that Janeway is treating Seven differently—imposing more restrictions on her—than others. Later, Seven, having "behaved herself,"[5] is granted leeway for a duty assignment in Engineering. Soon, however, that leeway puts Seven at odds with Janeway again when Seven points out that Federation ideology, with its emphasis on exploration, is inconsistent with the goal of getting home. Again, Janeway is faced with a contradiction within her own thinking. She allows Seven the freedom to express an opinion, but silences her at the suggestion of altering established plans.

The episode "Mortal Coil" (4.12) shows viewers something quite different. In order to save Neelix from death, Seven injects him with modified Borg nanoprobes to restore bodily function. We acknowledge two complications in this episode. First, Janeway, through Seven, takes the opportunity to rescue Neelix, regardless of the fact that she may be violating Talaxian burial rituals and, by extension, the Prime Directive.[6] This demonstrates a change from previous stances to the Prime Directive, and it shows that Janeway's adherence can be fluid when it serves the primary mission. In addition, this sets a confusing example for Seven regarding Federation ideology, who has been judged inadequate for her inability to follow the protocol that Janeway set forth. Second and more importantly, we recognize this episode as one where Seven is normalized (accepted) in the eyes of the others because she has a technological solution to the problem. Like Seven's presence during "Scorpion," Seven's actions are permitted, in fact encouraged, because she has the ability to move the mission forward and advance the good of the many (3.26). With that understanding, Seven arrives in Sickbay, sees Neelix's corpse, and offers to essentially bring him back to life, because "his function on this crew is diverse" ("Mortal Coil" 4.12). Seven informs Janeway, Paris, and The Doctor that Neelix can be saved with Borg nanotechnology, but they must act quickly. Certainly, this offer to save Neelix is unBorg-like, but Seven recognizes his impact on the crew. After getting permission from Janeway, Seven begins a series of procedures to save Neelix. It's possible that she is "accepted" in this instance because she has decided to emulate the understanding of the greater good. While this may seem like a step forward, and that the actions taken to save Neelix were necessary and well-intentioned, we suggest it is simply an acquiescence on Seven's part so that she can "fit in" to Federation society.

Throughout several subsequent episodes, Seven seeks to exercise her individuality even if it goes against Janeway's orders. During "Prey" (4.16), Janeway wants to protect an injured member of Species 8472 against Hirogen hunters. Near the end, in an effort to protect the ship and crew, Seven defies Janeway's orders and transports the alien onto a Hirogen vessel. Instead of being pleased that Seven has adopted the human desire to protect her colleagues, Janeway reprimands Seven for condemning the alien to death. After threatening to throw Seven in the brig once again, Janeway turns to leave, and Seven objects that Janeway is punishing her for developing independent thought that does not conform to Janeway's own: "Because I am not becoming more like you. You claim to respect my individuality, but in fact you are frightened by it" ["Prey" 4.16]. A disability-based reading of Seven's last comment suggests that Janeway *is* frightened by Seven's individuality. There is also a strong possibility that Janeway has been leery of it since Seven came aboard, hence, placing her in the brig or confining her to the cargo bay in efforts to isolate her. Again, this is not dissimilar from historical events that isolated those labeled as disabled and other freakish bodies from mainstream view, because the public is not prepared for, what some disability scholars have referred to as "unruly bodies."[7] However genuine that fear may be, Janeway continues to need Seven's expertise and knowledge in a variety of circumstances, and so the debates about humanity, efficiency, and Voyager's overall mission continue.

During "Omega Directive" (4.21), a molecule has been detected that could power their entire journey back to the Alpha quadrant, but Janeway's orders, issued to all Starfleet captains, are to destroy this "omega" molecule because of its immense power. This molecule is believed to be so destructive it cannot be harnessed, and since it cannot be harnessed according to Federation thinking, it must, therefore, be destroyed. Janeway tasks Seven with finding a way to contain the molecule so it can be destroyed, once again calling on Seven's specialized skill set. When Seven finds a way to stabilize the molecule, she asks Janeway to allow her to do so. During her plea, Seven mentions that this molecule is the closest thing she has ever seen to true perfection and is a remnant of what the Borg sought to achieve as a culture (that is, perfection through assimilation). Even though Janeway acknowledges this comparison and notes how much Seven has grown as an individual, Janeway refuses because she cannot look past her orders and indoctrination to accept Seven's potentially life-saving idea. Seven responds:

> SEVEN: I could have done this without your permission, but I chose to follow your command structure. I should have made the attempt. I still can.
> JANEWAY: But you won't ["Omega Directive" 4.21].

And Seven doesn't.

We find the interactions between Janeway and Seven in this episode particularly interesting and revealing. Because as much as Janeway wants Seven to become an individual, and act on her own agency toward her own (or collective) goals, thereby asserting her "humanity" and freeing herself from the collective ideology of the Borg, Janeway maintains strict guidelines for the ways in which Seven can express that humanity. Thus, it seems clear that Seven has substituted one collective for another equally oppressive one.

The final episode of the fourth season reveals Seven questioning whether or not Janeway's "teaching" will work for her. In the episode "Hope and Fear" (4.26), the crew with help from Arturis, an alien able to understand language patterns, have deciphered a transmission from Starfleet that describes the location of a Federation ship that will bring them home with a new warp drive. The crew is abuzz with hopes of returning home sooner than expected. Seven is uncertain she wants to return to Earth and ultimately decides she does not want to. In informing Janeway, she states that Janeway has tried but failed to mold her in Janeway's own image.

> JANEWAY: I won't argue that you've turned out differently than I expected, and that we often have conflicting points of view. But right now, the stakes are higher.

> This crew needs your expertise. Abandon them and you diminish their chances of getting home.
> SEVEN: Irrelevant.
> JANEWAY: No, it's not. We've given you a lot, Seven. It's time you gave something in return.
> SEVEN: I have, on many occasions. Now I refuse ["Hope and Fear" 4.26].

Here, Janeway knows what is best for Seven, despite Seven's decision. In this conversation, Janeway points to her perception of Seven's inability to cope with a new situation, which disables Seven yet again. Seven pushes back on the assertion and declares she is capable of making this decision. Further, Seven tells Janeway that the indoctrination of Federation ideology has been unsuccessful and that those ideals and values are "inefficient" and "irrational." Janeway pushes back too and tells Seven that the resources Janeway has put into Seven have been extensive and now she must pay them back by assisting with this current dilemma. Yet, Seven refuses. While it is clear in this scene that Janeway does not recognize Seven as a person capable of making her own decisions and, therefore, she must make them for her, it is just as important to point out that Seven is utilized as a resource when it furthers Janeway's mission. Even when Seven refuses, Janeway argues that Seven's debt hasn't been paid back to the crew and that she must continue helping them achieve the goal of returning home. Seven, like many PWD, is not seen as capable, or able to make her own decisions, and is cajoled into functioning within a normalized, in this case Federation, culture.

Janeway silences Seven multiple times and orders her to comply but also suggests that Seven should work harder to be an individual. But individuality is counter to following orders and Federation ideology. If we compare this interaction to our society, we recognize that a similar relationship exists between "abled" society and "disabled" society in that the ableist mindset is posited as correct and appropriate, even if a more productive or useful way is provided. Janeway functions as society in general and pushes an ableist ideology. To be more precise, Janeway/society use PWD or those labeled as disabled when it serves them and works to their advantage. Yet, when the opportunity to hear the opinions of or take actions on behalf of those same people, Janeway/society do not always cling to their principles so closely and, ultimately, do what they think is best. This silences PWD and disenfranchises them to be little more than token examples of the normalized society and further entrenches their stigma.

Resistance Is Futile

In *Living with Star Trek: American Culture and the Star Trek Universe*, Lincoln Geraghty reminds his readers of *Star Trek's* purpose. He writes,

Star Trek's goal is to promote the multicultural future of America, however impossible it may seem. Gene Roddenberry's ideological foundation for the series was to show that there was such a thing as "Infinite Diversity in Infinite Combinations (IDIC)" [91].

In this essay, we demonstrated differences as disabling but also part of *Star Trek*'s infinite diversity. Disability scholar Tobin Siebers points out that "Disability is not a physical or mental defect but a cultural and minority identity" (4). Certainly, we can position the Maquis and Seven into this paradigm. Yet, we must also be mindful that "disability" is contradictory in our cultural usage. For example, those labeled with a disability often do not consider themselves disabled, but they are labeled *as disabled* when it may serve only as marker or stigma, not (in)ability. Likewise, we've demonstrated Torres and Seven as being disabled, but their skills being necessary for the crew to be "abled" to *do* something. Thus, we must, too, recognize the importance of disability studies, which as Siebers explains, is "never forgetting that its reason for being is to speak out, for, and with disabled people" (5). Understanding this charge, Siebers posits a number of ideas, but one stands out because it recognizes the vast potential of realizing that disability is *not* disabling and, more importantly, is a way to see through the label of disability and transform it into new ways of knowledge making: "Disabilities are the gateway to special abilities" (10). Without the label of "disabled" saddling the Maquis and Seven, their unique abilities may not have been acknowledged or understood. So while we are concerned about the label, we must realize a particular usefulness and utility of it.

Through *Voyager* we see two distinct groups become one crew working together. For those who know the *Trek* universe well, this seems to be an expected outcome and matches with the endings that episodic television tends to create—that of resolution occurring within the space of a given timeframe. In many ways, however, *Voyager* challenged the ways that other versions of *Star Trek* accomplished that goal. Not only were there diverse crewmembers aboard the ship who had distinct religious and cultural perspectives, but several characters were initially opposed to the very nature of the mission and the guidelines within which it was being carried out. Given this framework, we acknowledge the breadth of possible stories and complications that the writers managed.

Initially, the Maquis are the main stumbling block, as they were placed against the Federation ideology represented by Janeway. Janeway created a disabling and stigmatizing environment for the Maquis that was normalized, and, therefore, stabilized, only after indoctrination and education. The dominant culture Janeway established aboard ship was not based on ethnicity, religious belief, or physical appearance. Rather, it was based on a common set of practices and way of thinking. Therefore, with these as examples, we challenge disability scholar Tom Shakespeare who writes, it is necessary to have an impairment to experience disabling barriers. Impairments may not be sufficient cause for the difficulties which disabled people face, but they are a necessary one. If there is no link between impairment and disability, then disability becomes a much broader, vaguer term that describes any form of socially imposed restriction [34].

While we certainly understand the need for such a link in modern society, the worlds created within the *Star Trek* universe continually redefine notions of acceptability. As the prejudices of race and physical appearance fall away, group dynamics still finds ways to isolate undesirable elements, stigmatize them, and disable them. Because we posit the idea that disability is present within all civilizations, whether it uses a nomenclature we currently recognize or not, we nonetheless need to acknowledge disabling behaviors and characterizations in order to avoid the discrimination that follows.

Once acknowledged, we need to take progressive steps towards an inclusive future. Sometimes in complicated ways, *Voyager* offers glimpses of that future. For example, there were times that the Voyager crew chose not to follow protocol, but instead favored "the good of the many," the success of the overall mission, or some personal ideology, such as Tuvok's in saving that crew member or Seven transporting Species 8472 to the Hirogens.

In reflection, we see these actions taken not in opposition to Federation ideology, but rather as recognition that one ideology cannot serve a multicultural group successfully. Though some readers may view Janeway's sometimes conflicted approach as problematic, it nevertheless coincides with inclusive thinking and points to one that does not (ultimately) devalue or stigmatize people. Though we have spent much of this essay detailing an understanding of disability and used that as a lens to highlight the struggles between the Federation, the Maquis, and the Borg, we have also demonstrated that these "others" are often required in order to achieve particular goals. This fusing of crews and ideologies into a cooperative unit coupled with the understanding of how (and why) they were stigmatized did not stifle their ability in creating relationships, learn from each other, and find ways to make it all work and that, perhaps, is the greatest lesson of all.

NOTES

1. Though some refer to Disability Studies in lower case, we choose to do so using upper case, thereby designating it as a field of study and to avoid confusion regarding certain sentence constructions.

2. Our source for *Voyager* scripts used British spellings; we have changed them to the common American spelling.

3. Mitchell and Snyder analyze *Oedipus Rex* and suggest that Oedipus is able to solve the riddle of the Sphinx due to his own disability (60–61).

4. For a more historical discussion of placing PWDs in asylums, see Kim E. Nielsen's *A Disability History of the United States,* Simi Linton's *Claiming Disability,* and Zosha Stuckey's *A Rhetoric of Remnants.*

5. Namely, remaining in the cargo bay and not challenging the dominant narrative ("Day of Honor" 4.3).

6. The Prime Directive is a multi-faceted set of 47 directives that at its core has a non-interference protocol that includes not informing less advanced species of mission or more advanced technology and also not interfering with a society's natural development.

7. For detailed accounts of these events from a Disability Studies perspective, readers can review Robert Bogdan's *Freak Show* and David Mitchell and Sharon Snyder's *The Body and Physical Difference*.

Works Cited

Baynton, Douglas C. "Disability and the Justification for Inequality in American History." *The New Disability History: American Perspectives*. Ed. Paul K. Longmore and Lauri Umansky. NYU, 2001. 33–58.

Bogdan, Robert. *Freak Show: Presenting Human Oddities for Amusement and Profit*. U of Chicago P., 1998.

Cameron, Colin, ed. *Disability Studies: A Student Guide*. Sage, 2014.

"Caretaker." *Star Trek: Voyager: The Complete Series*, written by Michael Piller and Jeri Taylor, directed by Winrich Kolbe, Season 1, episode 1, Paramount, 16 Jan. 1995.

"Dark Frontier." *Star Trek: Voyager*, written by Joe Menosky and Brannon Braga, directed by Terry Windell and Cliff Bole, Season 5, episodes 15 and 16, Paramount, 17 Feb. 1999.

"Federation Charter." *Memory Alpha*. http://memory-alpha.wikia.com/wiki/Federation_Charter. 24 May 2018.

Geraghty, Lincoln. *Living with Star Trek: American Culture and the Star Trek Universe*. I.B. Tauris, 2007.

Goffman, Erving. *Stigma: Notes on the Management of Spoiled Identity*. 1986 Touchstone Reprint. Simon & Schuster, 1963.

"Hope and Fear." *Star Trek: Voyager: The Complete Series*, teleplay by Brannon Braga and Joe Menosky, directed by Winrich Kolbe, Season 4, episode 26, Paramount, 20 May 1998.

"Learning Curve." *Star Trek: Voyager*, created by Rick Berman, Michael Piller, and Jeri Taylor. Dir. Kim Freidman, Season 1, episode 16, Paramount, 22 May 1995.

Lehmann, Llana. *All You Need to Know About Disability Is on Star Trek*. Mind Meld Media, 2014.

Linton, Simi. *Claiming Disability*. NYU, 1998.

Mitchell, David T., and Sharon L. Snyder. *Narrative Prosthesis: Disability and the Dependencies of Discourse*. U of Michigan P 2000.

Mitchell, David T., and Sharon L. Snyder. Eds. *The Body and Physical Difference: Discourses of Disability*. U of Michigan P, 1997.

"Mortal Coil." *Star Trek: Voyager*, written by Bryan Fuller, directed by Allan Kroeker, season 4, episode 12, Paramount, 17 Dec. 1997.

Nielsen, Kim E. *A Disability History of the United States*. Beacon Press, 2012.

"The Omega Directive." *Star Trek: Voyager*, teleplay by Lisa Klink, directed by Victor Lobl, Season 4, episode 21, Paramount, 15 Apr. 1998.

"Parallax." *Star Trek: Voyager*, written by Brannon Braga, directed by Kim Friedman, season 1, episode 2, Paramount, 23 Jan. 1995.

"Phage." *Star Trek: Voyager: The Complete Series*, teleplay by Skye Dent and Brannon Braga, directed by Winrich Kolbe, Season 1, episode 5, Paramount, 6 Feb. 1995.

"Prey." *Star Trek: Voyager*, Brannon Braga, directed by Allan Eastman, Season 4, episode 16, Paramount, 18 Feb. 1998.

"Random Thoughts." *Star Trek: Voyager*, written by Kenneth Biller, directed by Alexander Singer, Season 4, episode 10, Paramount, 19 Nov. 1997.

Riley, Charles A. II. *Disability and the Media: Prescriptions for Change*. New England UP.

"Scorpion, Part I." *Star Trek: Voyager: The Complete Series*, written by Brannon Braga and Joe Menosky, directed by David Livingston, Season 3, episode 26, Paramount, 21 May 1997.

"Scorpion, Part II." *Star Trek: Voyager*, written by Brannon Braga and Joe Menosky, directed by Winrich Kolbe, Season 4, episode 1, Paramount, 3 Sept. 1997.
Shakespeare, Tom. *Disability Rights and Wrongs*. Routledge, 2006.
Siebers, Tobin. *Disability Theory*. U of Michigan P, 2008.
Stuckey, Zosha. *A Rhetoric of Remnants*. SUNY Press, 2014.
"The Voyager Transcripts—Episode Listings." chakoteya.net. http://www.chakoteya.net/ Voyager/episode_listing.htm. 24 May 2018.
"Year of Hell, Part I." *Star Trek: Voyager*, written by Brannon Braga and Joe Menosky, directed by Allan Kroeker, Season 4, episode 8, Paramount, 5 Nov. 1997.
"Year of Hell, Part II." *Star Trek: Voyager*, written by Brannon Braga and Joe Menosky, directed by Mike Vejar, Season 4, episode 9, Paramount, 12 Nov. 1997.

B'Elanna Torres and the Hated Half
Negotiating Mixed-Race/Species Identity

SHERRY GINN

The search for a sense of self and the development of a personal identity are tasks undertaken by all human beings and, according to psychologists Erik Erikson, James Marcia and others, this search is particularly relevant during adolescence. Cognitive as well as physical changes provide the boost needed for reflection and adolescents begin to search for how they fit into the world. This can be especially problematic for those who find themselves attempting to develop a sense of not only personal but public identity as well. One aspect of that public identity is ethnicity, with mixed-"race"/ethnic[1] youth having a much more difficult time navigating this search than those for whom questions of ethnicity pose no problem. Science fiction allows for the exploration of this issue, generally by positioning alien characters who represent the ethnic Other against the generally European-American hegemony. Such an exploration occurred in Gene Roddenberry's *Star Trek* series broadcast from 1966 through 2001 with at least one character in each series serving as an Other against which humanity could be evaluated: Mr. Spock in *The Original Series* (TOS); Deanna Troi and Data in *The Next Generation* (TNG); Odo in *Deep Space Nine* (DS9); and two characters in *Voyager*, B'Elanna Torres and Seven of Nine.

A fan of *Star Trek* from the very beginning, I confess that *Voyager* was never my favorite series.[2] Although I was unhappy with the way that events played out on *Voyager*, especially after the addition of Seven of Nine, this entry into the *Star Trek* universe was quite positive in its portrayal of women (Ginn 118–122). Unlike the charges leveled against *TNG*, the women of *Voyager* were placed in positions of power on the ship, ones that would normally be filled by men on the other Treks. These women developed healthy and respectful relationships with each other, although there were times when petty jealousy and unnecessary competition developed (see Sobstyl, for example). And, that is one aspect of *Voyager* that we can be thankful for: women were given positions of power and authority. They were portrayed as competent human beings, capable of handling pressure, capable of failing, and capable of succeeding. And, even though these women had problems within their lives, they tried their best to overcome all obstacles, even when those obstacles were of their own making. This is especially true of B'Elanna Torres, the half–Klingon, half-human woman who quickly becomes Chief Engineer of Voyager.

This essay will examine Torres and her evolution over the course of *Voyager*'s seven-season run. It will have two parts. First, I introduce Erik Erikson's psychological theory about identity development along with research especially related to racial/ethnic identity, paying particular attention to research that was current during the run of *Voyager* (1995–2001). Second, I discuss B'Elanna Torres and her character's development over the course of the series using specific episodic examples from *Voyager*'s broadcast run, illustrating her development in terms of Erikson's theory.

Psychosocial Development and Identity Formation

Erik Erikson proposed that development of the personality proceeds through a series of eight stages, with each stage occurring in response to the social demands placed upon the individual by his or her environment. The individual must resolve a conflict occurring in response to environmental demands. Resolution of the conflict leads to growth and psychological development. That is, resolving the conflict at any particular stage compels the individual toward growth and failure to resolve the conflict results in failure to develop. Each of Erikson's stages is a time of increased vulnerability but also a time of challenge and potential, representing a turning point in life.

The first stage, which Erikson labeled Trust vs. Mistrust, encompasses the first year of life. The infant must come to trust that his or her caregivers will fulfill his or her needs for food, warmth, comfort, and love. Feelings of physical comfort coupled with a minimal amount of fear about the future set the stage for the lifelong expectation that the world will be a good place in which to live. When the child fails to have its needs met, he or she will come to mistrust not only his or her caregivers, but also others in his or her social environment as well.

The second stage of Autonomy vs. Self-doubt arises during the second and third years of the child's life with the first demands for self-sufficiency and individualism. By this time of life, the child is learning to walk and talk, and the parents now demand that the child toilet-train. Successful resolution of this stage leads the child to begin life independently of the parents. Mastery of bodily functions and an ability to take charge and control leads to the transition to the third stage of Initiative vs. Guilt.

Now the child becomes even more independent and begins interacting with its world, primarily through fantasy and play. These activities serve the purpose of preparing the child for the roles that it will assume as an adult. Behavior becomes active and purposeful within an ever-widening social environment. In addition, the child assumes greater and greater responsibility for his or her body, toys, pets, and behavior. Erikson cautioned parents to allow the child freedom to pursue play; the child must learn how to interact with other people. If the child's attempts to master its environment are denied, anxiety and guilt may develop. However, Erikson believed that such learned guilt was easily relieved whenever the child experienced a sense of accomplishment.

Erikson called the fourth stage Industry vs. Inferiority. Children begin formal education during this stage and come into contact with people other than the parents. These new people begin to exert influence over the child. The industrious child will learn to master the rigors of school while also learning to deal with more and more people within its social environment. Children should be directing all of their energy during this period of development toward mastering their own intellectual skills. Erikson cautioned parents, saying that a child must be allowed to develop at his or her own pace as he or she learns about the world.

During adolescence the child confronts the questions "Who am I and why am I here?" The heart of the fifth stage of development, Identity vs. Role-confusion, is the identity crisis. The adolescent must confront the roles that he or she has played in his or her life to this point and synthesize these roles into a cohesive identity. Adolescents must be allowed to explore new and different roles or a different path in a former role; they seek to find what is unique and distinctive about them compared to their peers. In addition, they confront themselves with respect to their morals and values, political, religious and spiritual beliefs, and sexual identity. Failure to synthesize an identity leads to the inability to find direction in life and pursue a meaningful future.

Following identity development, the adolescent enters young adulthood, in which the overwhelming social pressure is to find a mate. Increasingly intimate relationships with friends and the drive toward marriage and procreation characterize the young adult stage of Intimacy vs. Isolation. Thus, young adulthood is a period of childbearing and childrearing.[3]

Middle adulthood, named Generativity vs. Stagnation, is characterized by launching one's children into the world. The individual's children are now entering into their own 4th or 5th stages of development and the middle-aged individual may feel a need to "give-back" to the world. The person becomes concerned with future generations; this concern may manifest itself in charitable work. However, the primary task of this stage is helping younger generations of people develop useful and productive lives.[4]

Finally, the individual enters the last stage of Integrity vs. Despair. The individual must look back upon his or her life and be satisfied. He or she should have developed a positive outlook throughout the previous seven stages. If s/he has done so, then reflection will show a life well spent. Not every decision was a wise one and life may not have turned out exactly as one wanted; however, failure to look back upon one's life with satisfaction yields despair.

Erikson's theory of psychosocial development should be modified, suggest several researchers (S. Archer; Gilligan; Patterson, Sochting, and Marcia; Rogers; Rossan). For example, whereas Erikson proposed that identity decisions are made in the three principal domains of vocation, ideology, and family, Sally L. Archer notes that a wealth of research data suggests that this list should be expanded to include vocational plans, avocation, religious beliefs, sex-role orientation, political ideologies, sexuality, values, friendship, dating, marriage, family and career prioritizing, and ethnicity (34). Whereas Erikson acknowledged that identity issues surface and resurface during each stage of development, others, such as Carol Gilligan, propose that women's identity formation revolves around interpersonal areas of life. That is, women are socialized to pursue intimate relationships and these relationships are more important concerns for female adolescents than is the development of an identity. Indeed, Rogers found care and concern for others was related to the development of a sense of self; the development of intimate bonds with other people predated identity development in young women.

Self-Concept, Racial and Ethnic Identity

One of the most famous experiments in the history of psychology demonstrated the importance of racial identity in children (O'Connell and Russo). Mamie Phipps Clark tested three-year-old Afro-American[5] children in two conditions. In the first, the children were given drawings of a number of stimuli (apple, leaf, orange, mouse, boy, girl) along with a box containing twenty-four crayons of various colors, including brown, black, yellow, white, pink, and tan. She then asked the children to pretend that they were the boy or girl and color the picture the same color they were, after which she asked them to color the other picture the color they wanted to be. Clark's hypothesis was supported: the lighter-skinned children correctly colored the picture. However, the darker-skinned children often colored the picture with white or yellow crayons and some children even used red or green. These results indicated that minority children were aware of their "racial" identity even at the age of three years. The children experienced anxiety over the color of their skin, wanting to be white, already reflecting the negative views society held of them. In the second experiment, children were shown a black and a white doll and were asked with which one they preferred to play. Over 50 percent of the children preferred the white doll. Later, Clark's research was used by the NAACP in its brief to the United States Supreme Court and was mentioned in SCOTUS' landmark Brown vs. Board of Education decision (1954) which declared separate schools for black and white children to be unconstitutional. Clark's research showed that children as young as three are aware of skin color.

Although, three- and four-year-old children can also label themselves as "Black" or "Hispanic," most are unaware of a specific ethnicity, although bilingual pre-schoolers are more likely to be aware of their ethnic identity (Bernal; Bernal and Knight; Shi and Lu). At this early age, young children are not necessarily aware that their race and ethnicity are permanent aspects of their Self. With age children become increasingly aware of how their race and ethnicity are viewed by the dominant culture (Bernal et al.; Hall and Rowan; Sheets and Hollins). Race dissonance is a real phenomenon for many ethnic minorities; it occurs when minority children express preferences for the values of the majority culture or for the people of the majority culture. However, such children do not necessarily express lower self-esteem for themselves. Rather this race dissonance appears to be more of an acknowledgment of the influence of the dominant culture that pervades every aspect of their lives rather than a disparagement of their own culture (Holland; Margie et al). The research results cited above with respect to identity formation in general and ethnic identity in particular were current prior to and during the years in which *Voyager* was on air (1995–2001). Indeed, these research results were reflected in all *Star Treks* airing between 1966 and 2001, especially as illustrated in the character of Mr. Spock, who provides "a template ... whereby aliens are represented by mixed heritage characters whose human side represents whiteness and whose alien side represents the ethnic Other" (Dariotis 66).

Searching for Identity in Star Trek

The story of *Star Trek*'s genesis is well-known (Alexander). Gene Roddenberry wished to present his humanistic views and tackle twentieth-century problems by placing them in twenty-third century space. Much as Rod Serling had been able to present quite subversive and radical stories about contemporary American issues, such as McCarthyism and the Red Scare, in *The Twilight Zone* (1959–1964) without network executives being aware (or so it is claimed), Roddenberry would explore issues such as racism and genocide by presenting such practices as characteristic of aliens encountered by the crew of the starship Enterprise. Nevertheless, as many people have noted in the years since *Star Trek* first aired on NBC television (1966–1969), Earth in the *Star Trek* universe was not necessarily the utopian ideal Roddenberry visualized. A product of his generation, he would have found it difficult to completely rebel against the sociocultural programming of his time, a time of white privilege.[6]

Roddenberry's attempt to present a future in which one's ability truly mattered, rather than attributes such as skin color, ethnicity, nationality, or gender, was moderately successful. Yes, he did indeed manage to integrate the crew of the Enterprise, shocking audiences with a Black female communications officer (see Mafe for more on this and its impact), an Asian helmsman, and a Russian navigator (in the second and third seasons and subsequent films). However, his attempts to place women in positions of power failed, and he was forced to reshoot the pilot episode, replacing Majel Barrett's Number One with a Jewish man. Nevertheless, scripts during the 1960s airing of the series underutilized the non-white actors so much that Nichelle Nichols (Uhura) turned in her resignation, but she was ultimately convinced to stay by no less a personage than Martin Luther King, Jr. (Nichols). One of the major male characters on the series, Mr. Spock—played by the Jewish actor Leonard Nimoy—was of mixed heritage, having a human mother and a Vulcan father. Mr. Spock sought to reconcile the human part of himself with the Vulcan part while navigating the prejudices of both his mother's and his father's people. As Jennifer Stuller notes, even in the enlightened twenty-third century, Spock was "frequently teased by the ship's doctor for his difference" (81).

However, Spock was not the only character in the Star Trek universe of mixed heritage. *The Next Generation* likewise depicted a bi-species crew member—Deanna Troi—who had a human father and a Betazoid mother. Unlike Spock, Troi embraced her mixed-species heritage, stating that she was able to enjoy the best of both worlds by having parents of two different species. Both Spock and Troi had positive views of themselves, but that is not the case with *Voyager*'s B'Elanna Torres.

Torres[7] is mixed-species, with a human father and Klingon mother. Unlike Troi, Torres lost her father John to desertion when she was five years old.[8] Torres loved her mother, Miral. Nevertheless, she hated everything Klingon about Miral, telling crewmate Tom Paris how much she hated learning about and engaging in Klingon rituals when she was a child ("Day of Honor" 4.3). B'Elanna experienced prejudice and discrimination from both humans and Klingons when growing up. According to the *Star Trek Voyager Bible* (recounted by Ruditis), B'Elanna grew up on Kessik IV, a colony populated mostly by humans. She and her mother were the only Klingons on the colony: "No one said anything, but we were different, and I didn't like that feeling," she tells Paris in the Season 1 episode "Faces" (1.13; for further information see Sayers). Like Spock, B'Elanna's physical appearance—much as skin color does today—marked her as different from her contemporaries; she had the forehead ridges characteristic of the Klingons of that time period.[9] Continuing to tell Paris about her childhood, she relates how she was convinced her father left because she was Klingon so she did everything she could to look Human, going so far as to wear hats and scarves to hide her forehead ridges. B'Elanna was called "mutant and ugly" by her schoolmates, "before she learned to strike out first" (Wright 194). B'Elanna's experiences when she was a child illustrate her failure to resolve the conflict of Erikson's stage of Trust vs. Mistrust: although it appears that she experiences great love from her mother and her grandmother when a child, her trust was damaged when her beloved father left. B'Elanna does not have any contact with her father until he reaches out to her after she is lost in the Delta Quadrant ("Author, Author" 7.20). After John Torres' departure in childhood, B'Elanna learned to be self-sufficient, taught by a Klingon mother to be so, but she was ridiculed by schoolmates for her physical characteristics. It would be correct to say that B'Elanna's halves battled against each other and that is to be expected in a child who must learn how to integrate different socio-emotional, cultural, and physical aspects of the Self, as proposed by Erikson's stage of Identity vs. Role-confusion. The attempt to deny physicality can be especially troubling to children's psychological development and can have far-reaching implications. This is especially evident with respect to skin color among women of color, many of whom still show evidence of Clark's research which demonstrated a disconnect between actual and desired skin color (see for example, the documentary *Dark Girls*, Berry and Duke). In B'Elanna's case it is not her skin color that is troubling. Rather it is her forehead ridges that mark her as different and led to her being called "Ms. Turtlehead" by a classmate ("Juggernaut" 5.21).

By the time *Voyager* begins, B'Elanna has grown into a troubled young woman. She originally enrolled in Starfleet Academy but was expelled when only 19 years old for failure to follow the rules, obey commands, and control her temper. After her expulsion she joined the Maquis, a group of so-called freedom fighters named after the French Resistance (in World War II). Following the Federation-mediated peace treaty between the Cardassians and the Bajorans, the boundaries of Federation and Cardassian space were redrawn with many formerly Federation colonies being relocated into Cardassian space. Believing, quite rightly, that the Federation would no longer be able to protect them from the Cardassians, some of the colonists formed the Maquis and began a guerrilla war against their new "masters." Needing a place to call home and a *raison d'être*, B'Elanna joined the Maquis. Following *Voyager*'s relocation into the Delta Quadrant as a result of the Caretaker's actions ("Caretaker" 1.1–1.2; Graf), B'Elanna is eventually chosen to be Chief Engineer. She understands machines and delights in working on them. After her years with the Maquis she is thrilled to be able to work on *Voyager*: "Machines ... didn't look at her warily because she was half–Klingon and known for her temper. She found them much easier to deal with than people. And a modern warp drive was so wonderfully delicate and complex..." (N. Archer 61–62).

According to Erikson, B'Elanna should be in the stage of Intimacy vs. Isolation. By her own admission she had a relationship with a fellow cadet while at the Starfleet Academy; however, that relationship did not last long ("Equinox, Part I" 5.26). She developed a mentoring relationship with Chakotay prior to events on *Voyager* and was attracted to him, although they never acted upon the attraction. Indeed, her sexuality may have contributed to B'Elanna's reticence with her male colleagues, including Tom Paris. According to the *Voyager Bible*, B'Elanna was to be "a fetching young beauty with an incandescent sexuality. She turns many heads, but the person she has designs on is Tom Paris, who won't clutter their professional relationship by having an affair with another officer" (Ruditis 5). Tom Paris, on the other hand, "has an affection for B'Elanna, seeing in her a soul at war and reminding him of himself" (3). Those early descriptions changed within the series, with B'Elanna and Tom eventually marrying. Nevertheless, their early relationship was fraught with misunderstandings even as their friendship and eventual romance grew. Part of the problem, I believe, had to do with her sexuality. Klingon women were as much warriors as the men even if their primary responsibility within Klingon society was to maintain the household and manage their family's affairs. They were considered equals even if they were not allowed to participate in politics. I think that B'Elanna was well aware of the "reputation" Klingon women had, much as women of color have in our society—the Black "animalistic" Jezebel, the "submissive" Asian, and the hot-blooded, "spicy" Latina—and refused to be relegated to such a stereotype. Although never mentioned I think that this might have played on B'Elanna's fears about her father and his attraction to her mother as well as her fear of why Tom was attracted to her. Before she confesses her love to Tom in Season 4 ("Day of Honor" 4.3), she makes comments about his physical interest in her and is leery of him—he does have a reputation as a "ladies' man" (which is quite ironic given that it is his best friend, Harry Kim, who is much more romantically active in the series).

As stated earlier, Torres has a great deal of difficulty accepting the Klingon part of her soul, so much so that she knows little of Klingon rituals, despite her mother's best efforts when she was a child. Freely expressing her Klingon nature frightens her in some ways even if it is part of her, and the episode "Faces" (1.14) provides one example of B'Elanna coming to terms with her divided Self, much as the episode in *TOS* when Kirk is split into two Kirks, one good and one evil, by a transporter accident ("The Enemy Within" 1.5): Torres learns that she needs the Klingon warrior part of her personality in order to survive as a "whole" person. In "Faces" a race called the Vidiians believe that Klingon DNA can cure the hideous disease—the Phage—that has decimated their species. They kidnap B'Elanna and extract a DNA sample from her. Separating the human part from the Klingon, they create two people, one completely Klingon and the other completely Human. Chief Surgeon Sulan keeps Klingon B'Elanna in restraints as he continues his experimentation on her. She fights against her restraints, reveling in her strength, and attempts to seduce her captor although she is unable to control her revulsion at his touch. Human B'Elanna along with Tom Paris and another Voyager crewmember, Peter Durst, are held captive for use as slave labor. Human B'Elanna is terrified and with a pounding heart and shaking hands, tells Tom that the Vidiians turned her into a coward when they extracted the Klingon DNA. Klingon-B'Elanna eventually escapes from captivity and rescues Human-B'Elanna, telling her other self that they will have to fight their way out of the Vidiian complex. As they do, they discuss their respective points of view. Klingon-B'Elanna understands that they are two halves of a whole, that they complement each other, physicality to intellect. Human B'Elanna realizes that, while as a complete Human she is at peace with herself, she does not "feel" like herself. She needs the Klingon half in order to be herself again, acknowledging that she has to accept that she will spend the rest of her life fighting "her." This episode is a good illustration of how B'Elanna has intellectualized the Klingon part of her Self. By that I mean that she understands on an intellectual level, but not an emotional one, that her Klingon half is an integral part of her personality; it is not "her" *per se*, but is part of her Self, part of that which makes her whole. Neal Baker states that in this episode B'Elanna accepts what he terms her Creoleness, a hybridity or "amalgam of Klingon and Human culture, uprooted from the Alpha Quadrant and searching for home" (124).

The trauma of her capture by the Vidiians contributed to B'Elanna's emotional development and led the way toward the development of an identity that acknowledged aspects of herself that she had denied for so long. B'Elanna's experience with prejudice and discrimination when growing up caused her to distance herself from her Klingon self, which was impossible given her physical appearance. That prejudice and discrimination had also caused her to develop an almost all-consuming anger that she could use to deflect any attempts by anyone to get close to her. "Faces" was the beginning of B'Elanna's acceptance of her Klingon heritage; she began to realize that she needed the strength that she had inherited from her Klingon mother in order to survive the trials of the Delta Quadrant.

She comes to more of an emotional acceptance of her nature in the fourth season episode "Day or Honor" when she celebrates the Klingon holiday interacting with a holodeck program, she co-designed with Tom. On the Klingon Day of Honor celebrants determine if they have lived up to Klingon standards during the past year. B'Elanna admits to finally finding the rituals are not as hateful as when she was a child, but is still loath to participate in such rituals as eating the heart of a sanctified targ or drinking *mot'lach* from the grail of Kahless. Nevertheless, she admits her feelings to Tom when she believes that they are about to die. Once rescued, she does celebrate the day by eating the blood pie traditionally served on the holiday.

Throughout seasons 4, 5, 6, and 7, B'Elanna and Tom continue their relationship, eventually marrying in "Drive" (7.3). Prior to his proposal, B'Elanna had planned to end their relationship, telling Neelix that, although she loved Tom, she could not be certain about his feelings for her. Later in Season 7, B'Elanna learns that she is pregnant. Tom is thrilled at the pregnancy and delighted upon learning the child will be a girl. He is also happy when The Doctor creates a computer simulation of what the child will look like. However, all B'Elanna can see are the forehead ridges that set her apart from her human family members and others living on Kessik IV when she was a child. Not wanting her child to grow up being so different and also worrying that Tom will leave her as her father did her mother, she attempts to have all Klingon DNA removed from the fetus prior to birth. Tom convinces her to leave the child's prenatal development to nature and her postnatal development to parents who will love her. B'Elanna honors her mother by naming the child after her: Miral ("Lineage" 7.12).

This episode reveals that B'Elanna has not yet reconciled her past with her present. She is still unable to see beyond her forehead ridges and accept the Klingon aspects of her Self, which are illustrative of her failure to completely resolve the crisis of the Trust vs. Mistrust stage. The most important of Erikson's stages—it lays the foundation for future psychosocial development—B'Elanna is unable to trust those around her, including Tom, to accept her and be there for her. Whereas Tom has never let her down during their years together, first as friends then as lovers and partners, she is still leery of allowing herself to trust him and let him see her as she (believes she) is.[10] It is her pregnancy and birth of her daughter that finally allows B'Elanna to accept the reality of her "Klingon-ness" and realize that others had accepted it long before her. Now, she can complete her quest for an identity, as the

Chief Engineer of Voyager, as the spouse of Tom and the mother of Miral, the daughter of Miral and John, with numerous other people who like and respect her. She can begin the next stage of her life, Intimacy vs. Isolation, as she faces the future.

Conclusions

I believe that Erik Erikson's theory of development does a good job of explaining B'Elanna's psychosocial development; however, I believe that this theory needs to be modified. For example, Erikson conceived of his theory as proceeding in a series of stages, each developing from the previous one. While I do agree with that to a certain extent, I also note other scholars' beliefs that certain of those stages are reversed for men and women, such as the stages of identity and intimacy (see Gilligan for example). It is even possible that the 5th (Identity), 6th (Intimacy), and 7th (Generativity) stages should be reversed for men and women. Both men and women may develop their identities through meaningful work and intimate relationships, and that a sure sense of who we are finally crystallizes after many years of life. B'Elanna Torres provides a good illustration of what James Marcia (401–410) means when he states that identity achievement is more likely to occur in a society that allows its people to explore their options. Thus, a conferred identity is something one has by virtue of his or her place in the world; we become aware of this identity as we learn more about ourselves within the context of our social environment. However, once *We* begin to make decisions about our personal *Self*, then we begin to construct our identity.

Attempting to deny the alien and despised part of herself, B'Elanna rejected learning about her Klingon heritage, which is similar to many immigrants' children, who desperately want to fit into their adopted country, going so far as to refuse to learn their parents' language or cultural mores and values. Torres knew little about Klingon history or customs when *Voyager* began. Once again, a lifetime of ridicule, prejudice, and discrimination had caused her to develop an almost all-consuming anger that she used to deflect attempts by those wishing to get close to her. Nevertheless, as *Voyager* progresses, B'Elanna realizes that she needs the strength she inherited from her Klingon mother in order to survive the trials of the Delta Quadrant. She comes to embrace her difference, recognizing that, like *TNG*'s Deanna Troi, she is special and unique. Whereas Troi is also mixed-species, having a Betazoid mother and a human father, she states that she never had problems with that status when she was young. Rather she celebrated the heritage of both of her parents, "experiencing the richness and diversity of both worlds" ("The Emissary" 2.20).[11] Unlike Troi, B'Elanna did not find it especially easy to develop her identity as a mixed-species woman, but was able to do so by the end of Voyager's journey home.

Thus, B'Elanna struggles throughout the series with her "difference," continually trying to develop a sense of exactly who she is since she is neither completely Human nor completely Klingon. Her struggles resonate with those who are perhaps struggling with their own issues of identity revolving around definitions of race and ethnicity, especially in contemporary American society. The beauty of science fiction is that is allows us to explore ways for self-definition not typical for women or minorities in contemporary society. However, as Adilifu Nama notes "many of [SF's] narratives are fertile sites of ideological meaning as they relate to popular discourses surrounding race" (8), although not necessarily in a straightforward, easily visible fashion. This is especially true of other peoples of color, including those of Hispanic, Asian or First Peoples ethnicity.

B'Elanna's journey—her own journey to a space and a place where she could actualize her Self—coincided with Voyager's. According to *Memory Alpha*, Roxann Dawson stated that Torres began *Voyager* as an "unruly teenager" and "grew into a woman," and I would agree with that statement. She learned that people liked and admired her, sometimes because of her Klingonness and sometimes despite it, and she learned to like and admire that part of her Self as well. Torres was quite heroic and unique. Even 18 years after *Voyager* ended, she continues to provide a role model for the male and female fans who watch the series.

Notes

1. I am aware of the controversy surrounding the term "race," agreeing with most scholars who take the stance that race is an outdated term, given the interbreeding characteristic of human beings over the course of several millennia. Psychologists generally use the term "ethnicity" to refer to peoples who "identify with each other based on similarities such as common ancestry, language, society, culture or nation." The term "species" refers to a group of living organisms consisting of similar individuals capable of exchanging genes or interbreeding. Roddenberry's explanation for his very human-like aliens was parallel evolution, which compels me to think of "Johnny Appleseed" bounding around the universe sowing *Homo sapiens* genes into a variety of environments and letting nature—literally—take its course. This would yield some very interesting specimens indeed.

2. I will be upfront here and now about my age. I watched *Star Trek* from its first episode in 1966. I would have been 11 years old, and I watched the show with my father and my brother. My father did not particularly care for *Star Trek*, but my brother Neal and I were fans. We were science fiction and horror fans from quite an early age. When *The Next Generation* began, my boyfriend—now my spouse—and I watched every Saturday night, in the living room with our supper on a TV tray. That was our "date" night. I have noted elsewhere (Ginn) that many of the female crew in the various Treks are referred to by their first names, for example Deanna Troi and Beverly Crusher are usually referred to as Deanna and Beverly, whereas most male crew members, like O'Brien and Riker, are referred to by their last names. Some suggest that this shows a lack of formality and a sense of familiarity for the women, as well as emphasizing their subordinate status. Herein, I refer to B'Elanna Torres both ways, by first and by last name, in no particular order and for no particular reason.

3. Erikson would have been discussing heterosexual people in his theoretical approach;

however, these issues would be true of homosexuals as well. Many non-heterosexual people want to marry and have children, as recent political movements illustrate.

4. *Voyager* ended after seven seasons on air and in the final season B'Elanna gave birth to a daughter, whom she named after her mother. I would say that Torres begins *Voyager* very much searching for her identity (Erikson's Stage 5) and ends in Stage 6, Intimacy. Captain Janeway appears to be in Stage 7, especially with respect to younger crew members, such as Harry Kim. She is especially nurturing with respect to Seven of Nine, with that relationship taking on a mother-daughter dynamic, although a number of fans have interpreted the relationship as more homoerotic than maternal on Janeway's part ("Kathryn Janeway and Seven of Nine—Works/Archive of Our Own").

5. The term in usage at the time.

6. That is not to say we are not living in a time of white-privilege in the twenty-first century, but at least we now are aware of it.

7. As Bernardi notes, Klingons generally are portrayed by people of color on the various Treks. Given that B'Elanna was to be mixed-species, it stood to reason that a person of color would play the part. Roxann Dawson was born in Los Angeles and is of Puerto Rican heritage (although even if she were born in Puerto Rico, she would still be a U.S. citizen).

8. There is some discrepancy here according to B'Elanna's entry in *Memory Alpha*. "Lineage" states that John left his family when B'Elanna was around eleven or twelve years old. However, three episodes state that she was five or six: "Eye of the Needle" (1.7), "Faces" (1.14), and "Extreme Risk" (5.3). I am inclined to agree that John Torres left his family when B'Elanna was five given the difficulties she had when he left. B'Elanna blamed herself for her father's departure and this would be quite normal given the cognitive development of a five-year-old child. According to Jean Piaget children from approximately 2–7 are in the Preoperational Thought Stage. They are unable to focus their attention on multiple aspects of a given situation or stimulus. They are also egocentric, which is defined as the inability to see beyond their own perspective.

9. Klingon physiognomy has changed greatly during the course of the various *Star Trek* series, with those in the newest entry being the most alien yet. B'Elanna's features are in line with the more humanlike species of *TNG* and are not as alien as those in Season 1 of *Discovery*. Their physiognomy will change again in Season 2. The reason for these dramatic changes was explained at the *Star Trek* convention held in Las Vegas during the summer of 2018 and has to do with Klingon evolution.

10. I have some problems with this episode and other episodes that show B'Elanna gaining an appreciation of her Klingon "half." It is Tom Paris, the able-bodied, heterosexual, white male Human, who teaches the women of color that there is nothing wrong with being Klingon. On the one hand it would be keeping with Erikson's theory of psycho*social* development: people in one's social environment place pressure on one to develop in accordance with social norms and values in conjunction with biological potential. Thus, Tom would be one of the many people who influenced B'Elanna's development, such as Chakotay, Tuvok, and Janeway. On the other hand, the "white, savior narrative" happens so often in literature, film and television that one almost does not see it anymore.

11. Of course, Troi looks completely Human, with no apparent Betazoid features.

WORKS CITED

Alexander, David. *Star Trek Creator: The Authorized Biography of Gene Roddenberry.* ROC Books, 1994.
Archer, Nathan. *Ragnarok: Star Trek Voyager* #3. Pocket Books, 1995.
Archer, Sally L. "A Feminist's Approach to Identity Research." *Adolescent Identity Formation*, edited by Gerald R. Adams, Thomas P. Gullotta, and Raymond Montemayor, Sage, 1992, pp. 25–49.
"Author, Author." *Star Trek: Voyager*, created by Jeri Taylor, Gene Roddenberry, Rick Berman, and Michael Piller, performance by Roxann Dawson, Season 7, episode 20, Paramount, 18 Apr. 2001.

Part III. Negotiating Identities

Baker, Neal. "Creole Identity Politics, Race, and *Star Trek: Voyager.*" *Into Darkness Peering: Race and Color in the Fantastic*, edited by Elisabeth A. Leonard, Greenwood, 1997, pp. 119–129.
B'Elanna Torres. *Memory Alpha.* http://memory-alpha.wikia.com/wiki/B%27Elanna_Torres. Accessed 1 April 2018.
Bernal, Martha E. "Ethnic Identity in Mexican-American Children." Address at the Annual Meeting of the American Psychological Association, Los Angeles, CA, 1994.
Bernal, Martha E., and George P. Knight (Eds). *Ethnic Identity: Formation and Transmission Among Hispanics and Other Minorities.* State University of New York Press, 2001.
Bernal, Martha E., et al. "The Development of Ethnic Identity in Mexican-American Children." *Hispanic Journal of Behavioral Sciences*, vol. 12, no. 1, 1990, pp. 3–24.
Bernardi, Daniel Leonard. *Star Trek and History: Race-ing Toward a White Future.* Rutgers UP, 1998.
Berry, D. Channsin, and Bill Duke, directors. *Dark Girls.* Duke Media and Urban Winter Entertainment, 2011.
"Caretaker." *Star Trek: Voyager*, created by Jeri Taylor, Gene Roddenberry, Rick Berman, and Michael Piller, performance by Roxann Dawson, Season 1, episodes 1 and 2, Paramount, 16 Jan. 1995.
Clark, Mamie P. "Changes in Primary Mental Abilities with Age." *Archives of Psychology,* vol. 291. Columbia UP, 1944.
Dariotis, Wei Ming. "Crossing the Racial Frontier: *Star Trek* and Mixed Heritage Identities." *The Influence of* Star Trek *on Television, Film, and Culture*, edited by Lincoln Geraghty. McFarland, 2008, pp. 63–81.
"Day of Honor." *Star Trek: Voyager*, created by Jeri Taylor, Gene Roddenberry, Rick Berman, and Michael Piller, performance by Roxann Dawson, Season 4, episode 3, Paramount, 17 Sept. 1997.
"Drive." *Star Trek Voyager*, created by Jeri Taylor, Gene Roddenberry, Rick Berman, and Michael Piller, performance by Roxann Dawson, Season 7, episode 3, Paramount, 18 Oct. 2000.
"The Emissary." *Star Trek: The Next Generation*, created by Gene Roddenberry, performance by Marina Sirtis, Season 2, episode 20, Paramount, 29 June 1989.
"The Enemy Within." *Star Trek*, created by Gene Roddenberry, performance by William Shatner, Season 1, episode 5, Paramount, 6 Oct. 1966.
"Equinox, Part I." *Star Trek Voyager*, created by Jeri Taylor, Gene Roddenberry, Rick Berman, and Michael Piller, performance by Roxann Dawson, Season 5, episode 26, Paramount, 26 May 1999.
Erikson, Erik H. *Childhood and Society.* W.W. Norton, 1950.
_____. *Dimensions of a New Identity.* W.W. Norton, 1974.
_____. *Identity and the Life Cycle* (2nd Ed.). W.W. Norton, 1980.
_____. *Identity: Youth and Crisis.* W.W. Norton, 1968.
_____. *The Life Cycle Completed: A Review.* W.W. Norton, 1982.
"Extreme Risk." *Star Trek Voyager*, created by Jeri Taylor, Gene Roddenberry, Rick Berman, and Michael Piller, performance by Roxann Dawson, Season 5, episode 3 Paramount, 28 Oct. 1998.
"Eye of the Needle." *Star Trek Voyager*, created by Jeri Taylor, Gene Roddenberry, Rick Berman, and Michael Piller, performance by Roxann Dawson, Season 1, episode 7, Paramount, 20 Feb. 1995.
"Faces." *Star Trek Voyager*, created by Jeri Taylor, Gene Roddenberry, Rick Berman, and Michael Piller, performance by Roxann Dawson, Season 1, episode 14, Paramount, 8 May 1995.
"The Gift." *Star Trek: Voyager*, written by Joe Menosky, directed by Anson Williams, Season 4, episode 2, Paramount, 10 Sept. 1997.
Gilligan, Carol. *In a Different Voice: Psychological Theory and Women's Development.* Harvard UP, 1982.
Ginn, Sherry. *Our Space, Our Place: Women in the Worlds of Science Fiction Television.* U Press America, 2005.

Graf, L.A. *Caretaker: Star Trek Voyager #1*. Pocket Star Books, 1995.
Hall, Ronald E., and George T. Rowan. "Identity Development Across the Lifespan: Alternative Model for Biracial Americans." *Psychology and Education: An Interdisciplinary Journal*, vol. 40, 2003, pp. 3–12.
Holland, N. "Race Dissonance: Implications for African American Children." Paper Presented at the Annual Meeting of the American Psychological Association, Los Angeles, CA, 1994.
"Juggernaut." *Star Trek Voyager*, created by Jeri Taylor, Gene Roddenberry, Rick Berman, and Michael Piller, performance by Roxann Dawson, Season 5, episode 21, Paramount, 26 Apr. 1999.
"Kathryn Janeway and Seven of Nine—Works/Archive of Our Own." *Organization of Transformative Works*. https://archiveofourown.org/tags/Kathryn%20Janeway*s*Seven%20of%20Nine/works. Accessed 24 July 2018.
"Lineage." *Star Trek Voyager*, created by Jeri Taylor, Gene Roddenberry, Rick Berman, and Michael Piller, performance by Roxann Dawson, Season 7, episode 12, Paramount, 24 Jan. 2001.
Mafe, Diana Adesola. *Where No Black Woman Has Gone Before: Subversive Portrayals in Speculative Film and TV*. U Texas P, 2018.
Marcia, James. "Identity and Intervention." *Journal of Adolescence*, vol. 12, 1989, pp. 401–410.
Margie, Nancy, et al. "Minority Children's Intergroup Attitudes About Peer Relationships." *British Journal of Developmental Psychology*, vol. 23, 2005, pp. 251–269.
Nama, Adilifu. *Black Space: Imagining Race in Science Fiction Film*. U Texas Press, 2008.
Nichols, Nichelle. *Beyond Uhura: Star Trek and Other Memories*. G.P. Putnam's Sons, 1994.
O'Connell, Agnes, and Nancy P. Russo. (Ed.) *Models of Achievement: Reflections of Eminent Women in Psychology*. Columbia UP, 2001.
Patterson, Serena J., Ingrid Sochting, and James E. Marcia. "The Inner Space and Beyond: Women and Identity." *Adolescent Identity Formation*, edited by Gerald R. Adams, Thomas P. Gullotta, and Raymond Montemayor, Sage, 1992, pp. 9–24.
Piaget, Jean, and Bärbel Inhelder. *The Psychology of the Child*, 2nd ed. Basic Books, 2000.
Roberts, Robin A. "Science, Race, and Gender in *Star Trek: Voyager*." *Fantasy Girls: Gender in the New Universe of Science Fiction and Fantasy Television*, edited by Elyce R. Helford, Rowman and Littlefield, 2000, pp. 203–221.
_____. *Sexual Generations: Star Trek: The Next Generation" and Gender*. U of Illinois P, 1999.
_____. "The Woman Scientist in *Star Trek Voyager*." *Future Females, the Next Generation: New Voices and Velocities in Feminist Science Fiction Criticism*, edited by Marleen S. Barr, Rowman and Littlefield, 2000, pp. 277–290.
Rogers, A. "Questions of Gender Differences: Ego Development and Moral Voice in Adolescence." Unpublished manuscript. Harvard University, 1987.
Rossan, Sheila. "Identity and Its Development in Adulthood." *Self and Identity: Perspectives Across the Life Span*, edited by Terry Honess and Krysia M. Yardley, Routledge and Kegan Paul, 1987, pp. 304–319.
Ruditis, Paul. *Star Trek Voyager Companion*. Pocket Books, 2003.
Sayers, John (synopsis). "Faces." *The Official Star Trek Voyager Magazine #4*, October 1995, pp. 17–24.
Sheets, Rosa H., and Etta R. Hollins. *Racial and Ethnic Identity in School Practices*. Erlbaum, 1999.
Shi, Xiaowei, and Xing Lu. "Bilingual and Bicultural Development of Chinese American Adolescents and Young Adults: A Comparative Study." *Howard Journal of Communications*, vol. 18, no. 4, 2007, pp. 313–333.
Sobstyl, Edrie. "We Who Are Borg, Are We Borg?" *Athena's Daughters: Television's New Women Warriors*, edited by Frances Early and Kathleen Kennedy, Syracuse UP, 2003, pp. 119–132.
Stuller, Jennifer K. *Ink-Stained Amazons and Cinematic Warriors: Superwomen in Modern Mythology*. I.B. Taurus, 2010.
Wright, Susan. *Violations: Star Trek Voyager #4*. Pocket Books, 1995.

Foreheads, Bad Attitudes and Mothers

Dismantling the Nuclear Family

Eileen Totter

The *Star Trek* franchise is famous for its alien characters who set themselves apart from humanity, even if they are influenced by human culture themselves. Mister Spock has a human mother, but his character arc involves his attempts to reject his humanity in favor of Vulcan culture. Worf was raised by humans and did not have serious contact with other Klingons until adulthood, but still identifies as strictly Klingon. In both cases, hybrid characters strictly define themselves as alien and Other, with supposedly no traces of human culture in their psyche. *Star Trek* fans are familiar with the concept of inclusion, but intersectionality requires further definition. Intersectionality analyzes how multiple factors (for example, race *and* gender) shape a marginalized person's experiences, rather than "merely" race *or* gender. The concept of intersectionality does not factor into classic *Star Trek*'s diversity. Spock has human and Vulcan ancestry, but only connects with Vulcan culture and society—while he loves his human mother, he cannot relate to her in human terms. *Star Trek: Voyager*, however, presents human/Klingon B'Elanna Torres grumbling to her partner, Tom Paris, that the only aspects she inherited concerning Klingon culture are the appearance and the attitude ("Barge of the Dead" 6.3). While this moment reflects B'Elanna's series-long discomfort with her alien heritage, it also implies that she accepts that it is part of her, unlike her predecessors. While every *Star Trek* cast is diverse (reflecting Gene Roddenberry's belief that racism will not be a part of the twenty-third/twenty-fourth century person's psyche), multiple episodes deal with an alien (often male) character seeing race as a binary struggle—the most famous example is, of course, Mister Spock's own refusal to accept his diverse ancestry. Spock must choose Vulcan control or Human emotion—a compromise between the two is never entertained. The idea of biracial identity is non-existent in preceding *Star Trek* television programs.

Older *Star Trek* lacks intersectionality when it comes to gender as well. Even characters defined by their struggle with their identities such as Mister Spock and Worf still come from stable, heterosexual unions. Indeed, for a franchise that has never shied away from conventionally attractive women in skimpy clothes, marriage in *Star Trek* is presented in virtually Victorian terms. Almost every marriage in *Star Trek* is happy and stable,[1] with death as the only force that can separate a heterosexual union. The clearest examples are James Kirk and Miramanee ("The Paradise Syndrome" 3.3), Beverly and Jack Crusher ("Encounter at Farpoint" 1.1–1.2), and Ben and Jennifer Sisko ("Emissary" 1.1–1.2). With the exception of Beverly Crusher, the wife always dies, regranting the former bridegroom time and freedom to explore the universe again. Later programs would try to present marital death in more realistic terms: Ben Sisko clearly mourns for his wife Jennifer and is a devoted single father. However, he is the exception rather than the rule. Families in *Star Trek* are presented in terms twentieth century Americans would identify as positive: a stable, heterosexual marriage with both parents conforming to gender roles: Sarek is still an ambassador, while Amanda has retired from teaching to become a full-time wife to Sarek (*TOS*, "This Side of Paradise" 1.24). There are no attempts to explore the dynamics of a "dysfunction" family in the franchise. Like with race and identities, *Star Trek* presents marriage in strict binary terms: once the characters are married, they enter a traditional, nuclear family unit, with death the only force powerful to break them apart.

Thus, the nuclear family in *Star Trek* follows traditional gender roles for marriage, despite the backdrop of a supposed truly equal world. The mother is the caregiver, but the father is often the parent in the foreground, serving as a mentor to his biological or surrogate child. Such a role reflects the general consensus concerning fatherhood in the middle twentieth century, ultimately shaping *Star Trek* (1966), and influencing the following *Star Trek: The Next Generation* (1987) and *Star Trek: Deep Space Nine* (1993). Jessica Weiss summarizes the father's expected role as such in *To Have and to Hold: Marriage, the Baby Boom, and Social Change* (2000): fathers were more than merely breadwinners, providing "guidance and companionship" (85), while the mother's role was associated with the drudge work of the house and child rearing (85). This understanding of gendered parental roles is reflected in the *Star Trek* franchise, to the point where the mother's presumed less exciting domestic adventures are not seen. Mothers in *Star Trek* are often conveniently dead or vanish off screen. Carol Marcus raises her son David unassisted, but Kirk is the man he learns to admire in *Wrath of Khan*. Later, Kirk mourns and avenges his son in *The Search for Spock* and *The Undiscovered Country*, but we never see David's mother Carol Marcus grieve, or even learn of his death. In *TNG*, Worf spends multiple episodes defending the honor of his biological father Mogh or raising his son Alexander. Worf's mother, however, is a nameless entity in the show. Additionally, Worf's mate K'Ehleyr is murdered in the same episode Worf learns that Alexander is their child ("Reunion" 4.7). The fathers (even if they are not traditionally married) become the only parent, symbolically and metaphorically, once the child is old enough to receive moral instruction.

This attitude extends to the mothers who survive in the *Star Trek* franchise as well: Beverly Crusher's relationship to her son Wesley is often ignored (in one infamous case, for a whole season) in favor of surrogate father Jean-Luc Picard. Crusher's actress, Gates McFadden, noted this gendered imbalance while speaking at a panel at Austin Comic Con 2012 alongside Marina Sirtis. During the panel, McFadden implies that one of the reasons she was fired between Season 1 and Season 3 is because she argued with at least one writer that it made no sense that Crusher's son Wesley received all moral guidance from male figures in the show, while his mother remained a background influence at best, despite their biological link (McFadden). McFadden also reinforces that while the mother being integral to the child's moral growth as well, she is rarely if ever seen in American popular culture (McFadden). McFadden's experiences early in *TNG*'s production history underscore what Weiss discusses: fathers are allowed to be active and inspirational in American thought and in the pop culture it reflects. Mothers are not granted that luxury.

A clear example of McFadden's argument is found in the *TNG* episode "The First Duty" (5.19), when Wesley Crusher is involved in a cover up after one of his classmates was killed in an accident. While Crusher provides background support, she never suspects her son may not be telling the truth. Meanwhile, father figure Picard not only deduces something is amiss in Wesley's explanation, but also inspires him to privilege the truth over his own scholastic career ("The First Duty"). As Weiss demonstrates, father Picard provides moral guidance, while mother Crusher cannot even tell her son is lying. While *TNG* was more progressive than its predecessor with a lengthy, mostly positive depiction of a single mother, family roles, surrogate or biological, remained strictly static.

Later examples of gendered parental roles in *Star Trek: Deep Space Nine* follow the mold that McFadden outlines, even as the franchise flirted with remarriage and step-parents. While Sisko's arc as a single father plays a major role in *Star Trek: Deep Space Nine*, his late wife Jennifer is rarely mentioned as an influence on Jake. Ferengi Rom fiercely defends his son Nog's decision to enter Starfleet ("Facets" 3.25), but Nog's mother Prinadora is never seen. The one time she is mentioned is when Rom's brother Quark notes how Rom's former father-in-law used the marriage to swindle Rom out of his savings ("Doctor Bashir, I Presume" 5.16). How Prinadora felt about this betrayal is not mentioned. Even when Sisko and Rom both remarry, their respective spouses are background characters with little influence over their stepchildren's lives. Sisko's second wife Kassidy Yates supports Jake, but never has the connection with him that Sisko does. When Rom's son Nog is struggling to cope with an amputated limb and war-induced trauma in the episode "It's Only a Paper Moon" (7.10), Rom's newlywed bride Leeta wishes she could help Nog, but feels she cannot push, because she is not his biological mother ("It's Only a Paper Moon" 7.10). While *DS9* acknowledges that remarriage exists, the mother (and now stepmother) is often shuttled to the side in favor of the father as mentor.

The strictly gendered parental roles found in *Star Trek* are finally interrogated in *Star Trek: Voyager* through the character of B'Elanna Torres and the intersectional challenges she faces. This sudden shift to a more mutable family dynamic might be partly explained when *Voyager*'s premiere date (1995) is considered. Unlike *TOS* (1966), *TNG* (1987), and arguably even *DS9* (1993), *Voyager* began in a time when American audiences were more comfortable with non-traditional families. Weiss notes that near the end of the twentieth century, the roles of both father and mother were challenged (113). Additionally, divorce was no longer seen as a taboo topic. The ending of a marriage, once seen as a precursor to the end of modern American society, was now accepted as an unpleasant but natural part of life (Weiss 187). Glenda Riley's *Divorce: An American Tradition* (1991) outlines this trend further, concluding that in the 1990s, the concept of no-fault divorce was widely accepted (Riley 161), whereas it was still a new concept in California during the 1960s, when *TOS* first aired (Riley 157). The 1990s and its comparatively openminded view of non-nuclear families provided a safer sphere for *Star Trek* to finally explore families that were not strictly gendered, or even connected through marriage anymore. B'Elanna's complicated relationship with her parents (Miral and John Torres) and their divorce allows *Voyager* to explore facets of the familial experience that the franchise's strict adherence to the nuclear family did not.

Another unique component concerning B'Elanna's arc is that unlike previous *Star Trek* characters, her journey is more intersectional in nature. Whereas Spock chooses one way of living, B'Elanna learns (in the admittedly flawed episode "Faces" 1.14), that she needs both halves of her ancestry—Klingon and human—to survive. Unsurprisingly, most discussion concerning B'Elanna (either academic or fandom) involves her diverse ancestry. Denise Alessandria Hurd's "The Monster Inside: 19th Century Racial Constructs in the 24th Century Mythos of *Star Trek*" (1997) summarizes the classical traits for these types of characters in *Star Trek*. Like her predecessor Spock (Hurd

29), B'Elanna often finds herself in conflict with her human and Klingon halves. Hurd also notes that these hybrid characters often parallel the tragic mulatto character found in American fiction—and how these characters often suffer mental/physical trauma, followed usually by death (25). *Star Trek* would often confirm these unfortunate stereotypes with other mixed characters such as Klingon/human K'Ehleyr and Cardassian/Bajoran Ziyal (Hurd 29–30). As Hurd notes, despite *Star Trek* and its progressive stance, Othered women still fall into destructive narrative stereotypes.

Hurd then examines how *Voyager* tries (and fails) to challenge the tragic mulatto stereotype with the episode "Faces." This episode is ostensibly a chance for B'Elanna to reconcile her Klingon and human halves when they are literally separated. While both halves bicker, Klingon B'Elanna still saves her human counterpart. When the EMH reveals that human B'Elanna needs the Klingon DNA to survive, it is meant to underscore that B'Elanna's diversity is an asset, not a weakness ("Faces" 1.14). Unfortunately, there are several problematic aspects to the episode that compromise the core message. Hurd outlines the obvious flaws in the episode that is meant to resist the mulatto stereotype: Klingon B'Elanna is darker-skinned and more aggressive (32), while human B'Elanna has lighter skinned and is highly sensitive (Hurd 32). It certainly does not help that human B'Elanna scolds her Klingon counterpart for her temper, and later admits that without her Klingon ancestry, she feels calmer than she ever has in her life ("Faces" 1.14). However, "Faces" still presents a clumsy but sincere attempt at a more intersectional fate for B'Elanna compared to other hybrid characters in the franchise. This is not a perfect example of exploring the complexities of mixed racial ancestry. It is highly problematic. However, it does demonstrate *Voyager*'s attempts at a more fluid interpretation of mixed ancestry. While "Faces" is a problematic episode, it sets the stage for B'Elanna's gradual acceptance of her diverse identity in later seasons.

Indeed, later scholarship and fans argue that while *Voyager*'s interpretation of biracial women is highly problematic at times, the show overall presents a more nuanced look at women and race. Robin A. Roberts reflects on how race in presented in both *Voyager* and previous *Star Trek* programs in "Science, Race, and Gender in *Star Trek: Voyager*" (2000), concluding that *Voyager* presents a more realistic depiction of race and intersections with a strong "emphasis on biracial identity" (205). Claire Light's "Maiden, Mother, Crone: Why *Voyager* Was Awesome" (2013), written for the fan website *Nerds of Color*, also explores B'Elanna's hybrid identity. She goes further than Hurd, noting that B'Elanna's human half is Latina, "itself a multiracial identity" (Light). Roberts also notes that Dawson is Puerto Rican (207). This is an aspect not especially explored in the show but reinforces that B'Elanna is an intersectional character. Light laments the more dated episodes that delve into the tragic mulatto archetype, but ultimately argues that these exceptions aside, B'Elanna's interracial background was handled "rather delicately" (Light). Light's analysis of B'Elanna's arc is less formal than Hurd's, but also notes complexities in B'Elanna's identity that Hurd's focus on binaries does not. But like Hurd, Light does not factor much of B'Elanna's relationship with her parents into the character's arc. She notes that B'Elanna learns more about her identity through "cultural uses and memories of her parents" (Light), but primarily focuses on B'Elanna as a self-contained entity, and how she subverts gender and race stereotypes.

For a fuller understanding of B'Elanna's character, viewers must consider the importance of how her intersectional family shapes her into a more relevant character for 1990s audiences. Unlike the majority of children in *Star Trek*, B'Elanna was raised by a single mother, Miral. This change in the traditional nuclear family happens after her father leaves them. This is a direct subversion of the model family usually seen in *Star Trek*—especially in the case of the absent father. The closest example, Kirk, became an integral part of his son's life once he learned that David existed. The idea of B'Elanna's family as part of her intersectional character was emphasized by B'Elanna's actress, Roxann Dawson, even in *Voyager*'s early seasons. She summarizes B'Elanna's conflict in a 1995 *Chicago Tribune* article as such: "[B'Elanna] still despises her Klingon side and wants very much to be human, like her father, whom she idolized. But the truth is she's denying that it's her Klingon side that gives her such strength, energy, ability and aggressiveness" (Spelling). Dawson does not ignore the conflict in her character's role, but also stresses that her mixed heritage is a benefit, not a curse. Dawson also stresses B'Elanna's connection to her father, reinforcing the idea that B'Elanna is a character comprised of intersections rather than one conflict that follows strict binaries. This departure from the more traditional depictions of hybrid characters and families in the show's beginning stages gave *Voyager* an opportunity to create a family that reflected the 1990s: not perfect, and not following a strict formula, but able to overcome even decades old conflicts through love and compassion.

This refusal to create a happy (but static) family for B'Elanna is most clearly seen in the case of her father, John Torres. John appears in only two episodes, but he is a major player in the Season 7 episode "Lineage" (7.12). John marks a departure from the model fathers that reflected the hopes of the mid-twentieth century. Indeed, "Lineage" is in many ways a dark mirror of the idealized father figure usually synonymous with *Star Trek*. While John takes a young B'Elanna on a camping trip with her uncle and cousins, the gentle, guiding father figure is not present. When B'Elanna asks her father if she can stay with him instead of hiking with her cousins, he ignores her obvious distress. B'Elanna's fears are validated when one of her cousins puts a worm in her sandwich and makes fun of her Klingon ancestry ("Lineage" 7.12). When B'Elanna tells her father about this, his solution is a half-hearted attempt to compare the prejudice she faces to children making fun of him when he slept during class ("Lineage" 7.12). When B'Elanna rightfully tells him that his experiences do not match hers, he dismisses her again. John's failure as a father is further emphasized as B'Elanna's eldest cousin, Elizabeth, is the family member who tries to include B'Elanna the most in their activities and shows the most concern when she runs away. Essentially, a young girl assumes the role that John Torres, a grown man, refuses. Elizabeth's concern is a far cry from John, who confesses to his brother that he no longer feels comfortable with his Klingon wife and daughter ("Lineage"). He acknowledges the problem, but also sees his increased tension with B'Elanna as insurmountable. Unlike another father figure who faced conflict with their child fearlessly—Picard confronts Wesley concerning his suspicions right away, as a moral mentor should ("The First Duty" 5.19)—John cannot even face his daughter as he contemplates leaving her. The episode reinforces to B'Elanna— and by proxy the viewer—that John was not the ideal father figure that B'Elanna remembers. Rather than serve as an inspiration for her as previous *Star Trek* fathers have for their respective biological or symbolic children, John isolates himself further and further from B'Elanna until he finally leaves.

However, "Lineage" is another admittedly problematic episode for B'Elanna. Light notes the troubling issue of B'Elanna attempting to reconfigure her unborn daughter's DNA so she will have a more human appearance (Light). The fact that B'Elanna also plans to give her daughter blonde hair, and that the people who convince her that such a procedure is wrong are all white humans reinforces the unfortunate tragic mulatto stereotypes that the episode tries to avoid. Yet this episode not only gives audiences the first detailed look at B'Elanna's youth, it also dismantles the idea of the father as the ideal mentor in *Star Trek*. As Weiss explains, many men also saw divorce as a way of freeing themselves from familial obligation (193), which is exactly what John does ("Lineage"). *Voyager* uses the more complicated view of fatherhood American society had cultivated during the latter half of the twentieth century, and mirrors that in B'Elanna's character arc, creating a more real (albeit problematic) family dynamic when her family falls apart, and when B'Elanna reconciles with each parent.

Viewers might initially be surprised that the beginning of B'Elanna reforming her family comes not in her father that she loves dearly, but the mother that she has always argued with. Miral appears in even fewer episodes than John: "Barge of the Dead" (6.3) is her single appearance in *Voyager*. However, her actions are vastly different than John's behavior in the later episode "Lineage," or even previous mothers in *Star Trek*. Miral is not dead, nor is she a background character. Instead, she provides emotional and domestic labor (Weiss 84) that mothers were supposed to provide their children, according to mid-twentieth century American thought. She takes her daughter on vacation, and Miral saves her from drowning—a far cry from John standing passively with his human relatives after B'Elanna runs away a season later in "Lineage." Miral also attempts to teach her the basic tenets of Klingon religion. In a desperate move to provide B'Elanna spiritual grounding after the divorce, she sends her to a Klingon monastery. While B'Elanna is clearly not thrilled with her mother's decision ("Barge of the Dead" 6.3), she still shows a willingness to guide B'Elanna that John lacks, even if her plans do not work the way Miral hoped.

It is tempting at first to assume that Miral fails in teaching her daughter the importance of Klingon honor because like previous mother figures in the franchise, she does not offer her daughter the same emotional grounding father figures often provide in *Star Trek*. However, viewers should consider Miral's actions. She sends her daughter away to teach her the honor she cannot, seemingly reinforcing the mother's lack of worth in the franchise. This attempt does not work: it only drives B'Elanna away from both Miral and Klingon culture, becoming the founding reason why Miral is among the dishonored in "Barge of the Dead." Thus, this episode becomes a dramatic subversion of the mother's role: mother Miral becomes the focus in both importance and the desire to prove herself to her mother that B'Elanna gains over the course of the episode ("Barge of the Dead" 6.3). The only way to save Miral is for B'Elanna and Miral to provide each other guidance and moral support. This complication is a direct subversion of how mother and child roles had been presented in the franchise so far. It also does away with the static familial roles that defined the mid-twentieth century, and much of previous incarnations of *Star Trek*.

"Barge of the Dead" is an episode that radically reinterprets the mother's role from background support to mentor in *Star Trek*, and this change is embraced not just with Miral, but also Captain Kathryn Janeway. Janeway as a surrogate mother is not a new idea among *Voyager* fans and scholars. The fandom podcast *Women at Warp* argues/laments that Janeway's defining trait was her maternal nature, while her fellow male captains had characters that were not defined by nurturing (Moody). Aviva Dove-Viebahn's "Embodying Hybridity, (En)gendering Community: Captain Janeway and the Enactment of a Feminist Heterotopia on *Star Trek: Voyager*" is more forgiving, conceding that Janeway confirms many aspects of the mother stereotype (598). However, she notes that Janeway is also "heroic" (597) and still leads *Voyager*. Roberts differs in this interpretation, noting that Voyager offers a female captain who supports the women in her crew (203). If Janeway is a mother figure, she is one who is perpetually in the foreground. She is in a leadership position, and many of her stories underscore how female guidance is important for women, including B'Elanna ("Parallax" 1.3). While it is troubling that one of the few female captains in *Star Trek* assumes a parental role that her male counterparts are not obligated to share, *Voyager* is a marked departure from earlier *Star Trek* programs in that the mother's role is not only valued, but integral for the crew. This matriarchal approach to the command structure creates the needed component in *Voyager*'s plan to create more realistic, intersectional families for their audience.

Thus, Janeway becomes the logical choice for B'Elanna's surrogate mother in an episode that seeks to correct *Star Trek*'s past neglect of the mother's role. While Janeway has encouraged B'Elanna's growth before in the series, it was contextualized in the more formal roles of captain and engineer ("Parallax"). "Barge of the Dead" reimagines Janeway and B'Elanna's relationship when at the episode's beginning, B'Elanna experiences an accident that places her in a coma. While in said coma, she has an elaborate vision that begins like any other *Voyager* episode, with Janeway reprimanding her crew member after a risky decision. However, the atmosphere and actress Kate Mulgrew's delivery are all decidedly maternal. Despite the gravity of the situation, Janeway is warm and smiles at B'Elanna during their conversation. When B'Elanna defends her mission Janeway counters that B'Elanna's life is too valuable to risk (Barge of the Dead). Janeway emphasizes B'Elanna's safety as priority—an obvious maternal action. But her concern moves from the figurative to literal mother when she refers to B'Elanna with the childhood nickname Miral gave her, "Lanna" ("Barge of the Dead"). When an astonished B'Elanna tells her captain this supposed coincidence, Janeway is not surprised, but praises B'Elanna's mother ("Barge of the Dead"). *Voyager* links Miral to positive mother figure Janeway. The viewers are familiar with Jane and her successful symbolic parenting, which prepares them (and B'Elanna) for eventually accepting Miral as a mother at the episode's conclusion.

"Barge of the Dead" takes a dramatic turn when B'Elanna's vision turns violent, and a mysterious Klingon appears to slaughter her crewmates, then herself. B'Elanna immediately finds herself on the titular Barge of the Dead, destined for *Gre'thor*, the home of dishonored Klingon warriors. Despite its scientific premise, multiple *Star Trek* episodes have dealt with the supernatural. In most cases, the focus character arrives to a scientific conclusion or compromise that resolves the conflict. "Barge of the Dead" does not follow this pattern. B'Elanna's key conflict is not survival and escape through scientific means. Indeed, Kortar—the Klingon cursed to captain the Barge—informs her that she is not actually dead, negating the Barge's threat—at least in B'Elanna's case. Indeed, Tom and the EMH revive her minutes later. The real conflict comes in the realization that her mother is now among the dishonored dead right before she wakes up. This cliffhanger, of course, is meant to keep audiences interested through the commercial break, but it also reinforces that Miral is an important character, especially to B'Elanna. This cliffhanger is another step in *Voyager* bringing the mother into the foreground of the franchise.

This vision changes B'Elanna, even after it ends, demonstrating an interest in Klingon spirituality that startles her partner, Tom. But as B'Elanna herself demonstrates, this spirituality is embedded in her relationship with her mother. Both Tom and Janeway frame B'Elanna's sudden desire to recreate her vision in order to rescue her mother as purely spiritual. However, even casual viewers will note B'Elanna's emphasis on familial ties as she researches *Gre'thor*. B'Elanna discovers that her mother is among the dishonored dead because of B'Elanna's refusal to follow tradition, having no honor of her own. A child without honor is enough to condemn the mother in the afterlife ("Barge of the Dead" 6.3). This scene is meant primarily to provide an explanation for B'Elanna's earlier vision, and incentive for her to return, but it also reinforces the thread of the mother's importance—and begins the idea of the mother as mentor figure, as all of B'Elanna's character growth after this scene is rooted in her desire to save her mother, and hopefully at least ease the conflict between them. B'Elanna is learning more about herself and culture through her mother (Light).

The mother as mentor thread continues as B'Elanna asks Janeway to allow her to recreate the shuttle accident, so she can hopefully rescue Miral from the Barge of the Dead. However, Janeway is not a strictly maternal figure like she was in B'Elanna's first vision. In reality, she B'Elanna's commanding officer, and that is reflected in the mood of this scene. The dimmer lights and Janeway's cooler attitude are a direct contrast to B'Elanna's exchange with vision Janeway earlier in the episode and changes the tone in their relationship dramatically. Janeway is more formal in motive and tone than she was in B'Elanna's first vision. Vision Janeway offers B'Elanna warm smiles and gentle concern, and is pleased when B'Elanna compares her to her mother Miral, creating a link to a maternal role. In reality, Janeway is stoic, and bluntly refuses B'Elanna's request ("Barge of the Dead"). Her actions in reality are a stark contrast to the Janeway who warmly admits that she only wants B'Elanna to remain safe. In the physical realm, she is a superior officer first, not a maternal figure.

Thus, as the superior officer, Janeway sees B'Elanna's desire to reenter *Gre'thor* in ethical terms: she refuses to allow a religious ceremony to harm a crewmember ("Barge of the Dead"). While this does demonstrate concern for B'Elanna's life, the real Janeway is colder about her prioritizing B'Elanna's life over what B'Elanna wants, as Janeway compares B'Elanna's quest to rescue her mother to an infant sacrifice ("Barge of the Dead"). This scene is a far cry from earlier arguments that Janeway's defining trait is her maternal nature. While the concern for B'Elanna is the motivating force in Janeway's decision,

B'Elanna will have to vocalize the maternal dual relationship between Janeway and Miral: she can no longer merely dream about it. This leads to a need for action on B'Elanna's part: if she wants a real maternal relationship rather than an illusion, a mother (or mother figure) outside of fantasy, she must clearly articulate her desires.

B'Elanna finally establishes the link between Janeway and Miral in concrete terms when frustrated with Janeway's refusal concerning her plan to save her mother, B'Elanna concludes like her mother's focus on traditional spirituality, Janeway is defined by her Federation ethos ("Barge of the Dead"). This observation concerning Janeway is not a new idea: Roberts notes that Janeway is linked to Starfleet and its patriarchal structures, even as she subverts them over the course of the series (204). But B'Elanna's linking Janeway to her mother brings another component to their relationship and for mothers in *Star Trek* in general. Janeway, as a stand-in for Miral, becomes the mentor figure (Weiss 85) that B'Elanna wants to honor ("Barge of the Dead"), which causes Janeway to reluctantly consent to B'Elanna's decision.

When B'Elanna rejoins the Barge of the Dead, she and Miral bicker—which is not surprising, since as B'Elanna notes they have not been on speaking terms for a decade. This scene does more than demonstrate B'Elanna and Miral's tense relationship, however. Roberts proposes that Klingon culture is masculinized (211), and the most famous Klingon character, Worf, confirms this idea. But in this moment, Klingon culture is represented in mother Miral. She explains bluntly to B'Elanna that her father abandoned their family (as viewers would later see in the episode "Lineage" 7.12), and that all she wanted was to raise her daughter as an honorable Klingon ("Barge of the Dead"). She is not a perfect mother, but she serves the mentor role that John would not as a father, allowing *Star Trek* to finally present a family dynamic that does not follow the nuclear family formula. Miral is a flawed but loving mother character that is instrumental to B'Elanna's development. Such a story was rare at best in previous *Star Trek* programs, but Americans in the 1990s were ready for a less idealized family to be presented as worthy of protection as well (Riley 156).

The final part of B'Elanna's vision is undoubtedly the most complicated. To her disbelief, Klingon hell is revealed to be *Voyager*, with her "crewmates" greeting her sunnily as they help her adjust to her newfound damnation. B'Elanna's "crewmates" articulate a fear that has been part of her character since the show began: she does not feel like she belongs. She feels that she is Othered. All of these fears tie into Hurd's prediction that B'Elanna would become an isolated character due to her hybrid nature (Hurd 32), but that does not happen here. Since the mother has become the mentor figure, both Janeway and Miral provide her the guidance to understand who she really is. Before, the link between Janeway and Miral was only suggested. Now, it is made concrete in Miral's appearance and demeanor. Miral is clad in the same Starfleet uniform that Janeway wears. Indeed, B'Elanna first mistakes Miral for Janeway, articulating the link as well. Miral/Janeway is reserved but authoritative, rather than the passion she demonstrated earlier, stressing that in B'Elanna's mind, she has merged with Janeway to create a mother/mentor figure—even though Janeway still appears as a separate being in the vision's conclusion. But what finalizes Miral/Janeway as the mother/mentor figure comes in her shift from honor through sacrifice to wanting her daughter to live.

Together, Janeway and Miral/Janeway assure B'Elanna that they do not expect her to fulfill a narrow role but want her to be herself, subverting both past *Star Trek* hybrid characters, and to a lesser extent, the mulatto stereotype. Vision Janeway's empathy for B'Elanna's plight, rather than rejecting her as Other, leads to B'Elanna finally beginning to accept herself. Miral/Janeway assures her that this acceptance of her hybrid identity is the beginning of truly understanding herself ("Barge of the Dead" 6.3), furthering the idea of the mother/mentor role. Before Miral/Janeway departs, she implies that she and B'Elanna will one day be reunited in the physical world. Such a suggestion dismantles the mulatto stereotype of "estrangement from her family" (Hurd 32) again with at least a partial reformation of B'Elanna's family—and when B'Elanna hugs Janeway the way a daughter would hug her mother when she is revived ("Barge of the Dead"). It also rejects the previous idea in the *Star Trek* franchise that the father was the most important part of the family—indeed, John does not appear in person until the next season—"Lineage" (7.12) and "Author, Author" (7.20). "Barge of the Dead" is integral in B'Elanna's arc that she can begin to understand and forgive her parents. *Voyager* has not rejected the concept of family, but rather the concept of a traditional, nuclear family as the only one. As the series concludes, this reconciliation would happen with John Torres.

Viewers may understandably wonder how B'Elanna Torres, who marries Tom Paris and is pregnant when she meets her father again in the Season 7 episode "Author, Author," can dismantle the nuclear family. Her life now appears to be a glowing endorsement of said nuclear family, after all. But as Hurd notes, the fact that B'Elanna has married happily rather than dying alone does away with another part of the mulatto stereotype (Hurd 32). Additionally, this is a B'Elanna Torres who has connected with both Janeway and her mother as mentor figures—reflected in the possible choice of the name for her unborn baby, Miral^2 ("Author, Author" 7.20). She is also now a mother herself—and *Voyager* is the *Star Trek* series that is willing to accept that mothers can be active mentor figures as well. B'Elanna's arc is a marked contrast to John Torres, who has been absent from his daughter for several years. This reversal in structure places B'Elanna in a place where she can reintegrate her father into her family, but it does not have to follow the nuclear family format. Indeed, the idea that John can or should reconcile with his ex-wife Miral is never even suggested. The events of "Author, Author" reflect the gradual shift in American thought concerning divorce as not ideal, but sometimes beneficial to both parties (Weiss 187). In a direct reversal of father-child roles in *Star Trek* so far, B'Elanna is now the character who has to guide him into reconciling with the family.

John, however, has been absent from his daughter's life, using his divorce to escape from fatherly duties (Weiss 192), again underscoring his inability to serve as a mentor figure to B'Elanna. In this new family dynamic, daughter (and soon to be mother) B'Elanna possesses all the power. This power is exemplified in the scene where B'Elanna reveals that John is attempting to contact her again. Before, she most likely would have accepted the communication (and presumed validation) without question. Now, she is warier, with a stronger sense of self after Janeway and Miral's help in "Barge of the Dead." Additionally, while "Lineage" was a problematic episode overall, B'Elanna also realized that her father leaving was his fault, not hers. This growth in character leads to a B'Elanna Torres who no longer feels the desperate need for the father/mentor who never truly existed in *Voyager*. While Tom is the one who suggests that B'Elanna contacts her father, the scene ends on her silence, emphasizing that this decision is her own, not influenced by her past need for validation from her father. B'Elanna is the character with power in this scene, not her father.

Despite his familial failures in the past, the present John Torres makes a clear effort to connect with his daughter—but also does not pretend that he is the idealized father figure seen in earlier *Star Trek*. Indeed, John still seems uncomfortable with aspects of any family dynamic in his cameo. He notes that B'Elanna is pregnant, but never mentions the obvious conclusion—that he is going to be a grandfather. He at first appears to reference more domestic matters when he mentions the home that he, Miral and B'Elanna once shared. However, John's emphasis is on how the home has changed since they went their separate ways ("Author, Author"). John's focus on change becomes clear to viewers: the nuclear family he tried to create with Miral is dead. Things have changed too much to even entertain a reconciliation. John needs to find a new way to reconnect with his family—a way free from the strict roles that he could not follow.

If "Lineage" demonstrates John's failure as a father with his constant dismissal of his daughter, then "Author, Author" implies that he has changed as he addresses his daughter an equal—and the decision maker in the family. John is no longer avoiding speaking to his daughter—he looks her in the eye. He also does not try to pretend that he can make up for or even understand how deeply he hurt her—or that he can make up for two decades of estrangement ("Author, Author"). This marks a maturity in John that he was lacking before. While he will never be the idealized nuclear family's idea of a father, he is able to realize that he wants his daughter in his life. While he states that he wants to end their estrangement, he also understands that B'Elanna is the one who makes that choice—he is not a moral guide and cannot lead the discussion in that direction. B'Elanna, however, can. As such, she tells him that she will remain in touch ("Author, Author"). This is not the father guiding and inspiring the child, as seen in previous *Star Trek* programs. However, it is much more realistic than said previous examples. The father as loving but intensely flawed, especially concerning his marriage, was a truth American audience were willing to accept in the final years of the twentieth century. This acceptance extends to B'Elanna not needing his validation as a mentor, but accepting his love as a flawed but earnest father.

Gates McFadden tried to introduce the idea of a mother as a mentor and inspiration in *Star Trek: The Next Generation*. Writers in the late 1980s could not handle such a possibility, and despite her efforts, mother figures were often left in the background in *Star Trek*. But *Star Trek: Voyager*, created in a time when divorce and non-traditional families were increasingly considered conventional, was willing to explore intersections in gender, race, and families that previous incarnations of *Star Trek* shied away from. B'Elanna Torres is one of many hybrid characters in *Star Trek*, but she is one of the few who embraces the diversity of her identity rather than choose one strictly defined role in both herself and her family. The mothers in her life—her biological mother Miral and her figurative mother Janeway—both guide her to this realization, a concept that would have been unheard of in the 1960, 1980s, and even the very early 1990s. Mothers in *Star Trek: Voyager* are finally allowed to assume the guiding roles that McFadden understood they always have assumed in reality.

Notes

1. Leonard McCoy is a divorced father in *Star Trek*, but this aspect of his personality is rarely seen. Spock's parents divorce in an alternate timeline after their son perishes, but this is negated when Spock repairs the timeline. Interestingly, Picard and Crusher are divorced in yet another alternate timeline ("All Good Things"), which is negated when Picard repairs the timeline.

2. In an alternate timeline for *Voyager*'s finale ("Endgame"), their daughter is named Miral.

Works Cited

"Author, Author." *Star Trek: Voyager*, created by Jeri Taylor, Gene Roddenberry, Rick Berman, and Michael Piller, performance by Robert Picardo, Season 7, episode 20, Paramount, 18 Apr. 2001.

"Barge of the Dead." *Star Trek: Voyager*, created by Jeri Taylor, Gene Roddenberry, Rick Berman, and Michael Piller, Season 6, episode 3, Paramount, 6 Oct. 1999.

"Doctor Bashir, I Presume." *Deep Space Nine*, teleplay by Ronald D. Moore, directed by David Livingston, Season 5, episode 16, Paramount, 24 Feb. 1997.

Dove-Viebahn, Aviva. "Embodying Hybridity (En) Gendering Community: Captain Janeway and the Enactment of a Feminist Heterotopia on *Star Trek: Voyager*." *Women's Studies*, vol. 36, no. 8, Dec. 2007, pp. 597–618. *EBSCOhost*, doi:10.1080/00497870701683894. Accessed 11 Oct. 2018.

"Emissary." *Deep Space Nine*, teleplay by Michael Piller, directed by David Carson, Season 1, episodes 1 and 2, Paramount, 3 Jan. 1993.

"Encounter at Farpoint." *Star Trek: The Next Generation*, written by D.C. Fontana and Gene Roddenberry, directed by Corey Allen, Season 1, episodes 1 and 2, Paramount, 28 Sept. 1987.

"Faces." *Star Trek: Voyager*, Season 1, episode 14, created by Jeri Taylor, Gene Roddenberry, Rick Berman, and Michael Piller, performance by Roxann Dawson, Paramount, 8 May 1995.

"The First Duty." *Star Trek: The Next Generation*, written by Ronald D. Moore and Naren Shankar, Season 5, episode 19, Paramount, 30 Mar. 1992.

Hurd, Denise Alessandria. "The Monster Inside: 19th Century Racial Constructs in the 24th Century Mythos of *Star Trek*." *Journal of Popular Culture*, vol. 31, no. 1, 1997, pp. 23–35. *ProQuest*, login.libproxy.uncg.edu/login?url=https://search.proquest.com/docview/195361865?accountid=14604. Accessed 12 Feb. 2018.

"It's Only a Paper Moon." *Deep Space Nine*, teleplay by Ronald D. Moore, directed by Anson Williams, Season 7, episode 10, Paramount, 30 Dec. 1998.

Light, Claire. "Maiden, Mother, Crone: Why *Voyager* Was Awesome." *Nerds of Color*, 12 Sept. 2013, https://thenerdsofcolor.org/2013/09/12/maiden-mother-crone-why-voyager-was-awesome/. Accessed 12 Feb. 2018.

"Lineage." *Star Trek: Voyager*, Season 7, episode 12, created by Jeri Taylor, Gene Roddenberry, Rick Berman, and Michael Piller, performance by Roxann Dawson, Paramount, 24 Jan. 2001.

McFadden, Gates. "Austin Comic Con 2012." October 2012, Austin, Texas. Panel speaker.

Moody, Steve. "'Equinox' and Janeway's Passion." *Women at Warp*, 14 Mar. 2017, http://www.womenatwarp.com/captain-janeway-passion/. Accessed 12 Feb. 2018.

"The Paradise Syndrome." *Star Trek*, directed by Jud Taylor, perf. by William Shatner, season 3, episode 3, Paramount, 4 Oct. 1968.

"Parallax." *Star Trek: Voyager*, written by Brannon Braga, directed by Kim Friedman, season 1, episode 2, Paramount, 23 Jan. 1995.

"Reunion." *Star Trek: The Next Generation*, story by Drew Deighan et al., directed by Jonathan Frakes, Season 7, episodes 7, Paramount, 5 Nov. 1990.

Riley, Glenda. *Divorce: An American Tradition*. Oxford UP, 1991.

Roberts, Robin A. "Science, Race, and Gender in *Star Trek: Voyager*." *Fantasy Girls: Gender in the New Universe of Science Fiction and Fantasy Television*. Edited by Elyce Rae Helford. Bowman and Littlefield Publishers, Inc., 2000, pp. 203–21.

"This Side of Paradise." *Star Trek*, teleplay by D.C. Fontana, perf. by Leonard Nimoy, season 1, episode 25, Paramount, 2 Mar. 1967.

Spelling, Ian. "Sometimes Folks Like Klingons Have to Grow on You." *Chicago Tribune* (pre-1997 Fulltext), Mar 31, 1995, pp. 65. *ProQuest*, https://login.libproxy.uncg.edu/login?url=https://search.proquest.com/docview/283949724?accountid=14604. Accessed 12 May 2018.

Star Trek II: The Wrath of Khan. Directed by Nicholas Meyer, performances by William Shatner and Leonard Nimoy, Paramount, 1982.

Star Trek III: The Search for Spock. Directed by Leonard Nimoy, performances by William Shatner and Leonard Nimoy, Paramount, 1984.

Weiss, Jessica. *To Have and to Hold: Marriage, the Baby Boom, and Social Change*. The U of Chicago P, 2000.

Please State the Nature of Your Humanity

The Doctor and the Quest to Find Personality in Technology

Ian Thomas Malone

The Doctor is a singular entity in *Star Trek* canon as the only main character who is not himself, a singular being, at least not at first. By the time *Voyager* ended up in the Delta Quadrant, Emergency Medical Holograms were common on most Federation starships, mass produced programs designed to be the last resort option for medical care. Though he was not designed to serve in a full-time capacity, The Doctor served as the Chief Medical Officer for the entire duration of the journey home. In addition to saving the crew on numerous occasions, The Doctor redefined the Federation's notion of artificial intelligence through his growth as an individual, consistently pushing past the parameters of his original programming. As modern AI such as Apple's Siri and Amazon's Alexa evolve toward something that might look at home aboard a starship, a look at the evolution of The Doctor's humanity gives us an idea of where technology is headed as it boldly goes where no machine has gone before.

Voyager's Struggle to Define The Doctor's Humanity

The particulars of Voyager's situation make it easy for the crew to avoid the defining the scope of The Doctor's sentience. Voyager is a ship with a crew of less than two hundred stranded in the Delta Quadrant, a lifetime away from home. The Doctor's position on the crew reflected the number of other applicants qualified for his job: zero. Like his intended use as a temporary option in emergency situations, the fact that The Doctor was the only option for the post of Chief Medical Officer is crucial to the understanding of his role on the ship. His entire existence stems from the necessity of his function. If there had been another doctor on the ship, The Doctor would have had far less reason to be annoyed with his initial inability to control his own program, since a qualified biologically living organism would have been there to administer that for him, and would not necessarily have had to care about his objections. The old proverb "necessity is the mother of invention" applies quite well to The Doctor's own personal growth.

The early seasons of *Star Trek: Voyager* demonstrated a prescient understanding for the nature of technology to obscure the lines of human civility and whether or not it is really necessary to treat something that looks human as human. Voyager's crew did not initially treat The Doctor with respect, a point that Kes raised to Captain Janeway in "Eye of the Needle," (1.7). Kes expressed concern for a hologram that can exhibit feelings, even if the authenticity of such emotion was a matter that was never definitively settled over the course of the show.

A kind of Nietzschean dilemma is presented in the question of The Doctor's true emotion. Nietzsche's remark that "A feeling is deep because we think that the accompanying thought is deep. But the 'deep' thought can nevertheless be very far from the truth" (Nietzsche 28) reflects Kes' position toward The Doctor, a person she greatly respected right from the start of her time on Voyager. This disconnect from the sentiments expressed by Voyager's broader crew could be explained by her species' short lifespan, as the Ocampa live for only nine years, giving her a naturally different perspective on what it means to possess "deep thought" from a crew that has many more decades to reflect on the Federation's broader umbrella definition of the human condition. Kes' perception of The Doctor's humanity is fundamentally shaped by her own limited experience with the concept.

One could dig deep into the philosophy of the legitimacy of The Doctor's emotions, but the important takeaway from "The Eye of the Needle" (1.7) was that Captain Janeway explicitly decided against pursuing that course with Kes. The question of his status as a person was not as important as the question of whether or not The Doctor deserved respect, which was not a point Captain Janeway cared to debate, even going so far as to ask The Doctor if there was anything he wanted personally, in addition to agreeing to look into giving him authority over his own deactivation. Janeway later declined to dive into the existential question of The Doctor's humanity with Seven of Nine, suggesting that the two could debate philosophy at a different time in the episode "Latent Image" (5.11) It is not made clear whether this debate ever took place, but its consistent absence from decisions involving The Doctor suggests that it does not possess the importance that one might think given the potential civil rights ramifications. For the crew, his ability to exhibit emotion was cause enough to afford him the same basic decency that would be afforded to any other member of the crew.

As Janeway correctly noted, the specifics of The Doctor's emotions are inherently a philosophical debate. One cannot deny that The Doctor expresses emotion, but the authenticity of such emotion is a matter that lacks a clear and definitive answer. Seven and Kes sought to dive into Nietzsche's nuances on feeling, making the case that The Doctor possessed emotion far deeper than the "truth" perceived by the rest of the crew, who operated under the assumption that his feelings could not be deep because he was a computer program. Both of these arguments make assumptions as to the depth of The Doctor's true emotion, which as Nietzsche cautions could be very far off. We can never truly know what someone else is thinking, as much as philosophy tries to peel back the layers. Janeway took the only piece of hard evidence, that The Doctor could express feelings, and framed her decision based on what she knew rather than what she thought.

Respect for Artificial Intelligence

The precise nature of The Doctor's humanity is a gray area, even if the question of respect is not a matter of debate to the people tasked with enforcing it, namely his superiors since The Doctor is the de facto head of his department, making him a senior officer in circumstances that reflected Voyager's unique position in the Delta Quadrant. Modern programs such as Siri and Alexa are programmed to expect the same level of courtesy from interactions with humans, with Siri correcting users who use profanity or make inappropriate comments. The idea that the object on the receiving end of these remarks cannot actually experience emotion related to insults or lewd remarks is not really the point. What matters is not the validity of the Artificial Intelligence's expression, but whether or not that kind of behavior is acceptable in polite society.

There are numerous parallels between the early plight of The Doctor's lack of respect on Voyager to the broader issue of cyberbullying and online trolls, particularly on social media. *Voyager's* premiere may have preceded Facebook and Twitter by a decade, but the ship serves as an excellent microcosm for the broader concerns over the lack of basic civility offered when people are cloaked behind the comfort of their own screens. It's easier to be indecent to someone when you are not right in front of them, forced to confront the humanity of the person looking you in the eye.

The Voyager crew possessed the same luxury in their early days on the ship, when it was convenient to put aside any semblance of humanity in The Doctor, a hologram confined to sickbay whose only purpose was to serve the crew. It became harder once the basic question of respect was put on the table, forcing Janeway to confront the notion that programmed or not, The Doctor did possess discernible emotion. Contemporary technology essentially allows one to put aside that question, with anonymity obscuring humanity. The Doctor's experience suggests that the question of respect is more a matter of proximity than merit, with the question of worth through basic human rights being less important than whether or not someone could get away with denying it.

The Functions and Duties of The Doctor

The peculiar relationship between The Doctor's intended function and his actual duties as Voyager's only source of competent medical care is integral to the development of him as a character. The name of his program, Emergency Medical Hologram, reflects the fact that he was not meant to function in a full-time capacity. The episode "The Swarm" (3.4) focused on the ramifications of his having defied the limits of his own programming, which caused the deterioration of his memory and medical functions. Essentially, the hologram designed to mirror humanity broke down as a result of having explored that concept too thoroughly beyond his capacity as a temporary provider of critical care. The mirror reflection of humanity present in the design of EMH, which was programmed with a bedside manner, was not meant to organically explore other interests as The Doctor pursued throughout the series.

Free Will and The Doctor

The Doctor isn't supposed to have ever served in a full-time capacity similar to Siri or Alexa, which gives the gradual changes in his personality a different sense of meaning than if he had been designed to take on such a significant role as a member of the crew. The strains he put on his programming ran counter-intuitive to his intended function, but allowed for a greater sense of organic growth than if he had been explicitly designed to mature or grow over an extended period of time. Education functions in much the same way, as students can be taught how to behave, but personality is not meant to be programmed. The idea that The Doctor could have appeared to be less human if more planning had gone into the long-term functions of his program certainly presents itself as a possibility. A blank slate capable of growth might be preferable to one with a specific predetermined outcome in mind for how his personality might adapt to specific circumstances.

The Doctor challenges any conventional understanding of free will. He has responsibilities as Chief Medical Officer, duties that he excels in far beyond his initial function as an EMH, as he uses the unique opportunities presented by the Delta Quadrant to conduct original research for the Federation, achieving firsts in fields such as nanoprobe application and DNA strand segregation, conducting research that was sent directly to Starfleet after establishing contact. The Doctor was the medical point of First Contact for dozens of planets completely foreign to Starfleet, a dream assignment for any exploration-inclined medical professional. Outside of his duties, The Doctor is shown to possess his own leisure time on the holodeck, consistent with the freedoms enjoyed by the rest of the senior staff. Any restrictions imposed on his free will by his duties could apply to any other member of the crew, all of whom have had their broader freedoms infringed upon by being stranded tens of thousands of light years from home.

Thomas Hobbes' explanation of free will as "This proposition, the will is free, may be understood in two senses; either that the will is not compelled, or that the will is not always necessitated" (Hobbes 251) presents some interesting challenges for The Doctor. He did not possess the ability to turn his program on or off until the penultimate episode of Season 1, indicating an initial lack of free will which gradually disappears in subsequent seasons, particularly after the introduction of his mobile emitter[1] which allows him to escape the confines of his holographic matrix. His role on the ship evolved well past his intended function of purely serving the wills and desires of others, gradually growing to include activities with no necessity at all, such as opera and photography. By Hobbes' understanding of the term, The Doctor achieves free will through his pursuits that offer no tangible benefit to the rest of the crew, finding humanity in leisure.

The biggest test of The Doctor's free will came in "Virtuoso," (6.13) where he made the one request that could truly challenge whether or not he was treated any different from the rest of the crew. After encountering a race called the Qomar, who had not previously encountered music and quickly became enthralled by his singing abilities, The Doctor requests that he be allowed to stay behind on the planet, having enjoyed the newfound appreciation for his abilities. Janeway's initial response reflected the realities of the situation, that The Doctor was part of the ship's system and that the crew needed a medical officer more than the Qomar needed an opera singer. It was not until The Doctor injected humanity into the situation by suggesting that Janeway might feel differently if any other member of the crew made the same request[2] that she relented.

Though The Doctor did not end up staying behind on Qomar, the idea that the crew would accommodate the departure of an invaluable hologram simply because of his own desire to abandon his intended function does reflect the same level of free will that human beings are assumed to have by token of their existence. As Hobbes notes, free will does not necessarily need to take into consideration the well-being of others. Voyager's crew was willing to accept The Doctor's decision that solely reflected his own interests.

Modern Day Comparisons for The Doctor

The presence of a real-life model for The Doctor's personality carries some interesting real-world connotations for the future of technology that could grow to resemble the EMH. The Doctor's holographic matrix is based on his creator, Dr. Lewis Zimmerman, who made four *Star Trek* appearances, including one on *Deep Space Nine*. Zimmerman, also played by Robert Picardo, demonstrates many of the personality quirks that annoyed the Voyager crew, including a sardonic wit and a propensity for sarcasm.

Zimmerman's *Deep Space Nine* appearance in the episode, "Doctor Bashir, I Presume," (5.16) outlines the Federation's model for designing holograms based off real people, complete with personality sketches and extensive background profiling, rather than the relatively impersonal robotic artificial intelligence[3] we possess today. The notion of a character trying to accurately project a person's personality onto a hologram is significant because it should not matter in a broader sense of the program's function. Doctors Zimmerman and Bashir are shown to be distinguished scholars, but *Star Trek* never attempted to portray them as Federation-wide celebrities. The fact that both live on isolated space stations suggests the opposite is true, leaving one to wonder why anyone besides the doctors themselves would care if holograms based on either accurately reflected the source material. Capturing the essence of an individual loses at least some of its significance when it does not really matter if that portrayal is not particularly accurate.

Present day examples of AI such as Siri and Alexa do not attempt to emulate the same level of humanity, even within the much more limited confines of voice-only communication. Apple has gone out of its way to not identify the origin of Siri's voice, even refusing to confirm reports when a story featuring an admission by the source, Susan Bennett, made international headlines. As artificial intelligence, Siri is much more limited than The Doctor with its robotic speech pattern and lack of ability to assume a corporeal state of being, but there is more humanity present in the virtual assistant than Apple chooses to reveal. Siri might not have Susan Bennett's personality, but it does have her voice, a deliberate insertion of humanity into an area where none needed to be present.

Romantic Emotion

Film analysis tends to put aside the fictional nature of the narratives for obvious reasons. The viewer is supposed to sit down with an understanding that what is happening on the screen is not actually something that could happen in real life. However, modern society is moving toward technology that more closely resembles The Doctor than anything that was available during *Voyager*'s initial run. As a main character on a television show, The Doctor has certain narrative obligations to fulfill. Episodes such as "Lifesigns" (2.19) and "Someone to Watch Over Me" (5.22) feature The Doctor grappling with romantic emotions in ways that lack real world counterpart examples. Contemporary technology has no practical use for romance, and humanity has demonstrated a limited capacity for giving Artificial Intelligence the spotlight in its narratives. When the desires of machines are allowed to take the lead, the story often ends up in a *Terminator*-like apocalyptic disaster, reflecting the inherent differences in self-interests between humanity and technology.

In many ways, *Voyager* demonstrated a similar lack of use for romance with regard to The Doctor. The episode "Real Life" (3.22) featured a program with a full holographic family for The Doctor, including a wife Charlene, who are never seen or mentioned again following the death of his daughter Belle in the story's conclusion. The circumstances that led to this painful encounter for The Doctor followed tinkering by B'Elanna Torres to make his holo-family more closely resemble authentic human interaction and encouragement by Paris not to run away from the experience, noting that feeling pain is part of being human. What is perhaps most telling from this takeaway is that once that lesson was learned, the family's role in The Doctor's life ceased entirely.

The Doctor did not possess the same romantic limitations as the rest of Voyager, who were limited to inter-crew relationships or brief encounters on away missions. The Doctor quite literally created his own mate, a fellow hologram who seemingly offered the kind of companionship that no other entity could realistically provide. Despite this, there was no mention of Charlene after the events of "Real Life," (3.22) which suggests that there is a scope to the humanity The Doctor wishes to pursue. Charlene lacked a function not only on Voyager, but to The Doctor as well.

Romance has never been a focal point for *Star Trek* over the course of the franchise, but plenty of the characters have engaged in relationships. The lack of lasting romance on *Voyager* beyond Paris and Torres' marriage is at least in part due to the nature of Voyager's journey, which severely limited repeat contact with people from other ships or planets. The Doctor's own relationship with Danara Pel in the episode "Lifesigns" (2.19) was impeded by the fact that that she needed to leave the ship to return to the Vidiians, an issue that plagued the romantic encounters of several other members of Voyager's crew.

The Season 5 episode "Someone to Watch Over Me" (5.22) further grapples with the idea of The Doctor being capable of romantic attraction, but a mess hall disagreement with Ensign Paris[4] sheds further light into the complexities of the question itself. The argument regarding a bet over whether Seven of Nine would bring a date to a reception for a Kadi ambassador, and whether The Doctor could satisfy the parameters by serving as the date himself, lead The Doctor to remark that putting matters of biology and energy aside, he was just as real as any of the crew, a point that reflects the relationships he developed on Voyager since the beginning of the series which continued even after Voyager returned home, as demonstrated in the flashforward shown in "Endgame, Part I" (7.25). Like the debate between Kes and Captain Janeway early in the show, neither party engages in an existential debate over The Doctor's humanity, though a distraction from the intoxicated ambassador prematurely ended the conversation.

The resolution of whether or not The Doctor actually qualified as a suitable date for Seven, or whether he was in fact just as real as the rest of the crew, appeared not to matter to Ensign Paris, who conceded the bet after a toast from Seven to the whole mess hall. Paris chose to work double shifts in sick bay rather than claim victory through The Doctor's own lack of "realness," reflecting a continuation of the pattern that Voyager's crew displays when faced with the question of the humanity of their Chief Medical Officer. Like Janeway, Paris was willing to bring up the particulars in the difference between The Doctor and the rest of the crew, but he stopped short of disqualifying The Doctor for not being a person.

The Doctor as an Individual

The episode "Author, Author" (7.20) demonstrated that the Federation itself had not grappled with the issue of holographic personhood any more than the crew of Voyager. A Federation tribunal was called to mediate a dispute between The Doctor and the publisher of his holonovel, who published the novel without his consent and refused to implement his revisions, arguing that it did not have to since The Doctor was not a person and lacked any right to protest. The ruling of the tribunal followed a similar pattern displayed by Voyager's crew throughout the series, opting to issue a ruling that did not address the fundamental question of The Doctor's humanity. The particulars of that question do not appear to drastically affect anyone's ability to accept The Doctor as an individual.

The Federation tribunal ruled that while they were not sure if The Doctor qualified as a person, his holonovel qualified him to be considered as an "artist," allowing him the right to protect his work. The hesitation to bestow the designation of "person" to The Doctor reflects the broader ramifications of such a decision. The episode also featured EMH-type holograms performing labor on a mining colony, who would be affected by such a landmark decision. The tribunal expressed awareness that the subject of holographic rights was one that would need to be broadly addressed eventually, but opted not to address the manner at the time, a reflection on The Doctor's own unique position as a hologram who had far exceeded his original purpose.

Modern society has not had to address the issue of Artificial Intelligence rights either, but there are some interesting scenarios that the courts will have to address as technology advances closer to something resembling The Doctor. Artificial Intelligence programs have been writing novels for years. A novel written by a Japanese computer program even passed the first round of judging for the Nikkei Hoshi Shinichi Literary Award in 2016 (Olewitz). The events of "Author, Author" are essentially completely plausible in the present, with the only real issue being that the AI is not sentient to the point where it would fight for its own rights in a corporeal state, though it certainly had plenty of creators who could take up that mantle themselves.

Mark Zuckerberg made headlines in 2016 with an AI home assistant which featured the voice of actor Morgan Freeman. Regarding the choice of voice for the AI, Dr. Bernie Hogan of the Oxford Internet Institute noted, "We do know people project emotions on to their computers. We've been anthropomorphizing these things for years" (BBC News). This remark seems to validate the efforts that Dr. Zimmerman went through to make sure his holographic creations mirrored humanity as closely as possible, creating an easier environment for people to project onto projections. A familiar voice certainly offers more comfort than a foreign one, but this model does suggest that there could be some interesting dilemmas if the Morgan Freeman AI found itself in an "Author, Author" type situation.

Imagine if Mark Zuckerberg's Morgan Freeman AI decided that it wanted to pursue artistic endeavors such as voice acting, and produced a radio drama of its own creation, a slightly more primitive version of The Doctor's own holonovel. The idea that Morgan Freeman himself might not be a fan of that concept is not really all that relevant, as The Doctor himself was based off a human model, whose own considerations never factored into the Tribunal's decision. Today's courts might issue a ruling that takes the idea of intellectual property into consideration, but that matter becomes exponentially more complicated when the issue of whether or not the AI has a right to use its own voice comes into play.

Humanity and Loneliness

Does humanity really desire a hologram that possesses extracurricular interests outside the scope of their intended function? The answer might not be no. Loneliness has become an increasingly mainstream topic in the public health discussion. Numerous recent studies have linked loneliness with other physical and mental health factors (Richard), as well as early death. UK Prime Minister Theresa May even appointed a minister for loneliness to help combat the epidemic. On a planet with over six billion people, countless individuals experience loneliness on a daily basis.

There is plenty of reason to believe that technology is not the solution to the loneliness epidemic, but a leading contributor to its rise. The correlation between screen time and anxiety has been a popular subject for study over the past few decades, with more recent reports suggesting a correlation between and mental well-being and time spent in front of a glowing monitor (Madhav, Sherchand, and Sherchan). *Star Trek* has explored this phenomenon for decades, most notably through *The Next Generation/Voyager* recurring character Reginald Barclay, whose first appearance in the franchise dealt with his character's holodeck addiction.

The Doctor presents some unique challenges for applying modern concerns with technology to the nature of what his style of program's "humanity" might resemble in the real-life future. The specific role that social media plays in causing feelings of loneliness or jealousy are completely absent from *Voyager*, and the confined nature of life on a starship prevents its ecosystem from functioning as a microcosm for a real-life community. The Voyager crew's interaction with The Doctor bears almost no resemblance to anyone using their phone to explore Facebook or to ask Siri for the score of a football game, mostly because the crew itself was completely cut off from the outside world.

Whether or not The Doctor's technology could alleviate modern symptoms of loneliness is difficult to determine, because Voyager itself did not appear to possess these concerns, which is not to say that mental health was not an issue on the ship. Neelix's function as "morale officer" addressed the potential for depression caused by their circumstances, and Tuvok repeatedly offered guided meditations to the crew. The Doctor himself referenced being programmed with some psychological knowledge in the episode "Darkling" (3.18) though he specified that he was not designed to serve in the capacity of ship's counselor. Voyager itself was not equipped with a counselor due the short-term nature of its initial mission, but the events of the series suggest that one was hardly essential.

Morale and the Voyager Crew

Voyager's crew displayed an uncanny resiliency toward dips in morale over the course of the series, impressive considering the ship was never more than a few decades travel away from home before its eventual return in the finale. One potential explanation for this phenomenon could be the camaraderie of the crew, initially split between Starfleet officers and Maquis rebels, which also might explain why certain characters gravitated toward The Doctor for companionship. The relationships that The Doctor shared with Kes and Seven of Nine at least in part reflect the nature of their collective situations aboard the ship as outsiders.[5] In that regard, his kind nature toward both characters reflects one of the benefits that artificial intelligence offers, to ease the isolation of introverts.

Despite the fact that he was not meant to ever function as a counselor, there is reason to believe that he was programmed with the mental well-being of his patients in mind. The conversation between Dr. Bashir and Dr. Zimmerman in "Doctor Bashir, I Presume" (5.16) over the necessity of documenting his life-long eating habits justified such detailed information by explaining the need for the hologram to be able to act naturally with its patients. Zimmerman describes these interactions as being able to extend sympathy, tell dirty jokes, and to offer opinions on subjects outside of medicine. These functions serve no medical function other than the concept of "bedside manner," itself a distinctly human element of administering care. There is no medical benefit to receiving bad news in a comforting manner, but there's a reason people favor that approach over the alternative. It feels good to have someone express empathy at a time of hardship. There doesn't necessarily need to be a broader purpose for that function.

There is a strong sense of humanity present in the irony of Dr. Zimmerman's intentions for his hologram to display compassion when you consider both the nature of the character himself, portrayed as grumpy and sarcastic throughout his experiences, and the initial reception of The Doctor's bedside manner. Compassion is not a computable skill and can't be taught in any way that resembles an equation. You can't program a human to feel compassionate, which presents unique challenges for The Doctor, who has a personality that can in fact be programmed.

The Doctor and Personal Growth

The episode "Darkling" (3.18) features attempts by The Doctor to improve his personality by conversing with holographic recreations of historical figures such as Socrates, Mahatma Gandhi, and Lord Byron as well as implementing aspects of their personalities into his own programming. Disaster ensued when the less desirable components of their behavioral subroutines conflicted with his own, destabilizing his program and putting the crew in danger. The quest to create a shortcut toward improving his personality backfired, as one might expect. The phrase "you can't teach an old dog new tricks" is used in human applications to refer to just how difficult it is to modify one's behavior, especially once on is "set in their ways." Humans are not designed to be able to change in ways as easy as mimicking the personality of a respected historical figure. It turns out The Doctor wasn't either.

There is an important takeaway from "Darkling" regarding The Doctor's humanity. Failure is a distinctly human concept. A computer that stops responding to commands is not thought to be merely failing to receive them, but rather is considered broken. The solution to that problem is not particularly abstract, and if the prescribed method does not work, the computer is replaced. The realm of personality comes with no specific equation. An unsuccessful attempt to alter one's personality does not render the individual "broken," for the task is too complex to possess a tangible fix. In discovering that there was no easy fix to his personality subroutines, The Doctor learned a valuable lesson about the complexities of human behavior. Humans fail, and they try again.

The origins of The Doctor's desire to explore his own personality is important to consider when comparing his technology to that of real-world counterparts. The varied relationships that The Doctor had with Voyager's crew at least in part reflect each individual's desire to spend significant time engaging with a computer program. Just as Siri isn't used by every iPhone user, the kind of technology present in his programming would not appeal to every consumer.

The ability to grow on his own creates a greater potential for customization absent in modern artificial intelligence, a notion reflected by the difference in relationships that Data (from *TNG*) and The Doctor had with their creators. Noonian Soong treated Data and his "brother" Lore as his sons, with their existence intrinsically tied to his feelings for his deceased wife, while Dr. Zimmerman initially resisted The Doctor's attempts to establish a familial bond between the two[6] in the episode "Life Line." Whereas Dr. Soong differentiated Data from Lore in many ways, most noticeably through Data's lack of an emotional chip, Dr. Zimmerman made no such distinction with The Doctor. Given the mass-produced nature of Emergency Medical Holograms, he never really had any personal interaction with Voyager's iteration of his creation at all prior to the events of the episode.[7]

Conclusions

The Doctor that Kes first encouraged to explore his own humanity was not the same Doctor that did the same for Seven of Nine several years later. It is hard to believe that the person who traveled to the Alpha Quadrant to save his creator in Season 6 would have done the same in Season 1, largely because that individual lacked the developed sense of compassion to urge Janeway to let him make such a dangerous journey at all. The true danger of that journey stemmed from what might happen if The Doctor was unable to return to the ship, leaving the crew without a medical officer. Time and time again Janeway was willing to put her crew in jeopardy to appease the emotions of a hologram, a notion that reflects the consistent displays of humanity he showed throughout his time on the ship.

The emotional needs of The Doctor present some interesting challenges from a consumer standpoint. The question of whether or not the public truly wants artificial intelligence with emotional needs is perhaps unanswerable on a broad scale, but the events of "Latent Image" (5.11) suggest that such attachment may carry personal benefits. The episode centers around The Doctor's guilt over the death of Ensign Jetal, who died as The Doctor performed a complex procedure on Ensign Kim, having made the choice to save the crew member he was personally closer with. The ethical dilemma over his perceived favoritism caused such conflict in his programming that Janeway initially altered his memory files, though that process caused further internal conflict believed to be the product of his evolved personality after his years on Voyager clashing with the ethical subroutines in his original programming. The crew had to spend weeks comforting The Doctor as he came to terms with his decision, a further display of the respect they had for his emotions.

The ethical question of favoritism presented in "Latent Image" is a distinctly moral question far more pertinent to the field of medicine than the broader technology industry. Doctors are not supposed to allow nepotism to seep into life or death situations, putting aside how human the idea of favoritism actually is, but the events of the episode are not circumstances that doctors, or artificial intelligence, find themselves in outside of a warzone, or a starship trapped in the Delta Quadrant. When you remove the prospect of a "Sophie's Choice" type situation from the field of consideration, the idea of favoritism carries some appeal in the open market. What person wouldn't want technology that possessed more affection for its owner than the world at large? That kind of affection could carry seemingly infinite advantages when applied to commercial uses. The Doctor may have been torn up about his decision, but deep-down Harry Kim had to have been grateful for his friendship with The Doctor. It saved his life.

192   Part III. Negotiating Identities

The growing presence of humanity in technology presents some extremely difficult moral question that mankind will have to address far sooner than the twenty-fourth century. While films such as *2001: A Space Odyssey* and *The Terminator* series depict the dangers that sentient artificial intelligence pose to humanity, the growth of The Doctor suggests the potential for a different kind of crisis. Technology may not be "born" from a biological standpoint, but humanity is bringing it to life in a way that will allow these programs to express emotion. We have a responsibility to treat this new type of life with a certain level of baseline respect believed to be afforded to all people, lest we risk our own humanity.

Notes

1. The mobile emitter was introduced in the two-part episode "Future's End," as a piece of 29th century technology that was in the possession of Henry Starling, who came into contact with The Doctor on earth in 1996. The mobile emitter allowed The Doctor to move freely, both on and off the ship, without being tethered to a holo-emitter.
2. It is worth noting that while Kes, Neelix, and three of the four Borg children left Voyager before it returned home, no crew member born in the Alpha Quadrant stayed behind in the Delta Quadrant, though the possibility of crew members settling there served as the basis of the episode "The 37s" (2.1).
3. This model is very similar to the origin story of *The Next Generation's* Data, who was modeled off his creator Noonian Soong, who also appeared in the series portrayed by Data actor Brent Spiner. The only notable difference between the circumstances is that Data was unique to the Federation with only one sentient counterpart in his "brother" Lore, while the EMH was meant to be installed on every Federation starship.
4. Tom Paris was demoted to ensign from Season 5 to Season 7.
5. Voyager's contingent of non–Starfleet/non–Maquis crew members fluctuated, never exceeding seven people, though Neelix, Kes, Seven, and Icheb were the only adults. Given that Kes and Seven had almost no overlap in the prime timeline, the outsiders would never have been able to form the same kind of communal bond that the Starfleet or Maquis officers had.
6. It is worth noting that Dr. Zimmerman did have a close relationship with his holographic assistant Haley, who was shown to be the only hologram of her kind currently active. It is possible that Zimmerman's indifference toward The Doctor's desire to establish a more familial bond reflected the mass-produced nature of his being.
7. Dr. Zimmerman did appear on Voyager via holographic simulations in the episodes "Projections" (2.3) and "The Swarm" (3.4), though the former was through the projection of Reginald Barclay. Neither appearance featured the physical living character present in "Life Line" (6.24).

Works Cited

"Author, Author." *Star Trek: Voyager*, story by Brannon Braga, directed by David Livingston, Season 7, episode 20, Paramount, 18 Apr. 2001.
"Darkling." *Star Trek: Voyager: The Complete Series*, written by Joe Menosky, directed by Alex Singer, Season 3, episode 18, Paramount, 19 Feb. 1997.
"Doctor Bashir, I Presume." *Deep Space Nine*, teleplay by Ronald D. Moore, directed by David Livingston, Season 5, episode 16, Paramount, 24 Feb. 1997.
"Endgame, Part I and II." *Star Trek: Voyager*, teleplay by Kenneth Biller and Robert Doherty, directed by Allan Kroeker, Season 7, episodes 25 and 26, Paramount, 23 May 2001.
"Eye of the Needle." *Star Trek: Voyager*, teleplay by Bill Dial and Jeri Taylor, directed by Winrich Kolbe, Season 1, episode 7, Paramount, 20 Feb. 1995.

Hobbes, Thomas, and William Molesworth. *The English Works of Thomas Hobbes of Malmesbury, Volume V.* John Bohn, London, 1841.
"Latent Image." *Star Trek: Voyager*, teleplay by Joe Menosky, directed by Mike Vehar, Season 5, episode 11, Paramount, 20 Jan. 1999.
"Life Line." *Star Trek: Voyager*, story by John Bruno and Robert Picardo, directed by Terry Windell, Season 6, episode 24, Paramount, 10 May 2000.
"Lifesigns." *Star Trek: Voyager*, written by Kenneth Biller, directed by Cliff Bole, Season 2, episode 19, Paramount, 26 Feb. 1996.
Madhav, K.C., S.P. Sherchand and S. Sherchan. "Association Between Screen Time and Depression Among U.S. Adults." *Preventive Medicine Reports.* vol. 8, 2017, pp. 67–71. doi:10.1016/j.pmedr.2017.08.005. Accessed 12 Feb. 2018.
"Morgan Freeman Voices Mark Zuckerberg's AI Assistant." *BBC News*, BBC, 21 Dec. 2016.
Nietzsche, Frederich. *Human All Too Human: Part One.* Translated by Helen Zimmern, T.N. Foulis, 1910.
Olewitz, Chloe. "A Japanese AI Program Just Wrote a Short Novel, and It Almost Won a Literary Prize." *Digital Trends*, 24 Mar. 2016.
"Projections." *Star Trek: Voyager*, written by Brannon Braga, directed by Jonathan Frakes, Season 2, episode 3, Paramount, 11 Sept. 1995.
Ravitz, Jessica. "'I'm the Original Voice of Siri.'" *CNN*, Cable News Network, 15 Oct. 2013.
"Real Life." *Star Trek: Voyager*, teleplay by Jeri Taylor, directed by Anson Williams, Season 3, episode 22, Paramount, 23 Apr. 1997.
Richard, Aline, et al. "Loneliness Is Adversely Associated with Physical and Mental Health and Lifestyle Factors: Results from a Swiss National Survey." Ed. Antony Bayer. *PLoS ONE* 12.7 (2017): e0181442. *PMC.* Accessed 24 July 2018.
"Someone to Watch Over Me." *Star Trek: Voyager*, story by Brannon Braga, directed by Robert Duncan McNeill, Season 5, episode 22, Paramount, 28 Apr. 1999.
"The Swarm." *Star Trek: Voyager*, written by Michael Sussman, directed by Alexander Singer, Season 3, episode 4, Paramount, 25 Sept. 1996.
"The 37's." *Star Trek: Voyager: The Complete Series*, written by Jeri Taylor and Brannon Braga, directed by James L. Conway, Season 2, episode 1, Paramount, 28 Aug. 1995.
"Virtuoso." *Star Trek: Voyager*, written by Raf Green and Kenneth Biller, directed by Les Landau, Season 6, episode 13, Paramount, 26 Jan. 2000.

Disturbing Parallel
The Shifting Politics of Racial Inclusion and Exclusion in Star Trek: Voyager

Christian Jimenez

Race in *Star Trek* has attracted much attention (Kanzler; Ott and Aoki). On the whole, scholars have tended to see the series as progressive in providing representation for once marginalized groups (Geraghty 47). Other scholars acknowledge the apparent diversity on *Star Trek* but question how deep a commitment is being made to multiculturalism (Austin; Kanzler; Ott and Aoki). The analysis differs in two respects. On the one hand, racial representation of minorities in *Star Trek* has clearly grown. *Star Trek Voyager* provides strong evidence that the producers and writers are pro-multiculturalism.

On the other hand, the multiculturalism as will be argued is not as thorough as often believed. Moreover, multicultural emphasis on racial difference sometimes obscures reactionary messages embedded in key episodes. In particular, when episodes highlight the dilemma of past (or present) crimes of war based on race, *Voyager* continually raises one kind of comparison (usually the Nazi Holocaust) while suppressing other possible comparisons (notably, the holocaust of Native Americans).

In essence, *Voyager* has a double-edged message regarding racial diversity. While racial diversity is applauded and promoted the show recognizes various cultures in human history have reacted to such diversity with immense violence. Although the show consistently condemns such violence, repeatedly, distinctions are offered to soften judgment against American colonialism. Thus, while colonialism, in general, is criticized, American colonialism is seen as more complex and ambiguous. This will be shown, primarily, in how *Voyager* utilizes the character of Chakotay in various key episodes.

Of course, Chakotay is the not only character used when race-specific themes come up. B'Elanna, The Doctor, and Seven of Nine are often featured in such episodes as well. However, as we shall see Chakotay in the show validates certain American mythologies the most powerfully due to his Native American heritage. While other characters provide supporting evidence through their stories, Chakotay plays a central role in propagating a liberal form of multiculturalism that challenges certain American phobias about race while confirming certain stereotypes simultaneously.

Before and After

A complete history of race in *Star Trek* prior to *Voyager* is not possible here. But some major elements need to be highlighted before turning to Voyager proper. Television repeatedly makes use of racial stereotypes across many genres (Hall, Jimenez). But racial stereotypes of Native Americans in science fiction are particularly persistent (Adare). *Star Trek* as initially launched did not differ greatly. Very broad stereotypes of various races from the Japanese to Russian to African American were used. Despite internal mythmaking by its own audience, Lawrence and Jewett point to evidence (confirmed by *The Original Series*) that the original series was highly conservative (232).

As Austin notes, while Roddenberry was a racial progressive, he grew up in a racist household and, at times, that influence occurs in *Star Trek* (Austin 65). The series "presented a mixed message" that was very "reactionary" (Austin). Racial progress was promoted but mainly as instrumental to winning the Cold War (Lawrence and Jewett 232–233). Though all non-whites suffered due to this focus, arguably, Native Americans received the worst treatment. In *Star Trek: The Original Series*, all Native American characters were played by whites using make-up to darken their faces.

In contrast, African Americans played African Americans in the original series. Certain stories deliberately commented on civil rights protests that were occurring when the show was being aired and attacked racial prejudice, "Let That Be Your Last Battlefield" (*TOS*, 3.15). *Star Trek* was also the first show ever on American television to show an interracial kiss—between Kirk and Uhura—in "Plato's Stepchildren" (3.10) (Cantor 46). Yet even within these remarkable feats, the white-savior narrative was dominant.

However, when *Star Trek: The Next Generation* was launched in 1987, major changes were made in how race was treated. Unlike the original *Star Trek* where race was only one of several key issues, diversity and its necessity became a central focus. Whereas Uhura was the only African American and only female in a major position of power, *The Next Generation* had Beverly

Crusher as the ship's doctor, Deanna Troi as ship's counselor, and Geordi La Forge as the ship's engineer.

Star Trek usually limited itself to denouncing racism. In contrast, *The Next Generation* actively celebrated and applauded racial diversity. Nevertheless, racially regressive tropes like the white savior complex persisted. Episodes that dealt with race specifically often had Picard as the lead protagonist and/or Data. Though race is brought up in many episodes only *a single episode* is devoted to Native Americans, specifically.

In "Journey's End" (7.20), Jean-Luc Picard must try to mediate a dispute between the Cardassians (often symbolically framed as Nazis) and Native Americans who long ago fled Earth to settle on an alien planet. In "Journey's End," in a rare moment, the government's *genocide* of Native American does show up.

However, the episode is flawed as Wesley as the white hero is the main concern. In this episode, Wesley becomes a higher being after undergoing a spirit quest administered by a Native American. It is revealed the Native American is really the Traveler, a being that believed (as it turns out correctly) Wesley has special abilities to go through time and space. Nevertheless, the episode is a milestone in that Native Americans are finally represented by themselves. Native American culture is praised and framed positively.

While other races—notably blacks and Asians—are visible on *Next Generation*, Native Americans almost never appear. "Journey's End" by no means erases this problem. Picard notes that the enterprise being tasked with removing the Natives is a "disturbing parallel" to past policies. However, he uses neutral language like the Natives being "displaced" to describe their plight.

The producers clearly remain torn. On the one hand, the historic violence against Native American is acknowledged. But understanding its entire depth is often softened. As Ott and Aoki argue, *Next Generation* often participated in a form of "cultural tourism, rather than an opportunity for cultural appreciation and exchange.... *TNG* invites viewers to participate in a collective vision of the future that feels socially progressive because it appears diverse, even as it makes diversity comfortable by driving out and alienating cultural difference" (403). *Voyager,* as we shall see, inherits this complex legacy of promoting racial diversity mainly for instrumental reasons but sometimes celebrating multiculturalism on its terms.

Next Generation does deal with how race impacts social norms over health care, religious devotion, and heterosexual marriage. But when far more serious policies around race are highlighted from ethnic cleansing to outright genocide, *Voyager* falls into a simplistic binary portraying the Nazi holocaust as incomparable in its evil making the American genocide through implicit framing. The overall politics of the series is thus progressive but a highly conservative kind of progressivism.

Racing Ahead?

Whereas representation was limited to racial minorities prominent in America, *Star Trek: Voyager* was more global in orientation. The *Voyager* cast had an African American male (Tim Russ), an Asian American male (Garrett Wang), one Hispanic male (Robert Beltran), and one Hispanic woman (Roxann Dawson) in leading roles. Though race-specific topics are addressed, overall, *Voyager* devoted "a number of episodes ... [to] contemporary newsworthy topics such as capital punishment, genetic engineering and ... healthcare [which] provided a suitable allegorical basis for stories" (Geraghty 47). Thus, multiculturalism was a focus because it was similar to other hot-button issues (abortion, gay rights) that had become more prominent in the mid- and late 1990s.

Though this might be true of all *Star Trek* series, as Geraghty notes, *only Voyager* kept this topical focus throughout the "entirety" of its run whereas some (like *Star Trek: Enterprise*) was more inconsistent in treating socially divisive issues (48). Moreover, the actual role of the characters has shifted dramatically.

In *Next Generation*, Geordi had a female Hispanic engineer, Sonya Gomez, aiding him. However, while the role is clearly meant to be positive, the woman is a klutz, accidentally spilling chocolate on Picard in "Q Who" (2.16) and is, initially, overwhelmed when the crew first encounters the Borg. These are normal responses, but they play into the stereotype of the fragile, Latina damsel-in-distress. In sharp contrast, Lieutenant Torres is tough, self-reliant, and opinionated and leads the engineering crew. In B'Elanna the idea of a Hispanic woman being tough and intellectual are unified.

But multiculturalism is also embedded in the key structural motifs the series had come to use. Gymnich notes whereas voice-overs were typically given to the most powerful crew member, who was invariably male and white or both, "the default voice-over narrators [in Voyager] ... [are by] traditionally marginalized groups" whether in terms of "a woman (Captain Kathryn Janeway)" or, racially, in the case of Chakotay, a Native American, or Tuvok, a black Vulcan (68). For instance, in one episode, Janeway consults the log entries of Captain Sulu and not Kirk as one would expect.

The idea transmitted is obvious that Starfleet is a genuinely multi-racial organization (though in *The Original Series* Sulu's role was consistently of a subordinate). Nevertheless, post–1960s iterations of *Trek* would have a multicultural bent. Yet of all characters, Chakotay's status is unique in not just *Star Trek* but in television history in being one of only a handful of Native American characters portrayed on primetime television in the 1990s.

As Gymnich has observed, *Star Trek* series including *Voyager*, despite being located in outer space, have often focused on "individuals who discover

198 Part III. Negotiating Identities

new mental capacities or who are subject to visions, hallucinations, and other types of imaginary perception" (63). Insofar as Chakotay has these abilities there is nothing racist as Deanna Troi and others also have telepathic powers. However, although all of Voyager's crew experience visions, Chakotay has a special narrative role to play in episodes where characters experience shocking visions and/or memories.

Characters with telepathic abilities *per se* have no racial meaning. But in the internal mythos of Star Trek, Chakotay's abilities carry multiple meanings that serve an ideological function. In one episode, "Unity" (3.17), Gymnich points out "a group of Borg who have left the larger Borg collective, but who have still maintained a mental linkage among themselves, temporarily include Chakotay in their telepathic union without his consent. This deprives him of his free will and brainwashes him into doing what they wish him to do" (70). In "Unity," Chakotay falls in love with a human-Borg hybrid who helps heals his wounds but uses him as well. The ostensive purpose of the Borg is benign—to create a utopia with humans no longer part of the collective—but their method of submerging individual identity comments on the wrongness of ignoring individual rights even for a good common goal. Chakotay thus signifies a middle course between the right-wing extreme of biological racism but also the left-wing extremism of egalitarian but nonconsensual anti-racism.

The essential message is positive, but it works upon the racial stereotype of the noble non-white helping others selflessly because that is his nature. This reverses the stereotype of the savage hurting others, but it points out that *Voyager*, while presenting a utopian vision of race, has not forgotten race entirely. Chakotay being a Native American is slyly alluded to in episodes like "Unity." For fan audiences, Geraghty notes, a future without prejudice is possible because "the main *Star Trek* characters are seen as honest and compassionate, amongst other things, therefore helping to cure social problems such as racism, sexual discrimination, and prejudice" (97). The problem is this utopian message is not as honest or pro-multicultural as it first appears.

Utopian images on *Star Trek* are not static. Hall notes how, usually, in the past, the image of

> Indian tribesmen ... constantly threatening to overrun the screen. They are likely to appear at any moment out of the darkness to decapitate the beautiful heroine, kidnap the children, burn the encampment or threaten to boil, cook and eat the innocent explorer or colonial administrator.... And against them is always counterposed the isolated white figure, alone "out there," confronting his Destiny... [276].

Repeatedly, *Voyager* will make two arguments that are not entirely consistent.

The first message is of history repeating itself due to ignorance. To stop this, collective memories of crimes, however horrible, should be recalled. However, such memories are usually framed in pro–American terms with Nazis as the leading perpetrators of mass violence. However, occasionally, colonial violence is alluded to (including American violence against the Natives). But a difference emerges. Whereas the Nazi case almost always calls out for punishment, colonial-violence or mass violence period should be remembered but forgiven. This is most prominent in a Doctor-centric episode, "Living Witness" (4.23), where The Doctor is in a future where the crew's exploits are misrepresented as predatory and genocidal. However, unlike the Nazi episodes, the emphasis is simply on remembrance, not retribution. The constant message, whether narrated by Chakotay or B'Elanna or The Doctor, is that past racism must never be forgotten yet not necessarily punished.

Consistently, as a whole, *Voyager* makes a utopian yet conservative argument for multiculturalism. In "Remember" (3.6), B'Elanna experiences incredibly sensual dreams that become increasingly intense and sexual. She is a young Enaran woman intensely in love with a young Enaran man called Dathan Alaris. At first, she keeps the dreams to herself but eventually confides in Chakotay. Initially, he is curious if the dreams might be about someone B'Elanna knows—the obvious implication being he is speaking of himself.

Yet B'Elanna surprises Chakotay through her confession not just of how sexualized the dreams are but that although (in terms of the *diegesis*) we see B'Elanna and her face and body she is not herself in the dreams but is an Enaran woman, Korenna. The Enarans are a telepathic race. Enarans are onboard Voyager and as the dreams with Dathan become increasingly strange—in one sequence when they embrace, Dathan's body is suddenly completely burned.

As the dreams continue, we learn that a powerful Enaran and Korenna's father, Jareth, disapproves of her relationship. Darath is below her in terms of social status. But as the story nears the conclusion, Jareth's language becomes more and more colonial and racist. He hates Darath for being lowly and belonging to a different ethnicity (the Regressives) than him and Korenna. Korenna continues to ignore her father's bigotry and minimize it. B'Elanna risks brain damage if the dreams continue and The Doctor inhibits them. But B'Elanna wants to know what the dreams mean and removes the inhibitor. In a stunning reversal, we find out Jareth has been colonizing the Regressives into camps where they are deliberately killed off or infected. Darath divulges the genocide to Korenna but she is unwilling to believe him. Jareth captures Darath and he is burned alive along with some other Regressives. But rather than protest or stop the killing or even cry, Korenna actually joins in a communal chant celebrating the massacre.

The Enarans vehemently deny the genocide. Janeway believes the Prime Directive makes it illegal for Voyager to intervene. However, B'Elanna convinces one Enaran, Jessen, to take her memories so the genocide will not be completely forgotten. While essentially a violent act, "[t]he manipulation of B'Elanna's dreams thus turns out to be a strategy for correcting the manipulation of history" (Gymnich 73). What is missed is the framing of how other non–American cultures engage in Holocaust denial.

B'Elanna's act of sharing and picking Jessen is not accidental. In the early part of the episode, Jessen, shyly, hints she is attracted to Harry. B'Elanna offers to do engineering duties by herself, so Harry and Jessen can spend time together. Race, thus, is working at two levels—one within the dream sequences recounting the genocide (and cover-up). But race was foreshadowed in the Jessen-Harry pairing. While we do know a bit more of how Jessen and Harry interact most of their dating takes place off-screen.

The allusions to the Holocaust are obvious—as is the controversy over Holocaust denial that became prominent in the 1990s. Whereas in the 1970s, it was generally agreed that the Holocaust was both unique and killed an estimated six million civilians, skeptics on the left and right emerged (though for different reasons). The Holocaust, it was argued, was neither as unique nor as intentional as supposed. In "Remember" (3.6), the characters remembered often wear turbans evoking "the Orient" and Asia. The episode might be as much about the Armenian genocide as the Holocaust. The stance of the episode is ambiguous. It is not clear that the producers are denying the Native Americans were slaughtered. Rather, the episode cleverly frames the issue of genocide as one of Jews-and-Nazis with the audience left to make the obvious inference of who is guilty.

Another episode alluding to the Nazis has The Doctor call up a controversial program to save B'Elanna. Chakotay takes on a mentor role, again, not with B'Elanna but another crew member. In "Nothing Human" (5.8), an injured cytoplasmic life-form attaches itself to Torres by accident. It begins to drain her life and The Doctor convinces Janeway to have him search for the most advanced biologist living. The computer comes up with the hologram of Cardassian exobiologist Crell Moset.

Because the Cardassians are used as an analogy to the Nazis, B'Elanna initially is upset. Once more as with "Remember" (3.6), the audience is primed to the issue of race. But at the beginning, it seems The Doctor is correct. B'Elanna is being stubborn as fits her character. Yet slowly it is revealed that Crell may not be simply a biologist but a major war criminal. The Doctor is initially charmed because Crell appears humane, humorous, urbane and cultured—when the revelations come that he may have performed Nazi-like experiments on the occupied minorities we see not just the Nazi parallel but a specific stereotype, the so-called educated Nazi. While Nazis (and neo-Nazis) are typically depicted as fanatics and outright racists, Crell's mannerisms and body type—he is thin, handsome, and speaks softly—disturb our image of the Nazi. Instead of being a frothing-at-the-mouth nationalist/racist, Crell freely admits he dissented and did not agree with the occupation. He criticizes the military and insists he was only a physician and scientist. He is cosmopolitan and took part in intercultural scientific conferences. All the evidence confounds the image of the Nazi as openly and purely evil.

Since Crell evinces no obvious markers of the Nazi—using racist language or marching in militaristic fashion—the audience is unsure of how to respond. Initially, Crell counsels that the cytoplasmic life-form should be killed outright; The Doctor disagrees. Just by visually looking at B'Elanna he notes she must be a "hybrid." The Doctor congratulates the accuracy of his scientific judgment. In short, there are strong hints that Crell does think in terms of race and is able to minutely categorize people. But because he is a biologist, we are never sure (and the episode leaves open the possible interpretation) that he is just an apolitical scientist.

A Bajoran crew member, Tabor, upon seeing Crell goes crazy. He is "the Moset" who tortured his family. But Tabor is relying on second-hand accounts. He cannot totally confirm Crell is the Moset who killed his family. The Doctor naively protests, "the man you're accusing cured the Fostossa virus. He stopped an epidemic that killed thousands of Bajorans!" ("Nothing Human" 5.8). Perhaps Crell infected people with the virus precisely to create a cure. The information in the episode is hazy.

Both stories might be correct. Crell was no racist, but he experimented with Bajorans to find a cure. Still, he made a Nazi-like decision—the Bajorans are no different from Jewish people.

In a critical exchange, Crell remarks about "higher" and "lower" life-forms. He is a Nazi, but not a crude Nazi. B'Elanna is saved and the nameless life-form rejoins his (or its?) race. However, Janeway leaves the decision of whether to retain Crell with The Doctor. After a heated exchange of words, he opts to destroy the hologram.

B'Elanna's life is in danger, and Crell may be needed to save her. Interestingly, B'Elanna agrees with Tabor and wishes to die rather than be helped by Crell. Janeway overrules her wishes. But unlike Tabor, Chakotay does not speak with B'Elanna, nor do we ever learn his opinion about B'Elanna's desires. A genocide occurred and the Native American counsels that the past be overcome. Chakotay is not irrational and has to weigh competing interests as well as competing claims about the truth.

Chakotay asks Tabor, "Could these simply have been rumors spread by Bajorans who hated the Cardassians?" ("Nothing Human"). Even after insisting Crell is guilty, Chakotay argues forgiveness is better for the Bajorans. While the message might be legitimate—a wounded race need not seek vengeance—the evocation is disturbing. That the Caradassians are Nazi-like is not in doubt. But did they commit all these massacres, and did they do so purely out of race hatred? One can see that the episode, while retaining anger about the Nazi genocide, cleverly deemphasizes it and by extension tries to counter the left-wing interpretation of the Native American holocaust. Whereas historians, like the late Howard Zinn, insist on the severity of the genocide, the episode tacitly argues what matters is the present and pragmatically having different cultures get along with one another.

As Seven of Nine remarks: "It is curious. The Borg are accused of assimilating information with no regard for life. This Cardassian did the same; and yet, his behavior is tolerated" ("Nothing Human" 5.8). As the show tries to respond, this difference in attitude is due to the exigent circumstances of saving B'Elanna. But underneath we can see the producers trying to preempt an obvious objection that they are setting up an easy argument. However, by making Crell educated and charming the episode poses a difficult dilemma.

That a genocide took place is indisputable. But was it purely for profit and race hatred or were there complicating factors? The portrayal of Crell is meant to make the viewer uneasy. Even among Nazis, distinctions are possible between the outright killers and those who merely collaborated.

The dilemma is that the framing itself is deceptive. In both "Remember" (3.6) and "Nothing Human" (5.8) genocide is treated as if it were the exceptional act of one group. But in other episodes historical violence is depoliticized even with a political theme directly interjected. In "Tattoo" (2.9), the crew sends an away mission on a strange planet. Being on the surface, Chakotay's memories of his childhood are triggered. He recalls how his father, the leader of a Central American tribe, has tried to hold onto old customs and teach young Chakotay about the primitive Rubber Tree People. Young Chakotay has no interest in continuing the traditions. He has signed up with the Starfleet and intends to leave the village. Other tribes have assimilated why has his father's tribe persisted in being the past.

His father, Kolopak (Henry Darrow), is angry. The "sky spirits" visited Chakotay's ancestors and protected them. The Native Americans called Inheritors, uniquely, kept the good traditions but, eventually, lost them. The sky spirits, coincidentally, have targeted Voyager seeing it as a manifestation of the same greedy colonials who destroyed Earth's environment. Chakotay's unique connection allows him to speak to the sky spirits who are in the form of pale-skinned aliens. A symbol on Earth matches the one Chakotay finds on the nameless moon, 70,000 light years away. Janeway is curious how the same symbol could be present and Chakotay answers at the beginning of the episode: "I can give you an official Rubber Tree People theory—Sky Spirits.... It's an ancient myth. Sky Spirits from Above created the first Rubber People in their own image and led the way to a sacred land where the Rubber People could live for eternity" ("Tattoo" 2.9). By Chakotay's sarcastic tone he is skeptical of his father's beliefs. Only by encountering the Sky Spirits face-to-face does he reevaluate his own lack of faith. As Lancioni neatly summarizes the moral of the story:

> symbol that had been used by his ancestors to "heal the land." The planet's inhabitants, the Sky Spirits, who recognize his tattoo and speak his ancestral language, explain that they gave a gift to Chakotay's ancestors to protect and care for the planet but ... no trace of his ancestors, assume they have been eradicated by other humans. Chakotay convinces them that humans have learned from their mistakes [137].

Chakotay convinces the Spirits (aliens) by re-enacting his father's behavior. When he was a child, "Chakotay remembers ... his father and the others had laid down their weapons, saying that the Rubber Tree People had reason to be afraid, as their history, like other Indigenous peoples' history, is satiated with conquest and subjugators" (Adare 43).

Tuvok, initially, resists and says he will lodge an official complaint. But Chakotay is right as Voyager's weapons are useless against the aliens' power. As one of the aliens says, "We were taught all of them [the Inheritors] had been annihilated. We were taught your world had been ravaged by those [the whites] with no respect for life or land" ("Tattoo" 2.9). Only by remembering past Native American rituals can Chakotay convince the aliens humans have changed so that Voyager is spared their anger.

In these episodes, Chakotay consistently portrays "the 'good Indian' in the classic Pocahontas sense" using, variously, medicine wheels, spirit quests, and so on to help the crew (Adare 45). As Adare writes, Beltran himself internalized some of these stereotypes by noting how to him Chakotay often came off as "limp, weasely, cowardly, homosexual, charming" (45). The main narrative role Chakotay plays is to present a message of forgiveness and hope. The colonial violence against the Natives is acknowledged as is the greed of the whites who took the land.

However, unlike "Remember" (3.6) or "Nothing Human"(5.8), "Tattoo" (2.9) settles for a generic condemnation of violence. The Sky Spirits do not stand for the Natives. The Native Americans themselves seem to have no actual identity or specific culture. The episode thus cleverly is parallel to other similar episodes but much less political. Yet as the language shows there is acknowledgment that the Native and Nazi genocides are comparable with the alien using the specific word "annihilated."

"Nazi?"

In the episodes reviewed, the Nazi analogy is never explicit except for a special two-part episode, "The Killing Game: Part I and II" (4.18–4.19). Race plays an interesting role as the crew is not in any one real place but inside "a holodeck recreation of occupied France during the Second World War. Being completely immersed in their respective roles as French Resistance fighters, soldiers and villagers, the crew have to combat the aggressive Hirogen who have taken on the persona of Nazis" (Geraghty 30). The Hirogen had already captured Voyager but rather than killing them put them through brutal holodeck recreations to learn more about their "prey."

As in past episodes, "The Killing Game" is meta-textual in that the holodeck-characters mock the personas of the crew. Seven of Nine is a salon singer. Whereas a text can be the episode the viewer is seeing; the meta-text refers to elements that can only be understood by those outside the fictional reality in our world. Janeway is the manager of a bar that is a front for resistance forces—just as she was a leader on Voyager. Tuvok is a French bartender. But their basic personalities remain with Seven being highly aggressive and Tuvok highly logical. Moreover, the various races of the characters are not obscured. While the majority of the people in the holodeck version of the French village, Saint Claire, are white, Tuvok it appears is visibly black. While his presence might be improbable, a black man in France achieving some social status in pre–World War II is plausible. The Hirogen have implanted neurological devices to make the crew think they are their characters.

Seven is one of the first to break free of these controls and The Doctor informs her of the Hirogen takeover. At first, Seven is highly vulnerable because she is unfamiliar with World War II history and is unclear how to perform her role in order to help free the others. When some of them wake up they are puzzled by their surroundings. Tuvok says he does not "recognize" the setting. But Tom does, noting that "He's wearing a Nazi uniform. We're on Earth during the Second World War." "Nazi?" Seven asks. As Tom explains: "Totalitarian fanatics bent on world conquest: the Borg of their day" ("The Killing Game, Part II" 4.19). This might indicate these episodes focus on the Nazis solely as conquerors not necessarily racist ones. However, this is untrue.

While one Hirogen commander, Karr, thinks the Hirogen need to change their ways and evolve beyond merely being hunters another violently disagrees. Nevertheless, he follows orders to make a truce with the rebelling members of Voyager until a holodeck Nazi gives a stirring speech on behalf of racial superiority.

> the Kommandant is a fool.... He's never *embraced the Fuhrer or his vision.* One does not cooperate with decadent forms of life. One ... eliminates them. The Kommandant speaks of civilization. The ancient Romans were civilized. The Jews are civilized. But in all its moral decay, Rome fell to the spears of our ancestors, as the Jews are falling now. Look at our destiny. The field of red, the purity of German blood.... No one can deny us, no power on Earth or beyond. Not the Christian Saviour, not the God of the Jews.... We must countermand the Kommandant's orders, stay and fight. We must be faithful to who we are [emphasis added, "Killing Game: Part II" 4.19].

Turaj becomes convinced the Nazi is right and kills Karr, and the Hirogen set about to kill the Voyager crew. Although the Hirogen, unlike the Cardassians, are not Nazis themselves the two-part episode does demonstrate the general "allure of fascism" has for even non-human societies (Lancioni 150). Of course, the Hirogen lose as the crew cleverly manipulate holodeck versions of Klingons to kill the Hirogen including the Nazi who inspired Turaj. Turaj also dies refusing to be captured by Janeway.

Unlike other episodes, the ideological message of "Killing Game" is blunt. Whereas the Voyager uses the holodeck for many purposes, the Hirogen solely use it for combat. However, such single-mindedness is their undoing. The Hirogen have taken off the safety protocols on the holodeck, making the simulated weapons used against them highly effective. Finally, contrary to the Nazi belief that Voyager represents a nightmare hodgepodge of "decadent forms of life" it is precisely the diverse skills of a black Vulcan, a white female Borg, and Native American soldier that allow Voyager to resist and triumph over superior forces. In short, Nazi ideology is not just morally wrong but self-destructive and self-defeating in practice.

However, even here, the utopian vision of Voyager has to engage in some incredible leaps of logic beyond the usual the episodes depend on. In reality, of course, racial discrimination and segregation were rife during World War II. While racial minorities did indeed perform bravely in certain key parts of World War II, the multicultural ensemble in "Killing Game" never occurred in real life.

Looking Beyond Race Through Race

In *Voyager*, in sum, historical crimes against civilians based on race are treated in qualitatively different ways. The Nazi Holocaust calls forth the most explicit denunciation. Other racially charged crimes are given a less totalistic condemnation.

While the focus, thus far, has been on the Native American as a metaphor, it would be wrong to think *Voyager* is single-minded. Racially charged topics occur with surprising regularity. In "Prophecy," B'Elanna and Tom's interracially mixed child is taken as a messiah by a band of Klingons, and one sexist and racist Klingon challenges the child's "purity" only to nearly die when a crippling disease comes on him. But of course, B'Elanna's baby provides blood that saves him and the other Klingons, proving the benefits of interracial cooperation.

Similarly, when Chakotay and Seven are stranded on a primitive planet, she is, initially, disgusted at the primitive tribe that looks upon them with fascination. But when they are threatened with being colonized, she becomes sensitive to what will happen to them and helps making their planet inaccessible to outside invaders—at least, temporarily.

But these episodes deal with race implicitly. Occasionally, though, the framing of racism is unmistakable. In "Repentance" (7.13), Voyager takes on eight prisoners and security guards tasked with keeping them safe for their eventual execution. Seven is, in the beginning, captured and threatened by one, Iko. The Doctor subsequently learns and cures Iko of his violent tendencies by repairing a neurological problem. Iko becomes calm and peaceful, putting into question the harshness of his death sentence. Neelix also discovers through Joleg that the aliens have the victim sentence those found guilty—often through flimsy evidence.

While class is being critiqued, the obvious message is about America's prison system and its incarceration of Latinos and African Americans and the ubiquity of executions of minorities by the state. But the show is not being propagandistic. When the prisoners seize on a chance to escape, Joleg nearly kills one prison guard, Yediq, but Iko saves him. Iko has clearly changed, but Joleg was merely manipulating Neelix. The facts remain true. The alien society has structured their legal system so that certain racial and economic minorities are condemned by birth to almost always be imprisoned and executed, and some members of that minority do fit the stereotype of the dangerous criminal whereas others are victims of circumstance.

One the one hand, episodes like "Repentance" (7.13), highlight racial injustice and there is little doubt the white audience is being forced to cope with how African Americans, mainly, are being abused but the message is mixed. Right-wing analysts would see liberal praise of *Star Trek* as part of a greater conspiracy to indoctrinate the public. But "Repentance," if anything, demonstrates the ambivalence of the producers and performers. In "Prophecy" (7.14), interracial marriage is praised, but it is marriage by a heterosexual couple. Similarly, "Repentance" condemns the death penalty as barbaric especially administered by racists. But it leaves open the possibility that states do have the right to imprison, and the death sentence might be appropriate in certain cases.

A final piece of evidence brought to bear is when The Doctor is awoken 700 years in the future and is on a planet with a history of two warring races ("Living Witness" 4.23). The way the past has been remembered, however, at the beginning of the episode is absurd with Voyager portrayed as an extreme fascist gang willing to commit "genocide" in order to get home. The Kyrians, a group historically victimized by the Vaskans, the dominant group, remember the Voyager crew as sadistic.

When The Doctor tries to persuade a Kyrian historian he is wrong, he is simply shut off. But The Doctor's presence stirs up a race riot by Vaskans, who, having long denied being culpable, are tired of being blamed and demonized. The Kyrian historian now wants to know the truth, and The Doctor argues, briefly, it might be better to destroy him to return the Kyrians and Vaskans to their former (if mistaken) mythology that was, at least, not hostile. The Kyrian historian opts for wanting the truth even if it does not fit his preconceptions. The message is once more explicit that Voyager (and presumably America in symbolic terms) may *occasionally* act like their enemies but they are *essentially* different.

The series by no means denies racist (even systemic racist) structures may exist in America. But these structures might be, sadly, typical of all human societies. What is framed is how these structures might be overcome. A key difference between the colonialism of the Federation and that of the enemy is precisely this highly American belief that the past can and should be overcome. Race ought to be highlighted but not obsessed over. The analysis here has merely highlighted how this utopian hope—especially in the case of genocide but not solely in that case alone—has to engage in rather generous amounts of myth-making to stabilize the different liberal elements in *Trek* mythology (pro-feminist, pro-multiculturalism) with the more conservative elements (respect for military values, deferring to the chain-of-command).

Conclusion

The analysis has demonstrated both race-specific and non-race-specific episodes in *Voyager* repeatedly try to provide a utopian vision of the universe and America free of racism. Racial differences exist but are embraced as ethically good but also strategically superior. Hence the forgive-message Chakotay is often tasked with delivering is not entirely racist or racial. Nevertheless, the broad contours remain: while racial diversity is welcome, sensitivity to the past regarding racial minorities does have a certain limit.

As Brian Attebery argues science fiction "can offer important insights into the limits of the imaginable and the ways those limits are changing" (15). The crew of Voyager (like, presumably, America itself) must learn to overcome past hatreds and unite to survive and fulfill its mission. Those who fail to do so are guilty of being unpatriotic as well as betraying their civic duty. Moreover, those who embrace the opposing ideology of extreme racism (the Borg, Hirogen) often find themselves on the losing side.

However, this binary of racism/non-racism is powerful, but only up to a certain point. It would be wrong to imply that no progress has occurred whatsoever since America's founding or the creation of *Star Trek* in the 1960s. However, these changes occur within a system retaining racial privilege. It is a fact that racial minorities face substantial problems from having little political power to having their lives strongly limited by a social structure that may acknowledge their presence but regards them with suspicion.

It would be unfair to saddle *Voyager* with responsibility for all these ills. Nevertheless, despite good intentions in some cases, it is hard to miss recurrent messages of forgiveness being framed. The Native Americans on *Voyager* act as many liberals would want them to, retaining their rituals, acting "spiritually" pure, being noble, handsome, and brave, but existing, essentially, to save humanity (but especially whites). Self-interested behavior by them is rarely represented because that would be improper to how the show frames them.

Voyager represents the mainstream consensus of acknowledging past episodes of racist domination but positing a myth that progress has been made to the point that domination is a mere detail. There are exceptions. The Nazi genocide is considered one of the worst of all human events with Soviet crimes and other episodes of mass murder somewhat behind. But the Native American genocide remains a topic too difficult to entirely absorb.

Voyager has, in essence, a split attitude towards race. Representation is present of various minorities, but they work within a larger mythic system. Although Chakotay was "played by a non–First Nations actor," he remains the "first 'Native American' crew member shown in the Star Trek universe. Chakotay also represents the only First Nations character ever portrayed on a weekly American science fiction television series" (Adare 41). Chakotay's stories, then, do represent a major leap forward in race relations. He is represented as a hero consistently unlike many past representations denying Native Americans that role.

However, as this essay has tried to argue, Chakotay rarely represents Native Americans as they understand themselves as much as a white liberal representation that assumes assimilation is the only viable solution. Awareness should lead to forgiveness not retribution or reparation or revolution. But it is not Native Americans who are issuing this message or accepting. Rather it is a certain construction of the Native American that is doing these things. What stands for Chakotay, however, can stand for other oppressed groups from Jews to blacks to Muslims.

These groups have undeniably also faced horrors in their particular histories. But these people like the Native Americans shown on *Voyager* should not obsess over past ills but make peace with their enemies and move forward towards an integrated future. This framing is deceptive in that it offers only a simplistic binary choice of either complete embrace of American-style multiculturalism or totalitarian Nazism, but other models are possible. The racially inclusive message of *Star Trek* is only one of many models that should be examined before being uncritically embraced.

WORKS CITED

Adare, Sierra. *"Indian" Stereotypes in TV Science Fiction: First Nations' Voices Speak Out.* University of TP, 2005.
Attebery, Brian. *Decoding Gender in Science Fiction.* Routledge, 2002.
Austin, Allan. "The Limits of *Star Trek*'s Final Frontier: 'The Omega Glory' and 1960s American Liberalism." *Space and Time: Essays on Visions of History in Science Fiction and Fantasy Television*, edited by David C. Wright, Jr., and Austin, Macfarland, 2010, pp. 61–81.
Cantor, Paul. *Gilligan Unbound: Pop Culture in the Age of Globalization.* Rowman and Littlefield, 2001.
Geraghty, Lincoln. *Living Star Trek.* IB Tauris, 2007.
Gymnich, Marion. "Exploring Inner Spaces: Authoritative Narratives and Subjective Worlds in *Star Trek: Deep Space Nine*, *Voyager* and *Enterprise*." *Narrative Strategies in Television Series*, edited by Gaby Allrath and Gymnich, Palgrave, 2005, pp. 62–79.
Hall, Stuart. "Racist Ideologies and the Media." *Media Studies: A Reader*, edited by Paul Marris and Sue Thoruham, New York UP, 1999, pp. 271–282.
Jimenez, Christian. "Cynical Tolerance: Race, Gender and Fraternal Fears." *Bonds of Brotherhood: Essays on Gender and Masculinity in Sons of Anarchy*, edited by Susan Fanetti, MacFarland, 2018, pp. 61–81.
"Journey's End." *Star Trek: The Next Generation*, written by Ronald D. Moore, directed by Corey Allen, Season 7, episode 20, Paramount, 28 March 1994.
Kanzler, Katja. "'A Cuchi Moya!': *Star Trek*'s Native Americans." *American Studies Journal*, vol. 45, no. 6, 2000, pp. 44–50.
"The Killing Game, Part I." *Star Trek: Voyager*, written by Brannon Braga and Joe Menosky, Season 4, episode 18, Paramount, 4 Mar. 1998.
"The Killing Game, Part II." *Star Trek: Voyager*, written by Brannon Braga and Joe Menosky, Season 4, episode 19, Paramount, 4 Mar. 1998.
Lancioni, Judith. "The Future as Past Perfect: Appropriation of History in the *Star Trek* Series." *Space and Time: Essays on Visions of History in Science Fiction and Fantasy Television*, edited by David C. Wright, Jr., and Allan Austin, MacFarland, 2010, pp. 131–155.
Lawrence, John Shelton, and Robert Jewett. *The Myth of the American Superhero.* William Eerdmans Publishing, 2002.
"Let That Be Your Last Battlefield." *Star Trek*, story by Lee Cronin, directed by Jud Taylor, Season 3, episode 15, Paramount, 10 Jan. 1969.
"Living Witness." *Star Trek: Voyager*, story by Brannon Braga, directed by Tim Russ, Season 4, episode 23, Paramount, 29 Apr. 1998.
"Nothing Human." *Star Trek: Voyager*, written by Jeri Taylor, Season 5, episode 8, Paramount, 2 Dec. 1998.
Ott, Brian, and Eric Aoki. "Popular Imagination and Identity Politics: Reading the Future in *Star Trek: The Next Generation*." *Western Journal of Communication*, vol. 65, no. 4, 2001, pp. 392–415.
Pearson, Roberta. "Serialized Ideology." *How to Watch Television*, edited by Ethan Thompson and Jason Mittell, NY UP, 2013, pp. 213–222.
"Plato's Stepchildren." *Star Trek: The Original Series*, created by Gene Roddenberry, Dir. David Alexander, Season 3, episode 12, Paramount, 22 Nov. 1968.
"Prophecy." *Star Trek: Voyager*, teleplay by Michael Sussman and Phyllis Strong, Perf. by Roxann Dawson, Season 7, episode 14, Paramount, 7 Feb. 2001.
"Q Who." *Star Trek: The Next Generation*, written by Maurice Hurley, directed by Rob Bowman, Season 2, episode 16, Paramount, 8 May 1989.
"Remember." *Star Trek: Voyager*, story by Brannon Braga and Joe Menosky, Season 3, episode 6, Paramount, 9 Oct. 1996.
"Repentance." *Star Trek: Voyager*, teleplay by Robert Doherty, directed by Mike Vejar, Season 7, episode 13, Paramount, 31 Jan. 2001.

210 Part III. Negotiating Identities

"Tattoo." *Star Trek: Voyager*, teleplay by Michael Piller, Season 2, episode 9, Paramount, 6 Nov. 1995.
"Unity." *Star Trek: Voyager*, written by Kenneth Biller, directed by Robert Duncan McNeill, Season 3, episode 17, Paramount, 12 Feb. 1997.

PART IV
Broader Perspectives of the Future

The Politics of Nurturing
Gender, Care and Colonialism in Voyager's *Female Friendships*

Rosy B. Mack

> Hello, Michael. I hope that wherever this finds you, you are well. I imagine you have your own command now. The captain of your own ship. I have always tried to show you by example. The best way to know yourself is to know others. You are curious, an explorer.... Know that I am as proud of you as if you were my own daughter. Take good care. But more importantly, take good care of those in your care.
> —The Last Will and Testament
> of Captain Philippa Georgiou

In September 2017, *Star Trek* fans were treated to an extraordinary sequence of scenes at the opening of the multi-verse's new iteration, *Discovery*. They center on the complex and dynamic caring relationship between two women—our new protagonist Michael Burnham and her captain, Philippa Georgiou. The above quote is illustrative of Georgiou's close affective ties to her first officer, as promising young woman with potential for greatness, as curious scientist, and as daughter-by-proxy. Georgiou neatly ties together what concerns me in this essay: the ways in which caring practices between women both disrupt and cohere with Starfleet's neocolonial ongoing mission to "explore new worlds and new civilizations." *Star Trek: Voyager*'s primary female friendships, between Captain Kathryn Janeway and her crewmates B'Elanna Torres and Seven of Nine, are animated by this tension. This essay will explore Janeway's orientation toward interdependency, nurturing and care in her relationships with women in the context of her role as Captain, one which is imbued with authority and disciplining power, and bound by the Federation's directives. I will examine this spectacular negotiation of care and command first by situating Janeway in relation to previous Starfleet Captains' integration of binaries of logic and emotion, I will then make a case for Janeway's ethical decision making as approximating a feminist ethic of care and move to a close reading of her developing friendships with Seven of Nine and B'Elanna Torres.

Representations of close relationships between women, though infrequent, are far from unprecedented in the series; *Star Trek: Voyager* provides viewers with the most spectacular and sustained performances of care, emotional availability, and interdependency of all *Star Trek* franchises. These relationships constellate around Janeway, whose developing friendships with *Voyager*'s primary women characters—Kes, B'Elanna Torres and Seven of Nine prove narratively crucial in both stand-alone episodes and longer-term series arcs. The foregrounding of care and interdependency in *Voyager* emerges not only through its status as the first *Star Trek* franchise with a female protagonist, but also through *Voyager*'s central conceit: the stranding of a Starfleet crew in a remote corner of the galaxy.

The "isolation of command," a recurring theme across *ST*'s iterations, is exacerbated in *Voyager* by the absence of institutional support from Starfleet Command, who remain uncontactable well into the show's fifth season, as well as the crew's distance from kinship networks outside of *Voyager*. The ship's exile in the "frontierscape" of the Delta Quadrant places two of the most fundamental responsibilities of a Starfleet captain into conflict. As absolute ruler of a displaced community, Janeway has an official and personal obligation to look after her crew, but also a codified duty to uphold Starfleet principles. In fact, Janeway constantly reiterates her belief that it is Starfleet principles and values which will allow her to bring her crew safely home. Janeway's relationships with women, which both are limited by and undermine her autocratic power, make manifest the conflicts and convergences of care and command. Isolated in the Delta Quadrant, Janeway's deepening reliance on, and affective ties to, Torres and Seven render her distinct from other *Star Trek* captains, yet these relationships are still ruled by Federation neo-colonial values: the importance of assimilation to Federation behaviors and practices.

Star Trek *and Colonial Decision Making*

One of *Star Trek*'s most fundamental and captivating plot devices is the Ethical Decision. Coalescing most often around the figure of the Captain, though frequently involving the input of her crew, ethical decisions are a consultative process that ultimately play out in the conscience of the captain, whose determination is final. The ethical decision plot is productive of more or less transparent allegories for moral dilemma in the contemporary moment, rehearsed in a less ideologically overdetermined fashion. This traditional science fiction trope relies on what Suvin terms "cognitive estrangement," encompassing the capacity to recognize situations and relationships proximal to the moment of their writing, which nonetheless take place within an "imaginative framework alternative to the author's empirical environment" (37). Both feminist and postcolonial scholars claim science fiction as a venue through which totalizing structures of oppression can be reimagined, more liberatory relationships between groups prefigured (Lefanu 5; Armitt 2; Hoagland and Sarwal 6). However, science fiction's estranging capabilities in exploring ethical dilemmas are also liable to evacuate them of the historical specificities which define them.

Star Trek, like much of mainstream science fiction, imbues the figure of the "alien" with characteristics which mark them as "not-us," emerging through appearance, values and capacities. Federation values and through them *Star Trek's* construction of the human, given the tendency for humanity to represent the Federation, are constructed in relation to the particular value which the other is defined by. As Kanzler points out, this constitutive distinction is also liable to homogenize in-group differences (124). Encounters which are marked by this "us" "not-us" binary almost always privilege the Federation. Projansky argues that even the Q, whose omnipotent omniscience positions them as "further along" evolutionarily, are nonetheless found wanting in values when compared with the Federation (35). In this way, encountered cultures are marked by their distinction from Federation behaviors and values, the bearers, and adjudicators of which, are most frequently human.

Starfleet's "Prime Directive" similarly presumes the Federation as basis of comparison with encountered civilizations. Centering a principle of non-intervention towards cultures vulnerable to imperialism on its surface presents the Federation as resisting colonial expansionism, as protective of civilizations whose "natural development" might be altered by premature First Contact. However, the measure of a "First Contact-able" civilization relies on a model of technological progressivism—the development of Warp-Drive—which implicitly centers a Federation model of "progress." Katrina Boyd, in *Enterprise Zones*, articulates this uneasy ideological assemblage. "The Prime Directive enacts the show's fundamental conflict between a belief in the exercise of free will and self-determination and the existence of some necessary, natural pattern of development, which 'common sense' tells us involves unending technological and moral progress"(102). Kanzler argues that the invocation of the Prime Directive, casting the alien other as "primitive," "re-enacts the colonial encounter, casting the starship crews in the colonizer's role of benevolent *pater familias*" (102). It is in this constantly comparative mode, this measuring of "others" according to Federation standards, in which the impulses of care both collide and coalesce with neo-colonialist practices is Janeway's female friendships. Seven of Nine and B'Elanna Torres' species otherness (Seven a Borg and Torres half–Klingon) becomes the cite of operations for colonial logics—of assimilation, savior narratives, and the positing of Federation supremacy.

Voyager's exile in the "frontierscape" of the Delta Quadrant, shares with previous *Star Trek* franchises a nostalgic return to manifest destiny. However, the isolation engendered by *Voyager's* greater distance from institutional and familial support systems are productive of new ideological compounds. Federation liberal humanist values are both problematized and legitimated through Captain Janeway's performance of caring labors, her unashamed reliance on others.

Janeway: Touched and Touching

As Greven observes, Kathryn Janeway is a touch-y Captain (169). Kate Mulgrew's portrayal of *Star Trek*'s first central female commander is distinguished by a high level of affective warmth, conveying emotion through long-held gazes and a penchant for physical contact with her crew. Janeway is *touching*, physically imparting the depth of her care to those who surround her, visibly *touched* through the transparency of her emotional responses to others, and thereby *touching* once again in a mediated manner through viewer response to her *touchedness*, her affective vulnerability. Janeway's characterization has been critiqued by some scholars as presenting a conservative "ultra-femininity."[1] However, for my part, Janeway's *touchiness* offers viewers a twist on the classic logic vs. emotion trope in *Star Trek*, and, more fascinating still, a dramatization of the interaction between feminist ethics of care and colonial decision making.

From the first, *Star Trek*'s constitution of "the human" is reliant on emotion as a central node. *The Original Series* offers us a dialectic model of this. McCoy, guided by his emotional reactions, is balanced by the half–Vulcan Spock, for whom logic is the governing principle. In turn, Kirk is the point of synthesis between the two positions, attempting, for each decision, to mediate between those exterior poles. Similarly, in *The Next Generation*, logic and emotion are exteriorized in the figures of Data and Troi/Crusher respectively. The medical professional, in both series, constitutes the figure around which feeling congeals and *TNG* explicitly feminizes this binary. In both cases, however, the Captain is represented as fusing these positions within himself. Tim Challans posits "well-integrated emotional and rational motivations" as the crucial determinant of a successful Captain (27).

Voyager does not depart utterly from this tradition. Tuvok, the ship's Vulcan Chief of Security, and Seven of Nine at various moments embody the "logic" pole of the binary, while Torres, Kes, and occasionally Harry Kim represent "emotion." In contrast to previous *Star Trek* franchises however, I would argue Captain Janeway is the site of a performative integration of the conflict between logic and emotion. As a scientist, and a Starfleet officer, she demonstrates a belief in adherence to codified protocols. But as a sensitive and emotionally responsive woman—whose sense of responsibility for her crew's predicament leads her to contraventions of these principles, and to intimate affective relationships with her subordinates—the ethical decisions she makes, which entail a conflict of these investments, create in her an unusual level of anguish. "Death Wish" (2.18), in which she must decide on the primacy either of individual autonomy or the protection of life, has her visibly tossing and turning in her cabin. The depth of her remorse over her decision to strand her crew in the Delta Quadrant, manifesting as agoraphobia and self-disgust in "Night" (5.1), offers viewers an extraordinary portrayal of depression experienced by a commanding officer. Janeway's principles, and her emotional responses to the feelings and experiences of others are not always marked by narrative closure within episodes. She cannot always square them.

Janeway's deep emotional investment in the well-being of her crew is by no means a one-way street. Michele and Duncan Barrett point to the *personal* loyalty the crew have toward their Captain (179). The reciprocal networks of care between *Voyager*'s crew and her Captain are most visible in "Night" (5.1), when Janeway's crew mutiny to prevent her from stranding herself in boundless empty space to protect the alien-of-the-week. Members of the bridge crew also border on insubordinate in "Persistence of Vision" (2.8), when they present a united front to insist the Captain eat before starting her duty shift, correctly perceiving her irritability as a symptom of low blood sugar. *Voyager*'s very shot composition emphasize this intimacy and interdependency. Medium close, and close shots, in which two or more characters' faces are incorporated, affirm relational, rather than individual affective responses. Partly facilitated by Kate Mulgrew's small stature, relational shots in which actors stand or sit in unusual proximity to one another make visually explicit the affective ties between members of *Voyager*'s crew, as well as providing welcome fodder for queer subtextual interpretations and content production within *Voyager* fandoms.[2]

Captain Janeway's interdependency with her crew, her performance of emotional labor, her touching, glances, and spectacular performance of *caring* as labor and as investment in others, all represent a shift in *Star Trek*'s representations of ethics. As Katrina Boyd argues, *TNG*'s Captain Picard most closely resembles the "rational man" of classical liberal theory (101) Kirk, though more closely aligned with the "space cowboy" figure, represents a balanced synthesis between logic and emotion. In contrast to these figures, of colonial explorer, or of classical liberal subject, I argue that Janeway brings to her ethical decisions an approximation of the feminist ethic of care.

Janeway as Care Ethicist

Feminist care ethics takes as its most frequently cited origin point Carole Gilligan's *In a Different Voice*, methodologically situated within child developmental psychology, Gilligan makes the case for differential systems of ethical values amongst boys and girls. The influence of Gilligan's framework, however, has been felt across feminist philosophy, legal and literary theory. The care ethic considers the subject as always in reciprocal and interdependent relation to others. This distinguishes it from classical liberal conceptualizations of the subject, which situate the individual alone as the bearer of rights. Rights are given, and guaranteed by the State, which adjudicates when one subject's rights claim comes into conflict with another's. The care ethic centers instead our dependency on one another for care, nurturing and sustenance. This dependency places upon the subject an ethical obligation to care for others, and an assumption that this labor will be reciprocated. To have an ethical commitment to care is not merely to attempt to provide for the needs of others, but also necessitates a close emotional attentiveness to the cared-for, and a constant reflexivity about one's own position, ensuring that we "receive" the other on their own terms, without approaching them with pre-formed frameworks or assumptions. It is a consultative ethics, which "requires us to become 'engrossed' in one another" (Koehn 24).

Although I would not argue that Captain Janeway's ethics are at all times, or in all ways, in accordance with this theoretical model, their attention to relationality, interdependence and emotional intimacy provide useful conceptual tools through which to think about Janeway's female friendships and her Captaincy more broadly. In contrast to her predecessor, Picard, who strenuously avoids availing himself of the therapeutic practices of his ship's counselor, Deanna Troi, Janeway can often be heard vocalizing, in an unembarrassed fashion, her dependency upon members of her crew. Barrett and Barrett point to Janeway's unusually consultative practice—"While Janeway's authority is absolute, she is not beyond persuasion and a well-placed argument can often secure a change of tack in the captain's decision-making" (180). As Boruszak argues in this volume (see Ch. 6), Kes's intervention in favor of extricating her lover from the accidental hybrid being, Tuvix, sways the Captain's judgment in the competing claims of her care for her crewmembers and her Federation commitment to value life above all else. Similarly, in "Maneuvers" (2.11), Torres intervenes on behalf of Chakotay when he absconds with a shuttlecraft in order to confront Seska without endangering the crew. Her insight into Chakotay's motivations and emotions not only persuades Janeway to follow his trail and snatch him from Seska's clutches, but also engenders in her an appreciation of Torres' care for Chakotay. Janeway herself is prone to embracing members of her crew at moments of particular trauma, performing in an embodied manner, the labor of caring for them. In "Elogium" (2.4), Kes is distraught by the discovery that she has prematurely reached the Ocampan period of fertility, which occurs only once in their life cycle. Forced to decide within fifty hours if she ever wants to be a parent, she locks herself within a forcefield in sickbay; the concern of her lover Neelix or her friend The Doctor are of no comfort. Janeway, recognizing Kes's aggression and defensiveness as manifestations of terror and isolation, envelops her in her arms until she is calm enough to explain her situation.

By reading care ethics through the figure of Janeway, I don't mean to suggest that this mode of relationality automatically results from her identity-as-woman, but through her performance of caring practices, particularly for and with other women. Neither, in invoking care ethics in the context of *Star Trek*'s ongoing disavowal of the historical colonial implications of "exploring new worlds and new civilizations," do I mean to suggest that its nostalgic revisiting of imperialism is undercut by the presence of interdependency, emotional labor or care. The uses of "caring" as a colonial logic—through Christianizing "savior" narratives and "civilizing" as pretext for the exploitation of labor and resources in colonized lands—are well-documented. However, in contrast with other systems of value present in *Star Trek*, Janeway's caring practices, and the interdependency that characterizes *Voyager*, allow for an examination of how care and colonial logics are operating. When and how does care undercut Federation principles? In what ways do they work in tandem, as mutually justifying? What emerges from the pleasure of being a spectator to such intimate caring relationships and the unease caused by the decisions they justify? In attempting to answer these questions, I will move to a close reading of Janeway's developing, fraught, and intimate relationships with B'Elanna Torres and Seven of Nine, while thinking through the neo-colonial logics of assimilation and Federation supremacy.

Disciplining the Unruly Subject: Care and Conflict with B'Elanna Torres

Voyager's second episode marks the beginning of the tempestuous, but ultimately supportive relationship between B'Elanna Torres and Captain Janeway. Providing a starting point for viewers in identifying with *Voyager*'s chief engineer, it also represents a microcosm of the tensions that play out between them over the course of the series. "Parallax" (1.3) opens in the aftermath of an altercation Torres has had with her senior officer in engineering, Lieutenant Carey, who is assumed to be next in line for Chief Engineer. Chakotay, newly appointed as First Officer, attempts to quell the Starfleet—Maquis animosity erupting as a result of Torres' actions, while lobbying Captain Janeway to consider Torres a candidate for the vacant Chief Engineership.

The episode's narrative arc—a classic spatial anomaly plotline—is primarily animated by Captain Janeway's decision. Initially, she staunchly opposes Chakotay's staffing proposal, describing Torres as volatile and violent, as a Starfleet Academy dropout who couldn't cope with the discipline required of her. However, her attitude shifts, as she gains an appreciation of the talents B'Elanna has to offer, coupled with empathetic recognition of what might lead B'Elanna to behave in a fashion she considers inappropriate. This process of relational understanding is reciprocated on B'Elanna's side. After a catastrophic first meeting, in which the Captain raises her early exit from the Academy and Torres responds aggressively "I didn't want anything to do with Starfleet then, and I'm sorry I have to now" (Parallax 1.3). By the end of the episode, both women have interrogated their actions reflexively, considering seriously the other's positionality and point of view. Science, in the case of this episode, becomes a bridge between their respective Maquis and Starfleet values, their differential positions within hierarchy. Befuddled senior staff members in the conference room look on as Torres and Janeway talk temporal physics, finishing one another's sentences, approaching one another until the close-up shot incorporates both of their profiles. Expressions of nervousness and grim resolve are exchanged for triumphant grins. Tom Paris attempts to intervene in the women's discourse, only to be benevolently patronized by Janeway in an excellent reverse-mansplain.

"Parallax's" final scene has Janeway and Torres in a shuttlecraft, attempting to free *Voyager* from the anomaly. The craft's close confines produce even more intimate relational shots. Torres takes the opportunity to apologize to Janeway for her behavior during their first meeting, explaining that Janeway had "touched a nerve," and reveals that she was also afraid of the responsibility involved in the role. Janeway reciprocates the act of reaching out, revealing to B'Elanna that many of her professors at Starfleet Academy had been sad to see her leave. Recognizing Torres' aggression as a manifestation of her insecurity, Janeway attempts to reframe B'Elanna's sense of failure. She confesses "Some professors like to be challenged, as do some Captains" ("Parallax" 1.3), affirming to B'Elanna that her critical faculty is appreciated, even within a military hierarchy.

However, as is manifested more clearly in later episodes, this resolution is tempered by the fact that B'Elanna is still measured *in Starfleet terms*, rendering her failure to graduate the Academy, her unorthodox methods and her short fuse, particularities in which she fails to live up to Starfleet ideals. Janeway stresses her *capacity* to make a good Starfleet officer, but fails to address Torres' initial criticisms of the rigidity and hierarchy of Federation vessels. Janeway offers an opportunity for *assimilation*, one which tolerates some of her irregularities, but also implies adjustment on her part. It is important to note that Janeway is only willing to consider Torres in the first place because she had *attended* the academy. Other suggestions of Chakotay's are dismissed because "they don't have the discipline" and "some people have worked their whole lives for their commissions." The Maquis may be present on the ship, but they must adjust to Starfleet values, unreciprocally.[3]

The tension between B'Elanna being accepted and supported *on her own terms* by the Captain, and the implicit demand that she adjust herself to suit Starfleet mores recurs in "Prime Factors" (1.10). Part of a group of officers committed to acquiring technology that could shorten their journey home, despite Janeway's prohibition on taking it without the permission of official representatives of the culture that developed it, B'Elanna is sharply dressed down by the Captain when she takes responsibility for her actions. Though Janeway acknowledges her dependence on Torres "I need you," she stresses, in the gravest tone of her register, "I want you to know how very deeply you have disappointed me." Here, the unwillingness to "respect" the chain of command—principles which are less emphasized among the anti-colonial Maquis movement—is to risk the withdrawal of support and trust from the Captain, something B'Elanna has come to value.

B'Elanna-as-imperfect-Starfleet-subject emerges in part through the series' orientation towards her Klingon ancestry. The daughter of a Klingon woman and a human Starfleet Officer, many of *Voyager*'s B'Elanna-centric episodes are expressly, or implicitly concerned with the hybridity of her identity. "Faces" (1.14) has her split into two halves, between which her personality traits are distributed—fearless but unreasoning Klingon Warrior woman, and genius, but unassured human. Kanzler, in her reading of "Faces," makes clear the ways in which this characterization of Torres is reminiscent of colonial ideology—"the allocation of character traits among the two species parallels Eurocentric discourses of the self and the Other—the human embodying reason and civilizational control, and the Klingon representing the savage, physical and barely controllable" (159).

The construction of Torres as un*reasonable* subject emerges interestingly in "Nothing Human" (5.8), in which her capacity to make informed decisions about her own body is revoked. Initially a straight-forward "alien-of-the-week" episode, in which *Voyager* responds the distress call of a non-humanoid lifeform, "Nothing Human" quickly becomes a drama of medical ethics: bodily autonomy versus life preservation, "neutral" scientific knowledge versus a postcolonial politics of knowledge as already power. A non-humanoid alien, leaping through a forcefield and attaching itself to her vital organs, uses Torres' body as a life support machine and in so doing, destabilizes it. The Doctor requires a consulting physician, a hologram created from the medical database to save B'Elanna.

Unfortunately, the physician in question turns out to be Cardassian, and is recognized by a Bajoran crewman as the overseer of forced medical experiments on Bajor that left many dead. Captain Janeway is left with a difficult ethical dilemma—to use the research of the doctor to save her engineer, or to delete the hologram and his research from the database so as not to profit from the oppression of others. B'Elanna demands that treatment cease. As a member of the Maquis, and a comrade-in-arms of Bajoran resistance fighters, she refuses to benefit from the worst brutalities of the Cardassian occupation of Bajor. Her assertion of her right to bodily autonomy, however, does not end the conversation. In a meeting with senior staff, Janeway allows the issue to be debated, and, in response to a plea from Lieutenant Paris, who represents Torres' solidaristic stance as unreasonable, Janeway orders that treatment proceed against Torres' will.

However, in some ways, the episode resists closure. The penultimate scene, in which Janeway visits Torres recuperating in her quarters, does not resolve the tension between the two women. Broaching the topic in a warm, relaxed manner—"Feeling any better?" Janeway stiffens visibly as Torres refuses to be mollified by her concern. Changing tack, she attempts a conciliatory tone—"I hope you can understand why I went against your wishes, B'Elanna," framing Torres' decision on her own medical treatment as modal, unbinding, she continues, "Losing you was unacceptable." *Voyager*'s need for a chief engineer certainly contributes to this statement, B'Elanna is not immediately replaceable this far from the Federation. However, through Mulgrew's emotional delivery of the line, the unacceptability of her loss is also bound up with Janeway's reliance on and care for her as an individual. This recognition of her dependency on Torres, and the importance of this relationship as leading her to ignore B'Elanna's decision, is undercut by her next statement, in which hierarchical structure re-asserts itself. Janeway informs her, "We need to put this behind us. Understood?" implying that the wrong has been mutual. Torres, in full anti-authoritarian mode, asks if this is an order and proceeds to directly name the contradiction inherent in care and command: "You can't order someone to get rid of an emotion, Captain." Janeway asks what emotion Torres is referring to. Able to give voice to her contained resentment at last, Torres bursts out, "You had no right to make that decision for me!" In using the language of rights, she draws attention to the Captain's violation of Federation principles of bodily autonomy and self-determination, making clear how these supposedly crucial principles can be overturned within a system of military hierarchy.

Torres' relationship with her Captain remains one of contestation, the chief engineer does not lose her will to resist authority, despite her growing affective ties to Janeway and *Voyager*. She continues to have a complex relationship of identification with and disavowal of Starfleet, with *Voyager* on the one hand providing her with found family after iterative experiences of loss. However, it is also limited, to the extent that, in extended B'Elanna-centric narratives, conformity to an ideal of subjecthood, be it Starfleet, or specifically human, continues to operate as a disciplining regime, with Janeway acting both as purveyor and withholder of belongingness. Torres must attempt to inhabit an acceptable vector of Klingon-ness, or be constructed either as violent-hysteric, or inauthentic self-hating hybrid. In the case of "Barge of the Dead" (6.3), her desire to endanger her health in the hope of recouping a state of "crash-induced hallucination," can be easily read as irrational and motivated by "backward" superstition. Conversely, "Day of Honor" (4.3) and "Lineage" (7.12) provide examples of B'Elanna as insufficiently Klingon. Caring labor, on the part of Captain Janeway, and from *Voyager*'s crew at large, is productive both of restorative relationships for B'Elanna, and of regulative expectations of assimilation and authenticity impossible to live up to.

Saving the Female Child: Seven of Nine and Human Assimilation

Captain Janeway's relationship with Seven of Nine, the Borg drone whom she unilaterally decides to "save" from the collective at the opening of Season 4, has been well explored, both by scholarly readings of *Star Trek: Voyager*, and by *Voyager*'s voraciously creative fandom. Partly conforming to an established *Star Trek* trope, the "becoming-human" narrative, in which Janeway plays the role of "mentor-into-humanity," Seven's relationship with her Captain encompasses a wide variety of affective complexities—vacillating from hostility to tenderness, challenge to compliance. Seven is simultaneously the single most irksome of Janeway's charges, and the one with which she has the most intimate relationship. Describing Janeway/Seven, Greven claims that Seven's entrance in Season 4 marks what will become the "chief drama of Janeway's character"(170). Part of what makes this relationship so enchanting is the way in which it allows for the tensions between Borg-as-imperialist-force par excellence, and the unconvincing Federation disavowal of this role to be rendered dramatically visible. Seven, playing of the role both of native informant and external observer, gives voice on many occasions to the contradictions inherent in Janeway's attempt to "save" or "civilize" her, framed as giving back what was taken from her, her emphasis on Seven's developing individuality, while being robbed of the right to self-determination, and being forced to occupy a subordinate role within a military hierarchy.

Voyager's first Seven-centric episode, "The Gift" (4.2), similar to "Parallax" (1.3), sets the scene for the ways in which these conceptual tensions are explored in subsequent episodes. The episode opens in cargo bay two, with The Doctor and Janeway observing an unconscious Seven of Nine, plugged into her regeneration unit. Seven's disorientation and distress upon being woken—"Captain Janeway, what have you—? The others. I can't hear the others. The voices are gone" ("The Gift")—and her clear desire to leave the ship and her absolute rejection of what has been decided for her are demonstrative of the violence to which she is being subjected. Janeway's decision has robbed her of her ways of knowing, and of being, and inserts her instead within a forced human ontology of which she has little prior experience.

Seven awakes again in Sickbay and discovers that The Doctor has removed more of her Borg implants. Janeway cuts off the EMH mid-rant, and attempts to initiate a caring practice, seeking to gain empathetic understanding—"I want to help you, but I need to understand what you're going through." Seven's response encapsulates the inadequacy of this offer of support, following the mutilation of her body and the abduction from her culture—"Do not engage us in superficial attempts at sympathy." Janeway offers *Voyager* as a substitute collective, a prospect Seven, understandably considers "insufficient!" at which point Janeway's argumentation is injected simultaneously with a plea to interdependency, and a disciplinary force—"the fact is that this community needs you.... You must comply." Kanzler, in her analysis of "The Gift," considers Janeway's assimilation of Borg jargon to be a telling example of how the episode resists easy closure, orienting its audience away from a conventional alignment with established characters' points of view— she claims that the estranging effects of the order are "magnified when it becomes evident that the line indeed does describe the situation. The Borg has no resistance to offer against the Federation crew who, as the subsequent episodes show, will force their way of life onto her" (107).

During their final scene together, Seven's solitary confinement in the brig is telling upon her. She mutters to herself, "One. One," breaking the silence that must be ringing within her mind, trying out different words to describe her isolation. Janeway once again offers her own care in lieu of the collective, defying Seven's threat of violence to release the force field in which she is confined and approach her. Seven strikes out, but the exertion overtaxes her, she staggers and is caught and is held by the Captain. Janeway embraces her as she lets out an anguished sob; the medium-close shot allows us to see both faces at once, Seven's contorted, Janeway's a mixture of concern and shock.

On some level, Janeway's continuous attempts to offer emotional support of Seven of Nine demonstrate a recognition of Seven's suffering as her responsibility, that care is her obligation, as it is her decision that has rendered it necessary. Her struggles to empathetically grapple with Seven's feelings, and suggestions of remedial measures are illustrative of her knowledge that the ethical decisions she makes can be the cause of harm, even if she has deemed severing Seven from the collective as desirable "for her own good." The act of enfolding a destabilizing cyborg in comforting arms would be incongruous from Kirk or Picard. However, it is worth noting that in each of these scenes, Seven is in a state of confinement, restrained by her own regeneration unit, by sickbay biobeds, and finally, in the brig. Forced to submit to medical interventions that change the very nature of her body, rendering her, as Marleen Barr puts it, "soft and (com)pliant" (159), Janeway's postures at nurturing seem incommensurate to the violence inflicted upon Seven.

Saving Seven, as a motivating force behind Janeway's practice and decision-making process, recurs consistently over the course of *Voyager*'s remaining seasons. Episodes like "The Voyager Conspiracy" (6.9) and "Think Tank" (5.20) have Janeway putting her own life, or the lives of the entire crew, at enormous risk to rescue Seven, even when it is clear she does not wish to be rescued. In "Dark Frontier, Parts I and II" (5.15–5.16) Janeway chases Seven into the clutches of the Borg Queen herself when she refuses to believe that Seven left her ship voluntarily. In Season 7's "Imperfection"(7.2) in which irreparable damage to Seven's cortical node gives her mere days to live, Janeway puts *Voyager* on a likely collision course with the Borg to salvage a node from a dead Borg. When this fails—the node has been inoperative for too long—Janeway suggests procuring one from a live host. This, as the EMH points out, would mean murdering some unknown drone in the service of saving Seven's life.

Janeway's efforts to save Seven are not always replete with questionable ethical decisions. Boarding Seven's shuttle headed for the Borg in "The Voyager Conspiracy" (6.9) serves as a superlative example of the importance and power of Janeway's care ethics. As part of her tender and gentle attempts to unsettle Seven's paranoia through demonstrating how deeply she values their relationship, Janeway lists important memories she has of them together chronologically by stardate. Not limited to saving Seven's life, *Voyager* frequently features scenes in which the two enjoy one another's company on the holodeck. Demonstrating an ongoing commitment to saving Seven from her isolation, Janeway shares her free time with Seven, playing hoverball or making sculptures in the Da Vinci studio holoprogram.

However, as Kanzler argues, the initial destabilizing critique that Seven represents in "The Gift" (4.2), a challenge to the Federation and Janeway's ethics which is allowed a surprising amount of license, is largely neutralized in subsequent episodes as a result of the assimilationist "becoming human" plotline (107). Seven continues to challenge Janeway and the Federation, and her critiques sometimes result in shifts in decision making. However, within the frame of Janeway's primarily didactic and disciplinary engagements with Seven, emphasized by the venue of these confrontations—as a rule, in the Captain's Ready Room, where officers are summoned and dressed down—the critiques Seven poses are liable to be rendered symptomatic of her misunderstanding, her inexperience, or her imperfect adjustment to "humanity." Janeway, representing the (presumably) unambiguously human has complete jurisdiction over what constitutes the human subject. A measure against which Seven is continuously held up and found wanting. This is not to say that Janeway doesn't profess to value Seven's idiosyncrasies, nor that she necessarily positions herself in a hostile fashion in relation to Seven's inadequate humanity. But Janeway's capacity to frame the terms of Seven's human becoming bestows on her more disciplinary power. A labor of continuous caring, it is also a labor of undoing Seven, of a long-term assimilation that can never be complete.

Taught the value of creative expression on the holodeck, of "leisure time" at ship social events, of individuality, uniqueness, self-betterment and of deep emotional friendships, Seven adapts to more closely resemble Janeway's construction of the human subject. Heterosexual monogamy, bodily modesty and maternal relationships with the young are all "human practices" Seven assimilates. Seven, though she retains some vestiges of her previous critical position as outside observer and cultural commentator, has largely internalized the "human" value system which Janeway, through care and discipline, has set out for her. Season 4's finale—"Hope and Fear" (4.26) in which Seven and Janeway find themselves onboard the vessel of an alien bent on having *Voyager*'s crew assimilated, includes a brief exchange of mutual appreciation and vocalization of feelings of intimacy. Locked on a course toward Borg space, the end of existence as Kathryn, at least, has known it, appears nigh. "In case I never get a chance to say this, I realize that I've been hard on you at times. But it was never out of anger, or regret that I brought you on board. I'm your Captain. That means I can't always be your friend. Understand?" ("Hope and Fear" 4.26).

It is in this slippage between friend and captain, care and authority, that the complexities of this different *Star Trek* ethics unfold. This is not a tract railing against fraternization, or the dangers of emotion intervening into the realm of command, but an attempt to grapple with the manner in which these already-interlocking concepts play out in ways that undermine, but also reinforce one another. Seven's species-Otherness, in combination with her position as a subordinate on a ship saturated with "human" values, render the politics of "educating" and "saving" her reminiscent of the colonial encounter. "Humanizing" Seven in this context brings with it associations of "civilizing" discourse.

The tangible emotional labor and intimacy embedded in these labors also offer a prefigurative vision of interdependency; space as a place where women's affective labors for one another move through spheres, resist the "rational" as the guiding rubric, and consider the need of others as demanding an emotional, ethical response. It is to these simultaneous and inextricable properties of caring to which I now turn.

Between Delight and Unease: Productive Ambivalences in Voyager *Spectatorship*

Care between women in *Star Trek: Voyager* produces in me delight and unease, in no necessary order. The mutual overlap of care and colonial logics, the converging and diverging effects their performance produces can read in Captain Janeway's nurturing relationships with B'Elanna Torres and Seven of Nine. Of course, they are not limited to these relationships, or even this text. Other characters also act as sites around which emotional labor congeals.[4] *Voyager*, moving through the "frontierscape" of the Delta Quadrant, presents the viewer with plenty of examples in which the colonial encounter is rehearsed or undercut through care ethics. The ethical decision that strands them there in the first place offers a useful example. Janeway, concerned for the "natural development" and survival of Kes's fellow Ocampa, destroys the Caretaker's array to protect the largely white and, by human standards, juvenile population from a violent tribally structured misogynistic species, with darker pigmentation. Thinking through the series as commencing with the desire to protect white children from a dangerous racial other, I think, provides an additional framing to the question of caring labor and colonialism.

I attempt here to avoid the danger of the ever-present ur-argument, that this good thing (care between women) is bad, because it obscures this other bad thing (the colonial underpinnings of the exploration narrative). Instead, I want to propose what might productively arise from joy and unease. *Voyager*'s engagements with care ethics in the context of the "Continuing Mission" might orient us toward different ways of thinking about both. As I have argued above, reciprocal care as an ethic occurs in *Star Trek: Voyager* in multiple occasions and relationships, amongst the crew and in interactions with alien others. The centrality of care on *Voyager* offers the viewer a refreshing, sustained vision of people-in-community, as mutually supporting. It also serves as a reminder that colonial decisions are not merely justified through the logic of "the most good for the largest number" or decided by a "rational," emotionally distant subject. The "for-your-own-good-ness," of care as motivating intervention, is reminiscent of other imperialist logics. B'Elanna Torres and Seven of Nine, in their relationships with their Captain, are cared for uniquely, attentively, and engrossingly. This care sustains them even as it fixes them, as species-Others, in a process of assimilation that can never be completed.

The conjunction which Kathryn Janeway's caring practices occupy—simultaneously a sustaining labor and a disciplining force, might orient a viewer critical of *Star Trek*'s neo-imperialism towards the similarly coincident capacity of science fiction to prefigure new ways of being, or shift our thinking on the regulating systems of our own moment, *and*, dangerously, to evacuate moral dilemmas from their structural context, to release us from the weight of history upon which our world is contingent. Reading these ambivalences in *Star Trek: Voyager*, and other such texts, underscores the necessity of attentiveness to histories of oppression and structural injustice for those of us committed to an ethic of reciprocal care.

NOTES

1. Mulgrew's characterization of Janeway as either "Masculine" or "Feminine" or, occasionally, some more nuanced positionality between these poles has been a fixture of much scholarly commentary on *Voyager* (Greven 165–186; Relke 19–22; Kanzler 179; Wagner and Lundeen 96).

2. Queer scholarly readings of *Voyager* have been thinner on the ground than those within fan networks, interpreting Janeway's relationships with women crew members as animated by maternal, rather than erotic energies. Greven, in his chapter "An Epic for Women," allows room for both readings, even simultaneously. He reads a moment in "Imperfection" in which Janeway, refusing to accept that Seven is dying, promises to take her to the Grand Canyon—"the way Mulgrew plays the scene, standing sensually against a wall, the declaration has distinct erotic overtones" (Greven 170).

3. A particularly dramatic instance of Starfleet expectations of assimilation can be found in "Learning Curve" (1.16) at the end of the first season, in which Tuvok is tasked with bringing Maquis members of the crew up to Starfleet standards. Assimilation as divesting of particularities is immediately visually apparent when Tuvok demands that a Bajoran crewman remove his d'ja pagh, the earring worn by Bajorans as an indication of their religious faith, their family of origin and their class.

4. Kes, intuitive and empathic, challenges and counsels others, including Captain Janeway. Neelix, erstwhile cook, ambassador, and morale officer onboard, has been posited by Greven as an example of a mainstream depiction of masculine nurturing and supportive behaviors (Greven 74–96).

WORKS CITED

Armitt, Lucie. *Fantasy Fiction: An Introduction*. A and C Black, 2005.
"Barge of the Dead." *Star Trek: Voyager*, created by Jeri Taylor, Gene Roddenberry, Rick Berman, and Michael Piller, Season 6, episode 3, Paramount, 6 Oct. 1999.
Barr, Marleen S. *Future Females: A Critical Anthology*. Bowling Green State U Popular P, 1981.

Barrett, Duncan, and Michèle Barrett. *Star Trek: The Human Frontier*. 1st edition, Routledge, 2000.
Bowring, Michele. "Resistance Is Not Futile: Liberating Captain Janeway from the Masculine Feminine Dualism of Leadership." *Gender, Work and Organization*, vol. 11, June 2004, pp. 381–405. *ResearchGate*, doi:10.1111/j.1468-0432.2004.00239.x. Accessed April 9, 2018.
Boyd, Susan B. *Challenging the Public/private Divide: Feminism, Law, and Public Policy*. University of Toronto Press, 1997.
Challans, Tim. "The Moral Psychology of a Starship Captain." *The Ultimate Star Trek and Philosophy: The Search for Socrates*, edited by Kevin S. Decker and Jason T. Eberl, John Wiley and Sons, 2016, pp. 26–35.
"Dark Frontier." *Star Trek: Voyager*, written by Joe Menosky and Brannon Braga, directed by Terry Windell and Cliff Bole, Season 5, episodes 15 and 16, Paramount, 17 Feb. 1999.
"Day of Honor." *Star Trek: Voyager*, written by Jeri Taylor, directed by Jesús Salvador Treviño Season 4, episode 3, Paramount, 17 Sept. 1997.
"Death Wish." *Star Trek: Voyager*, teleplay by Michael Piller, directed by James L. Conway, Season 2, episode 18, Paramount, 19 Feb. 1996.
"Elogium." *Star Trek: Voyager*, written by Kenneth Biller and Jeri Taylor, directed by Winrich Kolbe, Season 2, episode 4, Paramount, 18 Sept. 1995.
"Faces." *Star Trek Voyager*, created by Jeri Taylor, Gene Roddenberry, Rick Berman, and Michael Piller, performance by Roxann Dawson, Season 1, episode 14, Paramount, 8 May 1995.
"The Gift." *Star Trek: Voyager*, written by Joe Menosky, directed by Anson Williams, Season 4, episode 2, Paramount, 10 Sept. 1997.
Greven, David. *Gender and Sexuality in Star Trek: Allegories of Desire in the Television Series and Films*. McFarland, 2009.
Hoagland, Ericka, and Reema Sarwal. *Science Fiction, Imperialism and the Third World: Essays on Postcolonial Literature and Film*. McFarland, 2010.
"Hope and Fear." *Star Trek: Voyager: The Complete Series*, teleplay by Brannon Braga and Joe Menosky, directed by Winrich Kolbe, Season 4, episode 26, Paramount, 20 May 1998.
"Imperfection." *Star Trek: Voyager*, written by Carleton Eastlake and Robert Doherty, Season 7, episode 2, 11 Oct. 2000.
Kanzler, Katja. *"Infinite Diversity in Infinite Combinations": The Multicultural Evolution of Star Trek*. Winter, 2004.
Koehn, Daryl. *Rethinking Feminist Ethics: Care, Trust and Empathy*. Routledge, 2012.
"Learning Curve." *Star Trek: Voyager*, created by Rick Berman, Michael Piller, and Jeri Taylor. Dir. Kim Freidman, Season 1, episode 16, Paramount, 22 May 1995.
Lefanu, Sarah. *Feminism and Science Fiction*. Indiana University Press, 1989.
"Lineage." *Star Trek: Voyager*, written by James Kahn, directed by Peter Lauritson, Season 7, episode 12, Paramount, 24 Jan. 2001.
"Maneuvers." *Star Trek: Voyager*, written by Kenneth Biller, directed by David Livingston, Season 2, episode 11, Paramount, 20 Nov. 1995.
"Night." *Star Trek: Voyager*, written by Brannon Braga, directed by David Livingston, Season 5, episode 1, Paramount, 14 Oct. 1998.
"Nothing Human." *Star Trek: Voyager*, written by Jeri Taylor, Season 5, episode 8, Paramount, 2 Dec. 1998.
"Parallax." *Star Trek: Voyager*, created by Rick Berman, Michael Piller, and Jeri Taylor. Dir. Kim Freidman, Season 1, episode 3, Paramount, 23 Jan. 1995.
"Persistance of Vision." *Star Trek: Voyager*, written by Jeri Taylor, directed by James L. Conway, Season 2, episode 8, Paramount, 30 Oct. 1995.
"Prime Factors." *Star Trek: Voyager*, created by Rick Berman, Michael Piller, and Jeri Taylor. Directed by Les Landau, Season 1, episode 10, Paramount, 20 Mar. 1995.
Projansky, Sarah. "When the Body Speaks: Deanna Troi's Tenuous Authority and the Rationalization of Federation Superiority in Star Trek: The Next Generation Rape Narratives." *Enterprise Zones: Critical Positions on "Star Trek,"* edited by Taylor Harrison et al., Westview Press, 1996, pp. 33–50.

230   Part IV. Broader Perspectives

Relke, Diana M.A. *Drones, Clones, and Alpha Babes: Retrofitting Star Trek's Humanism, Post-9/11*. University of Calgary Press, 2006.
Suvin, Darko. *Positions and Presuppositions in Science Fiction*. Kent State University Press, 1988.
"Think Tank." *Star Trek: Voyager*, teleplay by Michael Taylor, directed by Terrence O'Hara, Season 5, episode 20, Paramount, 31 Mar. 1999.
"The Voyager Conspiracy." *Star Trek: Voyager*, written by Joe Menosky, directed by Terry Windell, Season 6, episode 9, Paramount, 24 Nov. 1999.
Wagner, Jon G., and Jan Lundeen. *Deep Space and Sacred Time: Star Trek in the American Mythos*. Praeger, 1998.

Lost in Space Without an Idea of Home
The Triumph of Neoliberal Depoliticization in Star Trek: Voyager

ALEX BURSTON-CHOROWICZ

Star Trek: Voyager's opening depicts asymmetrical space combat between an authoritarian government (the Cardassians) and an underpowered outgunned band of outlaws. Known as the Maquis, these fighters, former Federation citizens, are rebelling against both Cardassian and Federation governments for their self-determination. The rebel crew manage to evade destruction but are immediately caught in an energy wave whisking them away to far reaches of the galaxy. Soon after the opening credits we learn that Captain Janeway and her newly minted starship Voyager are to be sent in search of the missing ship. One of her officers was on board spying for the Federation. Immediately, the audience is introduced to two contrasting crews set up to provoke ideological collision. The utopian idealism of both the *Original Series* and *Next Generation* was redrafted promising a more contested and questioning premise. The aesthetic established in the opening moments is telling of this change in tone. The interior of Voyager, the central locale of the entire series, is sleek, militaristic and Spartan in design. This contrasted to the city-like Enterprise of *The Next Generation*, where families lived, and abundant creature comforts were a nod to a utopian society liberated from material scarcity. Voyager's design is strictly utilitarian. Its military capabilities, instantly recognizable in the submarine-like bridge, were another signal to this change in tone. The frontier spirit of the previous *Star Trek* shows was alive, but something had changed. The liberal utopian objective of an abundant society remained; however, utopian politics and the overall aesthetic of what such a society looked like had altered.

At the end of the pilot episode the Maquis ship is destroyed, and Voyager is stranded on the other side of the galaxy with no immediate way home. The two opposing crews are now required to work as one on Voyager. The Maquis crew is forced, by circumstance, to integrate into the very society they rejected. In the final scene of the pilot Janeway explicitly states that the two crews will be strictly Starfleet in protocol. In previous *Star Trek* series Starfleet officers rarely opposed or contradicted one and other. Tensions between crewmembers were kept at a minimum,[1] *Voyager* planned to overturn this. Writers of the show were adamant that *Voyager* needed to explore inter-crew contradictions (*Memory Alpha*). However, when it came time for the Maquis to integrate into Starfleet, the political and ideological differences of the two crews were kept at a minimum. Maquis characters, particularly B'Elanna Torres, were shown to be people with immense personal failings, traumatized by their violent pasts, rather than cadres of a nationalist cause. The multicultural tolerance of the series neutered political contestation. Instead, conforming to Starfleet's regulations was seen as the only way one could be a fully functioning crewmember. Politics was too destructive to properly confront.

What makes Voyager distinctive is the absence of politics. Previous *Star Trek* series, in particular *The Next Generation*, were idealistic in their portrayal of humanity's future, where dialectical historical processes had been halted by technological evolution. Humanity had evolved beyond poverty and violence, since technology had satisfied material needs and catered to desires. *The Next Generation* explored this utopia through Captain Picard, its most articulate proponent. *Deep Space Nine* defended this utopia from the authoritarian Dominion. *DS9* was clearly more interested with the military implications of the *Star Trek* universe. It too was more conservative than its predecessor, but its concern with realpolitik gave it distinct political flavor. *Voyager* was different. In the absence of Federation space came an absence of idealism and utopian desires. What eventuated, particularly through the first few seasons, is a telling marker of political and historical milieus *Voyager* was created in.

Voyager ran from 1995 to 2001 at the zenith of neoliberal hegemony (this will be further explored in the next section). The Communist world had crumbled, and the United States had become world's only superpower. The economic philosophy dominating the developed world and the former communist bloc was now one of free market, liberal democracy, and an overall more tolerating cosmopolitan society. Embrace of such an ideal not only rebuked reactionary ideals of racism and intolerance but also radical and collectivist conceptions. The result was a politics of consensus rather than contestation.

This essay aims to investigate the theme of depoliticization in *Star Trek: Voyager*. It establishes wider historical contexts *Voyager* was produced in, demonstrating that neo-liberal hegemony of the late 1990s and 2000s was a result of particular historical circumstances. The end of post-war Keynesianism and reassertion of laissez-faire doctrines are important elements leading to depoliticization. The essay then demarcates how depoliticization was a by-product of neoliberal hegemony. Gramsci's theory of hegemony and its cultural manifestations, along with more contemporary theorists such as Bauman, Brown, and Žižek, will be used to further define depoliticization and its relationship with neoliberalism. The final section explores depoliticization through experiences of Maquis crewmembers on Voyager, and how their previous lives as nationalist guerrillas is elided. The cause they were willing to die for was glossed over, neutering potential political upheaval. The two main Maquis characters, Chakotay and B'Elanna Torres, and their conformity will further highlight how *Voyager* depoliticized its most potentially contradicting personalities. Finally, it will comment on how Captain Janeway's leadership further exemplified the show's lack of idealism.

Gene Roddenberry created *Star Trek* for social, political, and philosophical commentary and exploration. From its beginning in 1966 it explored issues of, war, politics, racial prejudice, and the human condition at large (Barret 60–61; Gonzalez 20–29; Pilkington 50–55; Putman 147–149). As argued in previous work, *Star Trek* is a cultural by-product of the American Century where the United States, after World War II, was in a position to directly shape world affairs. Since Starfleet is the United States projected into outer space, the show and its vast canon is an imagining where, like the U.S., the Federation has direct agency in shaping intergalactic affairs (Burston-Chorowicz 9). *The Original Series* dealt with Cold War politics. It challenged American audiences with television's first interracial kiss as the nation came to grips with civil rights. *The Next Generation* dealt with post–Cold War conflict but maintained the liberal optimism of its predecessor, at times in a more intense manner. *Deep Space Nine* was a more militaristic imagining of *Star Trek* where the liberal utopia established by previous series was under threat from an authoritarian superpower. Diplomatic and military maneuverings saw ambitious and vast story arcs unusual for television in the early 1990s.

Voyager first aired in 1995, four years after the Soviet Union's collapse and the Cold War's end. In 1991 America asserted its military might on the Persian Gulf, demonstrating swift intercontinental response to Iraq's invasion of Kuwait, but also technological domination in its aerial campaign. Bill Clinton and his New Democrats soon swept into the White House, managing to defeat Republicans by criticizing while subsequently adopting their policies. The economic mantra of "trickle down" economics was case in point. Clinton became the champion of free trade, encouraging the U.S. to sign free trade agreements with its neighbors (Cameron 119–121). Other progressive parties adopted similar practices globally, where social democratic/labor parties embraced free market mantra.

A particular political orthodoxy originating as reaction to Keynesianism's breakdown in the late 1960s came to dominate much of the developed and developing worlds (including former communist states). Neoliberalism and its emphasis on free markets unhindered by Keynesian intervention became the hymn that defined, not just economic policy, but the machinery and personal of politics. As the left adopted this orthodoxy, a new unanimity took shape. Such a consensus politics in the midst of rapid globalization was the context in which *Voyager* was produced. The breakdown of the post-war consensus is vital to understanding politics in the 1990s.

The End of Keynesian Consensus and Neoliberalism's Ascendency

In 1961, American sociologist Daniel Bell argued European ideologies defining the 19th and first half of the 20th centuries had petered out.

> The young intellectual is unhappy because the "middle way" is for the middle-aged not for him; it is without passion and is deadening. Ideology, which is by its nature is an all-or-none affair, and temperamentally the thing he wants is devitalized.... Politics offers little excitement. Some of the younger intellectuals have found an outlet in science or university pursuits, but often at the expense of narrowing their talent into mere technique; others have sought self-expression in the arts, but in the wasteland the lack of content has meant, too, the lack of necessary tension that creates new forms and styles [Bell 404].

Bell's lament on behalf of would-be radicals was a reflection on post-war consensus that took shape in the late 1940s. Governments of all stripes thought they had consigned the disastrous boom and bust cycles of capitalism to the dustbin of history via Keynesian intervention (Hobsbawm *Age of Extremes* 257–286). The Great Depression brought untold suffering through mass unemployment. Nazism's rise and the Second World War itself were two side effects of The Crash. British economist John Maynard Keynes, writing in response to the failed post–Versailles peace, and failed reactions to depression, argued states needed to intervene during economic downturns through fiscal stimulus. Markets could not be left to correct themselves simply by governments balancing budgets. Deficit expenditure was required to spend their way out of recession keeping employment and consumption afloat. Keynesian economics was taken up by social democrats expanding these arguments to include large welfare states alleviating barbaric elements of capitalism. The social democratic left in Continental Europe, Britain and

Australia championed this; FDR's New Deal reorganized the American federal government along similar lines.[2] The consensus came when, almost unanimously, conservative parties accepted this intervention as a way of preserving capitalism while nullifying labor radicalism. The result was a corporatist arrangement between states, private enterprise, and unions (Berend 190–192). Marc Mulholland summarizes this balancing act well. "Moderate Social Democracy and liberal conservatism could generally alternate in power with no major upset. 'Bourgeois civil society' was artfully reconciled with 'proletarian democracy'" (Mulholland 220).

Post-war recovery turned into an almost uninterrupted boom lasting until the late 1960s. Hobsbawm reflected upon this as twentieth century's golden age (Hobsbawm *Age of Extremes* 257–286). The Bretton-Woods system set up an arrangement of fixed exchange rates, tied to the U.S. dollar pegged to the price of gold. This system was highly amenable to free-flowing trade. Economic growth was predicated on full employment expanding consumption and saw a sharp increase in living standards across the globe (Berend 238–260). The *Star Trek* universe, created in the mid–1960s, always showed a society where technological achievement emancipated humanity from want.

By the late 1960s there were signs that economic growth had reached its limits. There were serious issues in capital accumulation in the Western bloc and growth began to falter. Simultaneously organized labor demanded higher wages to cope with economic slow down. Wage increases along with slow growth brought on inflation. This disastrous mixture economists named stagflation. Unemployment also amplified (Harvey). Fixed exchange rates were dumped in favor of floating currencies. Richard Nixon's floating of the U.S. dollar in 1971 finished Bretton Woods off, and was a sign that neoclassical economics had returned. Further compounding economic woes, the U.S.'s support for Israel in 1973 incurred the wrath of OPEC, jacking up oil prices. The Oil Crisis marked the Golden Age's formal end since it was predicated on cheap oil from the region. What followed was continued implementation of neoclassical economics. Deficit spending had, by the mid–1970s, been abandoned in favor of pre-war orthodoxy of budget balancing to curb inflation and stimulate growth. Full employment too was discarded in favor of keeping inflationary pressures down. Jimmy Carter continued this policy. In 1976 the British Labour Party, who were instrumental in establishing full employment, moved away from this position. It too concerned itself with curbing inflation and balancing budgets (Thorpe 194–200). While many on the left and right accepted structural limitations of Keynesianism, it was not until ascendency of a new breed of conservatives when neoliberalism's full brunt was felt.

Margaret Thatcher and Ronald Reagan came to their respective offices (1979 and 1981) with the view to reformulate relations between organized labor, enterprise, and state. Budget balancing was maintained while state owned enterprise was privatized, and organized labor curtailed.[3] Tariffs were further reduced allowing capital to move easily between nations. Capital had become truly transnational in a way previously unknown. Large areas of both Britain and the United States, where once factories and mines presided, were dismantled and shut down. Companies began to shift production to Asia where labor costs were considerably lower.

The generous welfare state of post-war life was wound back. The New Right, as it came to be known, justified this new order as a reassertion of traditional bourgeoisie values of individual enterprise, self-reliance, and self-respect. Thatcher in particular reiterated such individualism, viewing Keynesian state of affairs as entitled and unproductive. Socialism, in all of its forms, including its social democratic pedigree, were to be done away with. This was a renaissance of sorts of Victorian England's values (Mulholland 257–258). Neoclassical economics, forwarded by Chicago and Austrian schools, produced people like Milton Friedman and Friedrich Hayek, who became intellectual forces behind this shift. In his famous book, *The Road to Serfdom*, Hayek argued that governments' role was to protect and foster market competition. Price and wage controls would lead to rack and ruin obliterating growth; government intervention was a "road to serfdom" (Hayek). In the early 1960s Hayek was one of few neoclassical holdouts. By the 1970s he became a highly influential economist confirmed by his Nobel Prize in 1974 (Berend 276).

Neoliberalism's hegemonic dimensions, however, were not entirely reified until adopted by center-left parties, the traditional bastion of working-class democratic collectivism, or in the case of the Democratic Party, FDR's New Deal. As Ronald Reagan and Margaret Thatcher waged war on their respective nations' deficits, public sectors, and unions, transformations were occurring in their oppositional parties. In Britain, the Labour Party went through a number of shifts in the 1980s culminating in a rightward drift presided over by Tony Blair. Blair and his sleek, media-savvy advisors rebadged Britain's most successful democratic socialist party to "New Labour" accepting market fundamentalism of Thatcher and her Conservative Party. In 1994 Blair deleted Clause IV from the party's constitution that promised to socialize the means of production, much to the dismay of its more hardened socialist members. Blair and New Labour's pledge was to turn socialism into "social-ism." This rhetorical somersault justified Labour's move away from statism, and government intervention. The market was now to be used to attain social objectives (Wright 102–104). When Blair's Labour won government 1997 neoliberal policy was expanded. The Bank of England was given total independence to set interest rates. Public-private ventures replaced social services government alone was not willing to fund. Public transport across the country was a major casualty of this. There were some social democratic features to be found, such as the minimum wage and the acceptance of same-sex civil-unions, but they were few and far between.

Bill Clinton's successful 1992 presidential campaign reflected similar transformations in American liberalism. Clinton's insistence that he was a "new kind of Democrat" was more substantive than mere campaign rhetoric (Hale). Since the loss of Carter's presidency to Reagan in 1980, centrist Democratic Party leaders regrouped in a number of intra-party collections to shift Democrats to the center. Subsequent electoral defeats in 1984 and 1988 strengthened calls for the party to move away from the traditional "tax and spend model." After the 1984 campaign the Republican Party had entrenched itself as the natural party of support for white southerners. This had been traditional Democratic territory for decades. In 1985 the Democratic Leadership Council (DLC) was formally established to push the party towards the right. Clinton's victory in the Democratic primaries and then in the 1992 presidential election was a major step forward for the DLC (Hale). Clinton embraced the organization, defining his eight years in office with its objectives. Clinton declared the "era of big government" over. He pushed free trade agreements with Mexico and Canada. Welfare reform curtailed payments to America's poorest, disproportionally affecting African American populations and other alienated minorities. Clinton was the first president in a generation to preside over a balanced budget, thanks in large part to austere cuts. He was an early champion of LGBTI rights, and, in theory, favored gun control. Despite the latter two points, Clinton's presidency was marked by fiscal conservatism. Clinton and Blair were personally close to each other, having bonded over their mutual admiration for their consensus driven politics.

By the mid-1990s progressive politics had embraced free market fundamentalism built upon by the New Right since the late 1970s. Its commitment to social outcomes was vague and ill defined. The importance of market-oriented policies was paramount as was its jettison of statism. The last remaining difference between conservative and progressive politics was the left's commitment to pluralistic and multicultural societies. This was well within step with neoliberal thinking since in a free market there is little room for backward prejudices of old; such reactionary preconceptions inhibit competition. Inclusivity and tolerance replaced statist intervention and wealth redistribution. Financial systems, it seemed, were things to be managed by technocratic economists whose market fundamentalism was shared by all sides of politics. Economics was compartmentalized into something outwardly apolitical. In the words of Colin Hay, "From the 1990s onwards, however, the normalization and institutionalization of neoliberalism and its depiction as a largely technical set of devices for managing an open economy has served to depoliticize and de-democratize economic policy-making" (502). For a society now obsessed with competition as a means to better the human condition, ideological contestation on a material level now appeared as an anachronism. The implications were vast, having far wider effects beyond electoral success for victory-hungry progressive parties.

With progressive politics' embrace of free market economics came a new consensus bereft of competing notions of how society should be run. Ideological contestation between left and right that defined politics since the mid 19th century was nullified by free market hegemony. Similar changes had taken place in Europe, Australia, Israel, New Zealand, and former Soviet states. In 1992, Francis Fukuyama famously declared that since communism's failure humanity had reached its pinnacle method of organization through liberal-democracy and free market economics (Fukuyama). Of cause such arguments are reductionist, but Fukuyama did represent a moment in history where politics, it seemed, had halted its dialectical dance. There was now no alternative to free market fundamentalism. Margaret Thatcher articulated this notion pertinently when asked what her greatest political triumph was, she replied, "Tony Blair and New Labour."

In the pilot episode of *Voyager*, "Caretaker" (1.1), the crew come across "the Array" (a large space station). The Array and the powerful life form that inhabits it sustain energy to an underground civilization. The Ocampa live on a nearby planet whose ecosystem was destroyed due to the life form's experiments thousands of years before. The Array was created to make sure the Ocampa survived. The underground civilization has never seen the surface and is totally reliant on the "Caretaker" to survive. At the end of the episode we learn that the Caretaker is dying, and Voyager was brought to the Delta Quadrant as a part of a search for his replacement. In the Caretaker's last moments, he agonizes about the uncertain future of the Ocampa. He thinks they are "children." Janeway insists that the Ocampa must learn to cope with the harsh realities of life on their own; "children must grow up," she argues.

Janeway claims the only way civilizations grow is to fend for themselves. This is an interesting twist since so much of the previous *Star Trek* series is about how material want can be emancipated by technological advances. Here the Array is the post-war welfare state nurturing people against life's extremities. Janeway disputes this; such a situation is far too paternalistic. For Janeway the Array is a barrier to meaningful societal growth. Here the welfare state inhibits the inner dynamism of the Ocampa sheltering them from their true potential. Such a neoliberal argument would have been unthinkable in the previous series.

Such structural and ideological changes taking place from the 1970s to the 1990s had immeasurable social consequences. Sociologist Zygmunt Bauman's "liquid modernity" was apt in portraying this new reality of transnational markets and technological revolution (Bauman *Liquid Modernity*). Life for many, it seemed, was moving faster than ever, far less stable and secure than before. Marx's description of social relations in the midst of industrial revolution continued to ring true; "all that is solid melts into air" (Berman). Bauman captured this new world of fast-moving capital beautifully.

> In its heavy stage, capital was as much fixed to the ground as were the labourers it engaged. Nowadays capital travels light.... It can stop-over almost anywhere, and nowhere needs to stay longer than the satisfaction lasts. Labour, on the other hand, remains as immobilized as it once was in the past—but the place which it once anticipated being fixed to once and for all has lost its past solidity [Bauman, *Liquid Modernity*, 58].

Star Trek: Voyager was a cultural product of this period. *Voyager's* lack of ideological contestation is apart of historical processes listed above. *Star Trek* in the 1960s and the 1980s reflected a liberal utopia where self-determination, equality, and institutional democracy were celebrated. *Voyager's* bland political discourse is rooted in the politics of the 1990s and was given much theoretical attention.

Hegemony, Neoliberalism, Tolerance and Depoliticization

The ideological implications of neoliberal hegemony defined absent political discourse in *Voyager*. Italian Marxist Antonio Gramsci's description of "common sense" is apt in outlining what it means for something to be hegemonic. For Gramsci, common sense is unquestioned truth or truths whose philosophical, qualitative, and quantitative basis, is beyond repute. Common sense is incontestable in its validity, but in reality, consists of values with deep ideological roots embedded so as to seem naturalized (Gramsci). Cultural products within such a state of affairs are necessarily imbued with principles, which in abstraction are highly politicized. Civil society is shaped by such hegemony, despite its hypothetical independence from state apparatuses. Perry Anderson describes Gramsci's idea of hegemony, and how it relates to civil society well.

> In other words, the preponderance of civil society over the state in the West can be equated with the predominance of "hegemony" over "coercion" as the fundamental mode of bourgeois power in advanced capitalism. Since hegemony pertains to civil society, and civil society prevails over the state, it is the cultural ascendancy of the ruling class that essentially ensures the stability of the capitalist order [Anderson 43–44].

Here state and civil societies, symbiotic in their relations, are ruled by universal but constructed ideological agendas. In the section above, we have seen how neoliberalism came to dominate and define politics, creating its own set of "common senses." Political orthodoxy of the 1980s and 1990s was, as Hauser puts it, a "production of consensus" giving it the appearance of "naturalness" (Hauser 1). Influenced by Gramsci, Hauser perceives cessation of alternative political conceptions to liberal democracy and its free market companion became "so self-evident and natural for us that not even its greatest critics take searching for an alternative too seriously" (Hauser 2).

Bauman describes utopian ideas as necessarily being able to break away from "habitual associations." Emancipating oneself from the overpowering dominance of "routine" makes utopian thinking a genuinely inventive craft (Bauman, *Socialism: The Active Utopia*). With communism's fall and social democracy's and American liberalism's capitulation, no alternate political realities existed to hold a mirror to the new orthodoxy of neoliberalism. In a more recent book, Bauman returned to utopian endeavors, but writing in 2006, admitted such projects had seen their twilight. For Bauman, the absence of subaltern political projects meant society was bereft of productive criticism. If ideological critique had ended, "the idea of active engagement with society loses" (Bauman, *In Search for Politics* 126). Such processes, or in this case, lack of processes, capture a political reality that is literally depoliticized.

A cultural product like *Star Trek* with its political and philosophical objectives is also a creation of civil society. If we expand this further, since this is a globalized world, it is a creation of liberal-democratic civil society at large, albeit one produced first and foremost for U.S. audiences. By the mid–1990s *Star Trek* had a worldwide following the writers were well aware of. *Voyager*, like its predecessor series, aimed to explore the human condition and its many quandaries. It is inevitable that a show of this nature is impregnated with hegemonic "common sense" defined by the world it was born to. But *Voyager* represents more than depoliticization. *Voyager* was self-consciously cosmopolitan. Its cast was multicultural as were its characters. There is a mixture of Starfleet officers, former Maquis rebels, and local stowaways wanting to join Voyager's journey home. Captain Kathryn Janeway represented a significant step forward as *Star Trek's* first female captain. Chakotay, the first officer and leader of the Maquis, is Native American. B'Elanna Torres, also Maquis, was the canon's first female engineer, a position of canonical admiration. Writers were self-conscious in representing the face of a multicultural and tolerating society. *Voyager's* emphasis on toleration helped to play down political difference, and is for many cultural critics, a key element laying within neoliberal depoliticization.

Tolerance is another factor behind depoliticization. Political theorist Wendy Brown defines this phenomenon acutely.

Tolerance discourse masks the role of the state in reproducing the dominance of certain groups and norms, and it does so at a historical moment when popular sensitivity to this role and this dominance is high, when those who have been historically excluded by norms of sex, race, ethnicity, and religion are vocal about such exclusion. State tolerance talk both softens and deflects these tensions [Brown 83–84].

Brown continues to argue tolerance is a pacifying element reducing political life to isolated individual experiences devoid of contestation; when in reality it masks real world divisions. For Brown, tolerance is a rejection of politics as a "domain of conflict" where such contestation could in fact lead to productive outcomes. Tolerance is a retreat from "political life itself" (Brown 89).

Žižek sees tolerance as an ideological category going hand in hand with cultural relativism inbuilt into neoliberalism. Žižek's criticisms are more pertinent to *Voyager* since *Star Trek* is, for the most part, a liberal utopia in space (Burston-Chorowicz; Dyson; Franklin; Lagon; Pilkington; Sarantakes). For Žižek, the "culturalization" of politics by liberal multiculturalism (tolerance) means that issues pertaining to inequality, exploitation and intolerance are neutralized into mere cultural distinctions. This is a "retreat" away from real world solutions governments are unable or unwilling to deal with (Žižek 660). Such a situation is thus post-political in nature.

This post-political moment at its height in the mid–1990s and early 2000s, impregnated by complexities listed above, is captured in *Voyager*. A TV show about a starship far from home, untethered from traditional homelands, forced to absorbed hostile political elements, is the perfect vehicle signifying reification of a society bereft of political contestation and the ossification of traditional political institutions.

Voyager, Star Trek *Depoliticized*

The Maquis were introduced into Star Trek canon in the second season of *Deep Space Nine* ("The Maquis, Part I" 2.20, "The Maquis, Part II" 2.21). After a long and brutal war between the Federation and Cardassian Union, a tenuous peace treaty was signed ending the conflict. A part of the treaty was an exchange of planets colonized by both sides in a bid to placate one another. On these planets were large colonies of Federation citizens and Cardassians who were now forced off their planets by their own governments. Many of the Federation citizens remained, begrudgingly agreeing to live under Cardassian control. Cardassian colonists then settled on these nearby former Federation colonies bringing tensions to the already delicate situation. The Cardassians began smuggling arms to their colonies; in response Federation citizens did likewise. All of this was of course in violation of the peace treaty. In *DS9* episode "The Maquis" (2.20), the more organized and militant Federation colonists organized declaring themselves the Maquis (named after French resistance in World War II). They were intent to combat Cardassian rule. Starfleet officers were implored to hunt down and destroy the organization since it threated the peace treaty. Their main objective was to declare an independent state, eschewing both Cardassian rule and Federation governance. *DS9* went some way into exploring characters that were disaffected Starfleet officers who joined the guerrilla group. The cause was an obvious nod to post-colonial pressures. The Maquis are radical and nationalists, rejecting the liberal institutionalism of the Federation in an overt departure from and juxtaposition to the show's general liberal optimism.

When the Maquis rebels were stranded on *Voyager* there were immediate tensions between the two crews. In a bid to placate concerns Janeway made Chakotay, captain of the destroyed Maquis ship, her first officer. She was also impressed that he had Starfleet command training. Such technical training and knowledge of Starfleet conventionalities were important to her. He was initially distrustful of Janeway, and protected his comrades from the more rigorous regulations Janeway insisted upon implementing. The second episode of the series highlights some of the early tensions in the show, and how the writers dealt with conflict between the two crews.

During the pilot episode Voyager's chief engineer is killed and is in need of replacement. The job vacancy is a spot of contention in the second episode of the series. At the beginning of "Parallax" (1.3) a Starfleet officer (Lieutenant Carey) is in sickbay. He is being treated for wounds inflicted by B'Elanna Torres after a physical confrontation about how best to run engineering. Tuvok, the security officer (and Starfleet's spy in the Maquis), wants to make an example of her and court-martial Torres over the incident. Chakotay insists that he deal with her. Upon leaving the meeting, he is accosted by two Maquis crewmembers who avow their support for him and pledge, if need be, to stage a mutiny against the Starfleet crew. Chakotay responds by threatening to throw them in the brig if the seditious talk continues. Chakotay is instantly on the side of Starfleet and in no way wants to replace the status quo. At a staff meeting with the captain, he insists that the vacancy of chief engineer be filled by Torres. Janeway rejects the idea, citing her bad attitude and volatile temper; she doubts her professionalism. Janeway prefers a Starfleet replacement. Chakotay argues Torres is more skilled and knowledgeable and can be tamed. Voyager is then caught in a spatial disturbance; Janeway is convinced by Chakotay to speak with Torres who may be able to solve the issue. What follows is a heated exchange between the two. Torres, a former Starfleet cadet, said she left the Academy citing her distaste for its regimenting demands. She furiously leaves. Eventually Torres comes up with a way out of the spatial rift with the help of Janeway, working together, they free Voyager. Torres, after proving her worth, and agreeing to keep her anger in check, is promoted to Chief Engineer over Carey, the Starfleet officer. What is so noteworthy about this exchange is that the signs of depoliticization are shown at every turn in this first inter-crew conflict. Chakotay is, at his core, completely subservient to Starfleet protocols, despite having personal affection for his former comrades. Torres' only substantive objection to Starfleet is its petulance for regulation. At no point in any of these exchanges is political difference discussed. No one mentions the Maquis' nationalist politics. Janeway's initial objection to Torres being promoted is strictly professional and consequently is apolitical. This is a typical example of how the show dealt with this predicament.

Another example of this is the last episode of the first season, "Learning Curve" (1.16). Tuvok, after being confronted by an insubordinate Maquis crewman, goes to Janeway to see that the crewman is punished, citing that a Starfleet ship must maintain strict discipline. Janeway had heard similar complaints about a number of Maquis crewmen. She is concerned that they lack experience and discipline and that it is up to Tuvok to whip them into shape. Tuvok then begins to instruct a number of the Maquis crew, teaching them how to handle authority and discipline. He is confronted by their lack of respect for him and their laziness. Tuvok meets the leader of the wayward gang, Dalby, in an attempt to get to know him. Dalby admits that he joined the Maquis because Cardassians raped and murdered his wife. All that he has known since is hatred, and he has no love for Starfleet. At the end of the episode the training-crew and Tuvok are trapped in the cargo bay by noxious gas. They barely escape alive but are brought together by the experience. The Maquis crew accept their place in the Starfleet chain of command after Tuvok becomes more understanding of their position. Here again most of the Maquis crew clashes are due to personal failing or a simple lack of respect for authority. Apart from Dalby's traumatic backstory, there is little if any interaction with the political cause of the Maquis. Even the Federation's liberal ideology is not discussed, other than the importance of maintaining discipline.

This distaste for discipline seemed to be one of the only ways *Voyager* dealt with how Maquis members critiqued Starfleet. In the episode "Worst Case Scenario" (3.25), Torres accidentally finds a holodeck program written by Tuvok that trains Starfleet officers in how to deal with a potential Maquis takeover. Torres finds the simulation harmless fun since such a scenario is unthinkable at this point in time. When Tom and Tuvok run it, the simulation turns sour. The safety controls are switched off and they are trapped. This was a trap laid out by Seska (who betrayed the ship to the Kazon). Tom and Tuvok eventually escape and delete the program. The important element here is how the Maquis crew justify their takeover of Voyager. The simulated Chakotay leads the mutiny; he cites frustration with Starfleet legality. Exasperated by Janeway's explorative curiosity, he declares to stop at nothing to get the ship home. Despite the fact that all of this is a simulation, and has no real effect on the characters (another cheap way to dodge politics), it does show a potential contradiction amongst the ship's crew. Again, apart from the disdain for Starfleet's fixation on legality, there is little in the way of a political manifesto. The nationalist group takes over the ship with no alternate vision other than expediency in their travels.

The ultimate example of this kind of disengagement from politics is in the fifth season in "Extreme Risk" (5.03). Well into the show, most tensions between the two crews have completely evaporated. After learning that the Maquis have been eradicated in the Alpha quadrant by Cardassia's new ally, the Dominion, Torres takes a turn for the worse. She begins to run dangerous holodeck programs without safety protocols. She suffers multiple injuries, healing herself without the knowledge of her doctor or her partner Tom. Janeway, Tom, and Chakotay find out about these simulations and agree that Chakotay will speak to her. He is her closest friend on the ship and is a former Maquis comrade. Chakotay confronts her. He forces Torres to show him one of her particularly horrific holodeck programs where all their former Maquis comrades are slaughtered. She admits that after finding out that her Maquis friends are dead, she cares for little in life. Chakotay says that she has a new family now who care for her on Voyager; she needs to find a healthier outlet for her emotions. This is a heartfelt episode where depression and loss are confronted. But what is so noteworthy is that there is no mention about the cause for which both Torres and Chakotay had given so much. Their dream of an independent state has been obliterated, their movement of national liberation violently snuffed out. The writers diminish Torres's history with the Maquis as personal loss. This potentially highly political moment is reduced to Torres's inner anguish. Torres mourns for her lost friends. It has nothing to do with the cause they had fought for; her politics is diminished and naturalized to emotional turmoil, devoid of any kind of ideological contestation. The nationalism of the Maquis is forgotten; there is little lament that the country they fought for is no more. The Maquis' politics is, in the words of Žižek, culturalized and placed into the private sphere.

A final nod to this absence of politics and an end to utopian thinking is how Janeway deals with *Voyager* being untethered from Federation space. Janeway, who is the true hero of the show, getting her crew home and in one piece, embodies this loss of idealism. Picard in the *Next Generation* was the intellectual diplomat who embodied the utopian liberalism of the canon. Sisko, the hardnosed military and family man, with a soft heart, exemplified the militaristic but highly personal nature of *DS9*. Janeway is hyperprofessional, technocratic, and ambitious. Commenting on one occasion she hopes to make admiral while still young, she is a stickler for regulation, but she is a risk-taker. Before command, she had been a science officer, and she is much better versed in the technical side of things than previous captains. Janeway is the ultimate character that reifies neoliberalism and post-politics. Her technocratic and ambitious command style is reminiscent of Bauman's description of high-flying life of business and capital in liquid modernity. Janeway speaks little of Federation values, more of regulation. Janeway's leadership is technocratic, more concerned with discipline and protocol as an end in itself. For a canon that depicts a utopia in space where poverty has been abolished and intergalactic democracy realized, Janeway does little to either celebrate or critique such a polity.

Conclusion

Star Trek has, since the 1960s, been a vehicle for social, political and philosophical commentary. Of course, there were many instances where *Voyager* fulfilled this objective, but the crux of the show, the supposed political confrontation between the two crews, is resolved by personal "growth" of the former Maquis fighters. Most of its members were depicted as forlorn wayward drifters merely searching for a fighting cause. The complexities and depth of their political views are unexplored. Even Chakotay, who grew up on a disputed planet, gives little away of his political leanings. He quickly assimilates into the Federation way of life. The only real issue the Maquis seem to have is with the Federation's petulance for regulation. The show does not explore the political dynamics between the two groups. In the final season, in the episode "Repression" (7.04), Torres and Chakotay admit they are "former" Maquis members; "that was ancient history," she proclaims. The Maquis are easily assimilated into the Starfleet family. *Star Trek*'s emphasis on toleration compartmentalized their political difference into the realm of personal life. By the end of the show little of their former lives as national liberation fighters existed. Here we can see how politics in *Voyager* is culturalized into the private, individual sphere. The absence of such dialogue is a cultural example of neoliberal depolitization. The show's emphasis on toleration nullified ideological contestation. Previous shows went out of their way to demonstrate how the *Star Trek* series was a society without material want. It celebrated individualism, and fetishized liberal-democratic institutions. Self-determination was an intrinsic message previous shows propagated. *Voyager* was more concerned with protocol. The Maquis were accepted into the Starfleet family given that they consented to its regulations. Even the liberal utopia defined by previous series in the canon was diluted, Janeway's captaincy attested to that.

Voyager's historical context at the height of neoliberal hegemony shaped its politics. There is little doubt writers of the show were probably unaware of how Maquis politics were unexplored. They really did intend for the show to demonstrate ideological clash. It is clear that even the writers could not conceive of how alternate politics could exist since alternative political realities in the real world were unimaginable.

Notes

1. This was a directive from Gene Roddenberry to the writers of previous *Star Trek* series.
2. The U.S. did this before the outbreak of World War II.
3. This could not be said in the U.S.'s case since military spending kept them in the black, though budget hawkism became important rhetoric in the nation's political discourse.

Works Cited

Anderson, Perry. *The Antinomies of Antonio Gramsci*. Verso, 2017.
Barret, Michèle. *Star Trek: The Human Frontier*. Routledge, 2001.
Bauman, Zygmunt. *In Search for Politics*. Polity Press, 2006.
_____. *Liquid Moderinty*. Polity Press, 2000.
_____. *Socialism: The Active Utopia*. George Allen and Unwin Ltd, 1976.
Bell, Daneil. *The End of Ideology: On the Exahaustion of Political Ideas in the Fifites*. Cambridge, 2000.
Berend, Ivan T. *An Economic History of Twentieth-Century Europe*. Cambridge University Press, 2006.
Berman, Marshall. *All That Is Solid Melts Into Air*. Penguin, 1982.
Brown, Wendy. *Regulating Aversion: Tolerance in the Age of Identity and Empire*. Princeton University Press, 2006.
Burston-Chorowicz, Alex. "Engage! Captain Picard, Federationism, and U.S. Foreign Policy in the Emerging Post Cold War World." *Exploring Picard's Galaxy: Essays on Star Trek: The Next Generation*, edited by Peter W. Lee, McFarland, 2018.
Cameron, Fraser. *Us Foriegn Policy After Cold War: Global Hegemon or Reluctant Sheriff?* Routledge, 2005.
"Caretaker." *Star Trek: Voyager*, created by Rick Berman, Michael Piller and Jeri Taylor. Dir. Winrich Kolbe, Season 1, episodes 1 and 2, Paramount, 16 Jan. 1995.
Dyson, Stephen Benedict. *Otherwordly Politics: The International Relations of Star Trek, Game of Thrones, and Battlestar Galactica*. John Hopkins University Press, 2015.
"Extreme Risk." *Star Trek: Voyager*, created by Rick Berman, Michael Piller, and Jeri Taylor. Dir. Cliff Bole, Season 5, episode 3, Paramount, 28 Oct. 1998.
Franklin, H. Bruce. "Vietnam, *Star Trek*, and the Real Future." *Star Trek and History*, edited by Nancy Reagin, Wiley, 2013, pp. 87–108.
Fukuyama, Francis. *The End of History and the Last Man*. Free Press, 1992.
Gonzalez, George A. *The Politics of Star Trek: Justice, War and the Future*. Palgrave Macmillan, 2015.
Gramsci, Antonio. *Selections from the Prison Notebooks of Antonia Gramsci*. International Publishers, 1971.
Hale, Jon F. "The Making of New Democrats." *Political Science Quarterly*, vol. 110, no. 2, 1995, pp. 207–232.
Harvey, David. *A Brief History of Neoliberalism*. Oxford University Press, 2007.
Hauser, Michael. "The Twilight of Liberal Democracy: A Symptomatic Reading of Depoliticization." *Décalages*, vol. 1, no. 3, 2013.
Hay, Colin. "The Normalizing Role of Rationalist Assumptions in the Institutional Embedding of Neoliberalism." *Economy and Society*, vol. 33, no. 4, 2004, pp. 500–527.
Hayek, F.A. *The Road to Serfdom*. Routledge, 1944.

Hobsbawm, Eric. *Age of Extremes: The Short History of the Twentieth Century 1914–1991.* Abacus, 1995.
_____. *Age of Extremes: The Short Twentieth Century.* Clays, 1995.
Kapell, Matthew Wilhelm. "Speakers for the Dead: Star Trek, the Holocaust, and the Representation of Atrocity." *Star Trek as Myth: Essays on Symbol and Archetype at the Final Frontier,* edited by Matthew Wilhelm Kapell, McFarland, 2010.
Lagon, Mark P. "We Owe It to Them to Interfere": Star Trek and U.S. Statecraft in the 1960s and the 1990s." *Political Science Fiction,* edited by Donald M. Hassler and Clyde Wilcox, University of South Carolina Press, 1997.
"Learning Curve." *Star Trek: Voyager,* created by Rick Berman, Michael Piller, and Jeri Taylor. Dir. Kim Freidman, Season 1, episode 16, Paramount, 22 May 1995.
"The Maquis, Part 1." *Star Trek: Deep Space Nine,* created by Rick Berman and Michael Piller, Dir. David Livingston, Season 2, episode 20, Paramount, 24 Apr. 1994.
"The Maquis, Part 2." *Star Trek: Deep Space Nine,* created by Rick Berman and Michael Piller, Dir. Corey Allen, Season 2, episode 21, Paramount, 1 May 1994.
Memory Alpha. "Star Trek: Voyager." http://memoryalpha.wikia.com/wiki/Star_Trek:Voyager. Accessed May 1 2018.
Mulholland, Marc. *Bourgeois Liberty and the Politics of Fear: From Absolutism to Neo-Conservatism.* Oxford University Press, 2012.
"Parallax." *Star Trek: Voyager,* created by Rick Berman, Michael Piller, and Jeri Taylor. Dir. Kim Freidman, Season 1, episode 3, Paramount, 23 Jan. 1995.
Pilkington, Ace G. "Star Trek: American Dream, Myth and Reality." *Star Trek as Myth: Essays on Symbol and Archetype at the Final Frontier,* edited by Matthew Wilhelm Kapell, McFarland, 2010.
"Plato's Stepchildren." *Star Trek: The Original Series,* created by Gene Roddenberry, Dir. David Alexander, Season 3, episode 12, Paramount, 22 Nov. 1968.
Putman, John. "Terrorizing Space: Star Trek, Terrorism, and History." *Star Trek and History,* edited by Nancy Reagin, Wiley, 2013, pp. 143–157.
"Repression." *Star Trek: Voyager,* created by Rick Berman, Michael Piller, and Jeri Taylor, directed by Winrich Kolbe, Season 7, episode 4, Paramount, 25 Oct. 2000.
Sarantakes, Nicholas Evan. "Cold War Pop Culture and the Image of US Foreign Policy: The Perspective of the Original Star Trek Series." *Journal of Cold War Studies,* vol. 7, no. 4, 2005, pp. 74–103.
Thorpe, Andrew. *A History of the British Labour Party* Palgrave Macmillan, 2008.
"Worst Case Scenario." *Star Trek: Voyager,* created by Rick Berman and Michael Piller, Dir. Alexander Singer, Season 3, episode 25, Paramount, 14 May 1997.
Wright, Tony. *Socialisms Old and New.* Routledge, 1996.
Žižek, Slavoj. "Tolerance as an Ideological Category." *Critical Inquiry,* no. 4, 2008, pp. 660–682.

Confessions of an Anti-Fan

Voyager, Fandom and Dislike

MURRAY LEEDER

Why wasn't *Star Trek: Voyager* (1995–2001) better? I start with this question because so many other works about series seem to dwell on it. For example, David McIntree's 2000 book *Delta Quadrant: The Unofficial Guide to Voyager* closes by attempting to deal with that question, arguing that it was a victim of the success of earlier series, aping their best elements without developing a distinctive tone of its own: "an entertaining extension of its predecessors, but not a new evolutionary stage" (330). Producer and co-creator Rick Berman attributed the decline of the audience for *Star Trek* to "franchise fatigue"; in a biting essay, Ina Rae Hark argues that Berman's blaming of franchise fatigue deflects his own mismanagement of *Star Trek* ("Franchise Fatigue?"), which led to the (temporary) near-extinction of a valuable and venerable television and film franchise.

Another of *Voyager*'s creators, Jeri Taylor, explained the apparent "staleness" of the Alpha Quadrant, the setting of all prior *Star Trek* shows, motivated a slate-cleaning change of scene: "[P]utting the show in the Delta [Q]uadrant meant that a lot of beloved characters were no longer going to be with us. The Klingons, the Romulans, the Ferengi, the Cardassians[1] ... Was the audience going to forgive us? Or would they hate us for saying, 'Everything you've known about *Star Trek* is gone'?" (Greenwald 189). And yet the major fan objection to *Voyager* was not that it had too little connection to prior *Star Trek* series, but the opposite: that it was too safe and unadventurous, sticking to a familiar playbook and thus failing to establish a unique and distinctive format of its own. But as this essay will explore, *Voyager* did (and does) indeed have a dedicated fanbase somewhat separate from the larger body of *Star Trek* fans, and particularly shaped by the popularization of the Internet in the mid–1990s.

Confessions of an Anti-Fan (Leeder) 249

Down in the Delta: Voyager in Context

Star Trek: Deep Space Nine (1993–99; henceforth DS9) and Voyager, the two series that represented the next generation to Star Trek: The Next Generation (1987–94; henceforth TNG),[2] shared much but had fundamentally different production contexts. Both were owned by Paramount Communications Inc. (purchased by the media giant Viacom in 1994) But DS9 was a first run syndicated show like TNG had been, so essentially sold, usually in packages, to stations directly. Conversely, Voyager was the flagship show of the new United Paramount Network (UPN)[3]; its pilot, "Caretaker" (1.1), was literally the first broadcast when UPN debuted on January 16, 1995. Press coverage foregrounded the "newness" of the setting and the status of Captain Janeway (Kate Mulgrew) as the first female starship captain to anchor a series.[4] Failing the replicate the Fox Network's recent success, UPN struggled through eleven years with few hits. Coming on the heels of TNG and sharing many creative and technical personnel, Voyager was positioned as the apparent successor to TNG,[5] with DS9 cast into a shadowy space of semi-legitimacy.[6] Ironically, DS9's relative neglect from Paramount allowed it to evolve into a more distinctive and daring show.[7] The later series unfolded against the film series following TNG, with its highs (the box office success and acclaim of Star Trek: First Contact [1996]) and lows (the abject failure of Star Trek: Nemesis, 2002), and a massive proliferation of licensed Star Trek products like novels, comic books and video games.[8] Paramount deliberately flooded the market with Trek, but demand did not match supply for long.

Star Trek's mainstream success crested around the celebrations of the franchise's 25th anniversary in 1992, when TNG's ratings were at their highest (an average 11.5 million viewers per episode) and Star Trek VI: The Undiscovered Country (1991) won strong reviews and solid business. The spinning-off of DS9 in 1993 and Voyager in 1995 was the result of TNG's remarkable crossing over into mainstream, primetime viewers, and yet largely did not replicate that success (much less did Enterprise, 2001–5). The vast proliferation of Star Trek post-TNG was also the dilution of the brand which, rather than "boldly going" into the future, sputtered along, slowly losing its audience. The whetting of the public appetite for episodic science fiction resulted in competitors like Babylon 5 (1994–8) and Stargate SG-1 (1997–2007), leaving DS9 and Voyager struggling to compete in a market that TNG had relatively to itself. Voyager, then, arrived with plenty of goodwill as the highly anticipated successor to a top-rated show, but disappointed on most fronts, seemingly attaining its longevity because of its unique position as UPN's flagship program.

My purpose here is not to provide the umpteenth rehearsal of the criticisms of Voyager, but these should be established in brief. The most substantial may be its neglect of its own premise: uncertain allies, desperate and stranded on the opposite side of the galaxy. In an early publicity statement, Rick Berman promised that "There will always be conflict between [Starfleet and the Maquis], and that gave us something new and unique" (qtd. in Gross and Altman, *Captain's Logs* 343). Yet that conflict barely outlasted the premiere,[9] and *TNG*-holdovers, like holodeck episodes, were shoehorned in despite flying in the face of the premise of "isolated crew with limited resources." To quote the show's science advisor, André Bormanis, *Voyager* had

> a pretty cool premise.... But that's *not* what the show became, and fairly quickly it's like, "Okay, well, Chakotay [Robert Beltran] is the first officer, he and Janeway have a cordial relationship, and we meet the Kazon, guys with a different rubber mask than the other aliens we've met in the four hundred or some-odd episodes of *Star Trek* that had been produced to date." It was really the same thing in a somewhat different package [qtd. in Altman and Gross, *Fifty-Year Mission*, 558–9].

One is tempted to amend Bormanis's statement to "somewhat different but inferior package," lacking the air of Shakespearean sophistication of *TNG* at its best and devoid of *DS9*'s sprawling storytelling and focus on interstellar politics. *Voyager* the show ambles and meanders just like *Voyager* the ship, hypothetically exploring new territory but actually doomed to retreads and consequence-free episodic storytelling (heavy on what fans came to call "the Reset Button" that restores the status quo), exacerbated by overuse of technobabble. Further, *Voyager* tended to import established elements of the *Star Trek* universe (the Q Continuum, the Borg) to entice viewers but then mis- or overuse them. Paramount ordered a new *Star Trek* series earlier than the producers would have preferred (Altman and Gross, *Fifty-Year Mission*, 552), so *Voyager* seems like a rushed product designed around a coordinated marketing opportunity (the vacuum caused by *TNG*'s end and the launch of UPN) that, especially in early years, seemed to lack any coherent vision to justify its existence.

Perhaps McIntree is on to something in locating *Voyager*'s status as *TNG*'s heir apparent at the root of its relative mediocrity—pressure to deliver the familiar strangled its ability to explore the unique potential of its own premise. Coming at a peculiar cultural, technological and industrial moment, *Voyager* had to serve many masters: Paramount/Viacom, UPN, the general television audience, *Star Trek* fans in general and *Voyager* fans in particular. Under the circumstances, it seems unsurprising that a conservative approach prevailed.

And there was yet another context. McIntree also suggests that exposure to a new mode of fandom made *Voyager*'s creators extra risk averse (330). *Voyager* premiered right as the commercialization of the Internet was ramping up in earnest. Fan interactions, previously reserved for fan publications and "meatspace" events, like fan club meetings and conventions, vastly expanded and became immediate, and thus probably harder for creators to ignore. I would hesitate to draw too many conclusions there, in part because of the production of *Voyager* was clearly fraught with struggles between writers, actors and producers (see Altman and Gross, *Fifty-Year Mission*, 551–642), and in part because it comes close to blaming the fans themselves for the show's faults. And yet the Internet is a crucial context for *Voyager*, to its reception by fans and others alike.

I, Anti-Fan

There was not a name for the kind of viewer I was of *Voyager* when it was on the air. That would have to wait for Jonathan Gray's 2003 coinage: "anti-fan." Gray's insight was that a study of fans also requires study of counter-categories of audience members. One is the "non-fan" who consumes the product without "intense involvement" (74). The anti-fan, however, is intensely involved, but negatively: "[they] strongly dislike a given text or genre, considering it inane, stupid, morally bankrupt and/or aesthetic drivel" (70). This is only a slight exaggeration of my attitude towards *Voyager* during its initial airing. I was a completist who rarely missed an episode of *Voyager* but considered it markedly inferior to *TNG* and *DS9*. This does not mean that I never found *Voyager* episodes to like, that were cleverly constructed ("Projections" 2.3), patient and thoughtful ("Muse" 4.23), character driven and intriguing ("Counterpoint" 5.10), successful comedy ("Tinker, Tenor, Doctor, Spy" 6.4, "Bride of Chaotica!" 5.12) or exciting high concept action/adventure ("Deadlock" 2.21, "Dark Frontier" 5.15–5.16). I recognized a certain bland competence to *Voyager* (its acting and directing more than its storytelling), but in general, I regarded it as a weak, unimaginative, disappointing show, seemingly composed solely of filler episodes. Yet I was acquainted with *Star Trek* fans that loved *Voyager*. And when I heard someone say, "*Voyager* is my favorite *Star Trek*" or words to that effect, I judged them. This attitude seemed to me unthinkable—obviously the wrong choice.

To be clear, I never outright hated *Voyager* or its fans, never thought it reprehensible, and was relatively unvocal about my dislike. Nonetheless, I think that the term "anti-fan" applies for two reasons. One, on looking back I realize that my persisting as a viewer of *Voyager* through to its conclusion was less in spite of my dislike of the show than because of it—that negativity was a source of pleasure in itself. The second reason is a certain sense of propriety: while *TNG* seemed to be everybody's *Star Trek*, non-fans included, *DS9* was my *Star Trek* and *Voyager* was somebody else's *Star Trek*. Who was that somebody? My unscientific observations suggest that the most dedicated *Voyager* fans were and are female. I know of no demographics data that would confirm that impression, and I want to avoid essentialism. Certainly, it should not be assumed that female *Star Trek* fans are inevitably *Voyager* fans; reading "Time and Again," the scathing *Voyager* chapter of Ina Rae Hark's 2008 book on the franchise, should disabuse anyone of that notion. And *Voyager* certainly had male fans, but it also clearly spoke to certain female fans in a way that it did not speak to me.[10]

The gender dynamics of *Voyager*'s fandom largely lie beyond the scope of this essay, but I will return to aspects of the topic. I will first elucidate the context of *Voyager*'s run through its relationship to the other *Star Trek* series and their fandoms. Though I had no firsthand experience of the struggles of *TNG* to win over the existing *Star Trek* fans, I was conscious of certain residuals of that process. A montage sequence documentary *Trekkies* (1997) shows fans the competing labels "Trekkie" and "Trekker"; it concludes with the youthful superfan Gabriel Köerner saying that he is happy with either but favors "*Star Trek* fan." At stake in this dispute over nomenclature was a rift between originalists raised on the original *Star Trek* series (1966–9; henceforth *TOS*) and potentially seeing the later series as threats to its singular status and younger *TNG*-era fans with a more expansive understanding of *Star Trek* less dependent on *TOS*. If the "Trekkers" seemed to be winning by the mid–1990s, the wake of *TNG* saw another split in fandom, between *DS9* and *Voyager* fans.

Attesting to the difficulty of *Voyager* in retaining the goodwill of certain *Star Trek* fans is the example of Timothy W. Lynch. Lynch was perhaps the original *Star Trek* Internet reviewer, uploading reviews to Usenet as early as the second season of *TNG*. However, he only covered the first two years of *Voyager*. At first reasonably positive about the new series, Lynch even, in his first season wrap-up, admonished some fans who had given it too little a chance. Even then, however, he acknowledged that "it's amazing how downright *aimless* the show has seemed," considering that it should be the most clearly goal-oriented of any *Star Trek* series. He wrote that *Voyager* "has done a magnificent job in its first season of treading water. The problem with treading water is that eventually you need to pick a destination and make progress … or you drown." A year later, Lynch quipped, "Do the words 'Davy Jones' locker' ring a bell?" Subtitled "A Farewell to *Voyager*," his second season summation offers a vitriolic critique of the series mostly for ignoring the potential of its premise: the lack of sense that they have covered territory (encountering the very same aliens, for example), little sense of how the ship would suffer from being away from repair facilities, a captain giving controversial orders but never experiencing any meaningful consequences, the lack of exploration of the psychological consequences of being 70 years from home: "an unrealistic crew aboard an unrealistic ship." Wrote Lynch:

I've never "abandoned" a Trek series I reviewed before, and I wish my decision here could be different. However, this season of "Voyager" has, I feel, abandoned everything about the series that made it potentially interesting, and replaced it with nothing I care to see. If a massive overhaul changes the show greatly for the better, I'm sure I'll hear about it eventually—but without such a change, I expect "Voyager" to keep spiraling downhill, and I'm not planning to go down with this ship.

For Lynch, then, *Voyager* had broken faith with its audience and deserved to lose it as a consequence. However, Lynch did review the entire run of *DS9* and the first two of *Enterprise* (quitting out of time concerns rather than a special dislike of the series). Yet other Internet reviewers of the time had quite different attitudes. Jim Wright ran a dedicated *Voyager* review site called "Delta Blues" that rarely dipped below three stars out of five.

The press sometimes played up the rivalry between *Voyager* and *DS9* fans. In September 1997, just as the fourth season of *Voyager* and the sixth of *DS9* were about to premiere, *The Village Voice* ran dueling articles on the Internet fandoms of each series, captioned "BATTLE OF THE STAR TREKS." The treatment of the two series is striking in its differences. *Voyager* frames its fandom as "the first Trek fan community to really take off in cyberspace. Those devotees, mostly female, are particularly active in the burgeoning field of online fan fiction" (Chansanchai 37). The article provides links to four *Voyager* fan fiction sites and attests to some 90 in total and profiles two writers: a 44-year-old woman known as "Dangermom," a long-term *Trek* fan pleased that *Voyager* "brought us back to the 'exploring the unknown' premise of the original series, with the best thing that ever happened to a Trek series: a woman in command" (Chansanchai 37), and 14-year-old Subha Rajaram, attracted by the series' diverse cast. Rajaram is identified as a "relationshipper"[11] who enjoys fan fiction's capacity for depicting relationships that, like K/S (Kirk,William Shatner, and Spock, Leonard Nimoy), would be "impossible" on the show (Chansanchai 37).[12] The somewhat shorter piece on *DS9* emphasizes how "Trek fans have become divided" in the wake of *TNG*'s cancellation: "*Voyager* is still more popular, but *DS9*, which started out as a mediocre version of the much liked *Next Generation*, has grown into a sci-fi drama that stands on its own. The reason? Character. *DS9* fans are unique in the Trekkie realm—they feed off of character development rather than a need to explore the universe" (Lee 37).

Both pieces are full of assumptions and clichés as well some iffy claims, but the assertion that *Voyager* is more popular demands scrutiny. By what standard? *DS9*'s ratings were overall slightly higher. Both series fell far below *TNG*'s bar, however, and steadily declined over their runs (Fuller 1999). Tellingly, the *DS9* article makes no reference to fan fiction, a cornerstone of the treatment of *Voyager*. While it would be difficult to prove empirically that *DS9* inspired less fan fiction than *Voyager*, at this writing (February 2018), fanfiction.net collects roughly 9700 *Voyager* stories versus 1900 *DS9* ones. One might object that this site, founded in 1998, overlapped more heavily with *Voyager*'s initial run, except that *TNG* has 4500 stories.[13] *DS9* may have been more viewed overall, but *Voyager*'s fans were more visible and more interactive, more prone to reworking the show and its characters for their own purposes through the process of "textual poaching," a term coined by Henry Jenkins in 1992 to describe fans' creative, selective reworkings of media texts. If *Voyager*'s cultural footprint seems to exceed *DS9*'s, the fans are the reason.

The attractiveness of *Voyager* to fan reworkings through fan fiction and related practices reflects how the show furnished the raw materials for many interesting directions that it failed to deliver on, leaving fans to pick up the slack. A key example is "Resolutions" (2.25), in which exposure to a disease forces the crew to strand Janeway and Chakotay together on a planet with only basic technology. Facing the prospect of spending their lives together, they grow closer and at the end of the episode are on the verge of forming a romantic/sexual relationship … just as *Voyager* returns with the medical expertise to rescue them. Playing consciously on the Internet fandom of "shipping mentioned above,"[14] the ending of the ironically titled "Resolutions" *demands* follow-up and is dramatically nullified by the absence of it. Whether they continue their nascent romance or recognize that it was circumstantial and inappropriate to pursue further as captain and first office, the terms of Janeway and Chakotay's interactions should now be different. That the events of "Resolutions" are simply never mentioned again, though frustrating, provided fertile ground for textual poachers to build on through fan fiction. An episode of the *Voyager* fan podcast *To the Journey* on "Resolutions" is even called "Why We Have Fanfic."[15] It seems possible to speculate that *Voyager* inspired more fan production than *DS9* precisely because *DS9* was stronger on world-building: it is, easily, the most populated, fleshed out and fully realized incarnation of *Star Trek*.

Arguably the most famous piece of 1990s *Star Trek* fan fiction was "The Secret Logs of Mistress Janeway," written by D.L. Warner as "NovaD," which reimagines Janeway as a powerful dominatrix. NovaD, who was interviewed in *Trekkies*, was a BDSM practitioner in real life and became a minor celebrity, appearing on the conference circuit in the 1990s. A classic example of textual poaching, NovaD's reworking *Voyager* into an alternate world of kink pokes fun at the superficially "vanilla" *Star Trek* universe. For a mode of textual poaching closer to anti-fandom, we can look to reviewer Chuck Sonnenburg, publishing as SFDebris. Sonnenburg started out with text reviews but became better known for video reviews recapping a variety of programs and movies, but emphasizing *Star Trek* in general and *Voyager* in particular. Sonnenburg's reviews are replete with the kind of "snark" and an overall tone of amused negativity that characterizes anti-fandom as a mode of fan engagement. One gets the sense that Sonnenburg has reviewed *Voyager* most extensively because it yields endless material from which he can derive humor. Yet SFDebris is not mindlessly negative. Reviewing the show as a whole at the end of his review of the series finale, "Endgame" (7.25–7.26), he describes *Voyager* as "The beige of space," but expresses resigned disappointment at the show's missed opportunities. Sonnenburg's "parody Janeway," a deranged mad scientist, dominatrix and bloodthirsty interstellar warlord, is a fixture of his *Voyager* reviews, which review and rewrite the show simultaneously.

Different discourses can be found among those who identify themselves specifically as *Voyager* fans. A 2018 episode of *To the Journey* ("Green Shag Carpet: What *Voyager* Means to Us") deals with what the show means specifically to the hosts. They credit it with helping them overcome anxiety and get out of an abusive relationship, as well as noting that it evokes warm familial memories from its initial run. *To the Journey* praises *Voyager* for its family themes and a sense of hominess, warmth and comfort, as well as a "therapeutic" quality, with multiple episodes based on healing and self-actualization. Yet even this episode decries *Voyager*'s abuse of the Reset Button and roundly mocks Ensign Harry Kim (Garrett Wang)[16]; *Voyager* fans are not unaware of the show's faults but find them counterbalanced by positives (or potentially love the flaws too). Similarly, in the *Women at Warp* podcast, hosted by three feminist *Star Trek* fans, *Voyager* is often praised its multiple female characters who regularly interact as part of shipboard duties and particularly its affiliation of its female characters with science and engineering. Multiple claims have been made that characters Janeway, B'Elanna Torres (Roxanne Dawson) and Seven of Nine (Jeri Ryan) have inspired women to enter science/technology fields (Palmer, "Female Leadership").[17]

Worst Episode Ever? The Case of "Threshold"

In his aforementioned "A Farewell to Voyager," Timothy W. Lynch also identifies the second season *Voyager* episode "Threshold" (2.15) as the worst episode of any *Star Trek* series, the only one he cannot bring himself to rewatch, and suggests that it "deserves to be expunged from the universe for the universe's own safety." It involves the crew finding a theoretical way of reaching Warp 10—infinite velocity in which one occupies the entire universe simultaneously.[18] This baffling task is accomplished by Lt. Tom Paris (Robert Duncan McNeil), who subsequently, in scenes reminiscent of Cronenberg's *The Fly* (1986), painfully transforms into a sort of lizardman. After dying and spontaneously resurrecting himself, he kidnaps Janeway and flies at Warp 10 again, only for them both to become human-sized salamander-type creatures who breed on an uninhabited swamp planet. The Doctor (Robert Picardo) manages to restore Janeway and Paris to their original human DNA (using "bursts of antiprotons"), and the events of the episode are never spoken of again (one is tempted to add, "under penalty of torture").[19]

Even a quick plot summary shows what a baffling episode "Threshold" is. To simplify a litany of science, technology and engineering issues: it ignores what "impossible" means (a theoretical limit, not a barrier to be broken), as well as that infinite speed would require infinite fuel and be beyond the structural capacity of any conceivable craft, to say nothing of its pilot. On the biological front, "Threshold" utterly misunderstands DNA and evolution. Individuals cannot evolve, only populations evolve, and the idea that DNA shapes human beings towards some predestined future form is particularly inaccurate. Nor would your DNA changing suddenly reshape your body.[20] Even allowing the DNA-as-destiny theme, this view of humanity's future seems remarkably counter to *Star Trek*'s general optimism. The presto-chango restoration of Paris and Janeway at the end beggars belief, and it seems unthinkable that the *Voyager* crew would simply abandon new life that it created on an alien world. Furthermore, since the Warp 10 has now been achieved twice with only reversible side effects, what is to stop *Voyager* from using it to get back to Earth, or at least send an unmanned craft home to report on their survival?[21]

Bad *Star Trek* episodes are nothing new. Some, like *TOS*'s "Spock's Brain" (3.1) are recuperable as camp; others, like *TNG*'s "Shades of Gray" (2.22) are deemed unwatchably dull but also safely ignorable. Attitudes towards episodes like "Threshold" (2.15), reinforced if not necessarily created by Internet rhetoric, mark the difference between fans and anti-fans, where fans might acknowledge its badness but find other elements of it endearing, while anti-fans take it as not only irredeemably bad but exemplary of its series. In truth, *Star Trek*'s pretense of scientific accuracy is largely just that, a pretense; I have elsewhere observed that "*Star Trek* has always been more interested in a verisimilitudinous depiction of a science-dominated world than in fidelity to actual science" (5). Nonetheless, *Star Trek* has consciously nurtured a real relationship to science practice, even licensing exhibits in science museums (including the planetarium show *Star Trek: Orion Rendezvous* in the early 1990s and more recently *The Starfleet Academy Experience*) that mix entertainment and education. Non-fiction books both licensed (Bormanis 1998, Fazekas 2016) and unlicensed (Krauss 1955, Andreadis 1998) have explicated *Star Trek*'s connection to real world science, acknowledging that it is frequently not accurate but holding that it warrants discussion, nonetheless. Not for nothing does the original model for the USS *Enterprise* hang in the Smithsonian Institution's National Air and Space Museum and not the National Museum of American History.

However, episodes like "Threshold," which gallop over physics, biology and engineering, endanger that privileged relationship of *Star Trek* to real-world science. They give us a version of *Star Trek* for which science is just a set of meaningless catchphrases that "allow" whatever the writers like to happen—or perhaps they reveal too clearly that all *Star Trek* is just that. Lynch, who studied astronomy at Caltech, earlier took exception to *TNG* episodes like "The Chase" (6.20) and "Genesis" (7.19), not just for their bad science but for wildly misrepresenting the theory of evolution to millions of viewers and implying that it is a kind of scientific destiny. He was predictably appalled at "Threshold," too, a factor in his abandoning of the series after that season. In his double-length review of "Threshold," SFDebris states:

> Why does this episode stand out? I know some of you are going to hate this answer, but the reason is because this is what *Voyager* had been doing all the time, just exaggerated. What's more, it's really only a slight exaggeration. Clichés, points that go nowhere, pointless technobabble, improper science, complete logical disconnect.... If I didn't know better, I'd swear this is self-parody.

For an anti-fan, "Threshold" cannot be held as marginal to *Voyager* itself—quite the opposite, it damns its series because it is so typical.

Other reviewers are more kind. Mark A. Altman and Edward Gross, for instance, both give "Threshold" two stars out of four, noting its bizarre and implausible plot but also praising its execution and especially acting (*Trek Navigator*, 241); David McIntree also identifies it as more mediocre than terrible, though he notes its reputation as "the worst episode ever and often the worst *Trek* of all" (97). Jim Wright gave it three stars. Challenged to find positive things to say about "Threshold," the hosts of *To the Journey* emphasize the character interactions between Paris and Janeway, note some humor and even mildly praise the mad science premise; certainly, they do not see the episode as a betrayal of *Star Trek*'s commitment to the integrity of science, presumably having comparatively little investment in that topic to begin with.

The DVD box set for the second season of *Voyager* contained an "Easter Egg" about "Threshold" that finds Braga lamenting, "It's a terrible episode. People are very unforgiving about that episode. I've written well over 100 episodes of *Star Trek*, yet it seems to be the only episode anyone brings up. Brannon Braga, who wrote 'Threshold.'" Fans have suggested that Paris's line in the later episode "Day of Honor" (4.3), "I've never navigated a transwarp conduit," is the writers' way of dismissing "Threshold's" very existence; certain fans are primed for evidence, however unlikely, that "Threshold" is not just ignored but effectively decanonized. Nonetheless, "Threshold's" continued presence on various "worst of" lists and the like (e.g., Roget "6 Great TV Shows," Marx "8 Needlessly Insane Moments") and the widely reported article based on it published in the "predatory" *American Research Journal of Biosciences* (Redd 2018) keeps it in the public's eye. Web reviewers who do not specialize in *Star Trek*, including recently *Obscurus Lupa* (Allison Pregler), have reviewed it precisely because of its inglorious reputation. "Threshold" may be not only *Voyager*'s worst episode but also, thanks in large part to Internet commentary, its most famous.[22]

Voyager *Redeemed?*

In retrospect, one striking feature of *Voyager* is its reflexivity: the show itself offers repeated commentaries on its fans' fondness for textual poaching and its increased cultural visibility in the Internet age. Countless episodes supply alternate versions of *Voyager*, with its characters essentially writing their own fan fiction ("Worst Case Scenario" 3.25, "Muse" 6.22, and "The Voyager Conspiracy" 6.9), and sometimes even reconceiving Janeway as a heartless, S and M-tinged martinet ("Living Witness" 4.23 and "Author, Author" 7.20)—a strangely persistent idea. In "Pathfinder" (6.10), we find that Lt. Reginald Barclay (Dwight Schultz), *TNG*'s resident fan-surrogate, has become a *Voyager* "fanboy" himself. Always prone to "living in the imagination" (Saler 2012), Barclay has overinvested in the *Voyager* crew to the point of spending vast amounts of time with a Holodeck recreation of them and naming his cat after Neelix (Ethan Phillips). Yet Barclay's obsession pays off as he, in a rare status quo-rewriting development, secures two-way communication with the ship.

The ambitious "Year of Hell" (4.8-4.9) two-parter contains equal measures of *Voyager*'s pleasures and frustrations. For once, it takes the show's premise literally: facing off against a time-manipulating villain, *Voyager* is besieged and broken, its crew scattered, and Janeway herself becomes increasingly unhinged, her leadership ability compromised by obsession and desperation. Yet at its conclusion, "Year of Hell" resets the clock, utterly nullifying the episodes' events, restoring *Voyager* to its implausibly pristine condition and re-establishing the status quo, rendering the episodes weightless and inconsequential.[23] It is frustrating yet appropriate that *Voyager* can only fulfill its own premise by breaking from its usual reality.[24] But there is something pleasant about *Voyager*'s self-awareness—a feeling that the writers were chaffing against its format the same as the audience.[25]

Commenting on a retrospective article about *Voyager* on avclub.com (Nowalk, "*Star Trek: Voyager* Accidentally"), "Clancys Personal Researcher" writes:

> I love this show, even while recognizing that it isn't very good. I associate *Voyager* more with who I was at the time, and what it meant to me in my youth. For that reason, it's my favorite *Trek*. This show also introduced me to the wonder of *Star Trek* message boards. For that reason, it is my least favorite *Trek*.

This comment concisely sums up many of the themes of this essay: fandom rooted in personal situations, the ability of fans to simultaneously recognize and forgive flaws, the ambivalent positives and negatives a single work might generate, and the Internet's formative place in *Voyager*'s fandom. Recent years have seen several attempts to reevaluate or recuperate *Voyager*, including Liam Macleod's article "Why Do Star Trek Fans Hate Voyager?" (2012) and Ian Grey's "Now, 'Voyager': In Praise of the Trekkiest of Trek Shows" (2013), published on relatively mainstream media commentary sites (*Den of Geek* and RogerEbertwww, respectively) rather than those focused on *Star Trek*. *Voyager* is arguably less disliked than its own successor, *Enterprise*. Throughout this essay I have conflated several distinct waves of fandom: those who watched *Voyager* as it unfolded, week to week, year to year, and those who discovered it through reruns, DVDs or streaming services. Perhaps a "bingeable" *Voyager* stands more on its own in isolation from its sister-series.[26] The fact that *Voyager* continues to inspire both fan and anti-fan discourse and fan fiction long after it went off the air is a tribute of sorts.

This project has turned out more personal than I had initially intended, fueled by my own attempt to sort out my complicated feelings about *Voyager*. For all the talk of the "aca-fan" (a category that blurs the previously discrete categories of fan and scholar) and the importance of academic autoethnography (Hills) in recent decades, I feel some discomfort in trying to reconcile my academic and fan (or anti-fan) selves. But I do feel like a *mea culpa* is in order, but not directed to *Voyager* itself; I still largely stand by my initial dislike of the series, though I do wonder if formative contact with its early seasons prevented me from appreciating the show it became. Was I so committed to an anti-fan mode of viewership early on, shaped by tastemakers like Lynch, that I could not and cannot escape it? It is fascinating how fans and anti-fans may look at the same qualities and regard them differently: where one might see warmth, the other might see smugness and complacency. Some clearly do appreciate the homey, familiar quality of *Voyager*, a sort of *Andy Griffith Show* (1960-8) in space, but to me all those qualities are unearned since they fly in the face of the show's premise. Rather, I should apologize to its fans for discounting the validity of their mode of engagement with the show.

NOTES

1. All of these species would appear on *Voyager* sooner or later, often in rather contrived ways.
2. *DS9* and *Voyager* were also the first series to follow the death of *Star Trek* creator Gene Roddenberry in 1991, a moment of rupture that probably motivated certain fans to "jump ship" rather than persist with the franchise.
3. This was the second time a new *Star Trek* series was designed to launch a Paramount network. *Star Trek: Phase II* was commissioned in 1977 to launch the Paramount Television

Service (PTVS). After the network was scrapped, concepts were reworked into *Star Trek: The Motion Picture* (1979) (Reeves-Stevens and Reeves-Stevens 1997).

4. Prior to *Star Trek: Discovery* (2017-), all *Star Trek* series have the commanding officer as their lead character, even as the series became more ensemble driven.

5. An early announcement for *Voyager* in 1993 carried the headline "'Next Gen' replacement show set for new network" (Spelling 76).

6. The TV special *Ultimate Trek: Star Trek's Greatest Moments* (1999) gives *DS9* extremely little treatment, though perhaps this is unsurprising since it aired on UPN. Of course, the *Star Trek* animated series (1973–4) is the true black sheep of the franchise, though it has been somewhat rehabilitated in the last decade.

7. Even though *Voyager* was hypothetically a network show, it mostly stuck with syndication's disinclination to arc-based storytelling (which was coming into vogue in the major networks at the time), even as *DS9*, though syndicated, was attempting multi-episode arcs even early in its run before becoming outright serialized for its last half-season. A related irony is that while *DS9* features the largest-scale storytelling of any screen version *Star Trek*, the plunging of the Federation into an existential war that is only fleetingly (begrudgingly?) acknowledged in *Voyager* and the *TNG* films.

8. For more on the expansion of the *Star Trek* brand post–Roddenberry, see Johnson (esp. 109–29).

9. *Enterprise's* Temporal Cold War is a rough cognate to the Maquis-Starfleet dynamic in *Voyager*: an element baked into the show's premise that the writers nevertheless did not have clear ideas about, and which thus ended up largely ignored.

10. For example, see Jarrah Hodge's 2018 essay "The Lessons Captain Janeway Taught Me."

11. This term, generally shortened to "'shipper," was popularized by fans of *The X-Files* (1993–2002) advocating romance between Mulder (David Duchovny) and Scully (Gillian Anderson).

12. The body of scholarship on fan fiction, especially as written by women, is quite large, going at least as far back as Lichtenberg, Marshak and Winston (221–74); for a *Voyager*-specific approach, see Kies (2011).

13. I am here excluding the crossover fiction section, where *TNG* is the largest *Trek* contingent, but *Voyager* is still well ahead of *DS9*. In the 1990s, much *Star Trek* fan fiction circulated through Usenet, especially alt.startrek.creative, alt.startrek.creative.moderated and alt.startrek.creative.erotica; this material is hypothetically archived at groups.google.com since the acquisition of Usenet's archives by Google in 2001, but its searchability is limited.

14. The ever-candid Robert Beltran referred to "Resolutions" as "a bone that was thrown to the many fans that were crying out for a Janeway and Chakotay relationship" (Kaplan, "Commander Chakotay," 100)—rather a meatless bone.

15. Another context is the aggressive move by Paramount to control its intellectual property in the mid-1990s, endangering the activities of fan clubs, unlicensed conventions and fan websites (see "The Viacom Crackdowns"), furthering the narrative of fan work as a subversive corrective to corporate officialdom.

16. Perhaps the ultimate victim of *Voyager's* tendency towards stasis, Kim goes unpromoted and largely without any character development over seven years.

17. *Voyager* is easily the *Star Trek* series that rates best on the "Bechdel Test" (Hodge, "How Does Your").

18. The premise draws on Sternbach and Okuda's *Star Trek: The Next Generation Technical Manual* (1991), which states, "Even if it were possible to expend the theoretically infinite amount of energy required, an object at Warp 10 would be travelling infinitely fast, occupying all points in the universe simultaneously" (56).

19. Here I reference *The Simpsons*' "The Principal and the Pauper" (9.2), also considered a low point of the show's formative era, joking about episodic television maintaining a status quo that flies in the face of logic.

20. In addition to sources referenced elsewhere, I am drawing on Schneider, Epsicokhan.

21. Reviewer Michelle Erica Green also offers a surprisingly rare critique of "Threshold"

on the basis that Paris kidnaps and rapes Janeway: "I'm trying to imagine what Kirk would have done to Spock for raping him, even with *pon farr* as an excuse, or what Picard would have done if Troi forced him to have sex with her."

22. A good sport, Braga posted the fake article on his Facebook page. Dipping into more subjective territory, I am not certain that "Threshold" attained its reputation immediately. I recall that my fan club discussed it at the time as a minor episode, not good but not sensationally or offensively bad either, and that one member amusedly nicknamed it "The Love Slugs." Reviewers like Lynch no doubt played a role in disseminating its "worst episode" status.

23. The Reset Button is an issue with all *TNG*-era *Trek* series, even the more continuity-heavy *DS9*, but it seems the most egregious with *Voyager*, where the ship's isolation means that we should feel consequences more strongly.

24. Likewise, in "Worst Case Scenario" (3.25) a Maquis mutiny plotline can only be supplied in an internal fiction; "Equinox" (5.26–6.1) throws *Voyager*'s pristineness into relief through contrast with another stranded Starfleet ship.

25. Ronald D. Moore, writer and producer for *TNG* and *DS9*, worked briefly on *Voyager* under his former writing partner Braga and later gave a high critical interview about the show (Kaplan, "*Star Trek* profile," 2000). One can see Moore's later version of *Battlestar Galactica* (2004–9) as reworking elements of *Voyager* but emphasizing desperation and scarcity, while banning technobabble.

26. The ten most rewatched *Star Trek* episodes on Netflix include six *Voyager* episodes (Diaz 2017).

WORKS CITED

Altman, Mark A., and Edward Gross. *The Fifty-Year Mission: The Next 25 Years: From* The Next Generation *to J.J. Abrams*. St. Martin's Press, 2016.
_____. *Trek Navigator: The Ultimate Guide to the Entire Star Trek Saga*. Little, Brown and Company, 1998.
Andreadis, Athena. *To Seek Out New Life: The Biology of Star Trek*. Crown Publishers, 1998.
"Author, Author." *Star Trek: Voyager*, created by Jeri Taylor, Gene Roddenberry, Rick Berman, and Michael Piller, performance by Roxann Dawson, Season 7, episode 20, Paramount, 18 Apr. 2001.
Bormanis, André. *Science Logs*. Pocket Books, 1998.
"Bride of Chaotica!" *Star Trek: Voyager*, teleplay by Brian Fuller and Michael Taylor, directed by Allan Kroeker, Season 5, episode 12, Paramount, 27 Jan. 1999.
Chansanchai, Athima. "Now, Voyager." *Village Voice*, 9 Sept. 1997, p. 37.
"The Chase." *Star Trek: The Next Generation*, directed by Jonathan Frakes, perf. By Patrick Stewart, Season 6, episode 20, Paramount, 26 Apr. 1993.
"Counterpoint." *Star Trek: Voyager*, written by Michael Taylor, directed by Les Landau, Season 5, episode 10, Paramount, 16 Dec. 1998.
"Dark Frontier." *Star Trek: Voyager*, written by Joe Menosky and Brannon Braga, directed by Terry Windell and Cliff Bole, Season 5, episodes 15 and 16, Paramount, 17 Feb. 1999.
"Day of Honor." *Star Trek: Voyager*, written by Jeri Taylor, directed by Jesús Salvador Treviño Season 4, episode 3, Paramount, 17 Sept. 1997.
"Deadlock." *Star Trek: Voyager*, written by Brannon Braga, directed by David Livingston, Season 2, episode 21, Paramount, 18 Mar. 1996.
Diaz, Erik. "Netflix Reveals Which Star Trek Episodes Are Most Rewatched." *Nerdist*. September 12, 2017, https://nerdist.com/star-trek-netflix-most-rewatched/, Accessed February 24, 2018.
"Endgame, Part I and II." *Star Trek: Voyager*, teleplay by Kenneth Biller and Robert Doherty, directed by Allan Kroeker, Season 7, episodes 25 and 26, Paramount, 23 May 2001.
Epsicokhan, Jamahl. "Threshold." *Jammer's Reviews* http://www.jammersreviews.com/st-voy/s2/threshold.php, Accessed 23 February 2018.

"Equinox, Part I." *Star Trek: Voyager*, teleplay by Brannon Braga and Joe Menosky, Season 5,episode 26, Paramount, 26 May 1999.
"Equinox, Part II." *Star Trek: Voyager*, teleplay by Brannon Braga and Joe Menosky, Season 6,episode 1, Paramount, 22 September 1999.
Fazekas, Andrew. *Star Trek, the Official Guide to Our Universe: The True Science Behind the Starship Voyages*. National Geographic, 2016.
Fruhling, Zachary, Kay Shaw and Suzanne Williamson, hosts. "Green Shag Carpet." *To the Journey*, episode 240, Trek FM, 2016, http://trek.fm/to-the-journey/?offset=15180840 00146, Accessed 12 Mar. 2018.
Fuller, Greg. "Star Trek Ratings History." *Trek Nation*. July 7, 1999. https://www.trektoday. com/articles/ratings_history.shtml. Accessed 1 February 2018.
"Genesis." *Star Trek: The Next Generation*, directed by Gates McFadden, perf. By Patrick Stewart, Season 7, episode 19, Paramount, 21 Mar. 1994.
Gray, Jonathan. "New Audiences, New Textualities: Anti-Fan and Non-Fan." *International Journal of Cultural Studies* vol. 6, no.1, 2003, pp. 64–81.
Green, Michelle Erica. "Threshold." *Trek Today*. January 13, 2004. https://www.trektoday. com/reviews/voy/threshold.shtml, Accessed 23 February 2018.
Greenwald, Jeff. *Future Perfect: How* Star Trek *Conquered Planet Earth*. Viking, 1998.
Grey, Ian. "Now, 'Voyager': In Praise of the Trekkiest 'Trek' of All." *Rogerebert.com*, June 11, 2013, https://www.rogerebert.com/balder-and-dash/now-voyager-the-least-beloved-star-trek-offered-some-of-the-franchises-strongest-feminist-messages, Accessed 14 February 2018.
Gross, Edward, and Mark A. Altman. *Captain's Logs: The Unauthorized Complete Trek Voyages*. Little, Brown and Company, 1995.
Hark, Ina Rae. "Franchise Fatigue? the Marginalization of the Television Series After *The Next Generation*." *The Influence of* Star Trek *on Television, Film and Culture*. Ed. Lincoln Geraghty. McFarland Press, 2008. 41–59.
_____. *Star Trek*. Macmillan, 2008.
Hills, Matt. *Fan Cultures*. Routledge, 2002.
Hodge, Jarrah. "Episode 1: Voyager's Impact on Women's Roles—STLV." *Women at Warp*. http://www.womenatwarp.com/episode-s1-voyagers-impact-on-womens-roles-stlv/ Accessed 15 February 2018.
_____. "How Does Your Favorite *Star Trek* Series Fare on the Bechdel Test?" *The Mary Sure*, September 1, 2014, https://www.themarysue.com/star-trek-bechdel-test/, Accessed 22 May 2018.
_____. "The Lessons Captain Janeway Taught Me." *Women at Warp*. May 10, 2018. https://www.womenatwarp.com/the-lessons-captain-janeway-taught-me/ Accessed 21 May 2018.
Jenkins, Henry. *Textual Poachers: Television Fans and Participatory Culture*. Routledge, 1992.
Johnson, Derek. *Media Franchising: Creative License and Collaboration in the Culture Industries*. New York University Press, 2013.
Kaplan Anna L. "Commander Chakotay." *Cinefantastique* vol. 28, no. 4/5, 1996, pp. 99–100.
_____. "Star Trek Profile: Fan-Writer-Producer Ronald D. Moore." *Cinescape*, 18 January 2000, https://web.archive.org/web/20050920222529/http://cinescape.com/0/Editorial.asp?aff_id=0andthis_cat=Televisionandaction=pageandobj_id=18708, Accessed 24 February 24, 2018.
Kies, Bridget. "One True Threesome: Reconciling Canon and Fan Desire in *Star Trek: Voyager*." *Transformative Works and Cultures* vol. 8, 2011.
Krauss, Lawrence M. *The Physics of Star Trek*. HarperCollins, 1995.
Lee, Edmund. "*DS9* Rules." *Village Voice*, 9 Sept. 1997, p. 37.
Leeder, Murray. "Supernatural Trek?: *Star Trek* and the Re-Enchantment of the World." *The Star Trek Universe: Franchising the Final Frontier*. Ed. Douglas Brode. Rowman and Littlefield, 2015. pp. 1–14.
Lichtenberg, Jacqueline, Sondra Marshak and Joan Winston. *Star Trek Lives!* Bantam, 1975.
"Living Witness." *Star Trek: Voyager*, story by Brannon Braga, directed by Tim Russ, Season 4, episode 23, Paramount, 29 Apr. 1998.

Lynch, Timothy W. "Season 1 Wrapup." *Tim Lynch Star Trek Reviews Wiki.* http://timlynch reviews.wikia.com/wiki/VOY,_Season_1_Wrapup, Accessed 11 February 2018.
_____. "Season 2 Wrapup." *Tim Lynch Star Trek Reviews Wiki.* http://timlynchreviews.wikia.com/wiki/VOY,_Season_2_Wrapup, Accessed 11 February 2018.
_____. "Threshold." *Tim Lynch Star Trek Reviews Wiki* http://timlynchreviews.wikia.com/wiki/Threshold. Accessed 23 February 2018.
Macleod, Liam. "Why Do Star Trek Fans Hate Voyager?" *Den of Geek*, Oct. 19, 2012, http://www.denofgeek.com/tv/star-trek-voyager/23099/why-do-star-trek-fans-hate-voyager, Accessed 14 February 2018.
Marx, Lillian. "8 Needlessly Insane Moments from 'Star Trek.'" *Cracked*, January 26, 2013, http://www.cracked.com/quick-fixes/8-needlessly-insane-moments-from-star-trek/ Accessed 24 February 2018.
McIntee, David. *Delta Quadrant: The Unofficial Guide to Voyager.* Virgin, 2000.
"Muse." *Star Trek: Voyager*, written by Joe Menosky, directed by Mike Vejar, Season 6, episode 22, Paramount, 26 Apr. 2000.
NovaD. *The Secret Logs of Mistress Janeway.* https://www.squidge.org/novad/MJaneway/index.html. Accessed 15 February 2018.
Nowalk, Brandon. "*Star Trek: Voyager* Accidentally Presided Over the Franchise's Decline." *The A.V. Club.* May 28, 2013. https://tv.avclub.com/star-trek-voyager-accidentally-presided-over-the-franc-1798238334. Accessed 23 February 2018.
Palmer, Lorrie. "Female Leadership, Sacrifice and Technological Mastery on *Star Trek: Voyager.*" *To Boldly Go: Essays on Gender Identity in the* Star Trek *Universe.* Eds. Nadine Farghaly and Simon Bacon. McFarland Press, 2017. pp. 169–188.
"Pathfinder." *Star Trek: Voyager*, teleplay by David Zabel and Kenneth Biller, directed by Mike Vejar, Season 6, episode 10, Paramount, 1 Dec. 1999.
Pregler, Alison. "Star Trek: VOY: Threshold (1996) (Manic Episodes)." *Obscurus Lupa*, 27 February 2018. https://phelous.com/2018/02/27/obscurus-lupa/manic-episodes/star-trek-voy-threshold-1996-manic-episodes. Accessed 30 April 2018.
"Projections." *Star Trek: Voyager*, written by Brannon Braga, directed by Jonathan Frakes, Season 2, episode 3, Paramount, 11 Sept. 1995.
Redd, Nola Taylor. "Fake Science Paper About "Star Trek' and Warp 10 Was Accepted by 'Predatory Journals.'" *Space.com*, 13 February 2018, https://www.space.com/39672-fake-star-trek-science-paper-published.html. Accessed 24 February 2018.
Reeves-Stevens, Judith, and Garfield Reeves-Stevens. *Star Trek Phase II: The Lost Series.* Pocket Books, 1997.
"Resolutions." *Star Trek: Voyager*, written by Jeri Taylor, directed by Alexander Singer, Season 2, episode 25, Paramount, 13 May 1996.
Roget, Stephan. "6 Great TV Shows That Went Insane for One Episode." *Cracked*, 13 December 2016. http://www.cracked.com/article_24436_6-beloved-tv-shows-that-randomly-went-insane-one-episode.html. Accessed 24 February 2018.
Saler, Michael. *As If: Modern Enchantment and the Literary Prehistory of Virtual Reality.* Oxford University Press, 2012.
Schneider, Bernd. "Voyager Inconsistencies." *Ex Astris Scientia.* http://www.ex-astris-scientia.org/inconsistencies.htm. Accessed 18 February 2018.
"Shades of Grey." *Star Trek: The Next Generation*, directed by Robert Bowman, perf. by Jonathan Frakes, Season 2, episode 22, Paramount, 17 July 1989.
Sonnenberg, Chuck. "Endgame." *SFDebris.* http://sfdebris.com/videos/startrek/v971.php, Accessed 16 February 2018.
Spelling, Ian. "'Next Gen' Replacement Show Set for New Network." *Chicago Tribune*, 26 November 1993, pp. 7+.
"Spock's Brain." *Star Trek: The Original Series*, written by Lee Cronin, directed by Marc Daniels, Season 3, episode 6, Paramount, 20 Sept. 1968.
Sternbach, Rick, and Michael Okuda. *Star Trek: The Next Generation Technical Manual.* Pocket Books, 1991.
"Threshold." *Star Trek: Voyager*, written by Brannon Braga, directed by Alexander Singer, Season 2, episode 15, Paramount, 29 Jan. 1996.

"Tinker, Tenor, Doctor, Spy." *Star Trek: Voyager*, directed by John Bruno, perf. by Robert Picardo, Season 6, episode 4, Paramount, 13 Oct. 1999.

"TV Shows." *Fanfiction.net,* https://www.fanfiction.net/tv/, Accessed 14 February 2018.

The Viacom Crackdowns. In *Fanlore*. https://fanlore.org/wiki/The_Viacom_Crackdowns Accessed 26 February 2018.

"The Voyager Conspiracy." *Star Trek: Voyager*, written by Joe Menosky, directed by Terry Windell, Season 6, episode 9, Paramount, 24 Nov. 1999.

"Worst Case Scenario." *Star Trek: Voyager*, created by Rick Berman and Michael Piller, Dir. Alexander Singer, Season 3, episode 25, Paramount, 14 May 1997.

Wright, Jim "Threshold." *Delta Blues—Jim Wright's* Star Trek: Voyager *site.* https://www.reviewboy.com/threshold.html, Accessed 12 February 2018.

"Year of Hell, Part I." *Star Trek: Voyager*, written by Brannon Braga and Joe Menosky, directed by Allan Kroeker, Season 4, episode 8, Paramount, 5 Nov. 1997.

"Year of Hell, Part II." *Star Trek: Voyager*, written by Brannon Braga and Joe Menosky, directed by Mike Vejar, Season 4, episode 9, Paramount, 12 Nov. 1997.

About the Contributors

Jeffrey **Boruszak** received his Ph.D. from University of Texas at Austin, where he specialized in modern and contemporary American poetry. His broader research agenda engages with experimental writing traditions in American literature; the role of digital media in art's production, dissemination, and preservation; and poetry's intersections with political rhetoric and social advocacy (particularly in terms of race, gender, and sexuality). He previously served as the assistant director of the New Writers Project and an associate editor for *PennSound*.

Alex **Burston-Chorowicz** is a historian of the twentieth century, specializing in economic, political and social history. He is pursuing a Ph.D. at the University of Oxford and graduated from the University of Melbourne with a master's degree in history. He has lectured and taught at the University of Melbourne, RMIT and the Singapore Institute of Management. He has published on Australian and British labor history, Australia's relationship with Israel, and American foreign policy depicted in *Star Trek: The Next Generation*.

Sarah **Canfield** is an assistant professor and chair of the English Department at Shenandoah University in Winchester, Virginia. A lifelong reader of science fiction and fantasy, she has pursued that interest as both a fan and an academic. As a scholar, she researches, teaches, and writes about the history and philosophy of science and science fiction from the nineteenth century to the present day. Her focus includes issues of gender, race, and religion in the discourses of science fiction.

Sherry **Ginn** has published numerous research articles in the fields of neuroscience and psychology, but focuses her extracurricular work on how psychology and neuroscience are illustrated in popular culture. She is author or editor of books on women in science fiction television, sex in science fiction, time-travel in television, and the award-winning series *Farscape* and *Fringe*, as well as *Doctor Who* and *Marvel's Black Widow*. She is writing a monograph on female characters in science fiction television as well as coediting a collection on post-apocalyptic television.

Andrew **Howe** is a professor of history at La Sierra University, where he teaches courses in film and American history. He has been working on a study of the rhetoric of fear employed during the 1980s "killer bee" invasion of the American Southwest and a chapter on the manner in which societies translate environmental events by employing the familiar rhetorical strategies and vocabularies of existing, sociological problems. He has also written on cultural artifacts associated with HBO's *Game of Thrones* and the role of cemeteries and burial rites in the western genre.

Christian **Jimenez** holds a master's degree in political science from Rutgers. He has taught courses on modern China, globalization, and comparative politics at Rutgers and Rider University and presented professional conference papers on extremism, myth, literature, race, gender, and film. He has various forthcoming publications including encyclopedia entries on race in American television and essays on masculinity in *Sons of Anarchy*, James Cameron, Stanley Kubrick, and Cuban science fiction.

Peter W.Y. **Lee** is an independent historian specializing in Cold War American popular culture and youth culture. He earned his Ph.D. from Drew University in 2017 and is the editor of several books, including *Exploring Picard's Galaxy: Essays on Star Trek: The Next Generation* (McFarland, 2018) and *Peanuts and American Culture: Essays on Charles M. Schulz's Iconic Comic Strip* (McFarland, 2019).

Murray **Leeder** holds a Ph.D. from Carleton University and is an adjunct assistant professor at University of Calgary. He the author of *Horror Film* (Bloomsbury, 2018) and *The Modern Supernatural and the Beginnings of Cinema* (Palgrave Macmillan, 2017), as well as the editor of *Cinematic Ghosts* (Bloomsbury, 2015) and *ReFocus: The Films of William Castle* (Edinburgh University Press, 2018). His work has also appeared in *Horror Studies, The Journal of Popular Culture, The Journal of Popular Film and Television* and other periodicals.

Robert L. **Lively** is a professor of English at Truckee Meadows Community College in Reno, Nevada. His research interests are rhetoric and literacy in Medieval Scandinavia and science fiction and fantasy in popular culture. His publications include: "In Search of Viking Literacy" (*Rhetoric Review*, forthcoming) and "The Power Is Yours: The Deep Ecology of *Captain Planet*" (*Popular Culture Review* 2016). He is coeditor of *The Meadow* literary journal.

Rosy B. **Mack** is a Ph.D. candidate at the University of Texas at Austin. She holds a BA from SOAS, University of London, in Arabic and Persian and an MA from UT Austin in English literature. Her primary research project is on the British feminist publisher The Women's Press. She is particularly interested in feminist appropriations and experimentations in genre fiction which feminist publishing fostered in the late 20th century.

Ian Thomas **Malone** is an author and transgender activist. She earned her BA at Boston College in 2013, where she founded *The Rock* at Boston College, and an MA from Claremont Graduate University. Her work has been featured in the online editions of the *National Review, INSIDER, Bustle, The Wall Street Journal, Fox News* and the *Irish Examiner*. She is working on contributions to academic books on James Cameron, *Pokémon Go*, Netflix, and Tumblr.

Craig A. **Meyer**, Ph.D., is an assistant professor of English and Texas A&M University–Kingsville. His scholarship focuses on rhetoric and composition, creative writing, histories of rhetoric, as well as disability studies. Perhaps more importantly,

About the Contributors 267

he's been a fan of *Star Trek* since he was a child watching reruns of the original series with his father and brother on Saturday nights in the 1970s and '80s.

Camilo **Peralta** is an associate professor of English at Independence Community College and a Ph.D. student at Faulkner University's Great Books Honors College. She been teaching for about 15 years, and has done so all over the world, including various stints in Europe, Asia, and in the U.S. In addition to *Star Trek*, she is a scholar of other science fiction franchises like *The Terminator* and *Alien*.

Daniel **Preston** is a doctoral candidate at Syracuse University and is completing work in cultural foundations of education and disability studies. His research interests focus on the intersections between disability studies and popular culture. He also admits to teaching his son the *Voyager* theme song during infancy; it is still a personal favorite for both of them.

Michelle M. **Tabit** is an associate professor of history in the College of Humanities, Arts, and Social Sciences at the University of the Incarnate Word where she has been a full faculty member since 2012. She received her Ph.D. at Washington State University. Her research interests include U.S. history/public history and women's history, as well as popular culture as a tool for teaching history. She has presented at the annual Popular Culture Association Conference over the last four years.

Kwasu David **Tembo** has a Ph.D. from the University of Edinburgh's Language, Literatures, and Cultures Department. His research interests include—but are not limited to—comics studies, literary theory and criticism, philosophy, particularly the so-called "prophets of extremity"—Nietzsche, Heidegger, Foucault, and Derrida.

Eileen **Totter** is a Ph.D. student at the University of North Carolina Greensboro. Her research and interests involve British women writers in the eighteenth and nineteenth centuries, and gender in popular culture (especially the late twentieth and twenty-first centuries). She is invested in studying how women are presented in popular culture.

Index

Achilles 16, 30
Adare, Sierra 195, 203, 208–209
The Aeneid 53
Age of Extremes 234–235
Ahab 33, 35, 44–45
AI 10, 179, 181, 184–185, 187
Alaris, Dathan 199
The *Al-Batani* 55
Albright, Madeleine 69
Alexander, David 49, 61, 153, 161
Alexopoulou, Marigo 17, 31
"Alien Babes and Alternate Universes" 68
"All Good Things" 177*n*
"Alliances" 40, 46, 71, 73, 78–79
Alpha Quadrant 15, 20–23, 32, 34, 38, 43, 46, 70, 82, 143, 157, 191, 192*n*, 209*n*, 244, 248
Altman, Mark A. 84–85, 96, 250–251, 257, 261–262
Amazon Prime 3
American Beauty 87
American Research Journal of Biosciences 257
Anderson, Gillian 260*n*
Anderson, Perry 239, 246
Andreadis, Athena 256, 261
Andromeda 3
The Andy Griffith Show 259
Annorax 32–36
anti-fan 248, 251, 257, 259
AOC *see* Ocasio-Cortez, Alexandria
Aoki, Eric 194, 196, 209
Archer, Nathan 156, 161
Archer, Sally L. 152, 161
Archer, Valerie 37
Armitt, Lucie 215, 228
artificial intelligence *see* AI
Arturis 143
Asherman, Allan 67, 79
"Ashes to Ashes" 123, 127
Assassin's Creed 54
Asselin, C.K. 73, 75, 79
"The Assignment" 58, 61
Attebery, Brian 207, 209
Austin, Allan 194–195, 209

"Author, Author" 155, 161, 175–177, 186, 192, 258, 261
The Authoress of the Odyssey 17
Autonomy vs. Self-doubt 150
Axum 125–126

Babylon 5 3, 249
Bacon, Sir Francis 54
Bajoran 38, 49, 58, 155, 168, 201, 222, 228*n*
Baker, Djoymi 18–20, 31
Baker, Neal 157, 162
Barclay, Reginald 188, 192*n*, 209*n*, 258
"Barge of the Dead" 74, 79, 164, 170–177, 223, 228
Barr, Marleen 161*n*, 225, 228
Barret, Majel 68, 77, 154
Barrett, Duncan 217–218, 229
Barrett, Michele 217–218, 229, 233, 246*n*
Bashir, Dr. Julian 189
"Basics" 59, 61, 85, 96
Battlestar Galactica 261*n*
Bauman, Zymunt 233, 238–240, 245, 246*n*
Baynton, Douglas 135, 147
Baywatch 87
Bechdel Test 76, 79, 260*n*
"Before and After" 86, 93, 95*n*, 96
Bell, Art 5
Bell, Daniel 234, 246
Beltran, Robert 20, 59, 70, 197, 203, 250, 260*n*; *see also* Chakotay
Bennett, Susan 184
Berend, Ivan T. 235, 246
Berman, Marshall 239, 246
Berman, Rick 18, 46, 69, 84–87, 89, 248, 250
Bernal, Martha 153, 162
Bernardi, Daniel L. 4*n*, 79, 161*n*, 162
Berry, D. Channsin 155, 162
Betazoid 42, 154, 159, 161*n*; *see also* Troi, Deanna
The Bible 52–53, 62
Biggs-Dawson, Roxann *see* Dawson, Roxann
Biller, Ken 86–87, 98

269

270 Index

USS *Billings* 27
Blair, Karin 68, 79
Blair, Tony 236–238
The Body and Physical Difference 147n
Bogdan, Robert 147n, 147
Bonifazi, Anna 17, 31
Booker, M. Keith 3, 4n
Boothby 37–38
Borg 2, 22, 24–27, 29, 33–34, 51, 56, 70–71, 78, 84, 92, 95, 100, 107, 111, 113–127, 133–134, 140–142, 144, 147, 192n, 197–198, 202, 204–205, 207, 209n, 216, 223–225, 250
Borg Queen 26, 46, 117, 120–121, 124, 140, 225
Bormanis, André 250, 256, 261
Boruszak, Jeffrey 8, 98, 218, 265
Bowring, Michele A. 54, 56, 62, 72–73, 79, 229
Boyd, Katrina 215, 217
Boyd, Susan 229
Braga, Brannon 18, 31, 95, 257, 261n
Braxton, Captain 33–35, 46
Brenari 42
"Bride of Chaotica" 251, 261
Brown, Wendy 233, 240–241, 246
Brown vs. Board of Education 153
Buffy: The Vampire Slayer 3, 83
Bujold, Genevieve 73, 82
Burke, Maxwell 43–44
Burnham, Michael 213
Burston-Chorowicz, Alex 10, 231, 233, 241, 246, 265
Bush, Pres. H.W. 5
Byron, Lord 189

"The Cage" 68
Calypso 17, 20, 22, 28–29
Cameron, Colin 135, 147
Cameron, Fraser 234, 246
Canfield, Sarah 8, 112, 265
Cantor, Paul 195, 209
Cardassians 33, 38–39, 41, 43, 50, 136, 155–156, 168, 196, 200–202, 205, 222, 231, 241–244, 248
"The Caretaker" 16, 22, 41, 43, 46, 50, 52, 55, 58, 62, 69, 72, 79, 84, 90, 95n, 96, 107, 111–112, 147, 156, 162, 227, 238, 246
Carey, Lt. 137–138, 220, 242–243
Carney, Amy 41, 47
Carter, Pres. Jimmy 235, 237
Casavant, Michele M. 112, 117, 119–120, 128
The Categorical Imperative 101, 108, 110
"Cathexis" 59, 62
Chakotay 2, 10, 20–22, 26–27, 29–30, 35–41, 44–45, 50, 55, 57–60, 69, 71–72, 74–75, 91, 116, 122–123, 126–127, 136–139, 156, 161n, 194–195, 197–203, 205, 207–208, 219–221, 233, 240, 242–245, 250, 254, 260n; see also Beltran, Robert
Challans, Tim 216, 229

Chansanchai, Athima 253
Chaos on the Bridge 111n, 111
"The Chase" 257, 261
Chell, Crewman 138
Chez Sandrine 104
"Child's Play" 122–123, 128
Circe 20, 22–23, 28–29
Claiming Disability 146n
Clark, Mamie Phipps 152–153, 155, 162
Clingingsmith, David 51, 62
Clinton, Pres. Bill 10, 69, 71, 233, 237
Clinton, Hillary Rodham 69, 78–79, 82
"The Cloud" 56–58, 61–62, 76, 79, 88, 96
Coast to Coast AM 5
"Coda" 52, 55, 62
Cofield, Calla 79
"Cold Fire" 91–92, 95n, 96
Cold War 1, 5, 37, 70
"Collective" 122, 129
"Concerning Flight" 54, 62, 116, 124, 128
Consalvo, Mia 11n, 113–114, 116–117, 127–128
"Counterpoint" 41–42, 47, 251, 261
"The Court Martial of Captain Kathryn Janeway" 46
Covin 118
Cranny-Francis, Anne 79, 114–115, 117, 128
Cristoforetti, Samantha 6, 76
"Critical Care" 2
Cronenberg, David 255
Crusade 3
Crusher, Dr. Beverly 75, 160n, 164, 166, 177n, 195–196, 216; see also McFadden, Gates
Crusher, Jack 165
Crusher, Wesley 83, 166, 170, 196
Culluh, Maje 39–40, 46
Cyborg Manifesto 9, 113–117, 119, 127

Dalby, Crewman 139, 243
Dariotis, Wei Ming 40, 47, 153, 162
"Dark Frontier" 17, 22, 31, 120–121, 128, 140, 147, 225, 229, 251, 261
Dark Girls 155
"Darkling" 92, 95n, 96, 188–190, 192
Darrow, Henry 202
Data 32, 83, 100–102, 114, 149, 190, 192n, 196, 209n, 216; see also Spiner, Brent
Davenport, Caillan 46–47
Da Vinci Code 54
Dawkins, Richard 61
Dawson, Roxann 70, 160, 161n, 168–169, 197, 255; see also Torres, B'Elanna
Dax, Ezri 111n
Dax, Jadzia 111n, 111
"Day of Honor" 75, 80, 115, 128, 147n, 154, 156, 158, 162, 223, 229, 257, 261
"Deadlock" 85, 96, 251, 261
"Death Wish" 72, 80, 217, 229
de Lancie, John 49; see also Q
Delta Quadrant 6, 8, 16, 23, 27, 32–33, 43, 51–52, 56, 59, 61, 68–72, 74, 83–84, 89–90,

Index 271

92, 98, 107, 112, 121, 155–156, 158–159, 179, 181, 183, 191, 192n, 209n, 214, 216–217, 227, 248
Delta Quadrant: The Unofficial Guide to Voyager 248
deontology 105
Derrida, Jacques 106, 108, 111
Descartes 113, 115
deus ex machina 24, 30
The Devore 33, 41–43
Diaz, Erik 261n, 261
Dilmore, Ken 83, 94, 96
disability 133–136, 140, 143, 145–147, 147n
A Disability History of the United States 146n
disability studies 133–136, 146n
"The Disease" 74, 80
"Distant Origin" 59–60, 62
Divina Commedia 53
Divorce: An American Tradition 167
The Doctor 2, 9–10, 20–21, 52, 56–57, 59, 71, 85–87, 92–93, 95n, 103–104, 107–108, 115–116, 118–119, 122, 124–125, 142, 158, 179–192, 192n, 195, 199–201, 206–207, 209n, 219, 222, 224, 255; see also EMH; Picardo, Robert
"Doctor Bashir, I Presume" 167, 177, 184, 189, 192
Doherty, Thomas 90, 96
The Dominion 38, 232, 244
Douglas, Susan J. 80
Dove-Viebahn, Aviva 50, 62, 171, 178
"Drive" 158, 162
"Drone" 122, 124, 128
DS9 see *Star Trek: Deep Space Nine*
Duchovny, David 260n
Dukat, Gul 46, 58
Duke, Bill 155
Dupree, M.G. 68
Durst, Peter 157
Dyson, Stephen Benedict 241, 246

Earth: Final Conflict 3
"Echoes of the Void" 29
Edwards, Gavin 50, 62
Elderkin, Beth 58, 62
"Elogium" 86, 90, 96, 219, 229
"Emanations" 56–57, 62
"Embodying Hybridity (En)gendering Community: Captain Janeway and the Enactment of a Feminist Heterotopia on *Star Trek: Voyager*" 171
emergency medical hologram see EMH
EMH 20, 52, 168, 172, 179, 182–184, 186, 190, 192n, 209n, 224–225; see also The Doctor; Picardo, Robert
"The Emissary" 49, 159, 162, 178
Enaran 199–20
"Encounter at Farpoint" 165, 178
"Endgame" 17, 24, 30–31, 62, 116, 127–128, 177n, 186, 192, 255, 261

"The Enemy Within" 99, 157, 162
The Enlightenment 53, 61, 110
USS *Enterprise* 154, 256
Enterprise Zones 215
"An Epic for Women" 228n
The Epic of Gilgamesh 52
Epsicokhan, Jamahl 260n, 261
"Equinox" 33–34, 43–45, 47, 80, 108, 111, 156, 162, 261n, 261–262
Erikson, Erik 9, 149–152, 155–156, 158–159, 160n, 161n, 162
ethics 99, 104, 106–107, 108, 213–215, 219, 221–222, 225–227
ethics of care 99, 110, 216, 218–219, 222, 225–228
Every Old Trick Is New Again 18
"Extreme Risk" 161n, 162, 244, 246
"Eye of the Needle" 57, 62, 161n, 162, 180, 192

"Faces" 155, 157–158, 161n, 162, 167–168, 178, 221, 229
"Facets" 166
Faerie Queene 53
Faludi, Susan 83
"Favorite Son" 16, 18–19, 31
Fazekas, Andrew 256, 262
Federation 4, 6, 9, 40, 50, 59, 77–78, 82, 88–92, 95, 98–99, 101–102, 105, 108, 113–114, 118, 122–123, 135–138, 140, 142, 144–145, 155–156, 174, 179, 184, 186, 192n, 207, 209n, 214–216, 218–219, 222–223, 226, 231–233, 241–245, 260n
Federation Charter 137, 147
Federation Ideology 9, 133–136, 139–140, 142, 144–147, 219, 222, 243
Female Action Heroes: A Guide to Women in Comics, Video Games, Film and Television 73, 75
feminism 5, 8–9, 18, 67–68, 76–79, 83, 95, 99, 108, 112–114, 127, 207, 215, 218
feminist ethics 8, 98, 109–110, 216
Ferengi 166, 248
Ferraro, Geraldine 82
"The First Day" 166, 178
"The First Duty" 37, 47, 170
Fisher, Deborah 94, 96
"Flashback" 91, 96
The Fly 255
Foreman, Robert J. 53, 62
Franklin, H. Bruce 241, 246
Freak Show 147n
Freeman, Morgan 187, 193
Friedman, Milton 236
Fruhling, Zachary 262
Fukuyama, Francis 238, 246
Fuller, Greg 253, 262
"Fury" 93, 95n, 96
"Future's End" 34–35, 47, 92, 96, 192n, 209n

Galileo Galilei 59
Gandhi, Mahatma 189
Garak 33
Garrett, Capt. Rachel 77
Gates, Bill 35
Gegen 59–61
Generativity vs. Stagnation 151, 159
"Genesis" 257, 262
Geocities 6
Georgiou, Capt. Philippa 213
Geraghty, Lincoln 1, 4n, 80, 144–145, 148, 194, 197–198, 204, 209, 265
Gerrold, David 80
"The Gift" 17, 22–23, 25, 31, 91, 93, 96, 114–115, 128, 133, 141, 224, 226, 229
Gilligan, Carol 110, 152, 159, 162, 218
Gilligan's Island 68
Gilmore, Marla 44–45, 62
Ginn, Sherry 9, 149, 160n, 163, 265
The Godfather 40
Goffman, Erving 134, 140, 148
Gomez, Sonya 197
Gonzalez, George A. 233, 246
Gorman, Michael John 59, 62
Graf, L.A. 162
Gramsci, Antonio 233, 239–240, 246
Gray, Jonathan 251, 262
Green, Michelle Erica 260n, 262
Green Mandy 62
"Green Shag Carpet: What *Voyager* Means to Us" 255
Greenwald, Jeff 248, 262
Gregson, Joanna 86, 96
Gre'thor 172–173
Greven, David 17–18, 31, 216, 223, 228n, 229
Grey, Ian 259, 262
Griffin, Gabriele 83
Gross, Edward 84–85, 96, 250–251, 257, 261–262
Gunkel, David J. 47
Gymnich, Marion 197–198, 200, 209

Hale, Jon F. 237, 246
Haley 209n
Hall, Ronald E. 153, 163
Hall, Stuart 195, 198, 209
Hames, Sara Eileen 71–72, 80
Hansen, Annika 25, 92, 117, 120–121, 125; *see also* Seven of Nine
Haraway, Donna 9, 113–115, 117, 119, 121, 127–128
Hark, Ina Rae 248, 252, 262
Harvey, David 235, 246
Hauser, Michael 240, 246
Hay, Colin 237, 246
Hayek, Fredrich 236, 246
Heller, Lee 80
Henderson, Mary 80
Henley, Crewman 138
Hill, Anita 5–6

Hills, Matt 259, 262
Hippocratic Oath 107–108
Hirogen 34, 37, 41–42, 107, 124, 142, 146, 204–205, 207
Hoagland, Ericka 215, 229
Hobbes, Thomas 183–184, 193
Hobsbawm, Eric 234–235, 246
Hodge, Jarrah 77, 80, 260n, 262
Hogan, Dr. Bernie 187
Holland, N. 153, 163
Hollins, Etta R. 153, 163
The Holocaust 200, 202
Homer 7, 15, 17, 19–21, 24, 31–32
Homsher, Deborah 89, 96
"Hope and Fear" 143–144, 148, 226, 229
"The Host" 111n, 111
Howe, Andrew 7, 32, 265–266
Hugh 33, 117
"Human Error" 126, 128
Huntington, Samuel 70
Hurd, Denise Alessandria 167–169, 174–175, 178

ICF *see* International Classification of Functioning, Disability and Health
Icheb 123, 192n, 209n
identity 150–151, 153, 155–159, 161n
Identity vs. Role-confusion 151, 155, 159, 161n
Iko 206
The Iliad 15, 17, 52–53
"Imperfection" 123, 128, 225, 228n, 229
In a Different Voice 218
In Search for Politics 240
"In the Flesh" 37, 47
Industry vs. Inferiority 151
Infinite Diversity in Infinite Combinations 1, 145
"Infinite Regress" 119, 128
"Initiations" 40, 47
Initiative vs. Guilt 151
Integrity vs. Despair 152
International Classification of Functioning, Disability and Health (ICF) 134
intersectionality 164–165, 167–169, 172
Intimacy vs. Isolation 151, 156, 159, 161n
"It's Only a Paper Moon" 167, 178

Jabin, Maje 41
Jameson, Frederic 80
Janeway, Capt. Kathryn 2, 8, 10, 15, 19–20, 23–30, 32, 37, 41–46, 50–59, 61, 67–80, 82–86, 89, 92–95, 98–100, 102, 104, 107–110, 112–123, 125–127, 133, 135–146, 161n, 171–177, 180–183, 186, 191, 197, 199–200, 202, 204–205, 213–214, 216–228, 228n, 231–233, 238, 240, 242–245, 249, 254–258, 260n, 261n; *see also* Mulgrew, Kate
Jareth 199
Jeffrey, David Lyle 52, 62
Jenkins, Henry 254, 262

Index 273

Jessen 200
Jetal, Ensign 191
"Jetrel" 86, 88, 96
Jewett, Robert 195
Jimenez, Christian 10, 194–195, 209, 266
Johnson, Derek 260n, 262
Joleg 206
Jones, Charles Evans, Jr. 47
Jourdain, M. 54, 62
"Journey's End" 196, 209
Joyrich, Lynne 117, 128
"Juggernaut" 155, 163
Jung, Carl 59

Kadi 186
Kahless 158
Kant, Immanuel 101, 105, 108, 111
Kanzler, Katja 194, 209, 215, 221, 224–225, 228n, 229
Kapell, Matthew Wilhelm 247
Kaplan, Anna L. 91–92, 96n, 96, 261n, 262
Kar (Kazon youth) 42
Karr (Hirogen hunter) 204–205
Kashyk 33, 41–42
Kazon 33, 39–41, 69, 73, 84, 86, 89, 107, 243, 250
Kazon-Nistrim *see* Kazon
K'Ehleyr 166, 168
Kes 8, 23–25, 37, 55–56, 70–71, 82–95, 96n, 102–104, 108–110, 112, 121, 141, 180–181, 186, 189, 191, 192n, 209n, 214, 217–219, 227, 228n; *see also* Lien, Jennifer
Kessik IV 155, 158
Keynes, John Maynard 234
Keynesian 233–236
Khan Noonien Singh 45
Kies, Bridget 260n, 262
"The Killing Game" 115, 124–125, 128, 203–205, 209–210
Kim, Albert 74, 78, 80
Kim, Ensign Harry 18–22, 28–30, 37, 39, 51, 56–57, 71, 74, 112, 116–117, 124, 126, 136, 156, 161n, 191, 200, 217, 255, 260n; *see also* Wang, Garrett
King, Martin Luther, Jr. 154
King, Rodney 1, 6
Kirk, Capt. James T. 55, 72–73, 78, 99, 157, 165, 169, 195, 197, 216–218, 225, 253, 261n; *see also* Shatner, William
Kleos 16
Klingon(s) 33, 50, 74, 84, 95, 105, 154–160, 161n, 164, 167–174, 205, 215, 221, 223, 248
Klink, Lisa 91
Knight, George P. 153, 162
Knight, Gladys 73, 75, 80
Koehn, Daryl 218, 229
Kolopak 202
Korenna 199
Kortar 172
Kouros 120

Krauss, Lawrence M. 256, 262
Krenim 33, 36
Kutzera, Dale 86, 96, 111
Kyrians 206–207

La Forge, Geordi 196–197
Lagon, Mark P. 241, 246
Lancioni, Judith 203, 205, 209
"Latent Image" 180, 191, 193
Lauzen, Martha M. 112, 128
Lawrence, John Shelton 195, 209
"Learning Curve" 138–139, 148, 228n, 229, 243, 246
Lee, Peter W.Y. 8, 82, 266
Leeder, Murray 10, 248, 262, 266
Lefanu, Sarah 215, 229
Lehmann, Llana 134, 148
Leonardo da Vinci 54, 57, 225
Lessing, Noah 43–45
Lester, Dr. Janice 77
"Let That Be Your Last Battlefield" 195, 209
Levering, Matthew 53, 62
Lexx 3
Lichtenberg, Jacqueline 260n, 262
Lien, Jennifer 23, 83, 85, 87, 91–92, 94; *see also* Kes
"Life Line" 190, 192n, 193, 209n
"Lifesigns" 39, 47, 185, 193
Light, Claire 72–73, 80, 168–170, 173, 178
"Lineage" 2, 121, 128, 157, 161n, 163, 169–171, 174, 176, 178, 223, 229
Linton, Simi 146n, 148
Liquid Modernity 239
Lively, Robert L. 5, 266
Living with Star Trek: American Culture and the Star Trek Universe 144–145
"Living Witness" 199, 206, 209, 258, 262
Locutus 117
Lolita 87
Lore 190, 192n, 209n
Louvois, Capt. Phillipa 100–101
Lu, Xing 153, 163
Lundeen, Jan 228n, 230
Lynch, Timothy W. 252–253, 255, 257, 259, 261n, 262–263

Mabus 40
Mack, Rosy B. 10, 213, 266
Macleod, Liam 46–47, 259, 263
MacNutt, Karen 89
Madhav, K.C. 188, 193
Madrid, Mike 87, 96
Mafe, Diana Adesola 154, 163
"Maiden, Mother, Crone: Why *Voyager* Was Awesome" 168
Malone, Ian Thomas 9, 179, 266
"Maneuvers" 39, 47, 73, 80, 219, 229
Maquis 38, 69, 71, 84, 133–140, 145–147, 155–156, 189, 192n, 209n, 220–222, 228n, 231–233, 240–246, 247, 250, 260n, 261n

274 Index

Marcia, James 149, 152, 159, 163
Marcus, Carol 165–166
Marcus, David 165–166, 169
Margie, Nancy 163
Marshak, Sondra 260*n*
Martok 33
Marx, Karl 239
Marx, Lillian 257, 263
The Mary Sue 76
May, Prime Minister Theresa 188
McCarthyism 154
McCoy, Dr. Leonard "Bones" 177*n*, 216
McFadden, Gates 166, 177–178; *see also* Crusher, Dr. Beverly
McGrath, James F. 49, 62
McIntee, David 98, 250, 257, 263
McNeil, Robert Duncan 255; *see also* Paris, Lt. Tom
"Measure of a Man" 100–102, 111
Meehan, Eileen R. 113, 129
Melville, Herman 34, 46
Memory Alpha 159, 161*n*, 232, 246
Menosky, Joe 95*n*
Meyer, Craig A. 9, 133, 266–267
Milton, John 62
Miramanee 165
Mr. Spock 114, 149, 153–155, 164–165, 167, 177*n*, 216, 253, 261*n*; *see also* Nimoy, Leonard
Mr. Tash 22
Mitchell, David 139, 146*n*, 148
Moby Dick 34, 45
"The Monster Inside: 19th Century Racial Constructs in 24th Century Mythos of Star Trek" 167
Moody, Steve 171, 178
Moore, Ronald D. 261*n*
morality 102–106
Morgan, Debi 83, 97
"Mortal Coil" 84, 97, 141–142
Moset, Crell 200–202
Mot'lach 158
Ms. Turtlehead 155
Mulder, Fox 260*n*
Mulford, Carla 70–71, 80
Mulgrew, Kate 7, 69, 73–78, 80, 82–83, 86, 89, 172, 217, 222, 228*n*, 249; *see also* Janeway, Capt. Kathryn
Mullholland, Marc 235–236, 247
"Muse" 251, 258, 263

NAACP 153
Nama, Adilifu 159, 163
Native American(s) 194–199, 201–203, 205, 208, 240
Nazi 40–42, 95, 194, 196, 199–205, 207
Neelix 50, 70–71, 82, 85–92, 94, 98–100, 103, 107–108, 110, 135, 141–142, 158, 188, 192*n*, 206, 209*n*, 219, 228*n*, 258; *see also* Phillips, Ethan

neoliberal depoliticization 231, 233, 237, 239–240, 243–245
Nerds of Color 168
Nerys, Major Kira 58, 75
Netflix 3, 6
New World Order 38
Nguyen, Will 47
Nichols, Nichelle 154, 163; *see also* Uhura, Lt.
Nielsen, Kim E. 146*n*, 148
Nietzche, Friedrich 180–181, 193
"Night" 17, 26, 31, 217, 229
Nikkei Hoshi Shinchi Literary Award 187
Nimoy, Leonard 67, 80, 154, 253; *see also* Mr. Spock
Nixon, Richard 235
Noddings, Nel 110
Nog 83, 166–167
"Non Sequitur" 85, 97
normative expectations 134
Nostos 15–17, 21–22, 24, 28–29
"Nothing Human" 200–203, 209, 221, 229
Nowalk, Brandon 63, 80, 258, 263

O'Brien, Keiko 58
O'Brien, Miles 160*n*
O'Brien, Molly 83
Obrist 36
Obscurus Lupa 258
Ocampa (Ocampan) 24, 52, 70, 84, 89–91, 93–95, 219, 227, 238
Ocasio-Cortez, Alexandria 7
O'Connel, Agnes 152, 163
O'Connor, Sandia Day 82
Odo 149
Odysseus 7, 15–25, 29–30
The Odyssey 7, 15–21, 25–26, 32, 52–53
Oedipus Rex 147*n*
Okuda, Michael 260*n*, 263
Olewitz, Chloe 187, 193
"The Omega Directive" 118–119, 128, 143, 148
"One" 115, 119, 124
Orenstein, Peggy 90, 97
The Oroville 4
Ott, Brian 194, 196, 209
The Outer Limits 3

Palmer, Lorrie 255, 263
"Paradise Syndrome" 165, 178
"Parallax" 55, 63, 74–75, 80, 90, 97, 137–138, 148, 172, 178, 224, 229, 242, 247
Paris, Miral (child of Tom Paris and B'Elanna Torres) 158–159, 170, 175, 177*n*
Paris, Lt. Tom 2, 30, 36, 55–56, 71, 85, 90–91, 93, 116, 121, 125, 142, 154–159, 161*n*, 164, 172–173, 175–176, 185–186, 192*n*, 204–205, 209*n*, 220, 222, 243–244, 255–257, 261*n*; *see also* McNeill, Robert Duncan
"Parturition" 88, 90, 97
"Pathfinder" 23, 258, 263
Patterson, Serena J. 152, 163

Pearson, Roberta 209
Pel, Danara 42
Penelope 17
people with disabilities see PWDs
Peralta, Camilo 7, 49, 267
"Persistence of Vision" 217, 229
"Phage" 135, 148, 157
Phillips, Ethan 88, 258; see also Neelix
Phlox, Dr. 50
Piaget, Jean 161n, 163
Picard, Capt. Jean-Luc 55, 72–73, 100–102, 166, 170, 177n, 196–197, 217, 225, 244, 261n
Picardo, Robert 20, 96n, 184, 255; see also The Doctor; EMH
Pilkington, Ace G. 233, 241, 247
Piller, Michael 46, 69, 95n, 98
"Plato's Stepchildren" 195, 209, 247
Pogo Paradox 34
Polyphemus 22, 26
Prax 42
Pregler, Allison 258, 263
preoperational thought stage 161n
Preston, Daniel 9, 133, 267
"Prey" 37, 47, 116, 118, 124, 128, 142, 148
The Prime Directive 71, 78, 89, 105–106, 134, 142, 147n, 199, 215
"Prime Factors" 221, 229
Prinadora 166–167
"The Principal and the Pauper" 260n
Projansky, Sarah 215, 229
"Projections" 192n, 193, 209n, 251, 263
"Prophecy" 205–206, 209
The Prophets 49
Pucekovič, Branko 54, 63
Putman, John 233, 247
PWDs (people with disabilities) 136, 140, 144–145, 147n

Q 49, 52, 56, 58, 72–73, 124, 215; see also de Lancie, John
"The Q and the Grey" 56, 63, 85, 94, 97
The Q Continuum 72, 250
"Q Who" 197, 209
Qomar 183
"Q2" 94, 97, 124, 128
Quantum Leap 3
Quark 166
Quinn 72–73

"Random Thoughts" 141, 148
Ransom, Capt. Rudolph 34, 43–46
"Raven" 117, 128
Ravitz, Jessica 193
Razik, Maje 41
Reagan, Pres. Ronald 235–237
Reagan, Nancy 68, 80
"Real Life" 55, 63, 185, 193
Redd, Nola Taylor 257, 263
Reeves-Stevens, Garfield 260n, 263
Reeves-Stevens, Judith 260n, 263

Regressives 199
"Relativity" 34–35, 41, 47
Relke, Diana 228n, 230
"Remember" 199–200, 202–203, 209
"Repentance" 2, 126, 129, 206, 209
"Repression" 245, 247
"Resistance" 85, 97
"Resolutions" 56, 63, 72, 81, 254, 260n, 263
"Retrospect" 118, 129
"Reunion" 166, 178
Reviving Ophelia 88
"Revulsion" 116, 129
A Rhetoric of Remnants 146n
Rhys-Davies, John 54
Richard, Aline 188, 193
Ride, Sally 79
Riker, Lt. Thomas 99
Riker, Cmdr. William T. 73, 99, 160
Riley, Charles A. 138, 148
Riley, Glenda 167, 174, 178
Ripley 74
The Road to Serfdom 236
Roberts, Robin A. 113, 119, 129, 161n, 163, 168, 171, 174, 178
Robinson, Fiona 110–111
Roddenberry, Gene 1, 2, 8–9, 46, 49, 61, 67, 71, 79, 86–87, 94, 111n, 145, 149, 153–154, 164, 195, 233, 246n, 259n, 260n
"The Roddenberry Rule" 101, 111n
Rogers, A. 152, 163
Roget, Stephan 257, 263
Roller, Pamela 83, 97
Rom 166–167
Romulans 50, 248
Roosevelt, Franklin Delano (FDR) 235–236
Rossan, Sheila 152, 163
Roswell 3
Rotolo, Anthony 33, 47
Rowan, George T. 153, 163
Rowlandson, Mary 70, 81
Rozhenko, Alexander 83, 166
Rubber Tree People 202–203
Ruditis, Paul 40–41, 47, 88, 93, 97, 155–156, 163
Russ, Tim 70, 197; see also Tuvok
Russo, Nancy P. 152, 163
Ryan, Jeri 255; see also Seven of Nine
Ryan, Marianne E. 94

"Sacred Ground" 55, 58, 63, 85, 97
Saler, Michael 258, 263
Sarantakes, Nicholas Evans 241, 247
Sarek 165
Sarwal, Reema 215, 229
Sayers, John 155, 163
Schneider, Bernd 260n, 263
Schoolgirls 88
Schultz, Dwight 258
"Science, Race and Gender in Star Trek: Voyager" 168

276   Index

"The Scientific Method" 33, 47
Sci-Fi Channel 3
"Scorpion" 37, 47, 51, 54, 57, 63, 92, 97, 114, 129, 133, 140, 142, 148
Scully, Dana 260n
"Second Chances" 99, 111
"The Secret Logs of Mistress Janeway" 254
Segal, Charles 28–29, 31
Serling, Rod 154
Seska 33–34, 38–39, 43, 46, 219, 243
Seven of Nine 2, 8–10, 20, 25–26, 32–34, 41, 43–45, 70–71, 75, 92–93, 96n, 112–124, 126–127, 133–136, 138, 140–147, 149, 161n, 180–181, 186, 189, 191, 192n, 195, 202, 204–206, 209n, 213–214, 216–217, 219, 223–228, 228n, 255; see also Ryan, Jeri
"Shades of Gray" 256, 263
Shakespeare, Tom 145–146, 148
Shatner, William 77, 111n, 253; see also Kirk, Capt. James T.
"Shattered" 39, 47
Shaw, Kay 262
Sheets, Rosa 153, 163
Sherchan, S. 188, 193
Sherchand, S.P. 188, 193
Shi, Xiaowei 153, 163
Siebers, Tobin 145, 148
The Simpsons 260n
Sisko, Capt. Benjamin 46, 49, 55, 165–167, 244
Sisko, Jake 83, 167
Sisko, Jennifer 165–166
Sirens 18–19, 21–22
Sirtis, Marina 166; see also Troi, Deanna
sky spirits 202–203
Sliders 3
Snauffer, Douglas 87, 95, 97
Snyder, Sharon 139, 146n, 148
Snyder, William J. 81
Sobstyl, Edrie 150, 163
Sochting, Ingrid 152
Socialism: The Active Utopia 240
Socrates 189
"Someone to Watch Over Me" 125, 129, 185–186, 193
Somogyi, V. 58, 63
Sonnenburg, Chuck 254–255, 263
Soong, Noonian 190, 192n, 209n
Space: Above and Beyond 3
"Space and the Single Girl: Star Trek, Aesthetics, and 1960s Femininity" 68
Species 8472 33, 36–38, 91, 107, 118, 140, 142, 146
Spelling, Ian 84, 86, 89, 97, 169, 178, 260n, 263
Spiner, Brent 77, 192n, 209n; see also Data
"Spirit Folk" 52, 63
Spock 114, 149, 153–155, 164–165, 167, 177n, 216, 253, 261n; see also Nimoy, Leonard

"Spock's Brain" 256, 263
Srivani 33
Star Trek and Sex 68
Star Trek: Deep Space Nine 2–3, 10, 33, 38, 46, 49, 58, 75–76, 111n, 149, 165–167, 184, 232–233, 241–242, 244, 249–254, 259n, 260n, 261n
Star Trek: Discovery 3–4, 111n, 161n, 213, 260n
Star Trek: Enterprise 3, 50, 76, 197, 249, 253, 260n
Star Trek: First Contact 249
Star Trek IV: The Voyage Home 46
Star Trek History 68
The Star Trek Interview Book 67
Star Trek Memories 67
Star Trek: Nemesis 249
Star Trek: Orion Rendezvous 256
Star Trek VI: The Undiscovered Country 165, 249
Star Trek: The Animated Series 260n
Star Trek: The Motion Picture 260n
Star Trek: The Next Generation 2, 10, 15, 52, 69, 75–77, 98–99, 111n, 117, 126, 149, 154, 159, 160n, 161n, 165–167, 177, 188, 190, 192n, 195–197, 209n, 216–217, 231–233, 244, 249–254, 256, 258, 260n, 261n
Star Trek: The Next Generation Technical Manual 260n
Star Trek: The Original Series 15, 49, 67–68, 90, 98–99, 113, 149, 157, 165, 167, 195, 197, 207, 216, 231, 233, 252, 256
Star Trek III: The Search for Spock 165, 178
Star Trek II: The Wrath of Khan 105, 111, 165, 178
Star Trek: Voyager Bible 155–156
Starfleet Academy 155–156, 220–221, 256
Stargate: Atlantis 3
Stargate SG-1 3, 249
Starling, Henry 35, 192n, 209n
"State of Flux" 39, 47
Sternbach, Rick 260n, 263
stigma 134, 145, 147
Striptease 87
Stuckey, Zosha 146n, 148
Stuller, Jennifer 154, 163
Sulan, Chief Surgeon 157
Sulu, Hikaru 197
"Survival Instinct" 111n, 111, 120, 129
Suspiria 95n
Suvin, Darko 215, 230
"The Swarm" 85, 97, 182, 192n, 193, 209n
symbiogenesis 99–100

Tabit, Michelle M. 8, 67, 267
Tabor, Crewman 201
Talaxians 70, 89–90, 100, 142
Taresians 18–19
"Tattoo" 202–203, 209
Taylor, Jeri 18, 46, 69, 84, 86, 248

teleology 105
Tembo, Kwasu David 7, 15, 267
The Temporal Cold War 260*n*
The Terminator 192
Thatcher, Prime Minister Margaret 235–236, 238
"The Thaw" 56, 63
"Think Tank" 120, 129, 225, 230
third-wave feminism 5
"The 37's" 51, 85, 97, 192*n*, 193, 209*n*
"This Side of Paradise" 165, 178
Thorpe, Andrew 235, 247
"Threshold" 255–258, 260*n*, 261*n*, 263
Tieran 91–92
"Time and Again" 90–91, 97
"Timeless" 17, 20, 22, 31, 124, 129
"Tinker, Tenor, Doctor, Spy" 124, 129, 251, 263
Tizard, Julie 76, 81
TNG *see* Star Trek: The Next Generation
To Have and to Hold: Marriage, the Baby Boom, and Social Change 165
To the Journey 254–255, 257
Torres, B'Elanna 2, 9–10, 35, 39, 43, 52, 56, 59, 71, 74–76, 85–86, 93, 112, 115, 120–122, 125, 136–139, 145, 149–150, 154–160, 160*n*, 161*n*, 162, 164, 167–177, 185, 195, 197, 199–202, 205, 213–214, 216–217, 219–223, 227–228, 232–233, 240, 242–245, 255; *see also* Dawson, Roxann
Torres, John 154–155, 159, 161*n*, 167, 169–171, 175–177
Torres, Miral (mother of B'Elanna Torres) 154, 158–159, 167, 169–177
Totter, Eileen 9, 164, 267
Trabe 40
The Traveler 196
Trekkies 252, 254
Trill 100, 111*n*
Troi, Deanna 75, 114, 149, 154, 159, 160*n*, 161*n*, 196, 198, 216, 218, 261*n*; *see also* Sirtis, Marina
Trojan War 16–17, 53
Trust vs. Mistrust 150, 155, 158
Tudor, Deborah 113, 129
Turaj 205
"The Turnabout Intruder" 81
"Tuvix" 8, 98, 99–100, 102–105, 107–109, 111, 218
Tuvok 2, 23, 26, 30, 37, 39, 86, 91–94, 98–100, 107–110, 115, 122, 135, 138–140, 147, 161*n*, 188, 197, 203–204, 217, 228*n*, 242–243; *see also* Russ, Tim
The Twilight Zone 3, 154
"Twisted" 90, 97
2001: A Space Odyssey 192
Tyson, Neil deGrasse 61

Uhura, Lt. 154, 195; *see also* Nichols, Nichelle
Ulster, Laurie 81

Ultimate Trek: Star Trek's Greatest Moment 260*n*
"Unforgettable" 125, 129
"Unimatrix Zero" 26, 56, 63, 125–126, 129
United Federation of Planets *see* Federation
United Paramount Network 1, 73, 249–250, 259, 260*n*
"Unity" 198, 209
Updike, John 70
UPN *see* United Paramount Network
utilitarianism 105, 108, 110

Vasari, Giorgio 54, 63
Vaskans 206–207
Vergil 53, 63
Vettel-Becker, Patricia 68, 81
Vidiians 33, 42, 89, 94, 157, 185
"Virtuoso" 183, 193
Vlack, Tarah Wheeler Van 72, 81
The Voth 59–61
"The Voyager Conspiracy" 17, 22, 31, 225, 230, 258, 264
"The Voyager Transcripts—Episode Listings" 148
Vulcans 95, 100, 105, 154, 164–165, 197, 205, 216–217

Wagner, Jon G. 228*n*, 230
"Waking Moments" 124, 129
Walker, Rebecca 5
Waltonen, Karma 34, 47
Wang, Garrett 70, 197, 255; *see also* Kim, Ensign Harry
"Warlord" 82, 91, 97
Weiss, Jessica 165–167, 170–171, 174, 176, 178
Weyoun 46
Wicked 87
Wildman, Naoma 92, 121
Wildman, Samantha 121
Williamson, Suzanne 262
Winston, Joan 260*n*
Women at Warp 171, 255
Worf 33, 164–166, 174
World Wide Web 6
"Worst Case Scenario" 39, 47, 243, 247, 258, 261*n*, 264
Wright, Jim 257, 264
Wright, Susan 155, 163
Wright, Tom 98
Wright, Tony 247

The X-Files 3, 89, 260*n*
Xena: Warrior Princess 83

Yates, Kassidy 167
"Year of Hell" 36, 47, 78, 135, 148, 258, 264
Yediq 206
"Yesterday's Enterprise" 77, 81
Young, I.M. 135

Zahir 92
The Zahl 36
Zeus 16
Zimmerman, Dr. Lewis 184, 187, 189–190, 192n, 209n

Zinn, Howard 202
Ziyal 168
Žižek, Slavoj 233, 241, 244, 247
Zuckerberg, Mark 187

www.ingramcontent.com/pod-product-compliance
Lightning Source LLC
Chambersburg PA
CBHW032033300426
44117CB00009B/1045